Between Promise and Policy

Between Promise and Policy

Ronald Reagan and Conservative Reformism

John Karaagac

LEXINGTON BOOKS
Lanham • Boulder • New York • Oxford

LEXINGTON BOOKS

Published in the United States of America
by Lexington Books
4720 Boston Way, Lanham, Maryland 20706

12 Hid's Copse Road
Cumnor Hill, Oxford OX2 9JJ, England

British Library Cataloguing in Publication Information Available

Library of Congress Cataloging-in-Publication Data

Karaagac, John, 1963–
    Between promise and policy : Ronald Reagan and conservative reformism / John
Karaagac.
        p.   cm.
    Includes bibliographical references (p.) and index.
    ISBN 0-7391-0094-7 (alk. paper)
    1. United States—Politics and government—1981–1989. 2. Reagan, Ronald.
3. Conservatism—United States—History—20th century. I. Title.
E876.K348   2000
973.927'092—dc21   99-052930

Printed in the United States of America

♾™ The paper used in this publication meets the minimum requirements of American
National Standard for Information Sciences—Permanence of Paper for Printed Library
Materials, ANSI/NISO Z39.48–1992.

To my father

Contents

Preface

This work is highly biographical without being, strictly speaking, a biography. It is about Ronald Reagan to the extent that he is the unifying character from beginning to end, but it is about much more. The work is, in the broadest sense, a study of American politics in the fourth quarter of the twentieth century: it addresses foreign, military, economic, and even social policy, but the reader wanting a comprehensive survey of any category would be advised to consult more conventional works, for the simple reason that our interests here are the ways in which various aspects of statecraft did or did not come together in a comprehensive package. Furthermore, the basis of this work is not in original primary research as much as in the interpretation of information already available in a number of excellent monographs on Ronald Reagan.

Ultimately, this book can and should be read as a series of essays on American politics, and the unifying thread is not simply Ronald Reagan but, more importantly, Ronald Reagan as a reform-minded conservative politician. Reform is as much a policy commitment as a political style. The reformist impulse encompasses both moral outrage and the utilitarian urge for efficiency; it speaks to our self-improving ethos and the practical need to circulate our political elites. In fact, reformism is the quintessential political posture because, in one stroke, it can imply several things without being overly specific. Now a skeptic might suggest, with good reason, that when a word is subject to multiple meanings and infinite nuance then it is devoid of value but, in fact, the opposite is true; politics is not about precision but about an appealing vagueness, not about intellectual rigor but about maneuver and even outright plagiarism.

The reader may wonder where ideology plays into this narrative: it is inevitable that any work on Reagan is also a study of conservative ideas and practice. In politics, however, too much ideology is as bad as too little: the former leads to dogmatism and inflexibility, the latter to opportunism and cynicism. Many academic observers treat ideology as motive rather than a political tool; they forget that ideology itself is constantly being rewritten and reinterpreted according to changing circumstances. Political creativity involves such reinterpretation of tradition, and he who flagrantly steals his opponent's lines without even the appearance of reinterpretation is, in the end, simply a politician. In light of this, Reagan was never as consistent as his rhetoric suggested but, in politics, inconsistency often serves a political function.

An assemblage of political assets and liabilities, Ronald Reagan embodied all the contradictions of American reformism. Indeed, he exaggerated them and, as is often the case with such individuals, their exaggerations highlight the broad outlines of politics and thus serve a particularly useful function.

It is perhaps stating the obvious to suggest that the purpose of this work is, for lack of a better term, political enlightenment. We study the part to better understand the whole; we examine the present to understand both past and future. Indeed, the world of contemporary politics has changed remarkably little since Aristotle set out to study the Greek constitutions in the fourth century before Christ. Today, as then, politics is about power and principle; it is about ideas and policies, individuals and institutions, plans and contingencies. Today, as then, virtuosity in politics implies not mastering a body of rules or a set of techniques—which do not exist and never have—but in knowing what is both appropriate and possible and acting accordingly for the benefit of the party or faction, the state and, in the broadest sense, society.

Chapter 1

Introduction

There is a tendency for memory to exaggerate, and this is particularly true in politics. The years of the Truman and Eisenhower administrations, for example, were not the golden years that later Americans made them out to be; the Korean War, bomb shelters, "McCarthyism," segregation and Sputnik all hinted at a more ominous side to those allegedly halcyon years of peace and security. Nevertheless, Americans of a later generation could be forgiven for thinking that there was something charmed about this era, flush with postwar prosperity, and if a tad boring, at least boredom and predictability seemed part of the natural order of things. Halfway through the twentieth century, Henry Luce's hyperbolic claim of the "American century" seemed to contain an element of truth.

Within the space of under two decades, the easy optimism of the "American century" had given way to a different scenario—one characterized by foreign policy frustration and heightened domestic division. Perhaps because "Ike" had brought the troops home, Americans were eager to forget the inconclusive war on the Korean peninsula, but the subsequent war in Vietnam was a different matter. It created sharper divisions on the home front and, as the war dragged on indefinitely, it raised a host of problems that seemed to multiply and further confuse political alignments.

Arbitrarily taking the year 1973, the average American had good reason to look back on the Eisenhower years with nostalgia. The current news was dominated by the bewildering and complicated issues of the Watergate break-in and the Paris Peace Talks. Closer to home, OPEC oil shocks hit the American consumer, and for the first time in the postwar era, people queued up for gasoline; inflation was climbing; old flagship American industries were shutting down and transferring their production overseas.

In a more elusive sense, these uncertainties had a cultural dimension. Youth was disrespectful, and though this is universally true, there was an aggressive, culturally sanctioned edge to the rebellion. Ethnicity of all types was fashionable, and this seemed to subtly change the way Americans thought of themselves and their nation. Flags were burned; values were flaunted; history was "revised." So many seemed disaffected. People spoke of the Second World War as the "good war," of America becoming a "normal" country, and of the end of American "exceptionalism." Somewhere along the line, Henry Luce's "American century" vanished from public discourse.

It is easy to forget all this, in part because Ronald Reagan helped many Americans forget such things. This was one, if not the, ingredient in his astonishing success. Ronald Reagan's politics, and his vision of reform, touched on all these issues. He was not unique in his vision of conservative reformism, for he simply echoed ideas that had been building in conservative circles for some time. He was, however, unique in his ability to reach beyond this constituency and carry this vision of reform to the national level. Reagan's success rested on his own skills but also the milieu, which, to many, seemed right for his strident views on both foreign and domestic policy. In American politics, reformist talk is cheap and easy. Although he may not have had a mandate for radically changing the way Washington works—for, strictly speaking, there are no such mandates, let alone "revolutions" in coalition-based, American politics—few presidential candidates arrive at the national level with the type of support and perhaps even goodwill that Reagan carried with him to Washington in the middle of January of 1981.

I

Political reform is always a policy response to a problem, or a related set of problems. It bears repeating: the nature of the problem or problems shape, but do not determine, the policy. Franklin Roosevelt's New Deal reforms—which altered the relation between the citizen and the federal government—were a response to the worldwide economic recession of the 1930s. In the former Soviet Union, Gorbachev's tentative reforms of the 1980s, subsumed under both perestroika and glasnost, were the responses of a political elite that sensed a widening gap between Soviet economic performance and that of the Western democracies. FDR strengthened the power of the state over society; Gorbachev loosened it. Clearly, different contexts require different remedies, and to extrapolate from one experience a universal rule is to confuse the particular with the general—an intellectual fallacy.

America's recent political problems were fundamentally different, and in many ways more complex, from the above examples. America's problems were associated, not with economic crisis, as in the 1930s, nor with the breakdown of centrally planned economy, as in the final days of the Soviet Union, but with the more intractable problems that face all major powers as the costs and benefits of international commitments shift over time. Changing international commitments, in turn, raise questions of evolving domestic priorities and shifting coalitions.

If America shared any similarities with other past states, it was that the margin of power that Americans had inherited by luck and by design was bound to recede over time.[1] With that would come a reappraisal of assets, commitments and perhaps even purpose. Changing conditions in the international arena tend to stimulate domestic debates; put alternatively, favorable conditions allow policy makers to finesse pressing questions or transcend the "give and take" of the domestic arena whereas more "normal" conditions do not. Indeed, states that have often expanded rapidly in the international hierarchy of states are ones that have often channeled bitter internal divisions outward and into either military expansionism or an aggressive economic policy. Traditionally, the best way to patch up differences at home is to focus attention on a common, often half-imagined, foe.

By the mid-1960s and certainly by the 1970s, policy questions that had been finessed in the easy days of the 1950s had resurfaced. It was no longer sufficient to see the common foe as worldwide communism, operating out of Moscow and Peking. Increasingly, Americans themselves came to be divided on a host of domestic issues dealing with the share of government services and the defense of cultural symbols.

Opposition groups that are unhappy with the domestic status quo tend to be marginalized in periods of expansive foreign policy success: their discontent seems to be the grumblings of a marginal fringe. Changing conditions abroad, however, give these people a political opening to exploit to their own advantage. Politics—in both the international and domestic arena—is, after all, a struggle for succession (succession to the throne or the presidency, majority status, great power status, membership in NATO, primacy within an alliance, regional preeminence, etc.).

II

Returning to the arbitrary year of 1973, it seemed that the American postwar consensus on both foreign and domestic policy had begun to fragment. Pressures that made such realignment timely had been building throughout the 1960s. The presidency of Lyndon Johnson (1963-1969) was the first administration to show the tensions associated with leadership abroad and expanded government at home. Beginning in the 1960s and continuing throughout the 1970s, stresses in foreign and domestic policy were part of a larger breakdown, not of political order, but of older assumptions and alignments.[2]

In foreign policy, the bipartisan agreement that had been cultivated after 1948 was severely challenged by American involvement in Vietnam. In 1966, half a million American soldiers were fighting a protracted guerrilla war against an elusive enemy and in defense of a questionable ally. By 1968, large sections of the public saw the war as unwinnable and opposed not only the war but also President Johnson. Attacked within his own party and belittled by the opposition, Lyndon Johnson declined to run for a second term.

The ten-year war had a divisive effect in a way that the Korean conflict (1949-1952) never did, and the war was particularly troubling in ways that were hard to identify. Policy makers had long known that massive American military and economic power could be checked in many circumstances, and continental Asia was regarded by many military experts to be one such circumstance. Nevertheless, when Americans put their resources and "know-how" to a task, any task, they were supposed to succeed. After the Tet offensive in 1968, a majority of Americans understood that success in Vietnam was out of the question.

The Vietnam fiasco also came at an awkward time for American policy makers. By the late 1960s, a number of trends were gradually undermining the vast margin of economic and political power that the United States had previously enjoyed over its allies. This was both good and bad. In the years immediately following the Second World War, U.S. policy makers had promoted both democracy and economic development in the defeated Axis powers. This was an effort to spread postwar stability, to avoid a repeat of the autarkic situation of the 1930s and to buttress democratic governments against the specter of Soviet expansion. The success of this policy was evident in the postwar vitality of Western Europe and Japan. One inevitable consequence of this policy, however, was a growing independence on the part of the allies, as illustrated by German Chancellor Brandt's policy of dealing with the Soviets, his famous *ostpolitik*, and by de Gaulle's dramatic separation from NATO in 1966. From an American standpoint, this independence was perhaps more annoying than troublesome; by contrast, economic trends raised American anxieties.

Simply put, the economies of both Europe and Japan outperformed that of America, which had rested on a comfortable postwar technological lead. Japanese economic success and the "German miracle" contrasted with the high inflation, high unemployment and lower economic productivity of the United States in the 1970s—all of which were partial legacies of Vietnam era spending policies. Here was real cause for concern. Indeed, the relatively sluggish performance of the U.S. economy in these years, particularly in the 1970s, made the humiliations of Vietnam even harder to swallow. If Vietnam was a shock, the sense of diminished U.S. power created a subtle mood of doubt, lost prestige and even international impotence.

There was something even more pernicious. During the Vietnam years, the Soviets had achieved parity with, if not outright superiority over, the United States in its nuclear arsenal. While America was trapped in an unwinnable land war in Asia, the Soviets had strengthened their hand in Eastern Europe and in the nuclear arms race. For many Americans, the subsequent policy of détente with China, and détente with the Soviets, was an implicit recognition of this American weakness. To some on the right, détente was even a betrayal of America's alleged Cold War covenant. Whereas the economic growth of Western Europe and Japan carried positive implications for U.S. policy, nuclear parity with the Soviets did not. It shook the confidence Americans had in their own system and helped explain the visceral reaction that most conservatives felt for Nixon-Kissinger policies.

If this were not problem enough, the domestic assumptions of the New Deal were also starting to come apart. As with the Cold War policy of containment, the postwar domestic consensus rested on a broad bipartisan alliance that combined two coalitions: a Democratic majority and an essentially compliant Republican minority—a minority party that had tacitly endorsed the Roosevelt-era welfare state. All but the most conservative and cranky Republicans accepted unemployment insurance, banking regulation, public works from highway to irrigation projects and, above all, social security.[3]

The 1960s, however, revealed gradual cracks in this consensus, and these cracks widened as the decade wore on. Ironically, the breakdown of consensus was aggravated by extending New Deal policies to previously disenfranchised groups such as the urban poor and Blacks. The logical extension of New Deal policies, codified in President Johnson's Great Society legislation, took place at a time when trends in American political ideas and assumptions were moving subtly to the right. Though a radical departure in the 1930s and 1940s, the New Deal policies soon became an accepted part of American society. The very policy success of entitlement programs, coupled with postwar affluence and social mobility, promoted a degree of economic security, and even complacency. It was inevitable that the middle classes would become increasingly conservative by the 1960s. As a consequence, Johnson's activist vision of government seemed peripheral to the middle class.

To compound matters, the stresses on this coalition took place at a time of particularly sharp social upheaval and widening cultural division.[4] This strain was a result of anti-war dissent, the push for racial equality that became progressively radicalized, and the challenge to middle-class mores that was subsumed in the "counterculture." This drift of liberalism away from the political center and toward fringe extremes, as typified by the "New Left," worked to the political disadvantage of the left-leaning Democratic coalition.[5] Inevitably, troubles for the Democrats benefited the Republicans, and a particular type of Republican that was vaguely subsumed in the grouping, the "New" or "Radical Right." In this time of policy confusion, partisans of the New Right possessed both diagnoses of the problems and a prescription for restoring America's health and purpose. There are times when conviction itself is convincing; the collapse of the old and increasingly uncertain Democratic coalition was thus inseparable from the story of the New Right and, its then, relatively radically traditional proposals for reform and renovation.

Prior to examining both Reagan and contemporary conservatives, it might be helpful to step back from the narrative and make clear what we mean by "reform"—a term that we all use with such frequency that we implicitly assume its meaning is self-evident. Often, it is not.

III

Some readers here may find it inconceivable that Ronald Reagan could be considered a reformer. In American politics, reformism has been associated with a left-leaning agenda for so long that many of us implicitly assume that conservative precepts can only run counter to reform, that is, "reactionary." Reform, however, is more complex. It mirrors the larger debates of political life, which is after all, a recurring dialogue between competing interpretations of what is true, just and efficient. Consequently, reform agendas can be the property of both the left and right, both the self-styled modernist and his traditionalist counterpart. Both Reform and Hasidic Jews are partisans of "reform"—albeit radically different visions; the same applies for the liberal Muslim modernist and the radical Ayatollah. To return to the political realm, the liberal who wants to alter the status quo by radically expanding the welfare state and the conservative who wants to radically rollback such government interference are both partisans of reform, though both rest on competing conceptions of the normative "good."

One need not endorse a specific vision to acknowledge that it is reformist, though calling an ideological opponent's views reformist subtly enhances his credibility and, conversely, labeling them "reactionary" or "extremist" diminishes that credibility.

The Oxford English Dictionary defines reform as the "amendment, or altering for the better of some faulty state of things, especially of a corrupt or oppressive political institution or practice; the removal of some abuse or wrong." In politics, reform simply implies the attempt at substantive policy adjustment based on correcting specific abuses or bringing about an improved condition. Not all that passes as reform is worthy of attention. Indeed, many politicians identify their policies as reformist so as to reap the normative benefits inherent in the term, and perhaps disguise the real, or simply non-reformist, nature of their policies. This is true in democracy, and particularly in American democracy, where the argument of change for the sake of change is one of the stock accusations against the party in power.

To reiterate, a reformer is one who advocates substantial change in policy and acts accordingly in an official capacity. A candidate for the presidency who fails to win the election cannot be considered a reforming president for obvious reasons. Applying the same logic, a successful candidate who fails in his pledge for radical change and essentially continues the policies of his predecessors is not really a reformer, nor is the politician who frustrates the reform program of his opponents without offering a legitimate alternative vision.

The first criterion for judging the success of a legitimate reformer is with the criterion that he himself has set, that is, what the reformer has identified as a problem and the corrective policy. This "tells" us where to begin the analysis. The study of reform implicitly becomes the study of policy problems, such as economic stagnation, budget deficits, poor military performance, an excessive bureaucracy or even an undeveloped political system that does not respond to its citizens. The study of reform is thus the study of plans to correct problems.

For all the reasons listed, Ronald Reagan deserves serious consideration as a reform politician. Detractors, both political and academic, have often been unwilling to even acknowledge that there was anything reformist about the man, his entourage, and his ideas; for opposite reasons, fervent partisans of the "Reagan Revolution" have been unwilling to judge the record in terms of its discrepancies, let alone contradictions. This work, then, is an audit of Ronald Reagan as a reform politician. This, in turn, raises a curious question: what do we mean by politics?

IV

Politics is nothing more than the coordination of those institutions that make up the state. The state, in turn, is the aggregate of those institutions that guard territory—"provide for the common defense" as stipulated in the U.S. Constitution—and make the daily intercourse of civilized life both possible and predictable—that is, "promote the general welfare." The politics of reform simply means correcting and improving those state institutions. In the broader sense, the politics of reform implies improving those aspects of our social life that have an implicit political dimension—the economy, race relations, or even the moral "health" of society.

Implicitly, the expansive definition of what is "political" implies that politics is more than simply running institutions. In fact, the British philosopher Michael Oakeshott noted there are two dimensions to politics. There is the practical aspect, the coordinating activity of institutions and policies alluded to in the preamble to the Constitution. There is also the element of politics as discourse—that is a dialogue of competing or differing visions. These discursive aspects of politics run the gamut from political philosophy or treatises on government such as *The Federalist Papers* or Rousseau's *Social Contract* to the simple and often manipulative advertising of a presidential campaign. Sometimes, we speak of the practical business of politics as "governing" and the scramble for higher office as "politics." We tend to make distinctions between the statesman—somehow unsullied and above the din of the crowd—and the politician—implicitly compromised. The lines between the two, however, are wholly insubstantial. As one shrewd observer noted, a statesman is a politician who makes you forget how he got there.

One need only think of American politics to see both the practical and the discursive aspects inherent in the term "politics." Clearly, the candidate who is running for office is directly involved in the discourse of politics. He is attacking the ideas and record of his opponent; he is jockeying for the opportunity to govern but campaigning is, in itself, not governing. Should that man or woman win the campaign and assume the office, he or she, whether a legislator or an executive, becomes engaged in the practical business of governance. When the candidate is a virtuoso campaigner but an inept president or legislator, observers tend to make distinctions between "politics" and "governing" but, as suggested, the distinction is an artificial one. To govern involves not only practical skill but also an aptitude for discourse, that is framing policies and cultivating constituencies. This is true in all but the most absolute of monarchies as it is in a parliamentary democracy.

Now this is immediately relevant to the study of reform politics, which is after all a subset of politics. Reformers may suggest that they are above politics, but this is a deceptively political gesture that plays on the pejorative meanings often implicit in the term politics. Whether they identify themselves as politicians or not, reform politicians are always involved in both the discourse of politics as well as the practical business of running the state. Consequently, the analyst of reform must first look at both the candidate's ideas of what is wrong, his prescriptions for correction, and then his attempts to implement them. Any observer will probably find a disjunction between promise and performance in even the most well-intentioned and consistent of reformers.

This gap is particularly true in modern democracies where politicians achieve the highest office by a complicated process of negotiation and, in the broadest sense, advertisement. The study of politics is thus one of not only the rise to power but the continuities and departure from the pure, and often easy, discourse of the campaign trail to the more complicated task of public office, where the true abilities and deficiencies of the newly elected official are exposed.

Notes

1. Some observers chose to interpret these developments as symptomatic of declining American power. "Declinism," which has always been a recurrent theme in American history, was most recently popularized in the late 1980s. This was perhaps understandable: the Cold War was winding down and the costs of the conflict were revealed in huge budget deficits. Although the Soviets "lost" the conflict, the United States seemed the poorer for it. It seemed the chief beneficiaries of the long rivalry were the West Europeans and the Japanese.

Nonetheless, the idea of "decline"—an intellectually irresponsible term that describes an aggregate of trends, some of which are quantifiable and others of which are purely impressionistic—was oversold to an anxious public. Although historical analogies are useful, there is a distinct limit to the comparability of historical experiences.

In fact, there were a number of intellectual problems with the intellectual fad of "declinism." History is, after all, a series of reversals and progressions that defy the strict predictability of cyclical or teleological theory. Such theories can never be proved or disproved and as Robert Nisbet suggested, it is child's play to find facts, any facts, to support a theory that cannot be disproved. Moreover, the analyst who takes a commonsense truism (i.e., what goes up must come down, fortunes rise and fall, nothing stays the same...) and accordingly derives a theory, with all types of policy recommendations for "reversing decline," commits the fallacy of intellectual banality. Such theories are really pseudo-theories with policy recommendations, most of which are sensible, haphazardly tacked on.

2. Joan Hoff, *Nixon Reconsidered* (New York: Basic Books, 1994), 6-8.

3. Michael Schaller, *Reckoning with Reagan: America and Its President in the 1980s* (New York, Oxford: Oxford University Press, 1992), 11.

4. Paul Allen Beck, "Incomplete Realignment,"in *The Reagan Legacy*, ed. Charles O. Jones (Chatham, N.J.: Chatham House Publishers, 1988), 158-159.

5. Hugh Heclo, "Reaganism and the Search for a Public Philosophy," in *Perspectives on the Reagan Years*, ed. John L. Palmer (Washington, D.C.: Urban Institute Press, 1986), 36.

Chapter 2

The Intellectual Background to Conservative Reformism

Policy debates may seem tangential to the rough and tumble world of politics, but as argued in the previous chapter, politics is not only about the struggle for succession to power but about competing ideas. Inevitably, periods of political flux and dislocation, such as the 1960s, stimulate political debate.

The contemporary debate on political reform in America—that is competing interpretations of problems and subsequent prescriptions for policy change—is in large part one waged on the merits of both liberal and conservative principles. Modern American liberalism, for example, has evolved around the idea of liberty as a type of economic equality. In the twentieth century, American liberals have been committed to the proposition that the federal government can provide a form of social insurance; the state, liberals argue, can also be an agent of economic redistribution. By contrast, modern American conservatism has developed around the idea of liberty as a freedom from political constraint. Conservatives have been skeptical about the powers of the federal government and have emphasized local government and, implicitly, the family and church as the focus of particular attention. On the whole, conservatives have been committed to individual, as opposed to collective, rights.

Political ideals, however, can never be separated from the political context in which they appear. For this reason, purely intellectual debate about the left or the right often seem abstract and unreal; in fact, when political ideas veer too far from the shifting reality of politics, they begin to seem lifeless, remote and—most damning of all—academic. Not surprisingly, the ideas of left and right tend to be clusters of related ideas rather than propositions held tightly together by the rigorous application of logic. If there is one thing about these clusters of loosely related ideas, it is that they evolve and change over time and do so in unpredictable ways. Alliances shift; interest groups pick up a line of reasoning dropped by the other side; the whole equation changes. The left defines itself against the right; the right, against the left.

Reform: The Politician and the Intellectual

The roles in this continuous drama are typically performed by different players. In a crude sense, politicians are less concerned with doctrinal consistency as opposed to political expediency. They are interested in enacting policies, frustrating opponents, building coalitions and supervising the machinery of state. By contrast, policy-minded intellectuals are less concerned with dreary details of policy as opposed to the larger discourse. Policy-minded intellectuals are concerned with reconciling contradictions and framing argument for change in terms of principles, ideas and traditions.

Successful politicians need not be intellectually imaginative, but they must possess a keen sense of judgment about what is both appropriate and possible. The emotionally demanding craft of politics rewards an intellectual focus and single-mindedness that would appear unsophisticated, simplistic, and quite possibly tiresome, in intellectual circles. In fact, overly intellectual or cerebral politicians tend to vacillate and buckle under pressure. It is the stolid statesman—the one who knows a few simple truths but knows them well—who proves more resilient than the politician with a dozen dazzling ideas on his agenda but no capacity for follow-through.

If it is too much to expect politicians to be genuinely original thinkers, it is too much to expect intellectuals to possess the political discipline necessary for the often-tedious calculation and compromise that politics require. This is not to suggest that politicians are neither clever, nor intellectuals, nor calculating. The skills of the intellectual, however, do not translate well into politics. Indeed, intellectuals in politics often reveal unfortunate traits: dogmatism and doctrinal zeal, impatience and arrogance, tactical ineptitude and disorganization.[1] Although there have been cases of reformers who were genuinely original thinkers, such as the brilliant eighteenth-century Frenchman Turgot, they are relatively rare. The record of intellectuals in politics, other than in circumscribed advisory positions where the intellectual serves at the pleasure of the sovereign, is a relatively dismal one.

Richard Hofstadter noted that such populist skepticism has deep roots in American democracy, and it was telling that experts were attacked from all sides of the political spectrum.

From the left, Noam Chomsky and C. Wright Mills derided academics who were quick to enter Pentagon or State Department service as men who had made a Faustian bargain with "the establishment." Drifting to the left in the 1960s, the émigré academic Hans Morgenthau added to this argument. That charge had some merit, particularly as Johnson cynically used academics as intellectual cover for his policies. (The Johnson White House even had an "intellectual in residence," which took such policies to their comical conclusions.) With a gift for the neatly turned phrase, Chomsky derided such policy academics as the "new Mandarins," and Mills labeled academics like Henry Kissinger as "crackpot realists."

From the right, conservatives could deride the experts associated with Democrat administrations as "Ivy League liberals." Whereas leftists exposed the pretense of intellectuals seeking influence, rightists pandered to the prejudices of the democratic everyman. There was a certain truth to this charge, particularly when those policy elites were often to the left of the majority of American voters or allowed themselves to be portrayed as such.

By the late 1960s, experts had become the focus of a pronounced conservative backlash against Washington. This backlash was first associated, not with Reagan, but with Richard Nixon, who seemed to personify the democratic commoner against the Ivy Leaguer.[6] In the early 1950s, the Johns Hopkins and Harvard-educated patrician Alger Hiss had been a perfect foil for Nixon's clever communist baiting. A graduate of Quaker-run Whittier College in California and a strident anticommunist, Nixon had portrayed himself as the popular politician who stood up to the academic expert and the patrician, whether a Rockefeller Republican or a Kennedy Democrat.

For their part, many in the universities felt a profound distaste, if not loathing, for Richard Nixon, who was nevertheless adroit as president in recruiting academics such as James Schlesinger, Daniel Patrick Moynihan and George Shultz into government service. Nixon even went so far as to recruit Harvard professor and Rockefeller aide, Henry Kissinger, who had been openly disdainful of Nixon's presidential aspirations but was not about to refuse any administration post.

So-called experts were easy, and perhaps even legitimate, targets for the simple reason that many Americans were losing confidence in the policies that experts had advocated. Predictably, dissenting voices on both the left and right claimed that the American public was simply learning what they had known all along.

Those in the hard left, for example, had long argued that America's New Deal policies did not go far enough in the direction of redistributive liberalism.

In foreign affairs, they maintained that America's policy was one of economic imperialism: America deliberately subverted revolution in the so-called developing world in order to keep markets open and thereby preserve a global economic hegemony. For the hard left, more government at home and withdrawal from foreign affairs was the preferred prescription for policy change.

The arguments of the hard right were based on the reverse argument. On the foreign front, right-wing skeptics had long suggested that policy makers in Washington were unwilling to truly roll back communism. The right focused on the "developing world" to the extent that it was the arena of Soviet expansion and mayhem, and the United States was doing too little on this front. To conservative dissenters, Vietnam policies—based on incrementalism and gradual "mission creep" in the south rather than serious bombing of the communist bastions in the north—demonstrated an utter lack of will. Their argument was not with the principle of anticommunist containment, but with tactics they considered tepid and defeatist. America's Cold War bark, they believed, was worse than its bite.

Slowly and inexorably, the hard right argument for rolling back communism abroad dovetailed with the conservative argument for rolling back the welfare state at home. Many believed that the crypto-socialism of the New Deal was simply one step toward a greater collectivization of the economy and this needed to be fought in the American homefront as much as in faraway Vietnam. Whereas the far left wanted withdrawal from foreign commitments and activist government at home, the far right wanted aggressive activism abroad coupled to limited government commitment at home.

Those in the broad political center—middle of the road Democrats and Republicans alike—could look at the mounting attacks from both hard left and right and suggest, with much justification, that America's postwar consensus was unraveling. In political life, however, one group's loss is another group's gain. Those in the hard left, who had been without a real voice in American politics since the marginalization of Iowa's Henry Wallace in the late 1940s, believed that the collapse of centrist liberalism would clear the way for a more mature social democracy to develop on American soil. Those on the right, who were viewed as cranky and old-fashioned rather than really threatening, began to catch a glimpse of a mainline audience for their dissenting opinions on flaccid American policy abroad and the welfare state at home. Simply put, such groups were energized by the collapse of the "vital center." In the dialectic of domestic politics, it was time for the extremes, on both left and right, to emerge from their enforced and unwanted isolation.

With the increasing complexity of political and social problems in the 1960s, the Kennedy-Johnson policies began to fragment. Having achieved success at one set of problems, policy makers predictably moved on to more intractable ones. The domestic agenda of the 1930s, 1940s and even 1950s—expanded infrastructure, rural electrification and minimal social security entitlements—seemed manageable in contrast to the policies of this later era where the political objectives—eradicating poverty in Appalachia and the inner city—seemed elusive. Whereas the New Deal reforms provided minimal entitlements, the objectives of the Great Society were in some ways unattainable: to eliminate social pathologies that the wisest social scientists did not yet fully comprehend. In all complex organizations, the goals become more difficult, not simpler, with the passing of time, if only because proven success inexorably takes the organization in the direction of greater challenges.

It was not only the problems that were tougher to solve, but also that the left-leaning coalition was itself cracking. Reform depends on a consensus, which in turn depends on a coalition of voting blocs. Partisans of the Kennedy-Johnson policies saw the Great Society as the inevitable extension of the New Deal and there was much truth to this. The converse, however, could also be true: periods of reform often need to be followed by periods of retrenchment and consolidation. The consensus for extending reform—that is for altering the status quo—must be refashioned anew every generation and this requires greater skill than simple promising more of the same. Consequently, the gradual extension of reform legislation to new constituencies can often alienate the original ones, as the leaders of Britain's fratricidal Liberal Party learned in the early part of the twentieth century.

Tampering with a proven legacy of reform can be the salvation of a dying political party; it can also lead to political disarray and fragmentation. As with everything in politics, success is a function of vision, skill and good luck. Success comes from knowing when to take the offensive without upsetting the coalition, and when to beat a tactical retreat and call it victory.

When, in the course of the 1970s, Reagan argued that government was the problem, not the solution, he was implicitly touching on the creeping sense of alienation and disillusionment that many Americans had for these policies and their proponents. As usual, Reagan had an unerring sense for popular opinion.

It takes no great leap of imagination to suggest that, in a democracy, political parties whose intellectual luminaries and politicians alike diagnose problems with sympathetic insight but possess no clear plan of action other than more of the same will lose out to parties whose leaders and thinkers over-simplify or even caricature issues but who nevertheless possess clear plans of action and carry a certain confidence about the moral rightness of those plans.

Conservatives did possess policy remedies. However vague, conservative remedies were instinctively soothing to the broad sector of American society that felt increasingly alienated from liberal policies and policy makers alike. By

1966—the midterm verdict on Johnson and, it seemed, all that Johnson stood for—conservatives were already showing signs of electoral revival after being pronounced near dead in the 1964 electoral rout. Far from proving the inexorable progress of American liberalism, the Johnson landslide victory was beginning to seem more a function of Goldwater's electoral ineptitude. Not only were conservative arguments increasingly compelling to large segments of an insecure electorate, but Republicans were lucky in their opponents. Simply put, the moderate left was imploding.

It is one of the ironies of history that the most vicious ideological attacks are often reserved for close competitors. It was as if many in the "New" or the radical Left, which was in many ways a university movement, took a perverse delight in savaging old-time, mainstream Liberals. This reflected the contempt all self-styled radicals heap on "bourgeois" reformers, and in the end there was something comic about middle-class students at Cornell, Berkeley and Columbia taking on and thoroughly discrediting essentially liberal university administrations. Those same student agitators all but ignored conservative faculty members. There may have been a farcical quality to all of this except for the fact that militant twenty-year sociology majors themselves became part of the larger political debate—which may have been their intention all along. Campus radicals helped to discredit centrist liberalism by shackling it to all the excesses and cultural nihilism of the "counterculture." This was a gift to conservatives of all persuasions, not least of those being the up and coming conservatives on the "New Right."

The New Right was, in fact, a collection of conservative groups that were unified in large part by focused opposition to the postwar liberal "consensus."

The specific details of New Right positions on policy will be covered in the chapters that deal with questions of reform in the various functional areas of the state—foreign policy and defense, budgetary and fiscal policy, and particularly those issues that touch on values questions. Suffice it to note here, however, that the conservative arguments on what "ailed" American and how it could be fixed ran the gamut from fringe issues, which may have resonated with true-believing John Birchers but were anathema to the majority of mainstream voters, to issues that could indeed play with the broad majority. Beyond opposition to a type of generic liberalism, many conservatives themselves tended to splinter on specific issues. It is easy to exaggerate the ideological unity of these conservative groups, but in a country as politically diverse as the United States—one in which the two-party system hinders ideological uniformity and promotes coalition-building—ideological eclecticism is the norm.

The story of Ronald Reagan as a putative reform politician is the story of political maneuvering within the Republican Party—a broad coalition of center-right groups—and then within the wider electorate. The story is one of the evolving policy debate, for politics reflects not only the pull of contingent experience but also the push of ideas—intellectual attempts to understand, frame and shape that experience.

This debate set the tone for the Reagan platform of the 1980s, itself a crystallization of many themes dear to conservatives. His platform was a collection of loosely held together platforms and his policies were shaped by forces of which he was in large part a conduit. Nonetheless, Reagan's virtuoso abilities as a politician gave those ideas and policies a credibility that might have been altogether absent in the hands of a lesser, or perhaps different, individual.

Reagan's career as a would-be reformer illustrated the successes but also the glaring limitations of those conservative ideas translated into politics. It is one thing for a politician of either party to talk boldly about changing the "system" but quite another to put those reform ideas into action. In fact, politicians often talk about ideas that they only superficially understand, not from lack of insight but because ideas are only one small part of the political universe. Ideas of change—so important in the hustle to win office—often become encumbrances in governing. Like the character in Lewis Carrol's *Alice in Wonderland*, politicians may try to mean what they say and say what they mean, but the correspondence is bound to be an approximate one.

Given the prominence of Reagan in the recent history of American conservatism it seems only fitting to turn our attention to a brief biographical chapter on Reagan, the man, the actor and the politician.

Notes

1. In trying to counter such typical traits, intellectuals in politics—particularly in advisory positions—often become caricatures of political machismo.

2. Turn of the century "progressive" reformers were often well-educated professionals from patrician backgrounds. In political terms, this high-minded moralism made an easy target for reform opponents. In the cities of the northeast, reformers could be ridiculed as "Yankee," that is subtly distinct from the majority of voters in cultural and class terms. Beyond this region, reformers could be ridiculed as part of the "eastern establishment"—those who knew nothing about the middle and far west and the wrong things about the South. The Knickerbocker Theodore Roosevelt managed to neutralize this criticism; his robust assertiveness, his prairie and later wartime experience helped deflect charges of being an effete mandarin—charges that had always tarnished the reformist enterprise. See Richard Hofstadter's *Anti-Intellectualism in American Life* (New York: Alfred A. Knopf, 1963), 174-191.

Chapter 2

3. Stanley Hoffmann, *Janus and Minerva: Essays in the Theory and Practice of International Politics* (Boulder: Westview Press, 1987), 12.

4. Garry Wills, *Nixon Agonistes: The Crisis of the Self-Made Man* (Boston: Houghton Mifflin, 1970), 228.

5. Wills, *Nixon Agonistes*, 593.

6. Tom Wicker made this point in *One of Us: Richard Nixon and the American Dream* (New York: Random House, 1991), 106-109.

Chapter 3

Ronald Reagan:
The Citizen Politician as Reformer

Whether explicit or not, the study of a reform administration is also the biographical study of the reformer as an individual. It is the study of the path to power, the promises made, the alliances forged. This is particularly true in American democracy, with its loose party structure and its corresponding emphasis on personality.

Given his relatively late entry into state and then national politics, Ronald Reagan's path to the White House was an unlikely and even an implausible one. Public life was a second career for him. Nonetheless, American political culture mythologizes the citizen politician as the virtuous outsider bent on renovating Washington and its institutions. This was doubly true for Ronald Reagan, who articulated a particular strain of American political thought: conservative suspicion against big government. Indeed, Reagan rose to higher office on a declaratory policy of reforming government by scaling it back, and even dismantling it. In a country where reformism had been, for much of the twentieth century, a matter of placing more and more power at the federal level and perhaps doing so uncritically, Reagan reversed the political equation.

The Early Years: From the Middle West to Hollywood

With its vast size, American politics is strongly colored by regional politics: Reagan's political career can only be understood in light of his Midwestern antecedents and his subsequent migration to California, a state that has always absorbed people from other parts of the country, particularly from the Midwest. The facts of Reagan's life are familiar: born three years before the First World War, Ronald Reagan—the younger of two sons—spent his early youth in small Illinois towns on the upper Mississippi river. These Midwestern roots are partial clues to Reagan's appeal, both in his acting and in his later political career.

Many of the biographical details of Reagan's life resembled those of fellow Republican Richard Nixon. Nixon and Reagan were both born to Irish-American families that were religiously divided. Both Nixon and Reagan had fathers who were ambitious but professionally frustrated; both had mothers who were deeply religious and widely admired in their tight-knit communities; both men attended small religious colleges that were avenues of social mobility for members of their small denominations. The similarities, however, stop there, for there was something claustrophobic and even desperate about Nixon's youth in Yorba Linda, California, whereas those were not qualities that come to mind in surveying Reagan's early life in Dixon, Illinois. In politics and in life, Nixon struggled and wore his struggles as a virtue; Reagan, by contrast, conveyed the effortless ease and untroubled confidence that Americans admire.

Parentage offers one clue to political biography. Reagan's father was a genial, if not flamboyant, Irish-American shoe salesman.[1] Reagan senior was a driven man with an interest in amateur dramatics and the dream of owning his own business. He was also an alcoholic.[2] It is easy to exaggerate biographical details, but a recurring trait of children of alcoholics is the desire for harmony, the capacity to ignore unpleasantries and the emphasis on pleasing those around them.[3] It was telling that both Ronald Reagan and Bill Clinton were children of alcoholic fathers.

More influential in Reagan's life was his strong-willed mother. In contrast to Clinton's brassy and carousing mother, Nelle Reagan was a beloved figure in her community and strongly committed to her fundamentalists church, the Disciples of Christ. The church, the same one in which Lyndon Johnson was raised, was particularly strong in both Texas and the upper Missis-sippi—Illinois and Iowa. It was a pietistic church whose members were upwardly mobile, committed to good works and, above all, to temperance. Influential in her congregation, Nelle Reagan was also something of a frustrated actress who often staged minor church plays with redemptive and moralistic themes.[4] It was a style that would not be lost on her son in his second career as a politician; as Garry Wills noted, Reagan often gave a mythic, and even religious, aura to his stories and speeches.[5]

Considering his modest background, Reagan's collegiate career was a tribute to his ambition and his disciplined work habits. By working six arduous summers as a lifeguard and by working on a host of campus jobs, Reagan put himself through tiny Eureka College in central Illinois, a Disciples of Christ school. Unlike Nixon, Reagan was never a star student nor even aspired to be. He was, however, a quick study, which helped him compensate for the lack of time he devoted to his classes.[6] At Eureka, Reagan was on the swimming and football teams and dabbled in college dramatics and both of these seemingly trivial activities would later prove significant in his steady progression from sports announcer to Hollywood actor.

The Great Depression altered the lives of most Americans and Reagan's family was no exception. His father, a lifelong Democrat, lost his job but managed to gain employment with the state welfare office in Dixon. This only intensified the Reagan family's political loyalty to Franklin D. Roosevelt—itself a peculiarity in strongly Republican Dixon. Well into the 1950s, Reagan would remain a loyal Democrat. Throughout his political life, Reagan's political style, his buoyant optimism and even the cadences of his speeches echoed back to Roosevelt's confidence-inspiring rhetoric from the 1930s and 1940s.[7]

The Great Depression was an unlikely time for Reagan to enter the entertainment business, yet through persistence, discipline and a measure of good luck, he succeeded in breaking into radio announcing. With his dramatic and sports experience, this was a natural medium. First in Davenport, Iowa, and later in Des Moines, he was a well-known and highly regarded sports announcer—in part because he understood his audience. With an astonishing degree of pluck and ambition, Reagan decided to head to Hollywood and try his chances in the moving picture industry, which seemed to have been his desire all along. With the help of a Dixon associate, Reagan lied about his acting experience and subsequently landed a job at the Warner Brother's Studio.[8]

The move from Illinois to Iowa and then to southern California was not as dramatic as it might first appear. Garry Wills noted that Des Moines had always been a natural "way station to California."[9] Moreover, southern California had a long tradition of welcoming transplanted Midwesterners who had come to dominate aspects of its culture.[10] Lou Cannon noted that when Reagan came to California, "he brought the mid-west with him," and this would be a clue to his later political popularity.

This was perhaps the reason for Reagan's swift entry into 1930s Hollywood. In these years, the major studios were trying to alter their image with the public and, in doing so, trying to distance themselves from the risqué Hollywood of the 1920s. It was a matter of money. The studios wanted to appeal to wider American audiences, seeking diversion from the Depression years in wholesome and unthreatening entertainment. Strict censorship laws had just been introduced and, partly for these reasons, someone of Ronald Reagan's homespun manner, nonthreatening good looks and even priggish rectitude had a definite advantage at this particular time in cinematic history. Reagan's assets were particularly valuable for the studios that needed to get controversial films such as *King's Row*—a screen adaptation of a gothic novel whose plot suggested both incest and bisexuality—past the censors. For the studios, Ronald Reagan was also perfect for the light comedy roles, which he in fact disdained.

What is important at this stage in Reagan's career was his work habit: he was considered a particularly easy actor to direct because of his quick memory, his facility with scripts and his ability to follow directions while improvising when necessary. These were skills that would later serve Reagan on the speaking circuit and then in politics. On the other hand, Reagan spent his formative work years in a profession that required demanding stints of work, followed by equally long stints of rest and inaction. As governor and later as president, Reagan's work schedule reflected this—it was never consistently strenuous. In fact, it was quite unstrenuous. Of his eight years as president, Reagan spent nearly a full year at his ranch in the Santa Barbara foothills.[11] As president, Reagan was stubborn in resisting tight scheduling, just as he resisted ideas and evidence that challenged his deeply held assumptions. This high-lighted another problem with Reagan—he was a quick study but he was intellectually lazy.

The Birth of a Salesman: From Roosevelt Democrat to Goldwater Republican

During his Hollywood days, Reagan's political interests deepened. Involved with the Screen Actor's Guild, he later served as its president and helped lead a successful strike against the studios.[12] In these early days, Reagan's affiliations were entirely Democratic. In 1948, he campaigned for Harry Truman; in 1950, he campaigned for Helen G. Douglas, who ran against Richard Nixon for the California Senate seat in a particularly bitter race.[13] Reagan was also among those who tried to lure Eisenhower to the Democratic presidential ticket in 1952.[14] In fact, Democrat Party leaders had themselves urged Reagan to run for congress in 1946.[15]

It was in the course of the Eisenhower years, however, that Reagan gradually drifted toward conservatism. This was as much a function of his changing economic status as it was a conscious reappraisal of his earlier beliefs.[16] At the height of the depression, Reagan had been an ardent supporter of Roosevelt's New Deal; when he moved into a higher income bracket, Reagan just as easily, and perhaps unconsciously, became a vocal opponent of big government and high taxes.[17] This was particularly true of Reagan in the early 1950s, when he and his second wife, Nancy Davis, were, in the words of biographer Lou Cannon, "land-rich but cash poor."[18] At one point, Reagan had even worked as a Las Vegas emcee but, in this, he was something of a flop; unlike Dean Martin, Frank Sinatra, Sammy Davis Jr. or the other "Rat-packers," the nonsmoking, near teetotaler Reagan was not a natural lounge performer.

When General Electric proposed that he become host of its Sunday evening program on the new medium of commercial television, Reagan, who needed the income, eagerly accepted. This commitment, which lasted until the early 1960s, was important in that it allowed Reagan to master television in the same way that he had earlier mastered radio. In Reagan, GE found not only a genial television host but a spokesman for the company. Soon Reagan became a motivational speaker for workers at the geographically dispersed plants but also for the corporate elite at GE, which had a reputation for being conventional and conformist even by the standards of 1950s corporate culture.[19] Reagan's public relations duties at GE eventually merged into a larger position, in fact a set presentation known simply as "the Speech"—one he delivered at GE corporate meetings. In "the Speech," Reagan defended corporate America, criticized big government and demonized communism.[20] Garry Wills noted that by 1962, Ronald Reagan "lived to deliver 'the speech.'"[21]

In these years, Reagan also reached out beyond GE and moved toward a degree of political involvement that made his corporate employers nervous. By 1962, GE severed its relations with Reagan, who was not only increasingly partisan but who also appeared to have his own political agenda.[22] Even though still a registered Democrat, Reagan was beginning to speak on behalf of Republican candidates, as he did for Richard Nixon in the 1960 presidential campaign.[23]

It was fitting that Reagan's entry into national politics came through the new medium of television; in fact, Garry Wills noted that Ronald Reagan entered American politics right at the moment that it was absorbing "show business techniques."[24] In October of 1964, Reagan made a televised speech on behalf of presidential candidate Barry Goldwater, whose campaign had never caught on and had, in fact, stalled. Ironically, the Goldwater campaign was uncomfortable with Reagan's strident message and with Reagan himself: both message and messenger appeared too controversial for a campaign already mired in controversy. In addition, many Republican insiders looked askance at Reagan and viewed him as a mediocre actor out of his depth in national politics.

To everyone's surprise, however, Reagan's speech struck a deep chord among the Republican faithful, particularly those on the right who perhaps implicitly sensed that Reagan conveyed the conservative platform in a way that reassured, rather than antagonized the electorate.[25] The day after the debut speech, one million dollars in contributions flowed into the Goldwater campaign.[26] At the time, journalist David Broder called it one of the most impressive political debuts since Bryan's "cross of gold" speech in the 1890s.[27] Broder may have exaggerated, but the speech—"a time for choosing"—did signal the arrival of Reagan as the Republican right's up and coming man.

In many ways, Goldwater had been a poor messenger in 1964 and overwhelmed the conservative message, which rested on a visceral reaction to the status quo. "The element..." wrote Richard Hofstadter, "that unified Goldwater's foreign and domestic campaign themes was the argument that domestic demoralization, foreign failures, and the decline of our prestige abroad were together the consequences of a failure of the old virtues and the old moral fiber."[28] Writing in the early 1960s, Hofstadter was openly dismissive. Indeed, even mainstream Republicans and the right-leaning Scripps-Howard and Hearst newspapers rejected Goldwater's brand of strident conservatism. Nonetheless, Reagan repackaged in entirety Goldwater's campaign themes— themes that were broadly reminiscent of "the Speech"—and made them the basis of his first attempt at elected office.

Entering California Politics: The Path to Power

With the decentralized nature of American government, state and regional politics take on an importance that is often missing in other political systems. This is particularly true in the question of political reform, for reform administrations at the federal level have traditionally been extensions of experiments at the state and even municipal level. In the late nineteenth century, for example, Democrat Grover Cleveland was a reform-minded mayor of Buffalo. Before he was president, Woodrow Wilson was a reform-minded governor of New Jersey. Prior to the New Deal, Franklin Roosevelt was a governor in New York who experimented with state relief.

Ultimately, it was the Goldwater speech that cleared the path for Reagan's entry in to California politics. Moreover, Reagan's timing was good, for in the early 1960s, California Republicans imploded. Nixon's disastrous 1962 gubernatorial bid in California ended with his famous line about the press not being able to kick him around anymore. Indeed, California conservatives had long distrusted Nixon, particularly since he outflanked former California governor Earl Warren for the 1952 vice presidential position. Many California conservatives also saw Nixon as a political loser and something of an opportunist.[29] To complicate matters, in the early 1960s the two senior California Republican officials had been engaged in a fratricidal power struggle that weakened the state party.[30] Simply put, Republican leaders needed a fresh face and had approached Reagan for the 1964 senate election. For his part,

Reagan himself appeared to have his eye on some type of elected office. It was the statehouse, and not the senate, that appealed to him, perhaps because it was a better path to the White House. Highly ambitious, Reagan seemed to have contemplated the presidency even at this early stage.

Reagan also had the support of certain California kingmakers who "recruited" him to run for governor in 1966 and provided the financial backing for the campaign.[31] These wealthy backers were for the most part southern Californians, and included the car salesman and Oklahoma transplant Holmes Tuttle, retailer Justin Dart, industrialist Jacqueline Hume, oilman Henry Salvatori and Reagan's personal attorney, William French Smith, who later went on to become attorney general in the early 1980s.[32] These men saw in Reagan a telegenic candidate who could appeal to wide audiences and articulate a probusiness, low-tax platform, in short, the message of economic individualism that crystallized for Reagan during the GE days.

These men did not buy Reagan's nomination, but they clearly facilitated his political ascendancy—one that would have been improbable in any other state of the union. Because of its intentionally weak party structure, a man such as Reagan who had no connection to the state party apparatus and who had not worked his way up the legislature, could be catapulted to the nomination for the highest office in the state. As Lou Cannon noted, the idea of the "citizen politician" was particularly strong in California.[33] Because California was a state of migrants from other states, Reagan was also never tarred by the "carpetbagger" charge, as was Robert Kennedy in his 1964 New York senate bid.

Reagan's ascendancy rested as much on his credibility as a messenger as on the message itself. Unlike Goldwater, he reassured voters, even though his spirited platform was much the same as Goldwater's. Moreover, events since 1964 had further worked to Reagan's advantage: a number of trends that were subtly undermining the Kennedy-Johnson domestic agenda were beginning to play themselves out in 1966, and play out with a particular intensity in California.

As part of the rising economic and demographic power of the sunbelt region, California was bound to be part of a larger realignment in American politics, but the state was in a class of its own. In these years, California passed New York as the most populous state in the union. Depression era migrants, whether the impoverished "Okies" and "Arkies" from the Dustbowl, or later migrants seeking economic opportunity in the "golden state," had all benefited from the postwar economic boom. This inevitably altered the political climate of the state. Increasingly, political power shifted from northern to southern California, which absorbed most of the influx of people. Changing demographics meant that voters in newer suburban communities wielded more power and, with its low-tax and law and order image, the California Republican Party was poised to take advantage of these trends. As the Great Society experiments were put in to effect, disaffection with Washington and "intrusive government" became a Republican rallying cry.

To compound these trends, a sense of crisis shook middle-class Californians in 1966 in a way that was not true only two years before. In 1965, riots broke out in the slums of south central Los Angeles, and predictably this heightened middle-class fears.[34] It hardly helped that Governor Edmund Brown was, at the time, vacationing in Greece.

To many, however, the challenge to the status quo also had a cultural dimension. In 1964, the Free Speech movement was born at the University of California at Berkeley; this became the most conspicuous example of campus radicalism, which was further galvanized by the Vietnam War and student opposition to the draft. In 1965 and 1966, this movement drifted to the far left, and to many Californians, Berkeley seemed a dangerous breeding ground for radical student unrest. Student activists themselves played to public sentiment. The Free Speech movement soon degenerated into the self-styled "Filthy Speech movement" and succeeded in shocking middle-class public opinion. Riots soon shook the Berkeley campus, and Governor Edmund Brown's last-minute crackdown satisfied no one and alienated many. It was a veritable gift to candidate Reagan, whose declaratory policy was to "clean up this Berkeley mess."[35]

Reagan was, of course, helped by the particulars of the 1966 race. In many respects, Edmund G. "Pat" Brown, the father of Democratic gadfly Jerry Brown, was his own worst enemy. His political base was in San Francisco, and particularly the old Irish wards, which were no longer the epicenter of California politics.[36] Brown also fell into the trap of not taking Reagan's candidacy seriously until it was too late. Though a capable politician, Brown seemed strangely out of touch with both political trends and with the voters themselves. It was Reagan, the ostensible "citizen politician," who seemed in touch with the voter's desire to see government scaled back and taxes lowered.

Reagan's proximity to current trends was no accident. His well-financed campaign staff had pioneered the use of continuous polling that enabled their candidate to touch on the visceral feelings of targeted voters and groups.[37] The millionaire backers of Reagan's candidacy hired the well-known public relations team of Spencer and Roberts, a firm that had previously worked for Rockefeller's California nomination bid in 1964. Spencer and Roberts developed a battery of questions and tests to help mold Reagan into what they referred to as a "total candidate." The campaign staff formulated debating positions on flash cards and treated Reagan as if he were a professional rehearsing lines: the staff referred to this as "goof-proofing" their candidate and soon perfected techniques that Reagan would successfully replicate at the national level.[38] A trained actor accustomed to props and warm-up rituals, Reagan was infinitely easier to coach than Goldwater.[39] It was a testimony to Reagan's discipline and ambition that he accepted this "coaching" without question.

To the surprise of many in both parties, Reagan trounced the incumbent governor Brown at the polls and won by a million-vote margin. Reagan was thus part of a Republican national surge in 1966—a surge in which Republicans captured enough state houses to equal those held by the Democrats.[40] (In Maryland, Republican Spiro Agnew won his bid for the state house; in Georgia, Democrat Jimmy Carter lost his bid.) 1966 represented an ominous midterm verdict on the Johnson presidency, and foreshadowed Johnson's last-minute decision not to seek the Democratic nomination in 1968.

Reagan as Governor: 1967-1975

Reagan's two terms as governor are crucial in understanding Reagan, both as president and as putative reformer. Perhaps the most important characteristic of Governor Reagan was his astonishing lack of knowledge about state government. He had no interest, nor even curiosity, about legislation, the budget process or any of the technical details of administration. This was also true of Reagan as president. (As Lou Cannon suggested, he was perhaps the least curious chief executive in modern history.) Beyond ideological shibboleths and the eight-by-five notecards on which he relied, Governor Reagan's views on policy were surprisingly undefined when he arrived in Sacramento. This would have two implications for state policy: one, much of the work was delegated to his staff[41] and, two, many of his actual policies contradicted his professed campaign rhetoric. It was an interesting foreshadowing of his presidency.

In Sacramento, Reagan was, on the whole, well served by a campaign staff that hid his considerable weaknesses and emphasized his equally considerable strengths. The personal loyalty of Reagan's staff, which included press secretary Lyn Nofziger, chief of staff William Clark, advisor Ed Meese and, for a time, Caspar Weinberger as budget director, was in many ways the key to his successes.[42] When the staff worked well, Reagan did. When, however, the staff botched its job, Reagan was unable to fully understand or correct the problem. (This was an unfortunate pattern that was recreated in the White House during the Iran-Contra episode.)

It is no exaggeration to suggest that Reagan was something of a figurehead who was often uninvolved in policy details. Predictably, this meant that Reagan's two terms were more pragmatic than both supporters and detractors cared to admit. Reagan's two-term administration was actually much more liberal than his rhetoric might have suggested.[43] He signed the most liberal abortion law in California history, and instead of cleaning up the university "mess," and cutting back the university budget as opponents feared, he presided over a 136 percent increase in state spending on higher education.[44] Few legislators in Sacramento expected much from Reagan yet his genial manner disarmed legislative opposition.

Ironically, the Democratic controlled legislature was far more cooperative with Reagan than with either Reagan's Democratic predecessor or successor. Putting rhetoric and political differences aside, Reagan cooperated with the California legislature and pushed through legislation that introduced important, but by no means pathbreaking, reforms in the state's welfare and tax policies. Campaigning to lower taxes, Reagan in fact presided over the largest tax increase in California history or in the history of any state to date.[45] (He also made taxes considerably more progressive.) Moreover, his tenure continued, rather than reversed, the expansion of state government. All told, Reagan's tenure was hardly the radical restructuring of state government that he had promised.

In terms of his declaratory commitment to conservative reformism, Reagan's record could be interpreted in one of two ways. His record could be justified in terms of pragmatic adjustment to the realities of governing. Liberal critics could say, somewhat condescendingly, that Reagan "grew in office." Conversely, Reagan's flexibility suggested a gap between promise and performance and the difference between campaigning and governing. At the state level, this disjunction probably worked to the overall advantage of most Californians. (As president, the disjunction left an ambiguous legacy.)

Despite a decade of stirring anti-state, low-tax rhetoric, Reagan's reformist convictions at the state level were surprisingly thin. As with Bill Clinton, his commitment to reform was in large measure a function of campaign rhetoric and positioning and, as with Clinton, Reagan was a consummate campaigner.

Running for President: 1968-1980

Reagan's 1966 victory was perhaps the most conspicuous in a string of Republican upsets that year; not surprisingly, Reagan's political stock increased in the party's conservative wing. Soon members of the Reagan inner circle, such as Lyn Nofziger and Ed Meese, were touting Reagan's presidential potential for 1968.[46]

Shortly after the 1966 election, Governor Reagan faced newly elected New York senator Robert Kennedy in a televised debate on the Vietnam War.[47] Both conservatives and nonconservatives alike widely believed that Reagan "won" the debate, not so much on points but on emotion and style. As demonstrated in the Kennedy-Nixon confrontation of 1960, televised debates are often won on questions of credibility, ease and confidence of manner rather than substantive points and as with John F. Kennedy, Reagan was extremely telegenic.

Always coy about his own political ambitions, Reagan himself envisioned a challenge for the Republican nomination in 1968, but neither he nor his staff could have anticipated the astonishing political comeback of Richard Nixon. Outflanking Reagan and the other candidates at the Miami convention, Nixon directly appealed to the southern bloc, led by South Carolina senator Strom Thurmond. Moreover many including Reagan himself felt that he was not yet up to the challenge, nor did they want the loathed Nelson Rockefeller to benefit from split ranks on the Republican right. Reagan and his staff set their sights on the 1976 Republican nomination.

Reagan's second term as governor—which was supposed to be devoted to welfare reform—was completely dominated by presidential ambition. By 1974, however, the political scene had changed rapidly. The Watergate scandal, Nixon's resignation and the subsequent elevation of Michigan congressman Gerald Ford to the presidency, complicated matters for Reagan's planned 1976 nomination bid—a bid that now seemed out of the question.

It was at this time that Reagan, prodded from the right by conservative pundits such as William Rusher, was even contemplating a third-party bid. Implausible as it may seem in hindsight, conservatives felt marginalized in the GOP. True to his manipulative streak, Reagan was willing to contemplate many ways of getting to the White House. It was the furtive Holmes Tuttle, the head of the Kitchen Cabinet from the early days, who in fact put a stop to all talk of third-party campaigns.

It was an outsider to the Reagan Sacramento entourage, John Sears, who had been part of Nixon's team, who approached the Reagan people with the "heretical" notion that Reagan challenge Ford from the right in the 1976 Republican primaries.[48] Ford's choice of Nelson Rockefeller as vice president had raised conservative wrath and even gave a primary challenge from the right a certain legitimacy. The die was cast to challenge a sitting president of the same party, though one who had been appointed, not elected. Reagan portrayed himself as the candidate of the Republican right wing, which had felt squeezed out of the GOP during the relatively moderate, and even demoralizing, Ford years.

Nevertheless, the early 1976 primaries went badly for Reagan, who was overhandled by his campaign staff. After having experienced surprise losses in the early primaries, Reagan increasingly resisted the advice of his campaign handlers, particularly John Sears, to soften his political instincts and appear nonconfrontational. In bucking the advice, Reagan began to find his political voice right at the time when many considered his challenge to Gerald Ford effectively over. In the New Hampshire primary, Reagan hit on foreign policy themes, particularly Ford's inability to stand up to the Soviets and his Panama Canal "giveaway." Candidate Reagan started to rise quickly in the polls.[49] In staking out these positions, Reagan not only garnered support in the crucial North Carolina primary, where he was heavily endorsed by native-son Senator Jesse Helms, but he also tapped into a larger vein of discontent in the Republican right.[50]

Many on the far right had never trusted Ford's foreign-born secretary of state, Henry Kissinger, who not only began his career as an aide to Nelson Rockefeller, but whose manipulative style and ponderous accent seemed to confirm populist suspicions that diplomacy was somehow un-American. Reagan directed pointed attacks against "Dr. Kissinger"[51] and his policy of détente. Indeed, these attacks hit such a strong chord in the primaries that Ford's campaign managers expunged the word "détente" from Ford's speeches. Unfortunately for Ford, Reagan won a string of primary victories after the North Carolina race. In raising doubts about Ford's ability to stand up to the Soviets, Reagan was raising doubts about Ford's capacity to lead the party and this, in turn, raised questions about Ford's ability to bring down inflation and restore business confidence. With his benign but clumsy manner, Ford was the perfect foil for Reagan's certainty, strident patriotism and reassuring confidence.

Ford, however, enjoyed one advantage over Reagan. In exploiting the prerogatives of the presidency, Ford could promise federal "pork-barrel" rewards that Reagan could not and, in doing so, Ford won over the remaining uncommitted delegates. Moreover, the Reagan camp wanted to avoid a fight that might finish off Ford, but that would nevertheless weaken Reagan's own chances in November, were he to have won the Republican nomination. Simply put, the Reagan staff wanted to avoid the intraparty fratricide that had shaken the 1964 Republican convention. Many in the Reagan camp, probably including Reagan himself, hoped that Ford would pick Reagan as a running mate, but Ford's eventual choice of Kansas senator Robert Dole eliminated this option.

In making these tactical and accommodating maneuvers, Reagan was abiding by what Richard Hofstadter described as the code of American politics—one that all but forbids fratricidal party fights and instead encourages coalition-building, one that favors pragmatism over doctrinal purity. In playing by the code, Reagan's winning performance at the Kansas City convention further raised his political stock within the party. Though he had been thwarted twice in the nomination process—outflanked in 1968 and outcampaigned in 1976—Reagan's political strength had always been that he profited from his defeats. In fact, Reagan made defeat look as if it were a strength, and this curious inversion was key to understanding his later success as president. He understood the symbolic gestures of putting party above campaign, just as he knew the value of putting the nation above partisan politics or, at least, appearing to do so. Reagan was a consummate professional politician, for the simple reason that he never appeared to be one.

Events further worked to Reagan's advantage. In running against Ford, Reagan weakened the sitting president and, indirectly, helped elect Democrat Jimmy Carter, who echoed many of Reagan's own criticisms of Ford in both foreign and domestic policy. By 1980, however, Jimmy Carter's high-minded moralism, public introspection and often-agonized policy reversals wore thin. Compared to Ford, Carter proved an even better foil to Reagan's simplicity and buoyant straightforwardness.

Notes

1. Garry Wills, *Reagan's America: Innocents at Home* (Garden City, N.Y.: Doubleday & Co., 1987), 13.

2. Lou Cannon, *President Reagan: The Role of a Lifetime* (New York: Simon & Schuster, 1991), 208-209.

3. Cannon, *The Role of a Lifetime*, 227, 308, 401; Haynes Johnson, *Sleepwalking through History: America in the Reagan Years* (New York: W.W. Norton and Co., 1991), 43.

4. Wills, *Reagan's America*, 17.

5. Wills, *Reagan's America*, 166.

6. This was a trait he shared with the more intellectually ambitious Bill Clinton.

7. Lou Cannon, *Reagan* (New York: G.P. Putnam's Sons, 1982), 32.

8. Wills, *Reagan's America*, 137.

9. Wills, *Reagan's America*, 108.

10. Wills, *Reagan's America*, 113-114. It is worth noting that Richard Nixon was the son of transplanted Midwesterners; his father was from Ohio and his mother from Indiana. Whittier itself was a colony of Midwestern Quakers who transplanted themselves into rural Orange County, California. As Wills noted, Nixon was "'heartland' in his sympathies but un-anchored"; Wills, *Nixon Agonistes*, 175. The same could be said for Reagan, but for different reasons.

11. Schaller, *Reckoning with Reagan*, 3.

12. Cannon, *Reagan*, 72.

13. Cannon, *Reagan*, 86.

14. Cannon, *Reagan*, 91.

15. Cannon, *Reagan*, 72.

16. By contrast, Reagan's older brother Neil seems to have been a more focused conservative. He had worked for Goldwater and had long been active in conservative causes. See Johnson, *Sleepwalking through History*, 63.

17. Cannon, *Reagan*, 236.

18. Cannon, *Reagan*, 92.

19. Wills, *Reagan's America*, 281-282. Wills called GE "something of a Boy Scout Company."

20. Cannon, *The Role of a Lifetime*, 90; Johnson, *Sleepwalking through History*, 67.

21. Wills, *Reagan's America*, 285.

22. Wills, *Reagan's America*, 284.

23. Cannon, *Reagan*, 96.

24. Wills, *Reagan's America*, 179.

25. Cannon, *Reagan*, 98-99.

26. Schaller, *Reckoning with Reagan*, 12.

27. Cannon, *Reagan*, 13.

28. Richard Hofstadter, *The Paranoid Style in American Politics and Other Essays*, (Chicago: The University of Chicago Press, 1963; Phoenix edition, 1979), 118.

29. Wills, *Nixon Agonistes*, 94.

30. Wicker, *One of Us: Richard Nixon and the American Dream*, 216.

31. Cannon, *Reagan*, 104; Johnson, *Sleepwalking through History*, 65-71; Wills, *Nixon Agonistes*, 253.

32. Cannon, *Reagan*, 121.

33. Cannon, *The Role of a Lifetime*, 42.

34. Cannon, *Reagan*, 110.

35. Cannon, *Reagan*, 148; Cannon, *The Role of a Lifetime*, 534.

36. Cannon, *Reagan*, 109.

37. Cannon, *Reagan*, 113; Johnson, *Sleepwalking through History*, 71-72, 80.

38. Wills, *Reagan's America*, 295.

39. Wills, *Nixon Agonistes*, 254; Wills, *Reagan's America*, 192.

40. Johnson, *Sleepwalking through History*, 81.

41. Johnson, *Sleepwalking through History*, 71.

42. On William C. Clark, see Cannon, *Reagan*, 125; on Caspar Weinberger, see Cannon, *Reagan*, 167.

43. Schaller, *Reckoning with Reagan*, 15.

44. Cannon, *Reagan*, 160. It might be added that the state's economic expansion was in many ways dependent on university research.

45. Cannon, *Reagan*, 324; Wills, *Reagan's America*, 310.

46. Cannon, *Reagan*, 133.

47. Johnson, *Sleepwalking through History*, 54.

48. Cannon, *Reagan*, 192.

49. Cannon, *Reagan*, 212.

50. Wills, *Reagan's America*, 330.

51. Cannon, *The Role of a Lifetime*, 294.

Chapter 4

Foreign Policy and Reform:
The Conservative Vision

In 1980, foreign policy questions formed a central part of Reagan's message of reversing political trends in Washington. Although many critics ridiculed Reagan's view of the world as provincial, outdated and even dangerous, others maintained that Reagan had consistent beliefs and was free of Carter's hesitation and policy vacillation. With his promise to stand up to the Soviets, to stand tall for American principles and to make America proud, Reagan seemed to reject not only a host of recent foreign policy experiments but even a creeping doubt about the moral virtues that America has represented. Reagan's strength was not in nuance nor sophistication, but perhaps just the obverse—he articulated views that were both readily identifiable and represented a broader continuity with American political argument since the 1950s.

The Politics of Foreign Policy: Four Strategies

There is a tendency to see domestic politics, let alone the question of reform, as altogether divorced from foreign policy. Critics of an administration, for example, will argue that the president retreats to foreign affairs as an escape from the complicated realities of politics at home. According to this line of reasoning, President George Bush—who seemed to possess little interest or even ability for the domestic agenda and who had no inclination toward political reform of any type—could gravitate to foreign affairs as a means for evading his weaknesses as chief executive. In a similar way, Richard Nixon in his second term could play the role of world leader abroad and gain the illusion of momentary respite from mounting domestic headaches. In the euphemistic language of American politics, foreign policy success can make a leader look "presidential."

Nonetheless, foreign policy and political reform overlap in unpredictable ways and, depending on the context, can reinforce each other or work at cross-purposes. Foreign policy success can enhance the overall political credentials of a reform politician once he is in office: success can allow him to "buy time," which is necessary if reforms are to show results. One could argue that, in the mid-1980s, General Secretary Gorbachev needed the foreign policy success of a nuclear arms treaty in order to placate an unsettled populace that had not yet reaped the anticipated benefits of economic restructuring at home.

Conversely, foreign policy disaster can undermine a domestic agenda. After the First World War, for example, President Woodrow Wilson's ambitious plan for American involvement in a League of Nations tempered popular enthusiasm for an activist government at home. A majority of Americans in the 1920s hankered for a "return to normalcy" and elected, in consecutive order, Warren Harding, Calvin Coolidge and Herbert Hoover. In the 1960s, it was no coincidence that Lyndon Johnson's political difficulties on Vietnam—what he called a "piss-ant" country—progressively undermined domestic support for the Great Society. Foreign policy setbacks not only give domestic opponents of an administration a tempting target but, in a less partisan sense, they raise legitimate grounds for questioning the wisdom, ability or governing philosophy of any administration.

It would be unwise to develop any rule governing domestic reform and foreign policy other than suggesting that, at differing moments, both are important. Although they may be colored by ideological assumptions, all political choices are a function of shifting alliances and the contingencies of the moment. One need only look at the example of David Lloyd George, the Liberal British statesman, and his political acolyte Winston Churchill who, in the first decade of the twentieth century, both opposed big defense budgets that competed with domestic social spending; when war with Imperial Germany loomed, both men became ardent advocates of an ambitious and expensive naval buildup.

Of course, great politicians can reverse their positions without being captive to earlier commitments and positions—indeed, war and the rumor of war enable the politician to alter and reverse foreign policy pronouncements. Short of the most exceptional emergency conditions—in which national survival is justification alone—most presidents must nonetheless make a case or renew the arguments for overseas commitments. The president who treats foreign policy issues as a series of disconnected policies unattached to a larger political message at home is ridiculed, quite rightly, as a president without vision.

The question of vision is nonetheless bound to raise a problem. Academic writers, who implicitly emphasize ideas over process and theory over mundane politics, will speak of "grand strategy" as if foreign policy is part of a large operating blueprint worked out in the mind of foreign policy planning teams (implicitly staffed by "specialists") and implemented accordingly. The "grand strategy" metaphor, however, obscures the essentially ad hoc and contingent nature of foreign policy.

Here we get to the central point: the larger task of assigning priorities and articulating a vision, however "doctored-up," is not so much a function of foreign but domestic politics, that is selling a policy to a domestic audience. It is a matter of ideology and in foreign policy, ideology almost always exists for domestic consumption—it is a way of explaining but also justifying overseas commitments to the voters and taxpayers on the home front. Speechwriters and pollsters, rather than foreign policy "Mandarins," are thus the quintessential staff members. It is perhaps ironic that many professional observers and academic commentators fixated on the metaphor of the global chessboard and "grand strategy" fail to see how they, themselves, perpetuate a kind of public relations enterprise in which "highfalutin'" concepts—usually commonsense ideas dressed up in pretentious jargon, for example, "security architecture," "world order" and so forth, or simple value judgments camouflaged as "national interest" and affixed with the adjective "vital"—become usable material for the presidential speeches at college commencements or in front of congress, outlining the latest presidential "doctrine." (In the Cold War, every president had to have a doctrine—it conveyed substance.)

The politics of foreign policy is thus about both the policy itself—often immediate and contingent reactions to rapidly emerging and wholly unforeseen problems—as well as the broader discourse on that policy. It is debatable how far a president's domestic policy will resemble his foreign policy; what is, however, important is that the voter in the primaries and in the electorate understands that the often uncoordinated strands appear to fit some type of design.

The president who fails to master the discourse on foreign policy, quite distinct from specific policies, cannot be considered a success; in a democracy, inarticulateness is a fatal flaw. In any great power, foreign policy will always be a projection of domestic assumptions across the border, and this is particularly true in the United States, which has through its history demonstrated a clear missionary spirit, if not a slightly messianic streak.

Critics, and particularly Europeans, are liable to view this as American provincialism, which it perhaps is, but it is also the natural reaction of a great, landmass power that can, if it chooses isolate itself, from the world. Small powers are not ideological, for their survival depends on keeping their powerful neighbors at bay. Great powers, by contrast, are always ideological because they project their own domestic order abroad. As Raymond Aron argued, great powers must stand for something big.

American political debates about foreign policy intervention involve essentially four choices or, if one wants to sound vaguely official, and thereby convey a certain gravitas, "strategies."

1. *Foreign and domestic intervention*: Theodore Roosevelt was perhaps the archetypal politician calling for a robust American presence in world affairs and an aggressive, interventionist government at home. One would expect this activism in a newly rising world power as well as in a country that was turning official attention to social problems emerging in the wake of spectacular economic growth. Such a policy of foreign and domestic intervention is also a typical wartime policy—one that brings not only a concentration of energy in an overseas endeavor but also significant mobilization of domestic resources to meet stated objectives. For these reasons, wartime mobilization almost always accelerates social and political change—change that may or may not be reversed after the war.

2. *Foreign and domestic disengagement* is the obverse. It is often a postwar political strategy that suggests that, while mobilization and overseas commitment may have been necessary in times of crisis, it is unwise to make such policies semipermanent. Retreating from too many commitments abroad and at home was the response of the Republican presidents in the 1920s to the legacy of Woodrow Wilson's administration. As such, "no heroic plans," is often the political rallying cry of democratic governments after long and costly overseas wars: bring the boys back home and allow the postwar boom to take care of the rest. In these interwar years, American conservatives were committed to both isolationism and an old-fashioned laissez-faire economy.

3. *Foreign disengagement, domestic intervention* is a mixed strategy that calls for less government involvement abroad, precisely to free up resources for government activism at home. It is a strategy particularly appropriate to a long peace or a gradual winding down of extensive overseas commitment. In his first presidential campaign, Bill Clinton and his staff all chided President Bush with the undignified taunt, "it's the economy, stupid." The implication was that the patrician President Bush—an alleged master of foreign policy technicalities but, with his disjointed sentences and clumsy metaphors, a clear novice in the possibilities of political packaging—was oblivious to real economic conditions and the need for reform at home. When Clinton partisans made their facetious and even snide references to George Bush's "world tour," the implication was that health and welfare reform should take priority over foreign policy, deemed

lation as a kind of creeping, insidious homegrown socialism. It was also in these halcyon Eisenhower years that Reagan, however imperceptibly, moved to the right, although his transition from anticommunist Democrat to anticommunist Republican was a function of domestic issues rather than foreign policy. Beyond this, anticommunism was a convenient platform for Ronald Reagan. It allowed him to be both vague but also somehow involved: it was a way of signaling vigilance without criticizing the Eisenhower administration on the specifics of its policy.

The Foreign Policy Rhetoric of the Republican Right: Taking on Détente

Conservatives had been, on the whole, relatively restrained during the Eisenhower years. In 1960, it had been the Democratic challenger John F. Kennedy who charged that during the Eisenhower-Nixon administration, America had allowed its defenses to deteriorate and a missile gap to emerge.

By 1964, Republican challenger Barry Goldwater again led the conservative opposition and revived a number of themes he had initially popularized as early as 1952. Democrats and centrist Republicans, he argued, had become little more than appeasers and accepted communism as an inevitable fact, much as they had come to accept elements of crypto-socialism within the United States. Although the twin threats of spreading communism abroad and an unchecked liberalism at home constituted a powerful message to conservative enthusiasts, they failed to penetrate the political imagination of the electorate in 1964. Indeed, the message, coupled to Goldwater's reputation as a "reckless adventurer" with his hand on the nuclear trigger, brought electoral disaster for Republicans.[1]

Ronald Reagan's early rhetoric was no different from Goldwater's, but he was spared much of the negative publicity. Actually, the shifting political climate of the 1960s and 1970s proved favorable to Reagan's repackaging of the Goldwater message, provided that its hard edges were softened. By the late 1970s, the costs, uncertainties and complications of American power abroad, coupled with the growth of the federal bureaucracy at home, made the simple Reagan message increasingly even more appealing for confused and discontented voters.

There was, however, a missing link. In 1964, Goldwater called for strengthening American resolve abroad, but his revivalist platform was only half-developed simply because America had not really disengaged from its foreign policy commitments. To call Eisenhower or Kennedy an appeaser, as many ardent right-wingers had, was slightly farcical. True, the United States had not pushed for the "rollback" of communism as Cold War rhetoric had suggested, but America's military presence in Western Europe and the Korean peninsula, and indeed America's support for beleaguered South Vietnam, made charges of appeasement to communism seem almost ludicrous. By contrast, the policy of détente with the Soviets that emerged in the early 1970s and eventually dominated the foreign policy discourse for much of the decade gave Goldwater's accusation a credibility that had been altogether absent in 1964.

Détente was actually one of those rare policies that eventually drew condemnation from all sides of the political spectrum. Although essentially a conservative principle based on both balance of power statecraft and the practical need to manage superpower relations, détente never resonated with the Republican right wing: the policy seemed to subtly violate the code of American foreign policy because it was based on secretive negotiations and was not framed in terms of democratic principle. Détente seemed to suggest a type of military, let alone moral, equivalence between the superpowers—an equivalence that was intolerable for many conservatives. One can easily ridicule the "code" of U.S. foreign policy, but postwar political leaders had in fact justified America's role in the Cold War in terms of democratic principle, the defense of "the West," and American exceptionalism.[2] America and its democratic allies, they argued, faced an aggressive and totalitarian Soviet empire in a worldwide struggle. Although conservatives exaggerated and caricatured these themes, they did not misinterpret them. Although détente made strategic sense in the context of the 1970s, it also called for suspending, if not overturning, the assumptions that made America's participation in the Cold War politically possible in the first place. Therein was its greatest political weakness.

To complicate matters, détente was linked to Nixon who seemed, to many conservatives, suspiciously liberal, as demonstrated by his ideologically strange conversion to "Keynesianism" and wage and price controls. Although conservatives had always admired Nixon—one of their own who climbed to the top the hard way—they never loved him. Sensing discontent on his right wing, Nixon did everything to neutralize potential challengers like Reagan. It was telling that Nixon used Reagan as a foreign policy emissary to authoritarian strongmen Ferdinand Marcos of the Philippines and Francisco Franco of Spain. (This was a truly Machiavellian move that could alternately flatter Reagan but also marginalize him; the Franco meeting, in particular, further shackled Reagan to the radical, and less respectable, fringes of the conservative movement.)

For the right, Nixon's greatest sin was in appointing Henry Kissinger—heretofore an advisor to the liberal Republican Nelson Rockefeller—as national security advisor and, for all effective purposes, as chief foreign policy spokesman. Disgruntled conservatives had noticed that Kissinger seemed to be the darling of the Georgetown set and was widely admired by a host of relatively liberal journalists who were dazzled by the novelty of a Harvard professor in the Nixon White House. Kissinger's problems ran deeper, for his conservative vision of balance of power statecraft never resonated with the right. A naturalized American, Kissinger never understood that American nationalism was based on the idea, not of parity, but of exceptionalism—of the need to be somehow different and implicitly better than the rest of the world.

Actually, Kissinger personified everything American conservatives—and to be fair, most Americans—dislike about diplomacy. With his ponderous accent and his gift for historical metaphor, Kissinger was an academic expert from the social sciences whose sophisticated approach to foreign policy seemed to make foreign relations more difficult than they needed to be. As historian Richard Hofstadter noted, Americans implicitly trust policy analysts in the hard sciences but distrust policy analysts, the so-called experts like Kissinger, from the social sciences.

If this were not problem enough, the policy of détente with the Soviets had been subjected to further stresses. The political fallout from Watergate gave ammunition to critics, on both the right and left, who disliked the idea of secret and "un-American" diplomacy. Détente was thus mired in the political failings of the Nixon administration and the political weaknesses of the successor Ford administration.

On Capitol Hill, the benefits of détente had been oversold and its costs overlooked; support from congressional Democrats and Republicans alike was bound to disappear. In the Senate, Democrat Henry Jackson of Washington became a leading opponent of Ford's Soviet policy. An old-fashioned Cold War liberal, Jackson supported big government at home as well as big defense spending, thus appealing to both big labor but also defense hawks: two traditional Democratic constituencies left out of McGovern's 1972 presidential equation. Attacking détente was a way for Democrats aspiring to the 1976 presidential nomination to look tough by taking on the politically vulnerable Gerald Ford. It was also a way to distance themselves from the McGovern "dovish" wing that had gone down in flames in 1972. Eventually, the position that Jackson and Maine senator Edmund Muskie had tried to stake out was quickly usurped by outsider Jimmy Carter on the campaign trail in 1975 and 1976.

Even before Ford faced his Democratic challenger in 1976, he was assailed from the right wing of his own party—precisely what Nixon had feared. As recounted in the biographical chapter on Reagan, questions of détente and foreign policy gave Reagan's sagging 1976 primary challenge a second wind after the crucial New Hampshire primary. Not only had Ford picked the centrist Rockefeller and retained Kissinger as secretary of state, but he appeared to

kowtow to the Kremlin by refusing to meet with famed Soviet dissident and
Nobel prize winner Aleksandr Solzhenitsyn when he visited the United States.
For his part, Reagan played not so much on his own Cold War credentials,
which were frankly thin, but his rhetorical defense of traditional foreign policy
principle.

In the 1976 presidential election, it was Democrat Jimmy Carter who
campaigned on a rejection of the secret diplomacy of the Ford-Kissinger regime
and succeeded in convincing voters that Ford was somehow unable to stand up
to the Soviets.[3] Strength, but also honesty, would be the alleged hallmarks of
Carter's foreign policy.

Foreign Policy Debates: From Carter to Reagan

In spite of his tough talk against President Ford in the 1976 election,
Carter immediately put a priority on an ambitious, and perhaps overly idealistic, restructuring of American foreign policy—all to the detriment of the U.S.-
Soviet military rivalry. By 1978, if not 1977, it was thus easy, and even
respectable, to lampoon Carter as a muddle-headed and sanctimonious
missionary out of his element in the harsh world of international politics. Late
in his presidential term, Carter recovered the anti-Soviet hawkishness that he
had used so well in the campaign against Ford, but for many it was too late.

Unfortunately, a series of foreign policy setbacks further weakened détente
and strained relations between the two superpowers. The Soviets seemed to
interpret détente, not simply as a thaw in adversarial relations, but as a green
light to pursue expansion in what they deemed their sphere of influence. In the
late 1970s, Ethiopia fell to Soviet-backed rebels. By the end of 1979, the
Soviets had invaded Afghanistan. To compound matters, Soviet expansion took
place at a time of growing U.S. foreign policy frustration: the Shah of Iran fell
from power in 1979, and this led to the infamous hostage crisis, which created
an impression of U.S. powerlessness.[4] All together, these foreign policy
setbacks heightened public anxieties about Soviet expansion and even
America's superpower status. The debate was no longer simply one of U.S-
Soviet parity, but the question of how far the Soviets had surpassed the U.S. in
terms of military readiness. Inevitably, the debate about détente became
submerged in the larger perception that the U.S. had lost its commanding voice
as leader of the Western democracies.

It was doubly telling that, during the Carter years, the foreign policy
establishment was itself divided on the issue of détente and the overall course of
U.S. policy.[5] It is easy to exaggerate the uniformity of opinion within any
group, particularly when the group is an elite; it is doubly easy, to overstate the
degree of bipartisan consensus in American politics—a consensus that is

ultimately transient and must be continually reconstituted. Nonetheless, the natural divisions within the foreign policy elite widened in these years, and several strands of disaffection coalesced in support for Ronald Reagan's 1980 presidential bid. There were two overlapping reasons why a number of critics felt something was amiss in U.S.-Soviet relations: one, the nuclear parity, if not imbalance, with the Soviets that developed in the wake of détente and, two, the fact that the Soviets seemed to perceive détente as a demonstration of American acquiescence.

Many of those who were dissatisfied with Carter's arms limitation policy clustered around a group that was formed in 1976 and that went by the ominous sounding name, "The Committee on the Present Danger." The Committee included many that would later go on to serve in the Reagan administration, including both Caspar Weinberger and George Shultz.

In an interesting aside, more than half the group was composed of high-profile Democratic foreign policy experts, including arms control expert Paul Nitze, who would later go on to become Reagan's chief arms control negotiator.[6] With a patrician background and a distinguished history of service to the government, Nitze himself hearkened back to the older tradition of proconsuls and the "wise men" of Cold War lore.[7] In the 1970s, he had served Nixon as an arms negotiator; in 1976, he had been an advisor to Carter but failed to receive a positing commensurate with his background and service to the campaign.

During the Carter years, Nitze had lent his voice to the general charge that America had created "a window of vulnerability" that imperiled U.S. security. This became one of the biggest charges against Carter. If Nitze, a long-time Democratic stalwart, felt so strongly—and indeed there was a personal and even ad hominem edge to his criticism of Carter personnel—then this raised serious doubts.

Over time, critics of Carter-era foreign policy merged with the so-called neoconservatives who were in many ways the second generation successors to the original Realists of the 1940s and 1950s. As a group, the neoconservatives defy the neat categories that historians of intellectual trends tend to impose on events and movements. As in politics, intellectual trends are often loose coalitions that are defined against, rather than for, specific ideas and policies. Consequently, attempts to unify disparate strands of any group leave the analyst grasping at less and less, and perhaps this is why overly intellectual studies of political movements tend to break down into shades of nuance and finery that overlook the essentially tactical nature of political life.

Having said that, the neoconservatives of the late 1970s—like the Realists in the years immediately following the Second World War—emerged from the internecine turf wars of the left. (Like the Realists, a number of them had actually flirted with Marxism in their youth.[8]) What had started out as a movement to fend off the vicious attacks that campus radicals of the 1960s made against postwar liberalism gradually took on a life of its own. Many of the neoconservatives were Democrats who wanted to distance their party from the George McGovern-Eugene McCarthy wing; others wanted to preserve the idea of social liberalism linked to a robust interventionism abroad. One of the prominent writers of the neoconservative movement, Irving Kristol, editor of the journal *Commentary*, believed that Reagan could stand up to the Soviets in ways that Carter could not.

The background of a number of neoconservatives revealed their Democratic Party roots. Jeanne Kirkpatrick, for example, had been an advisor to Minnesota senator Hubert Humphrey, and Richard Perle was an aide to Washington senator Henry Jackson.

Identified with this group, Daniel Patrick Moynihan had worked for the Kennedy, Johnson and Nixon administrations. In the early 1970s, he had been ambassador to the UN, and from that platform he criticized the double standards imposed on the U.S. by both third world leaders and liberal elites within the United States itself. Moreover, Moynihan argued against the moral equivalence of U.S. and Soviet power and, incidentally, did in fact meet with Solzehnetsyn, thereby defying Secretary of State Henry Kissinger. In 1976, Moynihan was elected Democratic senator from New York and, during the Reagan years, became a passionate critic of Reagan's domestic policy. In fact, Moynihan's prominent role in the neoconservative movement suggests that the group was more than a simple cheering section for Ronald Reagan.

What is important here is that a movement among these Democratic Party activists, despite all nuances, gradually evolved into part of the coalition that supported Ronald Reagan. What the neoconservatives did was create an atmosphere that Reagan eventually exploited. Coral Bell noted that the Neoconservative movement was important in that it put an intellectual gloss on Reagan simplicities,[9] and in doing so, made them more appealing to the electorate.

The equation was not without some ambiguity. In fact, Reagan's pollster Richard Wirthlin observed that, on one hand, Americans had a general feeling that they were being pushed around in the international arena, but on the other hand, many voters also registered anxieties about Reagan's foreign policy stance—one that seemed overly confrontational. As a response, the Reagan team toned down their candidate's vulnerable image as a warmonger—something Carter tried to play up in the latter stages of the election when Reagan's huge lead began to erode. To some degree, Carter also appeared to demagogue on this charge, which in turn eroded his well-deserved reputation for trustworthiness and honesty, and thus the policy backfired over the longer term.

Fortunately for Reagan, he managed to escape the close foreign policy scrutiny that had irretrievably damaged Goldwater in 1964. Unlike Goldwater, who had an undistinguished legislative career but who left a veritable paper trail of extravagant foreign policy positions that alarmed both Democrats and Republicans alike, Reagan never had to confront complex foreign policy questions. As a state governor, he was not held accountable for a host of foreign policy positions and compromises. True, in 1965 Reagan argued that the United States could "level" Vietnam if it wanted to[10]—language more typical of a Curtis LeMay or a George Wallace than of a serious presidential candidate—but such gaffes were increasingly rare for Reagan, who had a capable staff that could tone down his more extravagant positions and groom him for wider audiences.

American presidential elections are rarely won on ideological mandates: candidates win general elections by softening their earlier positions, leaving them vague enough to allow subsequent maneuvering room. In this sense, Reagan won the 1980 election by soft-peddling his previous positions—such as opposition to the Panama Canal—and by campaigning on the noncontroversial position of making America strong again. The appealing vagueness of this platform contrasted with Carter's wearisome zeal for complexity.

As a candidate, Reagan's foreign policy position could be crudely summarized as this: emphasize the Soviet rivalry at the expense of all other foreign policy considerations and suspend all negotiations with the Soviets until the United States was strong enough to negotiate from a position of strength. Unlike Goldwater in 1964, Reagan in 1980 also had a number of issues to hammer away at an incumbent president: Carter's complex and overambitious foreign policy, the ambiguous legacy of détente, the Soviet invasion of Afghanistan, the containment of communism in the western hemisphere, the Iran debacle and, above all, the half remembered humiliation over Vietnam.

In the end, none of this would have meant anything had the messenger not been trustworthy. Ronald Reagan was, after all, the great communicator, and he communicated his heartfelt patriotism and his genuine belief in America's future in a way that a confused public could understand. In this sense, John F. Kennedy, not Barry Goldwater, is the right comparison for Ronald Reagan. Reagan's Cold War revivalism resembled Kennedy's bravura policy of closing the missile gap: Reagan's knack for framing foreign policy issues in broad expansive principle hearkened back to Kennedy's "New Frontier" symbolism.

Although both Kennedy and Reagan added a rhetorical flourish and personal policy adjustments, each essentially continued the broad policies of his predecessors. Both men understood that democratic politics is about the idea of change as much as change itself. Both men understood that foreign policy debates are not so much about fundamentally altering the established course but about pursuing it better than the other candidate. This poses a challenge, for if democratic politics is about the idea of change, it is also about the rhetorical distancing from previous administrations—the "packaging" of policy—even if policies are often broadly continuous. In this sense, the politics of foreign policy is in large part a game of public relations necessary to convince the public that inherited policies are actually new and improved.

One of the truths of politics is that leaders who rise to power espousing one set of principles often modify, if not wholly abandon, the very policies they advocated during their ascendancy to high office. This is particularly true in foreign policy, in which the dictates and pressures of international politics tend to make mockery of the easy and often careless promises that characterize domestic politics. Indeed, there is no better way of backtracking from the ideological enthusiasms of the campaign and, before that, the primaries than by appointing moderate centrists instead of ideological yahoos. By January of the first year, enthusiasm is out; competence is in.

Consequently, Reagan's foreign policy staff was never as conservative as either his rhetoric suggested or as liberal critics made it out to be. In foreign and national security policy, he generally tapped people from the Republican center, not from the hard right. Reagan did appoint Jeanne Kirkpatrick—who had won plaudits on the right for her 1979 *Commentary* article "Dictatorship and Double Standards"—to be UN ambassador, but Kirkpatrick was far from the White House and the center of policy.

Closer to the president was Richard Allen, who initially brought Kirkpatrick to Reagan's attention, and who was himself picked to be National Security Council (NSC) advisor. Widely regarded as the conservative figure in Reagan's foreign policy team, Allen was also considered something of an intellectual lightweight. In fact, his appointment suggested a downgrading of the position, which had been occupied by high-profile figures such as Kissinger and Brzezinski in the 1970s. (Rather than serving as the "honest broker" of foreign policy information that the NSC advisor was intended to be, both Kissinger and Brzezinski had become an institutional rival to the sitting secretary of state.) After a year in office, the unassuming Allen was compelled to resign after it had been revealed that he accepted a gift from a Japanese lobbyist. Allen's resignation inaugurated policy discontinuity at the NSC. In fact, Reagan had a total of six NSC advisors over the course of his two terms of office creating what I. M. Destler described as a revolving door at the NSC.[11]

The institutional weakness of the National Security Council revealed not only the internal foreign policy conflicts of the Reagan White House but also the problems with a hands-off chief executive on one hand and activist, almost freelancing operatives on the other. Eventually, Allen was replaced by Judge William Clark whose knowledge of foreign affairs was not only thin but almost nonexistent. Clark nevertheless brought a degree of administrative finesse and personal diplomacy to a fractious foreign policy team. He eventually left the NSC for the Interior Department where he soon managed to bring institutional damage control in the wake of James Watt's 1983 resignation. Clark was eventually replaced by Robert MacFarlane and then Admiral Poindexter—both of whom were damaged by, and contributed to, the Iran-Contra scandal in which the administration pursued a questionable policy of exchanging arms for U.S. hostages held in the Middle East. In the wake of that scandal, Weinberger's old assistant Frank Carlucci took over the NSC, purged the staff, downgraded its responsibilities and restored its integrity. When Carlucci replaced the retiring Weinberger at the Pentagon in 1986, General Colin Powell became Reagan's final NSC advisor.

The recurring thread through this administrative disorder was that the Reagan NSC advisors never had the institutional cohesion and clout of their 1970s predecessors. Instead, the Reagan foreign policy team coalesced at the cabinet level—the secretaries of state, defense, and the Central Intelligence Agency—rather than in the White House itself. For Defense, the Reagan transition team chose Caspar Weinberger, who will be addressed in the subsequent chapter on the Reagan peacetime buildup. At the Central Intelligence Agency, the Reagan team tapped Wall Street lawyer James Casey—an appointment that signaled the agency would play a prominent role in the shaping of U.S. foreign policy. (Vice President George Bush had been head of the CIA in the early 1970s and this, too, enhanced the agency's institutional prominence in the Reagan years.) Casey's prominence signaled a reverse of the late 1970s policy in which the agency emphasized pure intelligence gathering over operations, when internal morale plummeted and when public confidence in the counterintelligence apparatus was shaken. (Congressional hearings had revealed that the CIA had been involved in foreign assassination plots, though none were fully carried out, and, perhaps more troubling, had engaged in domestic surveillance.)

A former intelligence agent in the Second World War, who had earned a Bronze Star for his work with the resistance, Casey was also a man who had made his considerable fortune by writing "how-to manuals" on financial matters and tax shelters. In his colorful career, Casey had also treated lawsuits in a cavalier fashion—as part of the cost of doing business in a competitive world. He had also demonstrated a knack for skirting the boundaries of what was legally acceptable. Consequently, he left a paper trail of legal questions that raised a host of problems for him in his subsequent confirmation hearings in the early 1970s and, again, in 1980. Casey was admittedly effective and knew how to run an operation but he also exhibited a strange combination of traits that one might not have thought entirely suitable for espionage: he was indiscreetly brash but also conspicuously secretive. Indeed, it is not hard to imagine Casey, after several highballs, recklessly throwing his weight around. Like a number of Nixon administration appointees, Casey was something of a Wall Street tough-guy attorney who seemed to revel in the machismo of political life. At the same time, Casey had a penchant for covert operations—so covert that it is still hard to ascertain to what extent he was involved in both the alleged "October surprise" leading up to the 1980 election and the subsequent Iran-Contra debacle.

Recruited by Nixon in the 1970s for a number of tasks, Casey had eventually become head of the Security and Exchange Committee and held a number of second-tier appointments.

By 1980, Casey was brought aboard Reagan's 1980 campaign in order to bring financial regularity to a campaign that had been mismanaged by the well-intentioned but disorganized Meese. Like fellow Wall Streeter Don Regan, whom Casey promoted as a possible treasury secretary, Casey was the kind of Irish-American, self-made millionaire that Reagan liked and could understand. He was part John Mitchell and part Tip O'Neill. Nonetheless, Casey ran into considerable congressional scrutiny in the confirmation process and was almost undone early in Reagan's term by pushing through a questionable appointment for Senate confirmation. Secrecy is an essential part of espionage but Congress wants secrecy to be accompanied by an almost puritanical, priestly rectitude; the confrontational, outspoken Casey completely lacked the manners and tact of the "old boy" network that had been traditionally upper-crust WASP and "lace-curtain" Catholic. Even conservative Republicans like Goldwater were calling for his resignation early in the Reagan tenure, but Casey managed to weather the storm.

The Reagan State Department: From Haig to Shultz

At state, the Reagan team tapped former NATO commander in chief, Alexander M. Haig, who lasted less than two years and was eventually replaced by George P. Shultz.

Haig's appointment was the recommendation of former president Richard Nixon. In fact, rumors had long circulated that Haig had been something of a "regent" running the White House operations in the waning days of the Nixon administration. Haig's political appeal, which Nixon well understood, was his capacity to resist charges of softness. Like Kissinger, Haig believed that détente was politically feasible only when pursued from a position of confrontation,[12] and if the appearance of confrontation were necessary, then Haig was their man. A West Point graduate with a martial bearing as well as the brother of a Jesuit priest, General Haig possessed the rectitude, the looks and the Cold War credentials that history had denied Kissinger, who could never fully overcome the appearance of being a professor playing the game of nineteenth-century diplomacy.

Despite his reputation as a fierce Cold Warrior, Haig was really something of a foreign policy centrist who was highly regarded by the European allies—many of whom were anxious about the Ronald Reagan's "cowboy" rhetoric. Haig's appointment was doubly inspired because he satisfied both those who wanted a revivalist form of Cold War anticommunism and those who wanted practical foreign policy experience in the Reagan administration. He offered something for everyone—for the Republican right wing and the more centrist foreign policy establishment.

Haig, however, lacked only one thing necessary to succeed in the Reagan administration, and that was the temperament of a team player.[13] Almost exclusively a product of Washington's military bureaucracy, Haig scarcely understood how to play the insider game with the Californians, many of whom were new to the ways of Washington but who had nonetheless worked with Reagan since the Sacramento days and consequently knew his strengths and weaknesses. Rather astonishingly, Haig believed they would adjust to him rather than he to them.

Haig's big break had come in 1969, when he was appointed as a military aide to Henry Kissinger, then NSC advisor to President Nixon. Haig's years in the Nixon White House are the clue to his later, almost erratic, behavior as secretary of state. While Kissinger had basked in his semi-celebrity status of foreign policy *wunderkind*, Haig did the administrative grunt work that Kissinger himself disdained. Regularly putting in eighteen-hour days, Haig impressed Nixon, who valued self-discipline and drive over flash: he had the methodical discipline that Nixon referred to as an "iron butt." Increasingly, Nixon, who saw through and perhaps even encouraged Kissinger's vanities, began to play Haig and Kissinger against each other. By 1970, Haig had become deputy to H. R. Haldeman, Nixon's chief of staff, who eventually resigned amid the Watergate scandal. Eventually, Haig replaced Haldeman as Nixon's chief of staff—an astonishing ascent in the almost baroque drama of the Nixon White House.[14]

In the subsequent Ford administration, Haig had assumed the position of NSC advisor while Kissinger, who had been both NSC advisor and secretary of state, retained only the position at state. As NSC advisor, Haig proved adept at jockeying for the ear of the president. By 1974, Ford appointed Haig as NATO supreme commander in Europe—an astonishing promotion, over the heads of many officers senior to him, and despite his limited combat experience, which amounted to only a year in Vietnam. (At NSC, Haig was replaced by air force general and former Kissinger advisor, Brent Scowcroft.) Haig's surprise promotion was the triumph of the bureaucrat-soldier—along with Kissinger, the one true insider to come out of Watergate not only unscathed but with enhanced credentials. By then a four-star general, Haig retired from the army in 1979—right in time to join the subsequent Reagan administration after a brief and, even stormy, stint as chief executive at the defense contractor, General Dynamics.

Ironically, the very traits that had served Haig so well in the Nixon years became liabilities in the Reagan White House. Not only did Reagan never play members of his official "family" against one another, he found such conflict distasteful. In Haig's case, the bureaucratically savvy moves of one, politically dysfunctional administration became the slightly paranoiac behavior of another. Haig, in effect, managed to become his own worst enemy in the cabinet. He fought with everyone. As Michael Schaller noted, he, like Kirkpatrick, never quite made it into the inner circle of the White House.[15] It was, however, not from lack of effort.

Haig had started his campaign for the ear of the monarch, if not outright control of policy, on the first day of the new regime. On Inauguration Day, 1981, Haig submitted a memo to White House counsel Meese: the memo outlined Haig's plan for reordering the foreign policy decision-making and centralizing it within State rather than in the National Security Council. In effect, Haig's proposals turned out to be the Reagan policy in the initial years but Reagan never formally signed off on the memo: to do so would have strengthened Haig's hand. Indeed, Haig's campaign looked too much like a "power-grab"—one that alarmed the White House troika, particularly Chief of Staff Jim Baker.

From the start, Haig alienated budget director David Stockman by resisting any budget economies at State. Along with Weinberger, Haig resolutely opposed any cost-cutting whatsoever for the national security budget. Despite their tactical alliance against Stockman and the White House economists, Haig and Weinberger nevertheless had sharp policy differences. Haig had urged a naval blockade of arms going from Cuba and Nicaragua into El Salvador, whereas Weinberger—no apologist for the Sandanistas—felt that a blockade would raise international concern and be of limited strategic value. Regardless of the merits of the position, Haig was entirely right about Weinberger's interference; in fact, Weinberger had originally wanted to be secretary of state and took every opportunity to extend his influence beyond the Pentagon and into the sphere of foreign policy.

Haig may have had a legitimate complaint on this point, but like the boy who cried wolf, even legitimate claims were delegitimized when every thing became a matter of defending "turf" and territory. Demanding to be the "vicar" on foreign policy, he seemed to treat his cabinet appointment as the first step to greatness. Even Nixon suggested that Haig's own presidential ambitions were showing. After the 1981 assassination attempt on Reagan, Haig's press conference, in which he stated he was in the chain of command, came across as particularly bizarre.[16]

Haig was clearly on a collision course with the White House handlers, whose goal was to protect the president and to do everything that reflected well on him. When the messengers got in the way of the message, that created problems. Haig never understood this political equation. His objective was the control of foreign policy and when he felt undermined in this, he continually threatened to resign; eventually, Reagan accepted Haig's offer. It is probable that Haig had no intention of resigning and that Reagan simply called his bluff. Not a vindictive man in any sense, Reagan did not spare the reader the details of the Haig situation in his memoirs.

Haig was soon replaced by George P. Shultz, who had also been in the Nixon administration, but who had not been part of the White House cabal. Shultz and Haig could not have been more different; in fact, compared to rather colorful characters like Haig and Casey, Shultz appeared unassuming and conspicuously low-key and those were perhaps his greatest assets. One might well describe Shultz as the perfect secretary of state for the Reagan administration: he had strong conservative credentials; he represented the institutional interests of State in the foreign policy debates with rival power centers, that is, the Pentagon; he pushed the president in a direction that eventually brought a political payoff and that the White House handlers, particularly Jim Baker, wanted the president to take; he reassured European allies and, above all, he did not upstage the president who remained "diplomat in chief." The fact that there was no talk of a Reagan-Shultz foreign policy such as in the Nixon- and Ford-Kissinger years was a testament to his political finesse at State.

Like Jim Baker, Shultz was a Princeton-educated, former marine. Older than Baker, Shultz had served in the Pacific in the Second World War, after which he went on to receive his doctorate in industrial economics from MIT, where he subsequently taught. For a brief time, Shultz was on President Eisenhower's Council of Economic Advisors. After teaching at the free-market University of Chicago, and after serving as the Dean of its Business School, Shultz later migrated to Stanford, where he maintained close ties to California Republicans.

In late 1968, President Nixon tapped Shultz to be his secretary of labor. By 1970, he became director of the Office of Management and Budget, where he eventually implemented Nixon's wage and price controls, a policy he nonetheless opposed. By 1972, Shultz became treasury secretary but resigned two years later over policy disagreements—disagreements that only enhanced his reputation of high integrity.

During the 1980 campaign, Shultz had been one of Reagan's economic advisors, and there had actually been speculation that Shultz was the first choice of the transition team to be secretary of state. With his low-key but firm manner, his well-known anti-Soviet position, and his ties to the California entourage, Shultz would have been a natural choice. In the same 1980 memo that urged Haig's appointment, however, former president Nixon lobbied against Shultz for a cabinet appointment. There seems to have been bad blood between Nixon and Shultz. During the darker period of his presidency, Nixon was known to have belittled Shultz, who refused to use the Internal Revenue Service to harass Nixon opponents, by saying, "what does that candy ass think we sent him over there for?"[17]

At State, Shultz won wide applause from Democrats and Republicans alike for pursuing a cautious and competent foreign policy that steered clear of rhetorical excess but that was based on a skeptical view of Soviet intentions. Sharp differences existed within the administration, but they were not publicized to the extent that Vance-Brzezinski divisions in the Carter administration were.[18]

Shultz, for example, urged strong military action against states that had sponsored terrorism in the 1980s, whereas Defense Secretary Weinberger, who continued to take an active role in foreign policy debates, urged that the military not get dragged in to a conflict that he believed the U.S. public would not support. In the broader sense, Shultz urged that the administration think seriously about going to the negotiating table with the Soviets on nuclear arms limitations talks, whereas Weinberger—later backed by his old California associate, NSC advisor Clark—was more skeptical about any possibilities of negotiation. What unified both of Shultz's positions relative to Weinberger's was the idea of constructive engagement, that force was there to be used either to punish "terrorist states" or to get the Soviets to the bargaining table. Despite his reputation as a hawk, Weinberger was somewhat skittish about the use of force. His reluctance stemmed from his belief that the public was unwilling to support a large defense budget should a prolonged conflict or military setback take place. For Weinberger, the huge defense budgets of the Reagan era would be the first casualty of either (1) an unpopular conflict or (2) relaxed vigilance about the Soviet threat.

As president, Reagan was above such politics disagreements, which was both good and bad. It was good to the extent that Reagan's executive temperament contrasted with Carter's immersion in policy—an immersion that seemed somehow unpresidential. It was, however, bad to the extent that Reagan did not really understand the foreign policy debates swirling around him and this left him vulnerable to those—like Weinberger and Don Regan—who knew how to appeal to his basic instincts, often through anecdotes and irrelevancies. Reagan's real problem was not his intelligence but his intellectual laziness. Never a keen reader, Reagan was not pushed and, on the contrary, somewhat overhandled and protected. As Lou Cannon noted, the 1981 assassination attempt cut short his "learning curve" on foreign policy matters.[19]

It is to the operational aspects of foreign policy rather than the animating ideals that we now turn.

Notes

1. Hofstadter, *The Paranoid Style in American Politics* (Chicago: The University of Chicago Press, 1965; Phoenix Edition, 1979), 124-129.

2. Stanley Hoffmann, *Primacy or World Order: American Foreign Policy since the Cold War* (New York: McGraw-Hill, 1968), 19.

3. Gaddis Smith, *Morality, Reason and Power: American Diplomacy in the Carter Years* (New York: Hill and Wang, 1986), 31.

4. Smith, *Morality, Reason and Power*, 10.

5. Wills, *Reagan's America: Innocents at Home* (Garden City, N.Y: Doubleday and Co., 1987), 339.

6. Wills, *Reagan's America*, 336-338.

7. A veteran of the Roosevelt and Truman administrations, Nitze never quite received a position commensurate with his prominence in the early years of the Cold War, when he authored a controversial 1950 report that urged massive U.S. military spending to counter the Soviet threat. In the 1960s, he served Kennedy as an undersecretary at Defense despite having lobbied heavily for a cabinet position. In the Johnson administration, he was secretary of the Navy.

8. Wills, *Reagan's America*, 340.

9. Coral Bell, *The Reagan Paradox: American Foreign Policy in the 1980s* (New Brunswick, N.J.: Rutgers University Press, 1989), 12.

10. Schaller, *Reckoning with Reagan: America and Its President in the 1980s* (New York: Oxford University Press, 1992), 14.

11. See I. M. Destler, "Reagan and the World: An 'Awesome Stubbornness'," in *The Reagan Legacy*, Charles O. Jones, ed. (Chatham, N.J.: Chatham House Publications, 1988), 257.

12. Wills, *Reagan's America*, 346.

13. In fact, anyone reading the opening pages of Haig's colorful 1983 memoir will be struck by the author's touchiness and desire to prove himself against all odds, both real and imagined.

After West Point, Haig served on Douglas MacArthur's staff in Korea, later went to graduate study at Georgetown and, during the Kennedy administration, worked for Secretary of the Army Cyrus Vance. It is not hard to imagine Haig, the Philadelphia-born Irish-American, being touched by what Garry Wills called "Camelotitis." For their part, the Kennedys also had a soft spot for dashing military types such as General Maxwell Taylor, former Rhodes Scholar and White House warrior-in-residence. After his Washington stint, Haig did the (brief) mandatory tour in Vietnam and then served two years as assistant commandant at West Point. See Alexander M. Haig Jr., *Inner Circles: How America Changed the World* (New York: Warner Books, 1992).

14. Some have hinted that Haig was involved in wiretapping while working for Haldeman; more probable is the allegation that Haig, as chief of staff, persuaded Nixon to resign from office rather than face impeachment charges.

15. Schaller, *Reckoning with Reagan*, 40.

16. Haig had worked in the Kennedy administration and like another alumnus, Daniel P. Moynihan, understood the need for public reassurance after assasination attempts, the need for clarity in the chain of command and attention to detail necessary for later inquiries. Haig, however, was not reassuring and did not contribute to clarity.

17. Cannon, *President Reagan: The Role of a Lifetime* (New York: Simon and Schuster, 1991), 79.

18. On policy disagreements in the Carter administration, see Smith, *Morality, Reason and Power*, 245. On policy disagreements in the Reagan White House, see Cannon, *The Role of a Lifetime*, 306-309, 431.

19. Cannon, *The Role of a Lifetime*, 155-156.

Chapter 5

Foreign Policy: The Reagan Reality

Most studies of a president's foreign policy follow a sensible but rather predictable pattern that approximates an around the world tour where, after an introductory background chapter, each consecutive chapter knocks off the China policy, the ongoing Middle East negotiations, the evolving relations with the Kremlin and so forth. The names and faces change, but the style remains the same.

According to this pattern, one could write a competent and fair description of any administration but perhaps altogether overlook the president's inability to articulate a vision or, conversely, fail to recognize that policy neglect, if not outright disinterest, is in many instances an astute policy. The "round the world" approach also conceals the ways in which problems emerge quite independent of neat categories and tend to crowd in on one another at certain moments only to disappear for long stretches of time in other instances.

It is thus important to remember that almost every conflict—in Afghanistan, in Central America, in Europe—was, for the Reagan team, a refraction of the U.S.-Soviet rivalry, two great powers in competition. (Middle East policy was, perhaps, a partial exception.) In this sense, Reagan's policy was a calculated rejection of Carter's premature attempt to move beyond the confines of the Cold War. Even Carter, by 1980, had subtly repudiated his earlier position. (A rhetorically challenged politician who performs an "about-face" does so with difficulty.) In the broadest sense, Reagan's declaratory policy meant, not accommodation and dialogue, but selective confrontation—against communist insurgents, against Middle Eastern terrorists, and against Kremlin propaganda.

Continuing Carter's Policies

In many ways, the Reagan policy was roughly continuous with Carter's policy, particularly from the latter part of the Carter administration. This continuity extended even to areas where the Reagan administration quietly ignored Reagan's campaign rhetoric. Reagan had, for example, long pledged to support Taiwan and halt détente with mainland China. In office, however, he did neither. By 1982, détente with Red China was renewed,[1] and the anomaly of Reagan's earlier right-wing rejectionism was conveniently forgotten. In the same way, Reagan's rousing campaign opposition to the Panama Canal "giveaway" also conveniently faded from memory.[2]

For all the tactical repudiation of Carter, the Reagan administration, under both Haig and Shultz continued many of Carter's policies but did so with a focus that was altogether absent under Carter's watch. Moreover, the administration often committed more financial resources, and its supporters could say, with some justification, that although Carter may have talked tough late in his presidency, he never "spent tough." The Reagan administration, for example, continued and deepened aid to the Afghan rebels. Whereas the Carter administration provided thirty million dollars, the Reagan administration funneled six hundred million dollars into Afghanistan. After 1986, the administration even provided stinger missiles, despite the advice of many military experts who feared they would get into the hands of terrorists.[3]

This fit into an administration preference for covert operations, in effect returning to the Nixon Doctrine, whereby the U.S. used proxies in its Cold War confrontations. Afghanistan was actually the largest covert operation that the United States had launched since the Vietnam War, and offered clear evidence that Casey's tenure at the CIA was more than simply symbolic. Such covert operations were cheap, politically expedient and relatively effective. In Afghanistan, Mozambique and Central America, the Reagan administration used this policy with relatively favorable results.[4] The downside of such covert operations was, however, revealed in the Iran-Contra "back-channel" diplomacy—a policy that both Shultz and Weinberger directly opposed and took place, they claimed, without their knowledge.

In a sense, the Iran-Contra scandal was a direct result of the administration's Central America policy. Even in 1979, public alarm about Soviet involvement in the Western Hemisphere was rising, particularly when the presence of a Soviet brigade in Cuba was revealed. Upon learning of this, the Senate Foreign Relations Committee chairman, Democrat Frank Church of

Idaho, theretofore a "dove," had urged Carter to withdraw the arms control treaty with the Soviets from Senate consideration.

As president, Reagan underscored the strategic importance of Central America and urged support of the El Salvadoran government in its contest with leftist insurgents. Reagan had also urged support of anticommunist rebels, the Contras, in the then Marxist-dominated Nicaragua, which had predictably leaned toward Castro's Cuba.

Although Reagan strongly believed in supporting the Contras, several of his advisors, such as James Baker and Michael Deaver privately stressed its unpopularity in the polls. Reagan's convictions kept the topic alive; domestic realities kept it from being a central policy issue[5] as many, including Secretary of State Haig, who wanted a "line drawn in the sand," had hoped it would become.[6] More politically attuned to domestic trends than Haig, Baker knew that the idea of American military advisors in the jungles of South America, as well as official support for anticommunist insurgents trying to topple a government, raised not only the Vietnam but also the Bay of Pigs specter—two foreign policy nightmares that tarnished Democratic administrations in the 1960s but could nonetheless give congressional Democrats in the 1980s a wedge issue by which to challenge Reagan and the Republicans. In fact, congressional Democrats did precisely that by passing the 1982 Boland Amendment, which prohibited the CIA from funding the Contras. Increasingly, some in the administration looked for alternative ways to keep the pressure on the Sandinistas.

The second part of the Iran-Contra equation led straight to the administration's Middle East policy, a notably weak link in the administration's overall record. In 1982, a Lebanese suicide bomber managed to kill himself and more than two hundred marines—sent to Lebanon as something akin to peacekeepers—in a grisly attack. In the following years, Lebanese Shi'ite terrorists kidnapped a number of Americans and held them hostage.

To counter these moves, NSC staff members had, by 1985, developed a modern variant of the "King's secret," secret diplomacy that contradicted official foreign policy but that nonetheless carried the blessing of the monarch. Such policies—which echoed Nixon-Kissinger "back-channel" diplomacy and, in effect, subverted the bureaucracy—rarely succeed. In the case of Iran-Contra, the administration provided arms to Iran—thereby contradicting not only U.S. policy but one that the United States had urged on its reluctant allies—as a goodwill gesture to compel the Iranian clerics to prevail on its Shi'ite clients in southern Lebanon to release U.S. hostages and, in turn, to provide money to fund the Contras in their struggle with the pro-Marxist Sandinistas. The Byzantine details of this implausible, triangular plot are surely stranger than any fiction writer could conjure up. Indeed, it made one think the Reagan

National Security Council was staffed by keystone cops with security clearances.

The project was a predictable failure; after seven arms shipments, only three hostages were released and the negative publicity revealed to foreign allies and adversaries alike not only the divisions within the administration but the operational chaos within the White House. Still, it is hard to know what to make of the whole episode, which took place in Reagan's second term when the tight controls that had been imposed by Jim Baker were released and when Don Regan assumed Baker's position as chief of staff and subsequently proved administratively and politically inadequate to the task. Weinberger and Shultz both retained their positions in large part by claiming that they had initially opposed the policy and were innocent of subsequent developments that took place in the White House basement and back-warrens. Casey, who may or may not have known more than he let on, died in 1987, having suffered a heart attack after a particularly grueling line of congressional questioning.

There was a time when the Iran-Contra hearings threatened to turn in to another Watergate fiasco that could undo Republican gains and resuscitate the demoralized Democrats as nothing else could. Ultimately, the Iran-Contra scandal ended with a whimper, not a bang. Even if the means were highly dubious, if not outright illegal, the goal of gaining freedom for U.S. hostages nonetheless had its nobler aspects. In all probability, however, the perception that Reagan was not fully in charge as chief executive—something that had been initially revealed as early as November of 1981 in Budget Director Stockman's published asides on the supply-side fiasco—or even fully aware of foreign policy details, tended to exonerate him.

The immediate effect of the scandal was to straighten the foreign policy team from working at cross-purposes, as it had through much of the 1980s. This implicitly strengthened the hand of Shultz, who had been handicapped from pursuing arms control talks with the Soviets by administration hard-liners. Weinberger resigned in 1986, for reasons unconnected to Iran-Contra, and this further removed a source of friction that had kept the foreign policy team divided against itself.

Standing Up to the Soviets: Confrontation or Negotiation?

It has become almost a cliche to describe Ronald Reagan's administration in terms of the "Second" or "New Cold War" as if Reagan represented a radical rupture with previous administrations, or perhaps even a distinct step backwards. It might, however, be said with equal justification that Reagan—who like most Americans understood very little about nuclear policy—made détente politically acceptable and, in fact, built on the very legacy left by Richard

leaders in nearly eight years and while little was accomplished, it did lay the groundwork for another summit in the following year. In the October 1986 summit in Reykyavik, Iceland, Gorbachev launched a blitz of proposals that demonstrated how he had taken the public relations offensive and seemed more vigorous and certainly younger than Reagan. It became clear that Gorbachev wanted Reagan to abandon SDI and not engage in research for a full ten years but Reagan stubbornly refused to give in to this demand, much as he refused to give in on the Kemp-Roth tax cuts in 1981. When Reagan's mind was made up, there was no budging him.

This period was a time of continual jockeying for the rhetorical advantage. Following the lead of his mentor Andropov, Gorbachev tried to divide the West Europeans from the Americans by referring to the "common European home"—a slogan that may not have convinced the Hungarians and Poles but played to some constituencies west of the Iron Curtain. Not to be outdone, Reagan went on the offensive much as he had done in 1982. In Berlin, the cockpit of the Cold War, John F. Kennedy had once stood at the line demarcating democracy from dictatorship and intoned that he, too, was a Berliner. More than two decades later, Ronald Reagan stood at the foot of that same wall and implored General Secretary Gorbachev to tear it down. Gorbachev had done much to score a series of public relations successes, but with one simple declaration, Reagan called his bluff.

By early 1987, Gorbachev, who faced a number of pressures, effectively conceded SDI to Reagan and accepted the U.S. position on the zero-option that would eliminate all intermediate range nuclear weapons from Europe and that also allowed for on-site inspections. "Trust but verify" became Reagan's oft-repeated slogan.

It was telling that hard-liner Richard Perle had resigned from the administration in March of 1987 because of policy disagreements—ironic since he had himself proposed the zero-option as a means to scuttle détente but just the reverse had happened. The "pragmatists" had usurped his hard-line position; in a sense, it was the ultimate triumph of Paul Nitze who, as George Shultz's arms expert, turned perhaps the weaker of two options in to a sustainable treaty.

The successful orchestration of the superpower summits and the revival of détente were politically useful for President Reagan and General Secretary Gorbachev, both of whom were seeking to escape from domestic complications. Even before 1984, the White House staff and particularly Jim Baker sensed that the American public had to have something to show for the expensive arms buildup. Alarmed by Wirthlin's polls, Nancy Reagan even urged her husband to negotiate with the Soviets prior to the 1984 election. After the Iran-Contra scandal, Reagan needed to compensate for the botched policy with a major act of statesmanship. For his part, Gorbachev needed to compensate for the continued stagnation of the Soviet economy, the Afghan imbroglio and the exposure of Soviet technological weakness in the wake of the 1985 Chernobyl disaster.

The upshot was the famous Washington summit of 1987 that put forth the final INF treaty. At this time, Gorbachev, known almost affectionately as "Gorby" attained celebrity status. He even managed to bolt from his motorcade and pump hands with well-wishers along Washington's Connective Avenue. (The only bad blood at the summit seemed to be between First Lady Nancy Reagan and the relatively glamorous Raisa Gorbachev, who herself seemed ready to upstage her American counterpart.) The INF Treaty was soon ratified by the Senate.

As such, Reagan's second term was characterized by the virtual renewal of détente in all but name. It was fortunate for the Reagan White House that the second term coincided with the rise of Gorbachev, who facilitated the thaw in U.S.-Soviet relations. One wonders about the course of American-Soviet relations had Andropov or Chernenko remained general secretary through the 1980s. Both the perception of impenetrable Soviet military strength (dispelled in Afghanistan) and the ideologically accommodating tone of Gorbachev—the first Soviet leader that Americans knew as they might know an American politician—made it possible for a politically weakened Reagan to push through an arms treaty in a way that similarly weakened presidents before him could not.

Reagan as Diplomat in Chief

Reagan will probably be remembered more for his foreign policy accomplishments, which were clear-cut, than for his rather mixed domestic record. Nonetheless, the idea of Reagan as an astute diplomat is not a popular one—particularly among foreign policy experts, most of whom believed that Reagan was lucky to sit in the White House when the Soviet Union buckled and that his success was simply a function of the earlier policy of anti-Soviet containment. Reagan, they argued, was rewarded for abandoning his earlier stridency: he "grew" in office and, implicitly, distanced himself from his earlier and perhaps irresponsible rhetoric. Reagan, however, changed far less than imagined and much of his popularity can be located precisely in these continuities.

Reagan, it must be said, enjoyed a number of advantages denied his predecessors. He had the ability to extricate himself from disaster, such as the 1982 terrorist explosion in Lebanon when more than two hundred marines were killed by a suicide truck bomber. Since the Beirut tragedy was a suicide attack, it was perhaps also easy to dismiss as an example of incomprehensible Middle Eastern fanaticism rather than the tangible failure of Reagan as commander in chief. Moreover, Reagan was fortunate to have a quick, military victory in Grenada. Although the timing was purely coincidental, the U.S. invaded Grenada in the days immediately following the Beirut bombing, which had the effect of further distancing the administration from the Middle Eastern tragedy.

Second, it is easy to forget that Reagan was an expert negotiator and this helped him overcome his intellectual shortcomings. Indeed, Reagan was always at his best when the opposition underestimated his stubborn instincts and ability to bargain. Reagan had perhaps first learned these skills as a leader in the Hollywood Screen Actor's Guild, particularly during the stressful period of the Red Scare, which surely tested his skills of survivability. In Sacramento, Reagan had also surprised his adversaries by proving an astute negotiator with Democratic Assembly leaders. He was a good negotiator in large part because he fully believed in one-to-one dealings with other leaders; he knew how to compromise but also stand firm. Reagan combined both stubborn convictions and personal geniality, and it is not hard to imagine Reagan saying, as he did, that he saw a bit of Tip O'Neill in Gorbachev. In the larger sense, Reagan possessed a rather naive belief in the goodness of people and that free and open contact—between peoples and leaders—breaks down barriers. Of course, such a view oversimplifies much of human history, but in diplomacy, results count and Reagan brought results.

Third, Reagan was able to deflect foreign policy criticism and use it to political advantage and this, too, distinguished him from Carter. Traditionally, diplomacy has been the metier of kings and their ministers; in modern America, it has been the preserve of career bureaucrats and corporate lawyers with the occasional academic—hardly groups known for the common touch. For their part, foreign policy bureaucrats and academic commentators have tended to be dismissive of Americans' capacity to understand world events with any sophistication. Americans, so many critics lament, simply do not grasp the complications and burdens of world power.

Conversely, the foreign policy establishment often fails to appreciate the peculiar circumstances of American history, with its geographic insularity and democratic prejudices that subtly deprecate the craft of diplomacy. Indeed, the skills of the diplomat—nuance, agility, social poise, a capacity to straddle several social boundaries and to finesse confrontation—often seem elitist and "aristocratic" in democracies. It was no accident that American conservatives and populists have long ridiculed the American diplomatic establishment as "striped-pants" elitists and Ivy-League Anglophiles, as de-racinated Mandarins who are more comfortable in the Middle East than the Middle West. Free from the domestic liabilities of Kissinger-type diplomacy, Reagan could play to democratic prejudices. He never felt the need to lecture the public and thus brought a degree of tactical foreign policy disengagement to the presidency.

This, however, stemmed from a fourth trait: Reagan treated all foreign policy as derivative of the U.S.-Soviet rivalry. He provided the electorate with the sense that he could stand up to the Kremlin by freezing détente. Prior to the INF Treaty, Reagan was able to campaign in 1984 on the very issue of "having made America strong again," and a plurality of the electorate seemed to agree.

Disengagement from, and disinterest in, foreign policy detail coupled to anticommunist confrontation seem contradictory. One would think that disengagement and confrontation are dialectical opposites, but in fact, the two policies reinforce each other. Reagan's Cold War revivalism offered an ideological cover by which to disengage from the complexities of international involvement. Americans, noted Stanley Hoffmann, crave simplicity in foreign policy; they want what Hoffmann called a "simple activist type."[8] They want, not the balance of power calibrations of Nixon and Kissinger nor the tiresome complexity and anguished idealism of Carter, but a straightforward defense of American principles matched by an assertive use of military power.

That was Reagan to the core. He provided a simple, yet potent, position that both explained and justified the expensive arms buildup. Reagan's foreign policy offered a degree of strategic disengagement for an American public that wanted American muscle flexed against the Soviets but did not care to be drawn into peripheral conflicts where every small nation could gain something by taunting America. President Eisenhower—never preoccupied by face-saving or the need to project abstract notions of credibility—called this the "tyranny of small nations."[9] Great powers, Eisenhower believed, know how to endure the thousand indignities perpetuated by the weak and insecure. In a curious way, Reagan also avoided the tyranny of small nations and even small problems.

In practical terms, reform politicians are often most successful when they simultaneously bring disengagement from foreign complications and put priority on restructuring institutions at home. Every reformer must make a rough calculation of those relations that are important and those that are peripheral, those that can be postponed and those that must be addressed immediately. In keeping with Richard Nixon's pre-inauguration advice, the Reagan team decided to focus on domestic problems and postpone foreign policy questions until the second term.[10] For Reagan, the Cold War offered the best of both worlds—an excuse to focus exclusively on one rivalry, but also an excuse to postpone serious negotiations with the Soviets until America was stronger. It was a tactical retreat with the pledge of returning to the conflict at an unspecified, later date—the ultimate campaign promise.

In the end, Reagan's greatest asset was not that he had a sophisticated foreign policy—which never wins elections—but that he had a foreign policy strategy that meshed with his domestic agenda: less government at home and more anticommunism abroad. Reagan thus combined the platform of domestic disengagement with foreign policy revivalism and, in his rhetoric at least, never wavered. One can belittle such a policy, but that is to miss the point, for Reagan achieved a foreign policy success that had been denied all his predecessors dating back to John Kennedy. In 1988, Reagan was using the same rhetoric as he used in 1964: the times had changed but the foreign policy message had not.

Reagan's "philosophy" of foreign policy was grounded in the old-fashioned idea of the moral rightness of America—the very idea of "Americanism." Rare for diplomats, who are cosmopolitan and international in perspective, "Americanism" is at bottom a provincial outlook. The irony of history, however, is that provincial beliefs and even mythologies, penetrate the popular political culture of every great nation. For their part, diplomats, and the professional observer of the diplomatic scene, are often blind to the passions that drive domestic politics. Reagan, by contrast, celebrated these passions. Americans trusted Reagan to hammer out the INF Treaty, not only because the accords seemed to be made from a position of strength, but because Reagan believed that the negotiations represented a triumph of American principle. With his firm but reassuring manner, Reagan bridged the two expectations of the American public in the early 1980s: to get tough with the Soviets but also to reduce the nuclear threat.

Foreign policy—based on a dreary type of operational balancing and counterbalancing—is never emotionally satisfying and that is why experts often camouflage it in historical analogy and in metaphors such as "grand" strategy or as a "chessboard." (Foreign policy involves more perpetual tactics than strategy, more poker than chess; if there is a strategy, it is a function of domestic politics—something many experts dismiss if not subtly disdain.) Paradoxically, the professed "realism" of such experts is, at bottom, a romantic dressing up of fairly routine relations. In itself it is a harmless and even socially useful enterprise but it should not be used as the basis for ridiculing democratic prejudices as naive and provincial simplicities. Far more realistic than pseudo-academic "realism" is the selective projection of a domestic ideology onto world affairs—what all great powers invariably do. In this, Reagan was a near virtuoso.

While American leaders had not lost their faith in their professed principles (as the Soviet leaders appeared to do in the Brezhnev years) they had, by the 1970s, lost the political capacity to articulate them boldly and convincingly. As diplomat in chief, Reagan returned to the tradition of Kennedy, Eisenhower, Truman and Roosevelt. Reagan never tried to master diplomatic jargon—linkage, withdrawal, multilateral talks, credibility, renewable resources, countervailing force—but instead spoke of ideas and concepts that have emotional resonance with American voters.

Ultimately, Reagan was a professed believer in freedom—economic, political and intellectual. In this respect he was the inheritor of nineteenth-century classical liberalism with the easy and optimistic assumptions of a "harmony of interests" between free peoples. These assumptions applied equally to the Soviet people, whom he believed were the victims, rather than the beneficiaries, of their rotten government. Reagan's anti-Soviet Cold War stance was one built on optimistic foundations, not the paranoid pessimism of the fringe right. Herein was the success of Reagan's détente and, implicitly, the failure of Nixon and Ford's Soviet policy. If American nationalism is defined in terms of American exceptionalism, then détente of the 1970s—an uninspired type of operational balancing—was a subtle rejection of this nationalism. By contrast, Reagan's new détente with the Soviets was an affirmation of the very principles that Americans demand. In fact, Reagan was never more close to his idol, Franklin Roosevelt, than in his buoyant confidence about the inevitability of democratic values and the fall of totalitarian ones.

Notes

1. I. M. Destler, "Reagan and the World: An 'Awesome Stubbornness'," in *The Reagan Legacy*, Charles O. Jones, ed. (Chatham, N.J.: Chatham House Publishers, 1988), 241-242.

2. Lou Cannon, *President Reagan: The Role of a Lifetime* (New York: Simon and Schuster, 1991), 342; Michael Schaller, *Reckoning with Reagan: America and Its President in the 1980s* (New York: Oxford University Press, 1992), 18.

3. Cannon, *The Role of a Lifetime*, 371.

4. See Schaller, *Reckoning with Reagan*, 125-126.

5. Cannon, *The Role of a Lifetime*, 384.

6. Reagan, *Role of a Lifetime*, 344-345; Garry Wills, *Reagan's America: Innocents at Home* (Garden City, N.Y.: Doubleday and Company, 1987), 347.

7. Cannon, *The Role of a Lifetime*, 298; Wills, *Reagan's America*, 345.

8. Stanley Hoffmann, *Dead Ends: American Foreign Policy in the New Cold War* (Cambridge, Mass.: Ballinger Publishing Co., 1983), 82.

9. Garry Wills, *Nixon Agonistes: The Crisis of the Self-Made Man* (Boston: Houghton Mifflin, 1970), 134.

10. Reagan, *The Role of a Lifetime*, 78.

Chapter 6

National Security: The Conservative Vision

Assessing the foreign policy of the Reagan administration is impossible without also judging the nature of the "Reagan buildup." More than the matter of foreign policy—which rests on a set of relationships that are difficult to manage and ultimately impossible to fully control—military policy, which is centered on institutions, raises the question of reform in a direct, rather than simply a directional, sense. Throughout modern history, the military has been the one branch of the political apparatus where leaders who did not maintain an efficient level of preparedness nor innovate with new developments did so at their own peril. In fact, it is almost an axiom of politics to suggest that disappointments on the battlefield—somehow seen as the verdict on the "competitiveness" of a state or society—inevitably lead to soul-searching at home and the subsequent clamor for reform of both military and civilian institutions.

Not surprisingly, it was in the area of military policy that the Reagan administration was alleged to have its greatest reform impact. In the personified rhetoric of American politics, "Reagan made America strong again." Such rhetoric implied that Reagan's predecessors, particularly Carter, had allowed America to atrophy its military muscles. In democratic systems, this is the standard accusation of the outside party against the insiders—a pattern that was repeated by both parties throughout the Cold War.

"When I arrived in the White House in 1981," Ronald Reagan wrote in the opening, and thus crucial pages of his autobiography, "the fiber of American military muscle was so atrophied that our ability to respond effectively to a Soviet attack was very much in doubt... while the Soviet Union had created a war machine that was threatening to eclipse ours at every level."[1] The solution was to end the "hesitation and reluctance" and the "withdrawal" after the Vietnam and Carter years (implicitly, the two were linked). The solution was to send a clear message to the Soviets that their "violent campaigns of subversion" and "terrorism" could not be tolerated.[2] With his gift for bluntness, Reagan wrote that he wanted to let the Soviets know that "we were going to spend whatever it took to stay ahead of them in the arms race. We would never accept second place."[3]

Presidential memoirs tend to be the literary equivalent of a campaign speech pitched to future historians. It was telling that Reagan began and ended his work with the standard accusations of the military unpreparedness of his predecessors. Reagan, however, went on to take credit for his own administration's singular role in bringing the Soviets to the bargaining table and in terminating the Cold War. It was this, and not cutting deficits or scaling back government waste, that Reagan chose to emphasize in the opening and closing pages of his memoirs. Implicitly, Reagan revealed all the politician's tricks: belittle the predecessors, assume sole credit for the accomplishments of the administration and make a causal connection between policies taken and momentous events abroad.

The Politics of Defense: More or Better?

It is one of the tired truisms of American politics to suggest that "politics stops at the water's edge." True, partisan sniping is indeed unbecoming, if not unpatriotic, when American lives are at risk in some foreign field but the recriminations about who allowed the "loss" of China, who presided over military setbacks in Korea and Vietnam, or who failed to stand up to the Soviets gives lie to the truism.

Particularly during the Cold War, the president's ability to stand up to the Soviets and to be commander in chief of the U.S. armed forces was one of the central issues of any political contest: each election cycle afforded an opportunity for one party to challenge the incumbent by claiming to be more forceful in the defense of U.S. interests abroad. In 1952, for example, Republicans campaigned against Truman's handling of the Korean conflict: it was no accident that General MacArthur, who had clashed with Truman, addressed the Republican convention that year. In 1960, Democrat John F. Kennedy took advantage of the Sputnik scare and the public perception of Eisenhower's complacent foreign policy; Kennedy argued that Eisenhower, and by inference Vice President Richard Nixon, had allowed a missile gap to develop. In 1968, Richard Nixon reversed the argument and suggested that he, like Eisenhower, could bring the boys back home but could do so more effectively than Humphrey—explicitly linked to the failed policy of Lyndon Johnson. In 1976, even Carter managed to challenge Ford's competence in the "toughness" category. When, in the course of a televised debate, Ford suggested that Poland, still under Soviet tutelage, was never more secure than during his administration, it may well have cost him the election.

Despite this political posturing—a necessary part of the tactical positioning of democratic politics—the bases of U.S. military policy remained relatively constant from one administration to the next. The broad outlines of U.S. policy were shaped in the late 1940s and early 1950s when the United States committed itself to the NATO alliance and a permanent presence on the Korean peninsula. Containing Soviet expansion in both Western Europe and in the periphery of east Asia thus became the cornerstones of U.S. defense strategy: although there were tactical adjustments over the years, they were not broad departures in policy. By and large, the political debates from the late 1940s to the late 1980s were not about fundamentally changing U.S. defense policy but about how potential candidates measured up in the role of commander in chief. The candidate who seemed somehow out of synch with the accepted pattern flirted with disaster. Barry Goldwater, for example, had seemed too quick with the nuclear trigger and had seemed to favor aggressive rollback of communism; McGovern, by contrast, had appeared too dovish and even pacifistic. Both men lost in landslide elections.

It was not that politics stopped at the water's edge, but rather that the range for political positioning was narrow. Playing politics with defense issues became not one of questioning the assumptions, which were written in stone, but of trumping one's defense credentials and belittling the opponent's. The rule for the politics of defense was simply a variation on the general rule of American politics in which one aggressively attacked the opponent, remained vague rather than specific, and avoided defending a record too much, which looked defensive.

The politics of Cold War defense policy thus had very little to do with military reform and more to do with the perception of how forcefully the candidate could stand up to the Soviets without appearing too trigger-happy—who could contain the Soviets without getting the United States into an armed conflict. In one sense, it was the ultimate political equation, which involved splitting the difference between an aggressive and a conciliatory posture. "Peace through strength" was the intentionally vague slogan that the erstwhile candidate needed to convey.

The politics of defense is further complicated by the military's institutional role. Whereas the foreign policy establishment (the State Department and the Central Intelligence Agency) is seen as vaguely elitist, the military is somehow democratic. Moreover, civilian leaders may preside over the armed forces but they do so with the cooperation of the military brass; the idea of subverting or bypassing the military bureaucracy is thus unthinkable. The top slots in the Pentagon are reserved for careerists and that cannot be said for State, in which many of the top slots go to transient political appointees with ties to the party in power or the presidential entourage.

Consequently, the issue of reforming the military is rather delicate: the politician who does so walks a very fine line and risks appearing to be indifferent to the sacrifice and patriotism of the men in uniform. More than in any other category, missteps in military policy open the door for political attack: the feigned sense of outrage that anyone who would question the integrity of "our boys." For this reason, questions of military reform are seldom directly addressed in presidential politics. Instead, the question often becomes one of "buildup," that is the qualitative and quantitative improvements in the nation's defenses.

When issues of larger strategy are considered fixed and when questioning the institutional organization of the military itself is considered subtly inappropriate, then it is perhaps inevitable that reforming America's defense becomes a matter of greater funding. Military preparedness becomes measured in terms of dollars committed; negligence becomes a function, not of institutions or of miscoordinated strategy, but of civilian unwillingness to fund the services adequately.

One need not delve far into American history to see the flaws in this line of reasoning. Whereas America's participation in the Second World War—the standard by which military success is implicitly judged—was indeed a triumph of mobilizing vast resources and supporting a broad-based coalition, that same mobilization of resources proved strikingly inadequate in the very different environment of Vietnam. Moreover, the equation could also prove to be subtly antireformist since not all military problems are solved by more money. Indeed, financial excess often inhibits the hard choices and painful restructuring that keeps institutions at their peak performance. Too much money is as bad as too little. It was no accident that the serious reform of tactics and doctrine in the U.S. Army dated from the 1970s—a period of budgetary restraint and "build-down." As in corporations, the military is often made more efficient by downsizing and, indeed, the most disciplined reformers are often the most committed budget cutters. It is thus unwise to automatically equate bigger budgets with better defense: as with so much in politics, the case depends on context.

To reiterate, military reordering and reform is far more complex than simply a matter of approving bigger budgets. The massive funding of the Johnson years demonstrated the pitfalls of too much money in the service of a questionable military objective—one that was never clearly defined by civilian authorities. While the U.S. military was not defeated, its failure to prevail over the North Vietnamese and their collaborators was a traumatic experience for America. As with all military setbacks where great powers fail to defeat weaker adversaries, the Vietnam conflict became the genesis of an institutional readjustment within the services themselves within the 1970s—a period of rebuilding but also of political frustration because of lingering national divisions. It was inevitable then that institutional restructuring within the military converged with larger political debates at the national level.

In fact, President Carter's troubled tenure demonstrated the political liabilities often associated with institutional tinkering of the military and trying to readjust the code of defense politics during the Cold War. Conversely, Reagan's shining triumph during the late Cold War demonstrated the political windfalls of mastering the symbols of national security but also arraying himself behind the military as an institution.

The Politics of Defense Policy: From Carter to Reagan

President Carter was a classic example of the political technocrat: one whose knowledge of military affairs far exceeded his political skills and whose grasp of strategy was sophisticated but exceeded his ability to manage the powerful constellation of bureaucratic and political powers that are necessary in framing a strong defense policy. Though he immersed himself in the technical aspects of the 1970s military buildup, and contributed much to the fine-tuning of defense policy in the post-Vietnam era, Carter nonetheless failed to present a broad justification for both the use of American power abroad and the redirection of military policy that was begun under his watch. The Carter-era defense buildup was thus mired in the larger operational confusion, and even rhetorical ineptitude, that characterized his whole administration.

Still smarting from the legacy of Vietnam, the military was also not won over by Carter. Indeed, he seemed to begin his administration by taking on the military bureaucracy itself. This is a typical move for many civilian reformers, who are often right in viewing the established bureaucracy, satisfied with a status quo, as an obstacle to institutional reordering. As with all bureaucracies, the military changes only with difficulty: moreover, political appointees are often "captured" by parochial interests in the national security apparatus much in the way that civilian appointees are "captured" by the regulatory agencies that conservatives so often belittle.

A former governor of Georgia and one-time peanut farmer, Carter had a rather unique perspective on military affairs. A graduate of the U.S. Naval Academy, who also finished in the top 10 percent of his class, Carter had also been picked in the early 1950s to join the elite nuclear submarine division headed by Admiral Hyman Rickover. Founder of the modern nuclear navy, Rickover remained a towering figure in Carter's life; as a civilian and governor of Georgia, Carter would break in to a cold sweat when Rickover was on the phone. Abrasive, brilliant, demanding and unconventional, Rickover had a stormy history with the naval bureaucracy, in large part because he was contemptuous of the hierarchy and formality that is, by necessity, a part of military life. It is not hard to see how Carter learned the wrong lessons from his early years in the navy, which he eventually left upon the death of his father, who passed the family farm on to his son.

One can speculate that Carter—whose early ambition was to be the chief of naval operations—brought to the White House some of the earlier ambition to be the technocratic chief executive in the Rickover mold. (Nonetheless, Carter's leaving the navy early in his career was probably a blessing. Colleagues found him aloof and distant—hardly the type who "gets on" in the clubby world of the military where quiet reserve coupled to sanctimony seems "superior" and alienates fellow officers.) As president, Carter's astonishing mastery of technical detail amazed aides but often piqued the military and Congress, for it suggested—perhaps unfairly—someone who could not see the forest of strategy from the trees of technical detail.

Carter's problem, however, ran deeper. As in foreign policy, he interpreted the prevailing public moods of the 1970s correctly but failed to see how, if mishandled or if taken too literally, they could lead to contradictory policies. Carter was correct in his judgment that the public was skeptical of high defense budgets, particularly in the aftermath of the Vietnam debacle. The politician, however, has to tread a fine line between public skepticism about bureaucratic waste and inefficiency and a kind of crypto-pacifism that backfires politically. In the 1970s, Americans were skeptics but they were not pacifists. Trying to balance competing claims, Carter had promised to cut the defense budget between $5 and 7 billion. To achieve this without looking weak, the candidate must have an impeccable defense pedigree, a strong secretary of defense, a coherent vision for "projecting American strength" and clout on Capitol Hill. Carter had none of these assets. Indeed, the more he immersed himself in detail, the more he undermined his capacity to reassure and soothe public anxieties. The candidate who promises "better" as opposed to "more" may often have the moral high ground, but technical arguments rarely win the battle for public opinion. The partisan of "better" must work proportionately harder than the advocate of "more" who can often sit back and let the bureaucracy make the hard choices.

The problem was not so much with Carter's national security team—which included Cyrus Vance as secretary of the army, Harold Brown as secretary of defense and Zbigniew Brzezinski as NSC advisor—but with the president himself. By micro managing, and letting the military brass know that he was in charge, Carter inadvertently undermined the credibility of Secretary Brown, who seemed to lack the requisite clout with the commander in chief. Although a brilliant weapons expert and a keen strategic thinker, Brown did not possess the political personality to frame policy in broad terms and thus failed to compensate for his president's rhetorical weakness.

Carter's military-related initiatives demonstrated not only a high-handed rectitude, but also political clumsiness. His push for amnesty to Vietnam-era draft dodgers, so soon after the last American troops left Saigon, touched a raw nerve. He stunned the military high command by indicating he intended to see dramatic cuts in nuclear arsenals—cuts far beyond what Nixon and Ford had considered prudent. Then, Carter angered the European allies, particularly the West Germans, by going public with a new round of arms control proposals that bypassed NATO and the Europeans and that incidentally put both Brown and Vance in the awkward position of defending a policy that they had initially opposed. Finally, Carter—on the advice of Brzezinski—pledged to remove U.S. troops from the Korean peninsula and made the pledge against the advice of both the joint chiefs of staff and the State Department. This caused anxiety, not only in Korea and Japan, but even in communist China whose leaders felt that U.S. was behaving in an erratic fashion. Eventually, intelligence reports indicated that, contrary to Carter's earlier assertion, the North Koreans had in fact been raising defense levels. Carter eventually backed down from his provocative Korean policy.

Carter's problems did not end there. Immediately after Brown gathered NATO support for each member state to increase defense spending by 3 percent annually, Carter did the unthinkable. He followed through on his pledge to cut military spending by slowing down the defense budget that had been inflated by the outgoing Ford administration. The timing was terrible. Although fulfilling a campaign pledge, Carter's policy undermined Brown but, even more damaging, undermined U.S. credibility in several European capitals.

By 1978, Carter found himself on the political defensive. As the 1980 elections approached, conservative Republicans on the Senate Armed Services Committee, such as John Tower of Texas, increasingly sought broader political support by directly appealing to the military and by alleging that the nation's defenses were under threat. Republicans may have demogoged, but Carter paid the price for not cultivating support among the powerful Senate members and for having alienated leaders from all branches of the services. Indeed, Carter's call for parsimony and his acknowledgement of limited national resources clashed with the institutional aspirations of the various services that clamored for more funding and whose leadership often acted as if government waste and bureaucracy were foreign to the Pentagon.

To compound matters, Carter's larger political message was one that was subtly at odds with the American military's vision of itself. Early in his administration, Carter de-emphasized military power and anticommunist containment as the dominating theme of U.S. foreign policy. After the Soviet invasion of Afghanistan in 1979, however, he began to re-emphasize the military equation. His defense budgets rose substantially. He issued the famous, if not pompously titled, Carter Doctrine, which declared the Persian Gulf to be an American strategic interest, but it all seemed a last-minute conversion. (The trouble with the Carter Doctrine was that the U.S. had no base in the region to project its power—hardly the auspicious beginnings of a "doctrine.") Taken as a whole, the Carter policy tended to break down into uncoordinated strands.

In the 1980 election, the ideological albatross of McGovern (himself a World War II bomber pilot) was hung around Carter's neck. In these years, Democrats seemed destined to be "doves" and Republicans "hawks." Despite his being an Annapolis graduate, Carter came across as distinctly unmartial. By contrast, it was Reagan who seemed to be the natural man to restore military readiness and to stand up to the Soviets. In the popular imagination, Reagan seemed to provide everything that Carter could not.

Political appearances often deceive and, in a number of ways, Ronald Reagan was singularly unprepared to be commander in chief. Reagan's military experience was, to say the least, unconventional. In the 1930s, while still in Iowa, he joined the army reserves but did so principally to ride horses with a cavalry unit. When World War II came up, he was already a film star with Warner Brothers. Drafted in to active service, Reagan's myopia made him ineligible for combat duty and so he served his country in a way that put his considerable talents to good use: narrating propaganda films in Culver City, California, back lots.[4] A married man at the time with a legitimate health exemption, Reagan could easily have escaped military service had he made any effort to do so. Like other Hollywood actors—such as his friend wartime pilot Jimmy Stewart—Reagan joined the war effort out of a genuine patriotism and a desire to serve.[5]

Though he rose through the ranks and was eventually discharged from the army air force with the rank of captain, Reagan's experience in the services was nonetheless that of a propaganda filmmaker. He was thus insulated from the danger and tedium of frontline duty, the pettiness of interservice rivalry and the institutional sprawl of large military bureaucracy. In Reagan's world, the military could do no wrong and military experts were always right. This stood in strange contrast to his other gut beliefs that civilian bureaucrats could do no right and were always meddlers who interfered in business and individual life.

In fact, Reagan's wartime experience may have given him a romanticized vision of the military—one that reverberated in campaign messages, but one that also proved an obstacle to the more serious business of military reordering and reform. A skeptic could say that the Pentagon chiefs could get whatever they wanted from a credulous Reagan, whereas they could not with a cost-conscious Carter who was not about to be hoodwinked by the military brass.

To compound matters, Reagan had little curiosity about military details, whether in procurement, finance or strategy. Military advisors and congressmen alike were surprised by his inability to grasp even the rudimentary aspects of technical military questions.[6] While interviewing the president for the Tower Report, Ford National Security advisor Brent Scowcroft, Texas senator John Tower and former secretary of state Ed Muskie were all astonished by Reagan's inability to grasp the simple realities of military policy, let alone the details of the Iran-Contra episode.[7]

What Reagan did possess was an unshakable belief that the United States had allowed its defenses to deteriorate while the Soviets had rapidly expanded theirs. The United States, he argued on the campaign trail, had to spend fast to catch up.

Weinberger at the Pentagon: The Strange Disappearance of "Cap the Knife"

After Reagan's 1980 victory, the task of fulfilling the campaign promise for the military buildup fell to his California associate, Caspar Weinberger. For their part, conservatives and defense hawks were appalled by the specter of Weinberger at Defense. Head of the budgetary office in the Nixon White House and widely believed to have coveted Haig's job as secretary of state, Weinberger had a reputation of being a fierce budget cutter that garnered him the nickname "Cap the Knife." As Richard Stubbing noted, Weinberger's radical commitment to budget cutting in the Nixon years and his near profligacy at Defense in the Reagan administration made sense only in terms of his personality: he was zealous in pursuing any mandate given to him.

Weinberger was no stranger to politics. Growing up in San Francisco during the Great Depression, he was one of those precocious conservatives who come of political age at adolescence and never waver. The son of a successful attorney, Weinberger took both his bachelor's and his law degree at Harvard. When war broke out in Europe in 1939, Weinberger—captivated by the stirring rhetoric of Winston Churchill—tried to enlist in the Royal Air Force but was rejected because of poor depth perception. After the United States entered the war, he joined the U.S. infantry and eventually became a staff officer to General Douglas MacArthur. He later claimed that the experience of Britain's unpreparedness in 1939 had impressed on him that "it is an extremely risky and dangerous business for any country to allow itself to be unarmed and unready for war."[8] Indeed, the idea of preparedness and civilian support for the Reagan military buildup became something of an obsession for Weinberger in his seven-year tenure at the Pentagon.

In the 1950s, Weinberger was a California politician, although one who had not developed a statewide, let alone, national following. A Republican legislator from 1952 to 1958, Weinberger was both ambitious and politically astute in the relatively narrow confines of Sacramento. He was also media-savvy: from 1959 to 1968, he hosted a popular public affairs television program in San Francisco. As with Reagan, he had an ease of manner that played well on the new medium of television and this experience later helped him, as secretary of defense, pitch his policies to popular audiences through the media. As with his fellow San Franciscan, Pat Brown, Weinberger was also a northern Californian who was subtly out of synch with southern California sunbelt conservatism. Weinberger's brand was of the Herbert Hoover strain—without the populism and even fringe paranoia that characterized those California Republicans in the Goldwater camp.

Despite his media-savvy, Weinberger had the knack of getting on the wrong side of the rising powers within the state's Republican fold. He was a "Rockefeller Republican" at a time when that became a subtly pejorative term in California. Although vice chair of the state Republican Party, Weinberger alienated conservative fund-raisers such as Holmes Tuttle—Reagan's patron—by openly endorsing Rockefeller over Goldwater early in the 1964 primary: as state party chair, Weinberger was supposed to remain neutral in the primary fight. (For his part, Reagan was the chair of the state Goldwater committee.) Having been burned once, Weinberger might have learned his lesson. He didn't. In the 1966 Republican gubernatorial primary, he backed former San Francisco mayor George Christopher instead of rising right-wing star Ronald Reagan.

It is an understatement to suggest that Weinberger was not part of the original Reagan circle; he nonetheless proved persistent in trying to ingratiate himself in to the Reagan camp. He wrote in his own memoir that he felt the Reagan "magic at work" at their first face-to-face meeting in 1965, at San Francisco's Sir Francis Drake Hotel. Apparently Reagan's 1964 maiden speech on behalf of Goldwater had not proved magical enough for Weinberger to back Reagan in the 1966 primary.

Though he wanted a job in Reagan's Sacramento cabinet, Weinberger was treated as a persona non grata. It was only after a series of administrative embarrassments and a succession of ill-qualified appointments at the state budget office that Weinberger was finally brought aboard; by this time the

Reagan team—which had drifted in the first year—was desperate for the kind of administrative and fiscal order that Weinberger could bring. In 1968, he became the chief financial officer in California—the position he had sought from the very beginning.

From Sacramento, Weinberger was recruited to join the Nixon White House, first as budget director under George Shultz and then, in 1972, as director of the office in his own right. By 1973, Weinberger became secretary of the department then known as Health, Education and Welfare (HEW). In both Sacramento and Washington, he gained a reputation as a determined, if not ruthless, budget cutter.

In the Carter years, Weinberger (along with Shultz) left Washington for Bechtel, the California-based engineering firm with global, and specifically Middle Eastern, connections. Although conservatives had long viewed Weinberger as sympathetic to Nixon-Kissinger détente, it would be hard to call Weinberger soft on the Soviets. In 1977, for example, he spoke to San Francisco's Commonwealth Club and outlined his firm belief that the Soviet Union had outpaced America in every military category. It was the first salvo of many Republican attacks against Jimmy Carter's defense policy.

Despite long connections to the Reagan camp, Weinberger's appointment at Defense was in many ways a tortuous one. It was, in fact, his old patron Richard Nixon who recommended Weinberger for Defense.[9] (There was some initial speculation that Weinberger might have been given the post of Office of Management and Budget [OMB] director with cabinet status; he was offered Defense only after the transition team's first choice, Democratic senator Henry Jackson turned the offer down.) In a memo to Reagan, Nixon had urged that the president-elect make substantive cuts in the Pentagon's overgrown civilian bureaucracy and Nixon understood that Weinberger, with his anti-Soviet stridency and economizing instincts, carried the political clout to do what Carter appointees could not. Nixon also believed that Weinberger fulfilled any task given to him and would not be "captured" by the bureaucracy.

Despite Nixon's confident assessment, conservatives resisted Weinberger's appointment. Instead, they lobbied for the nomination of William Van Cleave, a California academic and a well-known defense hard-liner who had also served as Ronald Reagan's foreign policy advisor on the campaign.[10] When Weinberger was in fact picked by the transition team to be defense secretary, he resisted the idea that Van Cleave be his assistant. In fact, he fired Van Cleave from the transition defense staff. Instead, Weinberger chose, as his deputy, Frank Carlucci, who had worked for Weinberger at OMB and HEW in the Nixon years. A former Foreign Service officer, ambassador to Portugal and a deputy director of the CIA, the Princeton-educated Carlucci had a grasp of both domestic and international policy but was nonetheless new to the Pentagon.

Weinberger's 1981 confirmation hearing, which was more difficult than many had anticipated, indicated two things. One, many conservatives considered him too liberal for the job and, two, many powerful Republicans, such as Texas senator John Tower, the new chairman of the Senate Armed Services Committee, did not consider Weinberger sufficiently versed in defense matters. Critics argued that these two charges—that of insufficient conservatism and technical ignorance—subtly made Weinberger more royalist than the king, that is, made Weinberger an even more aggressive advocate for bigger defense budgets than he might otherwise have been. One might well wonder if Weinberger responded to conservative criticism by demonstrating the traits that had served him so well in his fence mending with the Reagan camp in the 1960s: on one hand, a persistence verging on stubbornness and a subtle type of sycophancy of the other. It was as if Weinberger had to suppress independent instincts and instead became a hired gun for the Pentagon in the funding battles—just the opposite of what Nixon had anticipated.

The Battle for Funding

Personally uninvolved in the interservice rivalries and doctrinal debates, Weinberger treated his position as simply a type of departmental fund-raiser rather than a coordinator of policy. His job was not a difficult one, for even the deficit hawks like Stockman conceded that part of Reagan's mandate was to boost defense spending. Early in 1981, budget director Stockman assumed that a 5 percent increase in real growth in Carter's 1980 budget would be sufficient. Weinberger, however, had other ideas. Perhaps to counter conservative suspicions, he grew progressively hawkish. Originally, he had favored the 5 percent budget increase promised by Reagan in 1980—an increase Weinberger saw as compatible with Reagan's pledge to balance the budget. On the campaign trail, however, Van Cleave, who had been the darling of the right, had urged a 7 percent increase. For whatever reason, Secretary of Defense Weinberger in effect adopted Van Cleave's position by early 1981.

Weinberger, however, not only annexed Van Cleave's higher position but upped the ante: in the initial negotiations with Stockman, Weinberger asked for a 9 percent increase in the defense budget but eventually settled on a 7 percent increase but with one string attached. According to Stockman, Weinberger and Carlucci shrewdly used a different base year than Stockman did. The Reagan campaign pledges were made with reference to Carter's 1980 budget, but for fiscal year 1981, Carter's last defense budget had already increased a hawkish 9 percent—in keeping with his desire to preempt Reagan's campaign accusation of Carter's having being soft on the Soviets. The end result was that in 1981, Weinberger managed to get a 7 percent increase on a budget that had already been increased by 9 percent. Consequently, Reagan's defense increase in the first year of his administration was projected to be actually double the 7 percent he pledged in the 1980 election.[11]

New to the executive branch budgetary process, Stockman was completely outflanked by Weinberger, veteran of the Nixon and Ford administrations and one who knew budgetary politics better than anyone. Stockman assumed that the bloated defense figures would later be revised downward, in keeping with the president's pledge for budgetary restraint. In this, Weinberger was still one step ahead, particularly since he padded the early budget with "insurance costs" and then subsequently did everything to prevent deficit hawks within the administration from modifying it downward. Weinberger, and the high-profile Secretary of the Navy John Lehman, understood that the political conditions favoring the huge buildup were temporary, and thus the budget had to "lock in" as many projects as possible. In this sense, it was the reverse strategy of Stockman, who realized that the political conditions favoring cuts in domestic spending were also temporary, and the administration had to use a tax-cut gimmick as a political cover to lock in as many nondefense domestic spending cuts as possible.

Ultimately, however, the administration's budgets needed to be approved by Congress, first in the labyrinth of select subcommittees and then on the floor. For Weinberger, this was phase two of the budget battle. Traditionally, most administrations ask for more than they can possibly get in full knowledge that the figures will be negotiated, but that never happened, for as Weinberger himself noted, "almost everything the president wanted was approved." Most Department of Defense officials believed that they would get substantial increases, but what they got was a budgetary increase amounting to thirty billion dollars more than the last Carter budget.

There was a simple reason for this. The 1980 election—in which issues of Soviet strength and American weakness played a prominent role—explained congressional acquiescence. Riding Reagan's coattails, Republicans won control of the Senate in 1980: the Armed Services Committee, headed by John Tower, thus became more conservative and central to the Reagan buildup. As Michael Schaller argued, bipartisan majorities also approved the budgets, in large part because congressional Democrats were in something of an identity crisis and unable or unwilling to challenge a popular president.[12] It was an unfortunate omission, for congressional oversight was necessary with so much money being pumped in to the defense budget.

For his part, Weinberger was also a particularly persuasive advocate for a huge budget increase at Defense. It is easy to imagine him—with his mastery of the arcane and often Byzantine federal budgetary process, with his reputation for cost cutting and his equally impassioned plea for rebuilding the nation's defenses—shepherding the gargantuan budget through the congressional committees. In his memoir, Weinberger's descriptions of the tedious rituals of the Senate Armed Services Committee suggest a savvy courtroom lawyer attuned to the mood of the judge and the concerns of the jury. Weinberger's gift was not intellectual subtlety but the lawyer's ability to craft a simple, focused message and repeat it ad nauseum. His skill was in wearing down any and all opposition, which soon irritated many in both the Reagan White House and then several on the Armed Services Committee itself.

The role may have actually gone to Weinberger's head. It was not hard to imagine him viewing his mission in vaguely Churchillian terms—warning of the totalitarian menace to sheepish Britons in the 1930s. Striking an exasperated note, Weinberger wrote: "Public support for defense expenditures in a democracy in peacetime is always very shallow."[13] For Weinberger, support was shallow even within the Reagan inner circle, where "several in the White House began to lose stomach for the build-up."[14] In Weinberger's equation, failure to endorse the highest rates of budget growth was tantamount to "losing stomach."

Moreover, Weinberger constantly harped on the Munich analogy: the argument that if the appeasing allies had stood up to the totalitarian menace of Hitler in the mid-1930s, World War II might have been avoided. The analogy implied that the 1970s policy of "appeasing" the totalitarian Soviets only encouraged Moscow's expansionism. The argument was a particularly useful one in countering the astonishing naivete of utopian disarmament advocates, but pushed to its extremes, however, the Munich analogy wore thin. If caricatured, the analogy became somewhat disingenuous: anyone who did not support higher defense expenditures could be painted as an appeaser, another Neville Chamberlain. The question of sufficiency—that is how much was needed to deter the Soviets—was thus eliminated from Weinberger's equation. To those who had spent their entire Senate careers on the Armed Services Committee, Weinberger's hectoring, his heavy-handed lecturing and his courtroom theatrics that masqueraded a relatively limited grasp of military policy became something of a liability.

It was inevitable that the battle for the mammoth defense budgets would play out in another round of debate within the administration itself— particularly because White House budget projections suggested that the bigger than anticipated defense expenditures coupled to smaller than anticipated tax receipts were going to balloon the forty billion dollar deficit inherited from Carter. Conceding the initial round to Weinberger, budget director Stockman subsequently immersed himself in the technical details of military policy. With

OMB defense experts, he put forth a slower growth proposal for subsequent years—a proposal that left the strategic forces (MX missile, Trident submarines, etc.) untouched but that did cut funding for a number of questionable weapons systems. Stockman's reasoning was that there could be no overall discipline, let alone domestic spending cuts, if there were no fiscal restraint at the Pentagon. To this end, Stockman enlisted the support of the troika—Baker, Deaver and Meese—Chief Economic Advisor Weidenbaum and Treasury Secretary Regan.

Although Stockman and the White House advisors managed to convince Reagan on the need for fiscal restraint, Stockman could in no way compete with Weinberger, who was backed by Secretary of State Al Haig, and who had worked with Reagan since the Sacramento days. Weinberger proposed that the issue be addressed at a formal meeting. Knowing Reagan's penchant for anecdotal evidence, Weinberger came to the August 1981 showdown not with standard charts but with cartoon graphs that obfuscated the issue and painted the choice between Carter-era appeasement embodied in the slower growth spending plan or Reagan-era strength embodied in Weinberger's higher figures. Stockman's cause was lost.

In his account of the Reagan years, Weinberger described Stockman, as a "quick study with a rather glib and authoritative way of answering questions or making his point.... What was particularly troubling," Weinberger continued, "was that he was most positive when he did not quite have his facts straight."[15] Ironically, this was precisely what many critics said about Weinberger. For his part, Stockman's feelings were mutually cool. Feeling that Weinberger had become a fund-raiser rather than a cabinet secretary making difficult choices, Stockman noted that "Cap the Knife had become Cap the Shovel."[16]

Despite intra-administration tensions, Weinberger accomplished his funding objectives. From 1980 to 1985, defense budgets increased by 50 percent beyond inflation. By 1985, the budget reached its zenith—the colossal sum of three hundred billion dollars.[17] Put another way, the rate of growth for the defense budget amounted to a 10 percent increase per year from 1980 to 1986. As Richard Stubbing noted, even at the height of the Sputnik scare—when American policy makers had good reason to be alarmed by Soviet technology—American defense spending went up only 10 percent over a five-year span.

In the next chapter, we shall consider just how that money was spent—a rather intriguing question that says as much about defense policy as any think-tank briefing or analytical piece in an esteemed journal ever could.

Notes

1. Ronald Reagan, *An American Life* (New York: Simon and Schuster, 1990), 13.

2. Reagan, *An American Life*, 266-267.

3. Reagan, *An American Life*, 267.

4. Garry Wills, Reagan's America: Innocents at Home (Garden City, N.Y.: Doubleday and Company), 162-166.

5. Moreover, Reagan's war service ultimately damaged his film career, for by the time he returned to civilian films, the studios considered him too old for the light, youthful comedy roles that they had type-casted him in. It would be wrong to minimize Reagan's commitment, or even sacrifice, as many observers have.

6. At his first meeting with the navy brass, for example, Reagan spent the first fifteen minutes talking about the submariners who served as technical experts to the film, *Hellcats of the Navy*, in which he and Nancy Davis both starred. It is hard to know what to make of the exchange. One could argue that it was an instance of Reagan trying to compensate for his relative ignorance of military issues or an instance of Reagan trying to put his audience at ease. The important point was that Reagan did not reassure the navy leaders—just the opposite.

7. Lou Cannon, *President Reagan: Role of a Lifetime* (New York: Simon and Schuster, 1991), 710.

8. Caspar Weinberger, *Fighting for Peace: Seven Critical Years at the Pentagon* (New York: Warner Books, 1990), 10.

9. Nixon bandied about Weinberger's name knowing that Weinberger had an "in" with the Reagan team. Nixon's first recommendation was his former protege, John Connally of Texas—who was universally distrusted in the Reagan camp.

10. Rowland Evans and Robert Novak, *The Reagan Revolution*, (New York: E.P. Dutton, 1981), 141-143.

11. In his account of the Reagan years, Weinberger addressed the issue in a footnote and dismissed Stockman's account of the budget negotiations as "fanciful." See Weinberger, *Fighting for Peace*, 49.

12. Michael Schaller, *Reckoning with Reagan: America and Its President in the 1980s* (New York: Oxford University Press, 1992), 128.

13. Weinberger, *Fighting for Peace*, 70.

14. Weinberger, *Fighting for Peace*, 66.

15. Weinberger, *Fighting for Peace*, 48-49.

16. David Stockman, *The Triumph of Politics: The Inside Story of the Reagan Revolution* (New York: Harper and Row, 1986; Avon Paperback ed., 1987), 300.

17. Schaller, *Reckoning with Reagan*, 128.

Chapter 7

Military Reform? The Reagan Peacetime Buildup

Having triumphed in the budgetary skirmishes, Weinberger had accomplished his objectives. Beyond that, he seemed to possess no particular vision other than countering the Soviet buildup of the Brezhnev years—a vision so broad as to include a number of options. In fact, finances, rather than an assessment of means to ends, drove the Weinberger strategy which was, for all purposes, a policy of buying everything the service chiefs wanted. In many ways, the Weinberger approach was the exact opposite of that of Robert McNamara—head of the Ford Corporation who took over Defense in the Kennedy administration. The McNamara years, which lasted until 1969, will be remembered as a period when the pseudo-scientific calculus of war—the "body count" in Vietnam and "systems analysis" within the Pentagon itself—became faddish in defense circles. For many in the military establishment, McNamara and his lieutenants were, rightly or wrongly, the "know it all" civilians who predictably botched their job and left the armed services to clean up the mess.

Putting aside the tragedy of Vietnam, Secretary McNamara nonetheless succeeded in his systematic reform of the Pentagon procurement system. He modernized the antiquated budgeting process and streamlined the sprawling bureaucracy. He was also astute in resisting calls for abolishing the different services precisely because he believed the military chiefs would have fought tooth and nail to defend tradition; instead he put people he considered dependable—such as Cyrus Vance, Paul Nitze and Harold Brown—at the key positions and supervised policy from there.

Weinberger, by contrast, consciously avoided "micro-management" of the department and instead adopted the opposite extreme, that of virtual non-management. This "hands-off" style actually aggravated the interservice rivalry that has plagued the Department of Defense since its inception in 1949.[1] During the Cold War, the changing nature of technology had meant a proliferation of functions: each branch clamored to accommodate air power and then nuclear weaponry. Consequently, each service learned to pursue its own agenda by developing client relations with powerful congressional members, particularly if that member had an air, naval or army base or a defense industry in the district or state. Nonetheless, strong secretaries, backed by the president, knew how to at least restrain interservice competition and pursue a relatively coordinated policy.

With no ambition other than raising the budget, Weinberger allowed the services to drive both their own agendas and spending priorities—a mixed blessing for the services in that such a "free for all" often erodes long-term support and perpetuates a "feast or famine" psychology in budgeting and assessing priorities. In one sense, it is hard to fault a bureaucracy for operating any other way; it was the pragmatic approach during an administration where the secretary abstains from enunciating priorities and working accordingly with the service chiefs. David Stockman correctly described this "budget driven" strategy as amounting to a "wish list a mile long"—one that included everything a "pyramid of clerks, colonels and generals sent to the Secretary of Defense's Desk."[2] Clearly, it was not what Nixon had in mind when he urged Weinberger's appointment: Weinberger, who had built his whole career on budget cutting, was in fact "captured" by the bureaucracy.

Because neither Weinberger nor Carlucci (nor Carlucci's successor after 1982, William Howard Taft IV) were well versed in the intricacies of defense policy and because of policy decentralization, administrative power drifted to a determined group of civilian appointees such as John Lehman, secretary of the navy, and Richard Perle, assistant defense secretary for international policy. (In the bureaucratic sprawl of the national security apparatus, the Pentagon had its own "little state department.")

It was ironic that the Reagan years represented the return of the "whiz kids" who had once wielded such enormous power within the Pentagon and who had once engendered such resentment among the uniformed leadership. These new "defense intellectuals" had first come to prominence by subtly sabotaging arms control agreements in the 1970s. Subsequently, the political climate of the early 1980s coupled to Weinberger's relative ignorance of strategy gave a third-tier appointee like Richard Perle enormous clout, so much so that he prevailed on Reagan to reject arms control representative Paul Nitze's 1982 proposal, the famous "walk in the woods" agreement. (Perle, not the military chiefs, pushed for the Strategic Defense Initiative, SDI, sometimes called the "Star Wars" defense.) The era of big budgets also allowed a civilian service secretary like John Lehman far more clout than is typical for the simple reason that increased funding brought a measure of complicity from a military bureaucracy. Instead of outlasting the civilian appointees, the bureaucracy suspended its semiadversarial stance in full knowledge of increased funding for pet projects.

The question thus becomes one of where the massive expansion of the defense budgets actually went. Contrary to critics and defenders alike, the big Reagan budgets did not go exclusively into big-ticket items like the MX missile, the B-1 Bomber and the Trident submarine, what defense experts call strategic weapons. In the Reagan years, funding for these projects amounted to approximately 10 percent of total defense budgets—considerably higher than the 7 percent average of the Carter years but not substantial enough to warrant the huge budget increases. Nor did increased funding go in to raising force structure: in 1985, force structure remained at 1981 levels.[3]

Increased budgets did, however, go toward improving service pay. From time immemorial, armies and navies have taken society's castaways; old regime recruiters and press gangs, for example, regularly rounded up drunks, vagabonds and petty criminals to dig the front lines and man the ships. The changing nature of warfare, however, mandated a better class of soldier and sailor than the era of press gangs. Increasing technicalization required a better type of recruit than the "category-4" types who filled the ranks in the post-draft services. In a more alarming sense, the U.S. military was itself corrupted by the abysmal quality of recruits in the 1970s. Drug use was rampant; functional illiteracy was common; armed forces recruiters were forced to take a high level of high-school dropouts, many of whom had criminal records. Desertion rates were extremely high and not publicized. Officers did not enter barracks unless armed, if they entered at all. As in the case of sexual harassment in the 1990s, the services, and particularly the army, concealed its disciplinary problems from public view. The Reagan budgetary windfall allowed each service to get better recruits. The average soldier's pay was 55 percent higher in 1985 than it was in 1980.

While increased pay was essential, it also preserved the existing bureaucracy, which was arguably overofficered and top-heavy with civilians. As such, the pay windfall of the Reagan years delayed the painful and inevitable reorganization that did not come until the Bush and Clinton administrations.

In a more mundane sense, much of the increased budget went in to replenishing stocks and supplies that had been neglected in the 1970s. Most of the increase, however, went for across the board modernization of weapons systems—systems that predated the Reagan administration. Such hardware, according to defense writer James Dunnigan, is easy to sell to congress. [4] Indeed, Richard Stubbing estimated that about half of the increases in the Reagan defense budgets until 1985—approximately one hundred and ninety billion dollars—went exclusively to the modernization of weapons systems.

It is important to examine how the services themselves spent the money on such modernization and how spending patterns did, or did not, influence institutional development and reform through the 1980s.

Distributing the Funds

The Army

The army had been the branch of the services most traumatized by the experience of Vietnam. Indeed, the army's experience in the Vietnam conflict was symptomatic of its difficult readjustment to Cold War realities in the 1950s—years when the thermonuclear arsenals of both the air force and navy seemed to make tank, infantry and artillery units old-fashioned and even redundant. Perhaps to compensate, the army experimented with counter-insurgency units that were, in degrees, drawn in to the Vietnam conflict. Sadly, the U.S. Army had inadvertently become an operational victim of the Cold War confusion between the Asian and European theaters; defending South Korea was one thing but defending South Vietnam was another matter altogether. By the 1970s, the army leadership began to rethink its mission and subsequently re-emphasized the centrality of NATO defense against a Soviet army that did put a heavy reliance on old-fashioned tank warfare.

In the late 1970s, both President Carter and Defense Secretary Brown believed in reordering priorities for such a conflict, which in part explained Carter's desire to have troop withdrawal from the Korean peninsula. The real doctrinal ferment, however, could be found among army planners who concluded that Vietnam had demonstrated a failure of military planning in which body counts and attrition tactics had replaced a winning operational vision. In the 1970s, then, the army undertook a systematic modernization program aimed at acquiring sophisticated tanks, guns and missiles—many of which had their congressional critics.

For his part, Weinberger gave a green light to everything the army wanted. The Divad radar gun, which cost $4 million per machine, and the Bradley fighting vehicle, which cost $1.7 million per machine, were but two white elephant projects that Stockman and OMB defense experts excluded from the "slower growth alternative." Weinberger, however, overruled the slower growth plan of Stockman, who was subsequently vindicated when the army finally canceled the Divad gun in 1985 after already investing $1 billion.[5] Perhaps more problematic was that the army procurement budget doubled in these years, but tank production increased by only an average of 200 tanks per year (to approximately 800). This was a significant increase but one that hardly justified doubling the procurement budget. Even more troubling, the Soviets in these years had built three times as many tanks and seven times as many fighting vehicles. It was fortunate for America and its European allies in the 1980s that the Soviets were bogged down in Afghanistan—terrain where they could not put their considerable tank advantages to best use—and were thus unable to put pressure on NATO, which was badly outnumbered in land forces.

By the late 1980s, the U.S.-Iraq war demonstrated the army's achievement in both doctrine and in coordinating policy with the air force. The Reagan bonanza years certainly did not hurt the army, and probably helped it, but not by as much as the Reagan rhetoric suggested. Looking at the post-Vietnam period, it would seem that the Carter administration was actually more inclined to favor the army within the overall defense posture than the Reagan administration, which really never made choices of weaponry relative to overall strategic needs but instead let the services push for their own big-ticket items. The army—the one branch without the big-ticket items—actually came out of the Reagan years as the big loser in the big-budget battles. It is ironic that the army, rather overlooked in the Cold War struggle, now appears particularly well poised to prosper in the post-Cold War environment—one that requires quick and massive force dispatched to relatively small conflicts around the globe.

The Air Force

Unlike the army, the air force had been a big winner in the Cold War funding battles and also emerged relatively unscathed from the Vietnam conflict. Created as an independent branch after the Second World War, it has been the branch most dependent on expensive equipment in large part because it was first entrusted with nuclear capacity in the early days of the Cold War.[6] In the interservice funding battles, the nuclear arsenal was the air force's ultimate trump card; the navy later clamored for its own submarine-based nuclear capacity, which it eventually got. Consequently, the air force and navy budgets have been generally 25 percent higher than the army's.

One key reason for the big air force outlays of the 1950s—the years of Eisenhower's "New Look"—was the actual cost-effectiveness of nuclear weapons as a deterrent to the colossal Red Army, which appeared poised to overrun the shattered democracies west of the Iron Curtain. In the 1950s National Security pecking order, the air force seemed the supreme branch and even enjoyed a certain mystique—sleek, technological and futuristic. The air force leadership was also active in pursuing institutional prerogative: of the three services, its leaders have been the most determined in circumventing civilian secretaries and approaching select congressmen in order to garner support deemed vital to national security.

While the U.S. military as a whole was focused on Vietnam, the Soviets has used the opportunity to build up their nuclear capabilities. After Kruschev's demobilization of the late 1950s, Brezhnev gave Soviet generals carte blanche power to expand the armed services and particularly the missile force.[7] (After Kruschev's abrupt fall from power, big defense budgets became a form of Politburo job insurance.) In the long run, the Brezhnev buildup probably bankrupted the Soviet economy, but in the short run, it strengthened Soviet nuclear capacity immeasurably. In some areas, the Soviets had actually surpassed NATO in the quantity, though perhaps not the quality, of weapons. Coupled to the huge Red Army, even numerical parity represented a distinct Soviet military advantage over NATO—something that the more enthusiastic proponents of arms control were liable to overlook.

In the 1970s, both Carter and Brown, who had also been secretary of the air force during the Johnson administration, clearly understood the shift and made plans to reapportion resources to counter the threat. Brown had been a Cal Tech physicist and Nixon's scientific representative at the SALT talks in the early 1970s; in the Carter years, he had William Perry, subsequently Clinton secretary of defense, as his weapons expert. Unlike Weinberger, Brown understood the details of the expensive hardware and how it did or did not affect the military balance. It was thus in the late 1970s, the alleged nadir of U.S. military power, that the air force began to develop a new generation of combat aircraft: the F-15s and F-16s.[8]

After 1980, the Reagan administration deepened several programs already begun by the Carter team, such as the Stealth Bomber, a plane designed to elude enemy radar systems. At the same time, the Reagan administration resuscitated the B-1 Bomber project that the cost-conscious Carter and many congressional critics considered redundant.[9] Critics had complained that the B-1 was not only prohibitively expensive but also projected to be obsolete by the early 1990s. Even in the early 1970s, Nixon's budget director Weinberger had opposed the B-1 on grounds of cost. One reason why the air force fought so hard for the B-1 throughout the 1970s was because its leaders did not like the alternatives, namely a whole new generation of guided, unmanned missiles and drones that could penetrate Soviet defenses and perhaps make piloted airplanes progressively redundant in the central conflict with the Soviets. Eventually, the air force leadership worked out a compromise whereby guided missiles could be deployed from a variety of launchers including piloted aircraft.

Carter's defense secretary Harold Brown, however, had supported the B-1 compromise, but urged that it be funded at very low levels and used as a bargaining chip in arms negotiations with the Soviets. With his utter refusal to bargain and compromise, Carter had overruled Brown and blocked the B-1, instead opting for upgrading the old B-52 force. In the 1980s, Weinberger in turn rejected both the Carter position and also the Brown compromise. With a complete about-face from his own position in the 1970s, he argued that the B-1 was absolutely essential to America's defenses.

It was in missile systems, however, that the Reagan team seemed to break most firmly with Carter precedent. One of the most persistent charges against Carter had been that he had allowed a "window of vulnerability" with the Soviets to open. Distinguished arms control experts such as Paul Nitze, and other members of the Committee of the Present Danger, had argued that Carter and his arms control advisors had rendered the United States strategically vulnerable to Soviet aggression. The "window of vulnerability" charge became Weinberger's mantra: it was both a testament to Carter's failed stewardship on defense and a justification for increased defense spending. In many ways, the "window" accusation obscured the reality. In the 1970s, both Carter and Brown had in fact taken specific steps to improve air defenses and proposed the creation of the MX missile system based in mobile launchers.

By contrast, the Reagan administration reversed Carter policy and urged that those missiles be placed in hardened silos. Most experts, however, believed the Reagan policy to be the less defensible of the two proposals. Ultimately, the Reagan administration altered preexisting plans, not for strategic reasons, but to satisfy elements of the Republican coalition. Western senators such as Paul Laxalt of Nevada and Orrin Hatch of Utah urged the administration to adopt the silo project and abandon the rail-based system of Carter.[10] In fact, the mobile MX system had been opposed from unlikely sides of the political spectrum—from environmentalists and from the Mormon Church, for the mobile system would have been based in the Utah and Nevada deserts.

In the long run, there seemed to be no consistent Reagan policy on the MX missiles. There was little coordination between Weinberger and the service chiefs, and it was clear that Reagan did not even understand what the MX policy entailed. His rejection of Carter's proposal seemed based on a strange assumption of guilt by association, that is, anything associated with Carter had to be unworthy. Weinberger played to this perception. Carter, who had allegedly allowed the nation's defenses to deteriorate, had actually asked Congress for 200 missiles, whereas Reagan had asked for 100; as time wore on, the administration sought assurances that 50 missiles could be funded. Moreover, the general public was itself bewildered about terms such as "densepack" and nuclear "fratricide." Members of the administration privately blamed Weinberger for the political morass, which raised public anxieties and left the service chiefs and Armed Services Committee members feeling that Reagan defense strategy was being directed by a virtuoso fund-raiser who did not seem to understand the strategic strengths and weaknesses of the programs he advocated.

It became increasingly apparent that the Reagan variation of the MX missile system was a white elephant. This created a dilemma. Key Republican supporters objected to it and objected to it for very good reasons, but endorsing the original Carter proposals would be awkward and an admission of political clumsiness. Abandoning the plan altogether, of course, raised questions about the need for massive defense spending: for Weinberger, this amounted to giving ammunition to opponents of the defense buildup.

The solution was to pass decision-making off to a select committee and let the problem languish—a typical Washington ploy for burying an issue with an aura of high-minded impartiality. Weinberger subsequently assembled a bipartisan committee headed by former air force general and Ford NSC advisor Brent Scowcroft. Probably the most capable NSC advisor in U.S. history (having served in both the Ford and Bush administrations), Scowcroft was a man of impeccably high integrity. Nonetheless, Weinberger also put the general in an awkward position that gave the appearance of a conflict of interest. Scowcroft was, in fact, a nominal Mormon, and the Mormon Church had opposed the mobile MX system—a position that would weigh on even the most impartial of judges. One might well wonder if Weinberger was, in effect, stacking the jury by personally picking a sympathetic jury foreman.

In 1983, the Scowcroft Commission effectively recommended against the construction of the Reagan proposal for the MX missile system. Even more important, however, the Scowcroft Commission quietly buried the window of vulnerability thesis. There was no vulnerability: the "window," which both Reagan and Weinberger had used to such effect in lambasting Carter's defense priorities, simply did not exist. Reagan's "window of vulnerability" was thus oddly reminiscent of John Kennedy's attacks on Eisenhower's "missile gap"—a gap that proved to be more campaign hype than reality.[11]

Nonetheless, nuclear defenses were perhaps not even the first priority of the Reagan-era air force, which spent more money on upgrading bombers than on missiles. There was a simple explanation for this: the upper ranks of the air force are dominated by pilots who put a priority on that which brought them to the top of the hierarchy. This illustrated one of the problems with letting the service brass choose their own priorities: they emphasize each services' bias (bombers for the air force and big aircraft carriers for the navy; the army's bias toward tanks is less pronounced) and such spending biases may not be congruent with the nation's long-term security interest.

As in army procurement, the air force's procurement record in the Weinberger years was riddled with problems. Indeed, Richard Stubbing argued that, of the three services, the air force had the most problems in getting value for money during the 1980s. Whereas the Carter-era air force had purchased 220 tactical fighter planes per year, in the first four years of the Reagan administration, the air force purchased only 172 per year. Some of the planes had more complex electronic systems; others did not, but the quantitative imbalance between the two administrations was hardly reassuring.

After the Cold War had wound down, the 1981 war with Iraq proved the utility of a whole generation of smart bombs and the utility of air power in tandem with a land-based force. (Iraq was also particularly good terrain for the use of air power.) Nonetheless, it would appear that the substantive technical innovations in air force capacity dated from the late 1970s—when President Carter, Secretary Brown and Undersecretary Perry all brought a sophisticated technical understanding to national security policy. Although the big spending Reagan-Weinberger years did not retard this progress, the claim of Reagan having rebuilt air defenses seems grossly inflated. Indeed, the erratic policy on the MX would even suggest a considerable step backwards in air defenses.

The Navy

If the air force came out of the big-spending Reagan years in relatively strong shape, the U.S. Navy illustrated some of the ironic problems associated with budgetary windfall. Directed by the thirty-nine-year-old secretary John Lehman, the navy pushed for a six-hundred-ship fleet that would guarantee American naval superiority over the Soviets who, during the 1970s, had surpassed America in the number of warships.

Unlike the secretaries of the army and air force, John Lehman was a high-profile player in the Reagan national security defense team and thus warrants particular treatment in ways that are not true for his counterparts.[12] Lehman was part of the new breed of ambitious civilians who climbed the national security apparatus in the 1970s and 1980s. Unlike earlier appointees to the navy, such as James Forestal or Paul Nitze, he was not an established proconsular type who had moved from Wall Street to the Pentagon. In fact, Lehman's rather astonishing rise was an example of bureaucratic maneuvering that would have been unseemly for an earlier generation of public servants. Lehman was the consummate operator—a national security Salieri, whose rise was promoted by Richard Allen, Reagan's NSC advisor for the first year.

While in the Nixon administration, Allen arranged to have Lehman, then in his late twenties and who had not yet finished his doctorate, work on the NSC staff. In time, Lehman became Kissinger's congressional liaison for the

NSC; after his NSC stint, Lehman moved to the Arms Control and Disarmament Agency, established to formulate and implement arms control policy. Though not the titular head, Lehman effectively took over control of the agency in lieu of the professorial Charles Ikle and it was widely surmised that Lehman, in collaboration with Perle and Senator Jackson, managed to secure a widespread purge of the agency's previous staff thus demonstrating the "capture" thesis in which opponents of a regulatory agency infiltrate it and undermine the original mission.

During the Carter years, Lehman worked for Allen's Washington-based defense consulting agent and was also a charter member of the Committee on the Present Danger. After Reagan's 1980 victory, he lobbied heavily to be secretary of the navy, but members of the transition team were dubious. It had been implied that Lehman had achieved his flyer's wings—he was a reserve naval pilot—by questionable means. Nonetheless, Allen lobbied actively on behalf of his old protégé. Eventually former navy pilot George Bush intervened and helped secure Lehman's appointment.

Whereas Allen was unassuming and tended to avoid publicity, Lehman was bent on leaving his mark. Mindful that both Teddy and Franklin Roosevelt had been assistant secretaries of the navy, Lehman—like Al Haig at Defense—seemed to treat his appointment as the next step to political greatness. Lehman, not the chief of naval operations, was in command.

With a fleet of a thousand ships in the 1960s—much of which was a legacy of the World War II shipbuilding boom—the U.S. Navy had fallen to approximately 466 ships by 1976. The age of many remaining ships mandated rearmament but the real question was about the type rather than the number of ships. Again, the question of the service bias got to the heart of the debate. The navy chiefs adore the mammoth aircraft carriers and, again, history offers the clue. Before World War II, the battleship had been the queen of the fleet but during the Pacific war the aircraft carrier replaced the battleship as the supreme naval weapon. The great sea battles of World War II were fought from carriers that were one-third the size of their modern variant but that made strategic sense in the wide-open seas of the Pacific theater and at a time when planes did not have long-range capacity and thus needed to base on these floating fortresses. By the 1980s, aircraft carriers no longer performed the same role that they did in World War II; aircraft carrier groups were important for "showing the flag" and patrolling sea lanes but in the Soviet conflict, they were in many ways eclipsed by the nuclear powered submarine fleet. Inspired by the glory days of World War II, old habits in the navy were hard to break.

The debate on U.S. naval policy was further complicated by the question of Soviet capability and intention. In the 1970s, a number of naval analysts had argued that the Soviet navy had begun to expand. Talk of the Soviets taking "command of the seas" or searching for "warm-water ports" was fashionable among both civilian and military analysts, who are more prone to intellectual fads that one might think. Gone was the quantitative language of systems analysis; instead the slogans of the late Carter and Reagan years dripped with geostrategic jargon straight out of turn of the century navalist Nathaniel Thayer Mahan but with just enough Tom Clancy to sound "cutting edge." Indeed, one would have though navy planners were envisioning a Soviet "blue water" fleet that would engage U.S. carriers in sprawling battles reminiscent of the 1940s.

As with the "window of vulnerability" charge, the threat of a Soviet carrier force was hugely overblown. In fact, the Soviet navy had long been a defensive force—something that the U.S. Navy knew since the early 1960s but, it has been alleged, suppressed for fear that is budgets would be cut. Receiving 20 percent less than its sister services, the Soviet navy was actually in woeful shape by the late 1970s. Its ships were rusting; its weaponry was inadequate; its troops prone to the same ethnic divisions, morale and alcohol problems as the Red Army. As with the Soviet land forces, its virtues were oversold and its liabilities ignored.

President Carter, a graduate of Hyman Rickover's elite nuclear submarine division, Secretary Brown, and Admiral Stansfield Turner, Carter's CIA chief, all understood that the U.S. Navy was sufficiently equipped to take on any naval challenge from the Soviets. It was telling that Carter and Brown tried to switch priorities from naval to air and land defenses, both of which they felt were indeed challenged by Soviet advances. Carter, by contrast, wanted to emphasize nuclear submarines to the exclusion of the carriers; he managed to increase funding for the nuclear navy only on the condition that it introduce administrative reforms—a telling contrast with the Reagan years.

Fixated on the idea of big carriers, navy leaders felt threatened by the change in Carter-era priorities. Carter, in fact, refused to add a thirteenth-carrier group that the navy had requested. Increasingly, the navy sought congressional allies to outflank the Carter-era policy and to this end, navy planners put forth Sea Plan 2000—a doctrine justifying a fifteen-carrier force. In fact, the threat of a massive Soviet flotilla continued to be the navy's biggest justification for budget increases, and their argument grew louder in the 1980s.

Once in office, Lehman, a naval reserve pilot, pushed full throttle for a six hundred-ship fleet based around two new aircraft carriers and their complement of support ships. To this end, he picked up the reasoning of Sea Plan 2000—a plan that involved moving away from the old "swing" plan of moving the Pacific fleets to the Atlantic as an escort for any land conflict in Western Europe and instead adopting a "forward strategy" whereby the U.S. Navy would use aircraft carriers to attack the Soviets from the Arctic circle. Though the British and Norwegians had envisioned this strategy in the 1950s, Lehman's official strategy made America's NATO allies nervous. It was highly doubtful that carriers and their complements could even penetrate Soviet defenses without getting blown out of the water by Soviet missiles; there was thus a kamikaze quality to the whole scheme. Many of the navy's top admirals were highly dubious, if not worried, about the proposal—which was after all more a public relations pitch than a coherent statement of doctrine. Richard Stubbing came closest to the truth when he described the plan as simply an elaborate excuse for more ships. Predictably, Weinberger backed the plan unequivocally.

In August 1981, Budget Director Stockman had tried to cancel one of the carrier groups proposed in the increased Weinberger budget but to no avail. By 1983, Lehman managed to receive funding for two more carriers, which cost a combined total of $7 billion but which defense writer Edward Luttwak estimated would cost another $6 billion each in hidden costs if one factored in the necessary complement of support ships, instruments, pensions and benefits for the requisite crews.[13] Not surprisingly, naval construction alone absorbed the largest share of the increased defense budgets. The Reagan administration spent $40 billion in shipbuilding alone between 1982 and 1984. It was also predictable that the costs of the equipment shot up dramatically, for both carriers and submarines were loaded with equipment; the Trident submarine, for example, cost nearly a quarter more in the 1980s than it did in the 1970s.[14]

The shipbuilding, however, was politically expedient in that it generated jobs in the shipyards of both the east and west coasts—regions of the country that did particularly well in the 1980s economy. Even more than Weinberger, Lehman was politically attuned to the possibilities of the national security pork barrel.

Although strategically questionable, the political payoff for naval construction was high. It was not surprising that naval expansion was given such a high priority in the Reagan years, for of all the services, the navy is perhaps the most conspicuous. Only the most jaded can remain unimpressed by the massive sea craft, which seem, however impressionistically, to stand for national muscle. Cruise missiles are too futuristic for the voter to comprehend and no politician breaks a champagne bottle while launching a tank. Ship launchings, by contrast, seem the patriotic-political gesture par excellence. Ronald Reagan—who mastered the rhetoric of national security symbolism like no other modern president—was often at his best at such launchings, particularly when his rhetoric hearkened back to the glory days of Halsey and Nimitz.

Stirring rhetoric, however, does not always make for good strategy. In 1982, a $200,000 Argentine Exocet missile hit and sunk a huge and hugely expensive British carrier equipped with the latest radar technology. It confirmed what military planners had suspected since the late 1960s—that the big carriers were more vulnerable than naval planners let on. (In fact, there had actually been an unwritten rule in naval war games not to report the full extent of damage that subs inflicted on carriers.)

It was predictable that Congress began to complain about the Weinberger-Lehman reliance on the big carriers. Democrat Gary Hart of Colorado argued in favor of smaller and mobile ships, and Hart was soon joined by an unlikely ally in the Armed Services Committee, Barry Goldwater. Navy luminaries such as former chief of naval operations Elmo Zumwalt lent their support. Murmurs of discontent bubbled up within the navy itself. One uniformed man who did speak out was the dauntless Hyman Rickover, who argued that the threats were exaggerated and the naval buildup was wasteful and uncoordinated. It had been alleged that defense contractors prevailed on Lehman to dismiss Rickover, who himself was vulnerable to the charge of being cozy with contractors. Ultimately, Lehman did dismiss Rickover—something that Lehman's predecessor, Paul Nitze, had tried to do in the 1960s but had failed. Nevertheless, Rickover's charges remained unanswered.

Unfortunately, the Reagan administration was concerned less about an appraisal of means to ends, what one normally thinks of as strategy, but instead doled out money. Defense writer James Dunnigan noted, "the post-Vietnam Navy did not reform as much as expand."[15] This, however, is typical of many periods of rapid naval expansion. More than land forces, navies tend to oscillate between budgetary neglect and lavish overattention. The neglect, alleged or otherwise, of one administration leads to the rapid buildup of another; although massive ship construction is often the most immediate expression of renewed commitment, such erratic spending patterns often retard institutional reorganization and a measured, sustainable expansion.

If the relatively underfunded army perhaps exceeded expectations in the Persian Gulf War, the overfunded navy was left in some ways without a mission. True, it was not a war that played to the navy's strategic strengths, but of the three services it was the least prepared for the post-Cold War world. During the abundant 1980s, it had all but failed to cooperate with the air force and army. In fact, such interservice cooperation often leads to unglamorous missions—such as conveying troops and providing naval backup for lightly armed coastal regions, not to mention the crucial task of mine clearing—missions that the navy must be prodded and pushed to fund.

In comparing the naval records of the Carter and Reagan administrations, one gets the impression that the Reagan years may have been ones of massive buildup but with little thought to long-term goals other than satisfying institutional prerogative. Far more than in the air force or army, the audit of the Reagan-era navy seems particularly troubling, not to mention extremely expensive. The short-sightedness of the Reagan years is that the huge behemoth carriers that Lehman emphasized and Weinberger seconded are increasingly irrelevant in the post-Cold War environment. Indeed, the heavy carriers seem unsuited to the evolving needs of protecting the shipping lanes—a task that can be performed by smaller ships and submarines, providing transport to ground troops, minesweeping and perhaps most significant of all coastal operations against lightly armed foes. Having received so much in the 1980s and having all but lost its chief foe, the Red Navy, which justified the big budgets, the navy put itself in an extremely awkward position to reorient doctrine. The Reagan buildup thus seems less than glowing with the passage of time.

Even before the 1984 election, members of Reagan's inner circle, particularly Baker and Deaver, had come to feel that Weinberger was hurting the president at the polls. The buildup was riddled with "horror stories" of waste, abuse and overcharging—perhaps small relative to the massive budget but symbolically damaging, and symbolism is central to political reform. Weinberger's stubborn advocacy—while successful in funding battles—began to wear thin, particularly when congressional committee members wanted more than a programmatic lawyerly response to complex questions. Having argued that every acquisition of military hardware was central to the nation's defense, Weinberger had subtly lost his credibility with the senators. Even Republican senator Goldwater—patron saint of the Right and retired general in the air force reserves—called Weinberger a "god-damned fool" and urged that he step down. In the House, Wisconsin Democrat Les Aspin became the chairman of the House Armed Services Committee in 1985 and began to direct greater congressional scrutiny to the administration's policy. In fact, the budget for 1985 proved to be the last of the big-budget increases. Citing both his wife's heath and his desire to return to California, Weinberger resigned from office and was replaced by his old assistant Frank Carlucci, who had left the Pentagon in 1982.

The Reagan-Weinberger Years: Buildup without Reform

Taken as a whole, the Reagan-Weinberger years were ones of aggressive across the board purchases rather than serious reform based on a coordinated assessment of the nation's strategic needs relative to both resources and threats. Critics suggested that it was more spend-up than buildup; one could argue that American military strength might well have been no different, and maybe even better, had the administration simply maintained the levels of the late Carter years. Indeed, it would seem the Reagan administration made some questionable choices. "Much of the money," noted James Dunnigan in 1993, "was spent on weapons and equipment that was then, and still is now, of questionable use for the rest of the 1990s." Dunnigan went on to state: "A case

One glaring problem of the Reagan buildup was that there was no overarching strategy; the helter-skelter buildup amounted to giving more money to every service.[24] Policy tended to be driven by bureaucratic operatives who pursued departmental objectives with relatively little control and supervision from the White House or from the secretary of defense. In fact, the Reagan defense team, beyond matters of fund-raising, revealed a surprising ineptitude at the practical business of political life. Furthermore, the administration was negligent in patrolling private sector waste and fraud that accompanied the increase in government contracts, which, in turn, eroded public support for the military buildup. In the international sense, the Reagan defense buildup demonstrated a failure to assess threats: the Reagan team all but failed to convey the deteriorating nature of the Soviet armed services and defense economy, for to do so would have eroded public support for the expensive buildup.

Understanding little about strategy, less about the military and even less about weapon systems, Reagan's problem was one of technological ignorance—itself understandable in this age of baffling complexity. In fact, Reagan had an almost superstitious belief that technology, and specifically military technology, would in itself solve problems. The idea that technology is implicitly good is a particularly American phenomenon. Since Reagan's noted aversion to "experts" never extended to the military, he was doubly susceptible to requests for more funding and more sophisticated hardware. He believed that, with the right technological breakthrough, the United States could render itself defensively invulnerable. This was the reason behind his fervent support of SDI—something that several members of the Joint Chiefs of Staff saw as chimerical and thoroughly illusory.

Moreover, Reagan also believed that increased financial commitment would, in itself, solve America's strategic problems. It was ironic that someone who had long condemned bureaucracy as both extravagant and wasteful should have suspended all judgment about military bureaucracy. Like many military planners, Reagan skirted the painful lessons of Vietnam, but military reform depends on such painful lessons, on setting priorities and sustaining policies beyond the simple election cycle. Consequently, Reagan's policy was characterized, not by the complicated negotiations with the various branches and interest groups, but a kind of sweeping fait accompli, guaranteed to bring maximum political returns with minimal work.

The "blitzkrieg" reform that the Reagan team pursued in defense policy—a suspension of the bargaining characteristic of most American politics and an emphasis on a sweeping change in policy under the rubric of semicrisis conditions—brings a type of institutional corruption, not only in practice and procedure but in judgment. It was no coincidence that the Iran-Contra scandal erupted in a White House governed by a "hands-off" president and where wide powers were given to subordinates without the corresponding institutional controls. Public trust is the first casualty of such policies, for when conditions are exposed as less than dire and institutions exposed as uncoordinated, the leadership loses its credibility, and credibility is crucial to reform.

Given these objections, one wonders why Reagan enjoys such continued popularity as a putative restorer of the nation's strength. His popularity seems to resemble the curious contradiction—what some call cognitive dissonance—in which Americans wanted Reagan to stand up to the Soviets but also negotiate. Although they saw it as wasteful, Americans liked the big buildup of the 1980s. In the broadest sense, however, it would be wrong to paint the Reagan tenure as simply an example of technical mismanagement coupled to political grandstanding—although there were indeed elements of both. Indeed, to look at the negative audit of Reagan as commander in chief is to miss the point of his success. The Reagan buildup must ultimately be seen in political, rather than exclusively military, terms—in a domestic, rather than in an international, context. (In this respect, it was fortunate that the United States in the 1980s faced a military rival, the Soviet Union, experiencing military crises of its own.)

In the end, Reagan's political success in defense policy emerged from three points. First, the Reagan military buildup did not rest on hard choices. Reagan was successful to the degree that he reaped the benefits of a policy drawn up in the late 1940s and early 1950s. Conversely, he was successful to the degree that he avoided the political penalties that would accumulate in the wake of the post-Cold War demobilization. Reagan never had to deal with the politically tricky maneuver of base closings or the economic consequences of lower defense budgets as his successor George Bush had. In this respect, he resembled those presidents who won the war but did not have to deal with the frustrations and psychological let down of the complicated peace.

A second and perhaps more compelling reason for Reagan's success was that his military buildup assuaged lingering resentments and anxieties over the Vietnam conflict—an inescapable backdrop to the late 1970s military buildup. One of the reasons that Carter had failed in the political packaging of the defense buildup was that he had seemed to be on the wrong side of the Vietnam issue. Typically, Carter sent an ambiguous signal by offering amnesty to those who had escaped the draft and moved to Canada: it was intended to be a symbolic message of healing but it could hardly have endeared him to the military bureaucracy or to veteran's groups. By contrast, Reagan's message on Vietnam was unambiguous. The war, he argued, was a just one and his unblinking certainty contrasted favorably to Carter's ambivalence.

The issue, however, ran deeper. America lost in Vietnam—so the reasoning went—not because of the military establishment but because it had been shackled by a civilian leadership that lacked will and had not rallied popular support. Indeed, Reagan echoed this when he wrote in his memoir, "We all felt that the Vietnam War had turned into such a tragedy because the military action had been undertaken without sufficient assurances that the American people were behind it."[25] These memories led inescapably to the real conflict—the U.S.-Soviet rivalry or, in more inflated terms, the conflict between the free world and communism. Inevitably, Reagan's enthusiastic military buildup reflected this. Mismanaged as it was, the Reagan military buildup thus served a larger political function. It put aside any nagging doubts or guilt that the public had not supported the military as allegedly happened in Vietnam. It was, in the end, the renewed campaign that banished the aftertaste of Indochina. As a technical military operation it was ill conceived and even rather amateurish, but as a political message, it was vintage Reagan.

Notes

1. Before 1947, the War and Navy Departments were represented by different cabinet secretaries.

2. David Stockman, *The Triumph of Politics: The Inside Story of the Reagan Revolution* (New York: Harper and Row, 1986: Avon Paperback Edition, 1987), 307.

3. Richard A. Stubbing, *The Defense Game: An Insider Explores the Astonishing Realities of America's Defense Establishment* (New York: Harper and Row, 1986), 43.

4. James F. Dunnigan, *Getting It Right: American Military Reforms after Vietnam to the Persian Gulf and Beyond* (New York: William Morrow and Company, 1993), 202.

5. Stockman, *Triumph of Politics*, 303.

6. In the Soviet military, by contrast, the missile forces constituted a fourth branch of the armed forces.

7. Dunnigan, *Getting It Right*, 158.

8. Dunnigan, *Getting It Right*, 200.

9. Dunnigan, *Getting It Right*, 201; Schaller, *Reckoning with Reagan*, 126-128.

10. Stubbing, *The Defense Game*, 384.

11. It was interesting that Paul Nitze, architect of the questionable proposal NSC-68—which rejected George Kennan's premise for containing communism only on the pressure points of industrial Europe and Asia—was involved in much of the hype surrounding not only the 1950s "bomber gap" but also the "window of vulnerability." Ironically, Reagan administration hard-liners used the "window" thesis against Nitze's own 1982 arms control negotiations.

12. Lehman was a poor choice to head the Navy. His high-profile career had been built around political ambition and hype, both of which are often detrimental to reform. Indeed, in the politics of reform, large things can be read into small acts: what was most

galling for many critics was the way Lehman passed himself off as a true-blue navy man, as a genuine naval aviator. (He wore a Vietnam service citation even though he had spent only four tours—each lasting several days—in Vietnam.)

Reservists, "weekend warriors," can never be part of the real military class and there was thus an element of fraudulence built into his rambunctious associations with the fraternity of naval fighter jocks, known in navy circles as the "airedales." Lehman's sham bravado, and his aggressive carousing at one of the infamous Tailhook conventions was not only inappropriate for a reformer, who must be clean as the driven snow, but for any political appointee.

13. Edward Luttwak, *The Pentagon and the Art of War: The Question of Military Reform* (New York: Simon and Schuster, 1984), 220; Stubbing, *The Defense Game*, 283.

14. Stubbing, *The Defense Game*, 46.

15. Dunnigan, *Getting It Right*, 223.

16. Dunnigan, *Getting It Right*, 190, 195.

17. Lou Cannon, *President Reagan: Role of a Lifetime* (New York: Simon and Schuster, 1991), 92.

18. Schaller, *Reckoning with Reagan,* 134.

19. Haynes Johnson, *Sleepwalking through History: America in the Reagan Years* (New York: W.W. Norton, 1991), 177.

20. In the course of the 1960s, partisans of the New Left picked up the threat of Eisenhower's critique on the military-industrial complex and grafted it on to a pseudo-Marxist analysis of American capitalism. In this sense, the New Left critique contaminated the debate for mainstream critics of the defense procurement process. Crudely put, anyone who criticized the Pentagon status quo became implicitly linked to the likes of Jane Fonda or Tom Hayden—to those more sympathetic to the Viet Cong than their own American compatriots. Indeed, the McGovern electoral disaster demonstrated what happened when Democrats allowed themselves to veer too far to the left in the politics of the Cold War defense posture. Subsequently, during the 1970s, congressional critics were somehow spooked on the accusation of being soft on defense. In the 1980s, however, reports of five-hundred-dollar tools and seven-hundred-dollar toilet seats gave critics of Pentagon procurement policy political "cover."

21. Johnson, *Sleepwalking through History*, 173-174.

22. On ethics charges in the Reagan White House, see Johnson, *Sleepwalking through History*, 184-185; Cannon, *The Role of a lifetime*, 801-802.

23. There were muffled voices of complaint within the White House. It was ironic that one of McNamara's "whiz kids" actually worked for Reagan although in economic, not defense, policy. William Niskanen—one of the highly regarded mainstream economists in the administration—worked for McNamara in the 1960s and then gravitated to the Rand Corporation, U.C. Berkeley and then the Ford Motor Corporation. Niskanen was well positioned to witness the skewed priorities that drove the Pentagon procurement process—which was not only wasteful and expensive but one in which strategy was often secondary to "turf politics."

24. Stubbing, *The Defense Game*, 382.

25. Ronald Reagan, *An American Life* (New York: Simon and Schuster, 1989), 466.

Chapter 8

Administrative Reform: The Conservative Vision

While strident anticommunism had been part of the conservative platform for a generation, that message was as much, if not more, about scaling back the scope and size of the federal government. Reagan's conservative reformism called for effectively reversing the half-century trend toward a centralized bureaucracy, one with progressively greater powers and functions. The real question, however, would be how far the Reagan redirection would go: would it mean slowing down the rate of federal government growth, freezing it, or even more audaciously, "shrinking the size" of government. As in the question of containing communism, the choice was between freeze or rollback. Reagan's political message—one of "getting government off the backs of the people"—made for appealing campaign rhetoric, but also fit into a larger debate about the role of government.

The Idea of Minimalist Government: From Left to Right

Reagan's message was an extension, and even an exaggeration, of the modern Republican policy that called for less government intervention in the economy, a smaller bureaucracy and fewer regulations. This was, in turn, an elaboration of the laissez-faire philosophy that eighteenth- and nineteenth-century liberals had first popularized. For these classical liberals, government intervention implied that the state had sided with powerful interests, such as aristocratic landholders or financial groups with immediate access to policy

113

makers. These liberal critics maintained that this was not only politically unfair, it was bad business: policies that were protectionist and interventionist hurt both consumers and efficient merchants who lacked social connections.

Consequently, liberal reformers believed that the state that governed best was the state that governed least; the state should provide only minimal functions such as police, sanitation and education. Liberty, the putative goal of liberalism, would be fostered by the removal of legislation that favored one group over the other. To pursue any other course, liberals argued, would be to penalize the hardworking, the industrious and the talented—all those who contributed to social progress.

Like political coalitions, ideas evolve over time and reflect changing political realities. By the late nineteenth century, rapidly expanding industrialization and the extension of the democratic franchise had created a new set of social and political problems for both policy makers and political thinkers alike. Consequently, a new generation of liberal reformers had begun to reformulate liberal political ideals in terms of collective, rather than individual, rights. Liberty, these reformers argued, could be achieved only by the state's breaking down income barriers and by helping the socially underprivileged improve their lot. They thus took the idea of a "level playing field" to its further conclusions and began to advocate elements of income distribution and equalization of opportunity.

Though there was much room for nuance in the positions taken, the newer generation of reform activists urged that the state assume a more vigorous role in society. No longer would the state act as a neutral umpire—one that provided minimal services and little more. Instead, the state would undertake an active role in promoting an agenda to minimize differences between groups and lift up the lowest strata. Liberty came to be defined, not in the removal of restraints that governed individual and collective behavior, but as the product of positive state intervention to promote social betterment.

Thinkers on the left thus emphasized the egalitarian aspects latent, but undeveloped, in early liberalism. They viewed the state as a means for social and economic leveling, that is, the provision of greater goods to greater numbers of citizens.

As reformers on the left drifted toward self-styled social democracy, older ideas of classical liberalism inevitably became the intellectual property of the right. Though superficially confusing, this process was a logical one. It is perhaps predictable that when state intervention in the economy is linked to a left-leaning political agenda, parties of the right invariably adopt a position of minimalist government—opposition to increased taxation and government plans for redistributing wealth. In this period, the ideas of the right were not so much the ideas of radical change, but the policies of a status quo that had proved successful. In the evolution of ideas, the reformist vision of one generation becomes the tried and true conservatism of another.

Consequently, the debate on the role of government, and implicitly the direction of reform, became a debate between the competing strands of liberalism: the older, libertarian and the later, collectivist vision.

Since the time of Thomas Jefferson, the Democratic Party had been strongly committed to state's rights and strongly opposed to the centralizing power of the federal government. By the 1930s, however, the Democrats had become the party of expansive central government. Countering that broad platform, the Republicans, the party of Abraham Lincoln and Theodore Roosevelt, came to position themselves as the party opposed to an extensive federal bureaucracy. Not all Democrats were collectivist liberals nor all Republicans free-market conservatives—American political parties are simply too inclusive to have simple litmus tests. Nonetheless, in the middle decades of the twentieth century, Democrats tended toward activist government whereas Republicans tended to criticize big government as overly intrusive.

In the years immediately before and after the Second World War, this situation worked to Democratic advantage. The reversal enabled the party of Franklin Roosevelt, Truman and Kennedy to remain the established majority party, even if it did not always control the White House. By contrast, in the years after the Vietnam War, the political and social climate undermined this Democratic ascendancy and worked, however subtly, to Republican advantage. Despite Goldwater's landslide defeat in 1964, the larger pattern of American politics was moving to the right in the years of Reagan's rise to national prominence.

The gradual waning of the previous Democratic ascendancy and the rise of increasingly conservative factions in the Republican camp directly touched on the question of the state's role in both economy and society. Would reform involve continuing the precedents of the New Deal and expanding them to new areas or would it mean resisting this trend and even rolling back legislation?

The move to the right, and with it the growing skepticism about the virtues of big government and post-New Deal liberalism, took place in fits and starts. Like many changes, it was the cumulation of a number of subsidiary developments and unlikely events that, over time, left their mark. In fact, the symptoms of political transformation might not have been readily apparent at the time. Central to all of this was the story of Barry Goldwater's rise and fall, which foreshadowed, and even facilitated, the rise of Ronald Reagan.

The Attack on Big Government: From Goldwater to Reagan

Modern conservatives in a variety of countries have succeeded in portraying themselves as defenders of both national stability and private property, of practical competence rather than grand vision. Compared to the left, which veers toward an almost utopian internationalism, the right has generally been emotionally committed to the symbols of national unity and herein is a main source of its vitality. Nonetheless, it may be particularly hard for the non-American to fathom how professed conservatives like Ronald Reagan could be so stridently opposed to big government, that is, antistatism. It is perhaps best to begin a study of Reagan's antistatist ideas with a study of his ideological precursor: Barry Goldwater, who was the first modern conservative to successfully link big government to an intrusive liberal agenda.

Goldwater will, perhaps, always be remembered for his "shoot from the hip" stridency in the disastrous 1964 presidential election. For many liberals, the Goldwater phenomenon proved how eccentric, and even how quixotically self-destructive, conservatives could be once they tried to move away from the easy insularity of "standpat" Republicanism. For many conservatives, however, the Goldwater loss will forever go down as the Alamo of the movement: a galvanizing defeat against all odds that stirred them to further action.

Both groups were right. Despite his excesses, Goldwater did in fact represent a grassroots conservative movement that was coming of age—a movement that would have been unthinkable only a decade before. What Goldwater began, and what Reagan continued, was a determined political offensive against the idea of big government that both men explicitly identified with a liberal agenda. Goldwater and Reagan articulated, and articulated brilliantly, the "gut" urge to reform the so-called welfare state by selectively dismantling it. In the context of the 1950s and early 1960s, this was a minority opinion even within Republican ranks, and one wonders what happened to make a minority opinion within a minority party an accepted part of the political mainstream.

Politics is, in large measure, an endless game of competing half-truths waged in order to gain control of the state and thereby influence policy. It is a game of tactical positioning, of downplaying both political liabilities and intraparty disagreements and acquiescing to the dominant ideas of the day, even if they contradict established party dogma. For political reasons, the generation of Republicans in the 1940s and 1950s had been compelled to make peace with both New Deal programs and the idea of a substantial federal presence in the economy. Inevitably, Republicans had come to accept and even endorse social security, unemployment and bank deposit insurances, federal works projects and grants to both state and local governments.

Increasingly, however, minority voices of dissent bubbled up. One such voice, Barry Goldwater, believed in rolling back part of Roosevelt's New Deal and much of Truman's Fair Deal,[1] but Goldwater also illustrated the frustrations of conservatives within the Republican Party during the very nonideological Eisenhower years.

Representing the moderate Thomas Dewey wing of the Republican Party, President Eisenhower would have none of Goldwater's brash vision of dismantling the New Deal. Indeed, Eisenhower's political fortunes rested on the appearance of consensus rather than partisan confrontation. Although he never publicized his policy disagreements, Goldwater viewed Ike as a "standpat" Republican who did not have a platform to separate himself from the Democrats.[2] Conservative critics grumbled that this type of complacency was not only a sellout to genuine conservative principle but a recipe for keeping the Republicans a perpetual minority party. There was much truth to their charge. From routine, ingrained habits of thought and subtle acquiescence, minority parties often fail to develop a mind-set for electoral victory. Safe and predictable, Goldwater was not, and for many conservatives, that was his very appeal.

Coming from a Democratic-dominated state, Goldwater had needed something more positive than "standpat" Republicanism. A native westerner, born when Arizona was still a territory rather than a state, he had become a natural spokesman for those populist conservatives who had been politically marginalized in the interwar years. In fact, Goldwater's conservative populism hearkened back to an older rift in the GOP coalition—one that echoed the late-nineteenth-century rancor between the farmer and rancher on one hand and the big banks, railroads and corporate trust on the other. The rift between Main Street and Wall Street had pitted the insular, isolationist Republican Party of the heartland, Great Plains and Far West against the internationalist "Eastern" wing of the party. In fact, the very vindictiveness that some conservatives still reserve for the term "Rockefeller Republican" can only be understood in terms of older antagonisms that southerners and westerners had for the cultured and often Anglophile easterners who understood more about the other side of the Atlantic than the other side of the Mississippi or the Mason-Dixon Line.

With a flair for marketing, Goldwater had repackaged these older populist prejudices for conservative consumption in 1950s America. His ideas were not for everyone, to be sure, but he slowly began to build a market niche. He began to rally conservatives around policies of robust national security even as he criticized the federal government. Indeed, Goldwater built on a very American notion—one enshrined in the constitutional arrangements granting a separation of powers—based on suspicion against the corrupting influences of centralized power. Goldwater's platform was not only one of less intrusive government but one of greater political accountability and, implicitly, greater political virtue. The state, he argued, needed to be pruned back in order to restore the country.

Goldwater entered the Senate in 1952, a year when Republicans charged the Democratic Truman administration with having lost China to the "Reds" in 1949 and having bungled the liberation of Korea from the communists. Predictably, these became questions, not only of foreign affairs, but of internal subversion. In a shrewd move, Goldwater had connected big government at home, the so-called welfare state, to a type of crypto-socialism. In doing so, he began to drive an ideological wedge between the interests of the state on one hand and business freedom on the other. Here Goldwater took a huge stride toward solving two critical problems of older American conservative populism: first, he minimized its regional emphasis and directed it against ideological accomodationists; second, he turned it in to a potentially probusiness policy—one in which government, not the big industrial trusts, formed the real threat.[3]

In the deeper sense, Goldwater directly criticized the idea of redistribution and economic interference in the marketplace. His was not in opposition to the traditional functions of government, such as infrastructure development, law enforcement or national security, but to economic redistribution for purely social as opposed to regional purposes. Traditionally, the federal government had subsidized military garrisons, railroad construction and huge water irrigation projects—all of which had been crucial to the economic development of the western states. It was telling that Goldwater's criticism of the welfare state had developed in the period when this region was well on the way to affluence and thus no longer fully dependent on Washington. Critics have thus pointed to conservative arguments against big government as not only ahistorical but even somewhat hypocritical. These critics, however, ignore the reality that political ideals change with time: just as increasingly economic affluence had weakened the old New Deal consensus, the increasing economic autonomy of the West had weakened its political ties to Washington. Inevitably, western conservatives began to flex their political muscle by appealing to a nationally based conservative audience. In doing so, they used the older individualistic ideas of classical liberalism as a rallying cry against the social-democratic aspects of the modern variant of liberalism.

Like Reagan, Goldwater was something of a citizen-politician. Although he was a salesman by profession, he was a proselytizer by temperament and his political faith rested on self-improvement, local initiative and private sector action.[4] Nonetheless, Goldwater's very attributes in rallying the Republican faithful became liabilities in the 1964 presidential race, when his message spun out of control.[5] He became easy to parody and marginalize—two of the risks of the conviction politician. Although he appealed to the party faithful, where authenticity counts most, he also raised doubts in the wider electorate. [6]

In classical drama, the tragic character is the one whose strengths become liabilities, the one who becomes his own nemesis. In his demise, the tragic character devolves his powers to others—the lesser members of the drama, who are in turn strengthened and even emotionally cleansed in the process. Regardless of what one thinks of Goldwater, his crashing defeat in 1964 was the genesis of the modern conservative movement and he, their martyr. In San Francisco's Cow Palace, where the Republicans had their convention, many outside observers saw Barry Goldwater as more square jawed Cleon than a Pericles from Phoenix, more caricatured Cold Warrior-cum-ranter than serious statesmen. Nonetheless, Goldwater's famous phrase, "extremism in the defense of liberty is no vice"—words taken from Cicero—warmed the heart of every right-wing Republican fed up with "standpat" centrism. "A choice not an echo," and "in your heart, you know he is right"—these were the emotional endorsements of those conservatives who felt disenfranchised by the bland, tepid centrism of postwar politics. It was the battle cry of those conservatives fed up with communist assertiveness abroad and an insidiously spreading socialism at home.

Politics, however, is about reigning in the passions, about negotiating with others and about forging coalitions. While a little passion is a very fine thing in rallying the troops, too much leads to political vendetta and fratricide. That was precisely what happened at the Republican convention, what Robert Goldberg called the "Woodstock of American conservatism."

It is true that great defeats give the vanquished cause for reflection, but great victories also bring hubris for the victors. In the zero-sum game of American electoral politics, Goldwater's landslide defeat became Johnson's landslide victory of 1964. The Democratic victory, and the memory of the assassinated president, became the driving forces behind Johnson's stunning domestic legislative agenda then described, almost heroically, as "the Great Society." Though Johnson's push for civil rights was noble, his drive to expand social welfare was also unprecedented in its ambition. Party leaders who win elections by landslides can rarely resist the temptation to overreach—it takes a rare form of political self-discipline to refrain from doing so. An ambitious agenda was also problematic precisely because the Democratic coalition had begun to show signs of stress. Whereas ambitious agendas often mend coalitions that have fragmented in times of crisis, ambitious legislative agendas often aggravate intraparty differences in more "normal" times.

Crudely put, Johnson's Great Society legislation gave the Goldwater Republicans, still licking their sores after 1964, a real target for the first time. It was, in fact, the Great Society, with its subtle departures in social policy that made the Goldwater rhetoric about the welfare state ring true for a new generation of post-Eisenhower conservatives. These new programs did not directly stimulate business growth and, in the deeper sense, represented a subtle challenge to the accepted public philosophy of transfer payments. In short, the Great Society took right-wing discontent about the "intrusive" role of the state in society and made it a progressively mainstream concern. Indeed, the Great Society became, in one way or another, a Republican target in every election after 1968; it was this, as much as the Democratic differences over Vietnam, that contributed to the Republican ascendancy.[7]

Whereas many Republicans in the 1950s and 1960s could only win office by stating their guarded fidelity to the New Deal, Republicans and even astute Democrats who came of age in the 1970s were almost compelled to advertise their opposition to the excesses of government transfer payments. Reagan and many in the Republican right wing were increasingly assertive in their rhetorical opposition to the "liberal welfare state"—a phrase that became something of a political mantra. The term "welfare state" became a code word for handouts to the urban poor and blacks; it was implicitly deemed government expenditure that—unlike defense spending, federal water projects, or interstate highway construction—did not promote regionally based economic growth but became a type of perpetual handout to the underclass. The welfare state thus became a code word for big government that supported every liberal interest groups and cause: the connection was made.

Picking Up the Goldwater Legacy: Reagan and the Idea of Minimal Government

Ronald Reagan's move from the far reaches of the Republican Party to become its standard-bearer in 1980 illustrated not only the changing political climate but also the opportunities made possible by Goldwater's political path-clearing. Reagan's story begins with his conversion on the political road to Damascus. In the 1930s and 1940s, he was a staunch defender of the New Deal and the ameliorative benefits of government intervention in the economy. He voted four times for President Roosevelt and, by his own admission, saw the government as a necessary bulwark against big business. To repeat, Reagan, the Roosevelt Democrat, saw big business as a threat to be contained and, in this, he echoed an older strain of midwestern populism.

By the 1950s, however, Reagan's stock speech excoriated big government as an unnecessary intrusion and even symptomatic of centralized planning. The speech was more than the conventional chamber of commerce fare that Republicans had long used in defending the small businessman and farmer. In Reagan's "Speech," big government was the New Leviathan: a threat to both the democratic way of life and American values. As with Goldwater's rhetoric, the rejection was total and unequivocal and therein was its appeal. Reagan's speeches were a call to arms made by a private citizen with name recognition; they were a statement of belief made by a convert to a new cause. In the game of political proselytizing, converts are needed to showcase the faith. Like Winston Churchill, who went from conservative to liberal then back to conservative, Reagan articulated the message of his newfound political creed with a gusto that more staid members of his party could not.[8]

Reagan always cited his own experience with higher tax rates—which he described as a disincentive to work and to productivity—as the beginning of his disenchantment with the welfare state. A number of other points, taken together, also help explain Reagan's "born again," antistatist convictions.

First, Nancy Reagan, like Rosslyn Carter and Hillary Clinton, had a considerable effect on her husband's political development. Nancy Davis's adoptive father, Dr. Loyal Davis, a millionaire Chicago neurosurgeon, had resettled in Arizona. Davis was not only active in conservative causes but was a neighbor of Barry Goldwater, and it was Davis who introduced Reagan to the rising conservative senator.

Second, Reagan's character—his penchant for optimism and his belief in personal initiative—translated in to a vague belief in conservative self-help. Originally, he had seen the New Deal as a handout to needy people in times of hardship and a policy that inspired hope. He was also a believer in the power of individual perseverance. Eventually Reagan had come to believe that government programs of the 1930s, which were confidence-inspiring measures during the darkest periods of the Great Depression, became a crutch in times of prosperity. The son of a frustrated shoe salesman with the dream of owning his own business, Reagan also came to have an almost transcendent faith in the regenerative powers of the market.[9]

A third factor in Reagan's conversion was sheer opportunism. What is clear is that Reagan, in his varied career, demonstrated a high capacity to rationalize changes that would get him ahead. It was no accident that his rousing defense of corporate America and his criticism of government interference crystallized while he was a spokesman for GE. By the time his corporate employers grew uncomfortable with the message, Reagan had since moved on to bigger, and more directly political, audiences.[10]

As a speaker, Reagan also had an unerring sense of his audience. In politics, he often managed, or planned, to follow a weak act. It was fitting that Reagan's political coming of age corresponded to the fall of Goldwater in the Republican Party. Having become the darling of the Goldwater wing, Reagan benefited from a number of opportunities denied to the movement's originator.

Reagan's first advantage was timing, for Goldwater's attack on the welfare state was premature in 1964. The Great Society legislation after 1965, coupled with riots and growing unease over Vietnam, all paved the way for Republican gains in 1966. Reagan thus had the advantage of Goldwater's having "market-tested" ideas and slowly creating consumer loyalty.

Reagan's handlers could also learn from Goldwater's tactical mistakes. In 1965-1966, the team of Spencer and Roberts could tone down the stridency of the Goldwater message and groom Reagan for the swing vote. In 1965, Reagan had given a speech to California conservatives in which he branded Rockefeller Republicans as the "traitors" who cost the Republicans the 1964 election. Spencer and Roberts, who had handled the California Rockefeller primary campaign in 1964, had a showdown with Reagan; they would work for him only if he abandoned the allegedly self-destructive conservative purity test, which played to the conservative base, but alienated more moderate Republicans. It was a testament to Reagan's ambition that he fully repudiated this purity test as Spencer and Roberts required.[11]

Another advantage was Reagan's political platform and base. Though a sun-belt native, Goldwater was also a U.S. senator and thus in an awkward tactical position to attack Washington. After all, the framers of the constitution had intended that the Senate be the legislative body that diminishes regional loyalties and tempers strident positions. Consequently, the Senate lends itself to bargaining and deal making over statements of ideological purity. Bored by the drudgery of legislative life, Goldwater's brashness seemed out of keeping with Senate practice and by the time he was propelled to the national spotlight, he seemed both unprepared and reckless.

By contrast, Reagan's tenure in Sacramento minimized his liabilities and emphasized his strengths. Figuratively and literally, he was the outsider to Washington, nor was he held accountable for a host of foreign and domestic issues that would have exposed his lack of knowledge and experience. The statehouse, rather than the Senate floor, was a better platform for this erstwhile citizen-politician. In Sacramento, Reagan could do what he did best—act as the overseer and perhaps even figurehead who could articulate a political platform for less government but who could also leave the details of implementation to his cabinet and capable assistants.

Governing in Sacramento: The Push for Less Government?

Reagan's first act as governor came in early 1967: he initiated a 10 percent across the board budget cut in all government departments. This was a response to the massive state deficit that was, by accounting details, concealed by departing governor Pat Brown. Nonetheless, Reagan's reckless and indiscriminate budget cutting proved, not only quixotic, but an insufficient palliative to balance the books. (It was telling that Reagan had three budget directors in his first year in office.) Moreover, Reagan and his staff implemented a number of drastic cost-cutting measures in state services, such as the policy of releasing the marginally mentally ill from institutions. In many instances the costs (not to mention hidden social consequences) were simply passed on to local authorities who were fiscally and administratively unprepared for these duties. Deficits persisted and Reagan was soon compelled to increase taxes, a policy that contradicted his campaign pledges. Nonetheless, Reagan helped make state taxes more progressive—part of a serious change in tax policy that many, including Reagan, viewed as his main legislative achievement during the first gubernatorial term.

The details of the Sacramento days are important only to the extent that they demonstrate a discrepancy between Reagan's vague promise to curtail the "behemoth" of spreading bureaucracy and the reality, in which he preserved the status quo. Reagan proved less the radical outsider than either liberals feared or determined conservatives wanted. Although Reagan did slow the growth rate of the state workforce, the state budget nevertheless rose from \$4.6 billion to \$10.2 billion[12] and this in a state where the governor had line-item veto power, in effect, the power to block select appropriations.

If there was one thing that gave Reagan bragging rights about being a reformer it was his attempt at welfare reform, which his aides saw as a political platform for his planned 1976 presidential bid. California's welfare problem had been an astonishing rise in the caseload of Aid to Families with Dependent Children—one that aggravated budget deficits. The upshot was the California Welfare Reform Act of 1971, which was probably Reagan's strongest legislative achievement, and which won plaudits from both left and right.[13] The Act was intended to achieve four things: (1) raise the amount of money given to the truly needy—payments that had declined in relative terms since the program's founding in 1957; (2) require receivers to undergo job training; (3) equalize health payments; and (4) ideally, strengthen the family unit. The Welfare Reform Act reduced the caseload, tightened eligibility requirements but also increased benefits for the truly needy. Ultimately, the 1971 Welfare Reform act was a sound piece of legislation that qualitatively improved the welfare status quo but did not radically overhaul it. Although it demonstrated Reagan's skill in dealing with a Democratic controlled assembly as well as his staff's ability to craft a piece of substantive technical reform, it was not the heroic overhaul of the bureaucracy that Reagan would later brag about in his bid for the presidency.

Running as an Outsider: 1976 to 1980

Little in Reagan's Sacramento past suggested a capacity for radically scaling back government—something that both detractors and supporters seemed to overlook. What he did, however, possess was a declaratory commitment to scaling back government and a haphazard record of cutting off the funds that perpetuated the inevitable growth of bureaucracy. Reagan's political virtues were more in the plane of ideas and ideology rather than in the implementation of policy.

This bears repetition. Reagan's success was in standing against things rather than proposing his own corrective policies: he was most adept at capturing a general and often vague indignation against the status quo. When it came to translating promise into policy, the results always seemed more meager and even more disappointing than the bold rhetoric had suggested.

Despite this, Reagan was afforded a measure of political maneuvering room in the early 1970s, particularly as President Nixon had angered conservatives by implicitly legitimizing aspects of the Great Society. Reagan, for example, challenged the Nixon administration's block grants to the states. In doing so, Reagan garnered support on the Republican right wing. It was telling that California's 1971 Welfare Reform Act strengthened the power of California relative to the federal government.[14] This made Nixon nervous, particularly since Republicans had fared poorly in the 1970 elections, and since Nixon wanted to eliminate any chances of a primary challenge from the right.

Nonetheless, Reagan's 1976 primary challenge against President Jerry Ford demonstrated the pitfalls of campaigning against big government when the incumbent was a Republican. Reagan was forced to the right and, in doing so, he adopted rather reckless positions that seemed unpresidential. In a 1976 speech in Chicago, Reagan claimed that ninety-billion dollars could be cut from the bloated federal budget but he failed to specify where those cuts would fall. Stu Spencer, who had helped craft Reagan's 1966 gubernatorial bid and who was then advising the Ford camp, urged Ford to focus on the ninety billion gaffe and thus underscore Reagan's lack of preparedness for the nation's highest office.

To be truly successful as the putative outsider attacking the welfare state, Reagan needed to campaign against a Democrat whom he could deride as a true tax and spend liberal. This was precisely what Jimmy Carter offered Reagan in 1980—a perfect foil for Reagan's "outsider" assault.

For his part, Carter had initially campaigned for the presidency on a broad message of political, and even moral, skepticism about the powers of the federal government. The former Georgia governor had portrayed himself as the outsider not wedded to the tainted ways of Washington. As with military and foreign policy, however, Carter's ambitious message outstripped his limited political base and his equally limited rhetorical capacity. He was doubly handicapped by his inability to put together a cohesive White House staff that could negotiate with a Democratically controlled, but nonetheless fractious, Congress. Long on ambition, short on political insight, Jimmy Carter self-destructed and when a politician self-destructs, intraparty tensions that are meant to be finessed soon metastasize into fatal contradictions.

Carter had another problem. The candidate who had spoken of a new era of restraint and limitation and who had run against the Washington status quo, had also established two new cabinet departments, Energy and Education. These actions, coupled to Carter's ambitious energy policy, which he likened to the moral equivalent of war, seemed out of keeping with his declaratory skepticism about big government.

Reagan rejected this ambitious but difficult duality of both more and less government. Instead of Carter's anguished nuances, Reagan repeated the standard shibboleths about less government and about bringing more individual freedom and business growth. Ronald Reagan, not Jimmy Carter, had the winning formula for the age of limitation, when less was allegedly to be more. In 1980, Reagan outflanked Carter on the domestic agenda much as he had outflanked him in foreign and military policy. Put bluntly, Reagan was both a better Cold Warrior and a more focused Washington outsider. Of course, none of this would have registered with voters had the economy been booming and had Carter the capacity to drive permanent wedges in Reagan's coalition. With inflation astronomically high, with legislative gridlock the norm, with an ambitious but botched energy policy and with the political ear of a tone-deaf technocrat, Carter's natural incumbent advantage eroded.

In many ways, President-Elect Reagan in 1980 was remarkably similar to Governor-Elect Reagan in 1966; he had made bold pledges but had little real idea of how to translate campaign promise in to policy. Fourteen years, however, had given Reagan not only an entourage of loyal advisors but also a cadre of veterans from the Nixon and Ford administrations that brought "institutional memory" and direct Washington experience to the transition team and then the administration.

Notes

1. Robert Alan Goldberg, *Barry Goldwater* (New Haven, Conn.: Yale University Press, 1995), 87, 105.

2. Goldberg, *Barry Goldwater*, 112.

3. It was important to note that the critique against big government was never applied to the national security apparatus. In fact, the huge outlays of defense related

dollars had made the Arizona economy boom in the 1950s and 1960s. It was not until the 1980s that a politically secure Barry Goldwater began to be troubled about the economic and fiscal complications of the defense budgeting.

Most conservatives make an implicit distinction between the welfare state, that is, domestic meddling, and the national security apparatus that protects America from external threats.

4. As a Phoenix city council member in the 1940s, Goldwater was the leading Republican officeholder in then solidly Democratic Arizona. He had entered politics as a prominent businessman chafing under government restriction and labor laws: indeed, Goldwater had resisted attempts to introduce federally imposed labor regulations. Nonetheless, the Goldwater Stores had been a model of enlightened management-labor practices, what Goldwater biographer Robert Goldberg described as a "show case for welfare capitalism."

After Goldwater's surprise election to the Senate, Republican Party leaders sensed a rising star with unusual abilities. By 1955, they gave him, then a junior senator, unprecedented responsibilities as chairman of the Senate reelection committee. Young, handsome, blunt, Goldwater the wartime pilot and businessman was just the right kind of Republican to travel the country, rally the constituents and spread the conservative gospel—lower taxes instead of social leveling, individual freedom instead of collectivist planning, private initiative instead of the welfare state. See Goldberg, *Barry Goldwater*, 50, 81, 110.

5. Goldberg, *Barry Goldwater*, x.

6. Actually, Goldwater believed that he would be ready for the presidential race only in 1968. He allowed himself to be drawn in to the 1964 race only to stop Nelson Rockefeller's nomination. Although centrist Republicans and most party leaders, such as Eisenhower, tried to discreetly block Goldwater's ascendancy, the party delegates from the southern and western states were strongly behind Goldwater.

7. In politics, names always carry a symbolic value. The "New Deal" or "Fair Deal," for example, implied a covenant between taxpayers and the government; they hinted at post-war prosperity and the possibility of moving to the suburbs. It was easy for Democrats to marginalize opponents of these "Deals" as "economic royalists" opposed to the little man.

By contrast, the very term "Great Society" suggested not so much a deal or a covenant but a type of social planning and even vague social utopianism.

8. Political conversions made on ideological grounds almost always bring political payoffs. Unlike John Connally—former Democratic governor of Texas turned Republican and one whom nobody could mistake as an ideologue—Reagan was never considered a "turncoat."

9. Unlike Goldwater, an astute marketer, Reagan had never run a business and, one suspects, would have had no clue about the technical details involved. Reagan's strength was in selling the idea of business and, conversely, in demonizing government interference.

10. Reagan's financial situation had also markedly improved, so much so that he no longer needed GE. In fact, Reagan became truly rich in the years immediately before his entry to public office. Southern California land deals negotiated by wealthy

friends—the very cronies who facilitated his entry into the 1966 Republican primary—made Reagan a millionaire by the early 1960s.

11. One wonders if this was the basis of Reagan's self-proclaimed eleventh commandment: never speak ill of fellow Republicans. The "commandment" was also something of a smoke screen for party unity, but Reagan never had any trouble dropping inconvenient connections. In the early 1960s, Goldwater could never bring himself to repudiate the John Birchers in his ranks. Reagan, by contrast, easily did so.

12. Lou Cannon, *Reagan* (New York: G.P. Putnam's Sons, 1982), 185.

13. Cannon, *Reagan*, 177.

14. Dilys M. Hill, "Domestic Policy in an Era of 'Negative' Government," in *The Reagan Presidency: An Incomplete Revolution*, ed. Dilys M. Hill and Phil Williams (New York: St. Martin's Press, 1990), 169.

social amelioration. These programs targeted two groups: the elderly and the urban poor. Social policy, Myer argued, thus moved away from the "social safety net" approach to a "social engineering" philosophy. The programs aimed at the elderly, who received the majority of funding, yielded substantial success. By contrast, programs directed toward eliminating poverty in the urban ghetto—poverty complicated by de facto segregation, family breakdown and diminishing job opportunities—proved strikingly less successful.

With this second point in mind, conservative critics of the Great Society almost invariably focused on transfer payments to the urban poor rather than the politically popular transfer payments to the elderly. Critics shrewdly and selectively focused on the welfare check, not the old age pension. Beyond this, critics attacked the premises of the Johnson-era departures in social policy in a number of ways. First, they argued that the programs did not meet their objectives, but this was only partly true. In fact, diminished poverty amongst the aged has perhaps constituted the crowning achievement of modern social policy. Second, conservative critics pointed to waste and fraud in the administration of these programs. This, however, was in many ways a nonissue, for transfer-payment programs typically involve the disbursement of checks, usually have low overhead costs and seldom involve the creation of a new bureaucracy. Third, and perhaps most damning, critics argued that these programs created a disincentive for both work and economic betterment by keeping the receiver in a type of economic dependency.

This third point was precisely the type of argument that Barry Goldwater had popularized in the 1950s, namely that government programs would sap the worker's economic vitality and incentive. Critics such as Goldwater argued that, although the tax-paying citizen may indeed get a return for his higher taxes in terms of both expanded government services and a social safety net, this only masqueraded the long-term costs to economic productivity and the subtle losses of political freedom as states and localities ceded power to Washington. This, however, was a difficult argument to make in the 1950s—a period when Washington underwrote the expansion of the national highway system, when memories of the Great Depression were still strong, and when government transfer payments invariably meant unemployment insurance or a social security check directed to those who had paid into the system. Although Goldwater's arguments played to certain business and conservative groups, they did not touch a sharp nerve in the wider electorate.

By the 1960s, however, the Great Society departure changed the political climate and simplified the task of opposition to the "welfare state." In fact, the running argument against big government and the welfare state took on inescapable racial overtones: it was easy for the average white middle-class voter to question the validity of transfer payments directed to a black underclass and, indeed, to the urban poor of all races. Whereas in the 1950s, it had been difficult to criticize rural electrification, old age pensions, farm subsidies and the local military base as egregious examples of the welfare state, it was easier in the 1960s to attack the Model Cities Program, Aid to Families with Dependent Children and Head Start as "handouts" to people who received far more from the government than they contributed. To risk stating the obvious, the underclass was not a powerful political constituency; its members did not vote in great number and tended to be concentrated in Democratic strongholds.

There was, however, a deeper problem—one that defenders of the Great Society could not overcome. Simply put, too many Americans had an unspoken, and often gut disagreement with the assumptions of Great Society transfer payments. It would be wrong to say that Reagan changed popular thinking; what he did, instead, was articulate popular, often latent, grievances. Alone among politicians of the era, he credibly challenged the assumption that able-bodied individuals of working age should receive unconditional subsidies without both time constraint and without reciprocal responsibilities that have come to be known as workfare. (Looked at in retrospect, one wonders if Great Society programs to the underclass and to the urban poor had any political resonance in popular culture at all.)

Critics of the Reagan-era shift in priorities argued that he and his cohorts were either "turning back the clock," or turning their backs on the underclass. What they were, however, doing was turning their back on the implicit assumption that able-bodied adults—not children, the infirm or the elderly—have a right to government subsidy in perpetuity. It was this very assumption, one implicitly accepted in the post-1960s welfare policy, that Reagan had challenged as early as his first term in Sacramento.

Detractors of this "rollback" charged Reagan—whose own father worked on a government assistance program in the 1930s—with a large measure of hypocrisy. Such criticism is unwarranted. Reagan's position on government assistance was perfectly consistent. He believed government subsidies should be a stopgap in times of distress but not, as it is sometimes called, "a way of life." Although Reagan's position was consistent on transfer payments, he nonetheless demagogued on the Great Society: his rhetoric often focused on alleged "welfare cheats," a subtle code word for poor blacks on government assistance.

Conservative critics, however, could hypothetically address the welfare status quo without recourse to such demagoguery and without demonizing the recipients (many of whom were making the simple economic calculations that free-market economists extol). To this end, the drug metaphor became an appealing way for conservatives—genuinely concerned about bringing economic change to the underclass—to challenge the legitimacy of an allegedly bankrupt system. For critics, the "welfare trap" was a form of dependency; the recipient became the addict; the provider of the services, that is, the government welfare bureaucracy became the pusher. Conservatives, and often black conservatives, noted that a system of perpetual handout without incentives for upward mobility kept many in the black community in a type of demoralizing dependency that corroded the sense of self-worth and dignity.

For his part, Reagan added nothing to this debate nor did he do an iota to reach out to black conservatives—which perfectly demonstrated the thinness of his commitment to lasting welfare reform as opposed to making easy and cheap electoral calculations. In keeping with this pattern, Reagan campaigned in both 1976 and 1980 on the issue of an alleged Chicago "welfare queen" who had bilked the system. It was the type of anecdote that Reagan loved, yet such anecdotes reinforced his intellectually lazy assumptions and his unwillingness, unless prodded by staff, to focus on the technical details of policy. (Reagan's famed anecdotes were often based on complete misinformation, something that caused his staff considerable grief.)

In the White House, Reagan's policy toward the welfare state was one of simple "rollback" rather than the more politically demanding craft of shaping policy echoing traditionally conservative ideas of empowerment, individual initiative and self-help. In absence of a controlling vision, the administration instead pursued the argument of fiscal savings: the welfare system thus became part of the targeted reductions in nondefense domestic spending. Nonetheless, the White House was careful to preserve the social safety net. On February 10 of 1981, one month into the new administration, the White House issued a list of seven programs that would not be cut:[9] social security retirement benefits, Medicare, veterans benefits, supplemental aid to the elderly poor and disabled, the Head Start program, free school lunches and the youth summer jobs programs.

What the White House did do was cut back funding for groups that lacked political clout. Although the White House cut Medicaid by only 5 percent, it cut Aid to Families with Dependent Children (AFDC) and Food Stamp programs by 13 percent and slashed child nutrition programs by 28 percent. It was thus easy for critics to complain that Ronald Reagan was trying to balance the budget on the backs of America's children. That ignored one problem that conservative critics of these programs pointed to, namely that many of these programs had expanded beyond their original intent. Conservatives argued, for example, that bureaucrats expanded programs intended as nutrition supplements for children beyond their original mandate into a food supplement program for the whole family, in effect, a type of camouflaged income supplement.

Consequently, the Reagan administration tightened eligibility for programs such as AFDC and in doing so excluded half a million families from the lists.[10] This echoed Reagan's California welfare reform project in which the state applied a new stringency even as it substantially raised benefits for those it deemed truly needy. In Washington, the administration also reorganized many of the approximately five hundred grants to the states into approximately thirty programs. Indeed, one of the administrative problems was that the welfare program was spread through Washington's Byzantine bureaucracy. The Department of Agriculture, the fourth largest department in Washington, ran the Food Stamp program whereas Health and Human Services administered Medicare, Medicaid and AFDC.

In real dollar terms, calculated after inflation, domestic spending on social programs remained constant through the Reagan years although the caseload of services increased. Nonetheless, the administration reduced the proportion of the federal budget devoted to programs that are commonly though of as "welfare" services. At the beginning of Reagan's term, the United States spent 28 percent of the federal budget on non-social security welfare payments but by the end of Reagan's term, the United States spent only 21 percent on such payments. (The proportions spent on defense were the exact obverses: 21 percent at the beginning and 28 percent at the close.) In terms of budgetary priorities, the Reagan administration succeeded in effectively reducing the more recent entitlement programs as a national priority. Instead of reforming the welfare system, it was slowly marginalized. In itself, neglect is a conscious form of action though it would be hard to describe it as an ideal, or sustainable, path to reform.

By the mid-1980s, Congress eventually blocked further cuts in welfare entitlement programs. It was telling that congressional defense was made, not on the merits of the program but on the extremity of the Reagan cuts. Though they halted further Reagan budget trimming, most congressional Democrats did not raise a philosophical defense of the established welfare system. Like their Republican counterparts, many either viewed the programs as symptomatic of government helplessness in the face of intractable social problems or, indeed, contributing to a culture of poverty. It was as if many Democrats, outside of those urban districts, had themselves lost faith in the Great Society.

The United States, along with much of the industrial world, experienced a growing economic inequality between the richest and poorest strata in the 1970s and 1980s. Conservative critics pointed to this deepening poverty and suggested that the Great Society programs had failed in meeting stated objectives. By contrast, liberals feared that poverty would deepen if Great Society social programs were slashed. Compelling arguments could be made for both sides but this, implicitly, put a burden on liberals, for the simple reason that Great Society programs aimed at nonelderly poverty did not bring the immediate benefits that liberal proponents had promised.

In the 1980s, one of the most vocal Democrats on the issue was New York senator Daniel Patrick Moynihan. In the Johnson years, Moynihan had written the famous and widely misunderstood White House memorandum on the fragmenting black family—a memorandum that had direct implications for urban poverty. As Nixon's Domestic Policy adviser, Moynihan had been instrumental in the Nixon-era innovations in welfare policy. By the 1980s, Moynihan argued that the current system was the best that could be done under present circumstances. Do no harm, he noted, should be the best policy, and in this he echoed qualms that conservatives usually voice about radical experimenting. Nonetheless, Moynihan also captured some of the fatalism of those who defended the status quo. No longer was welfare a way to lift people up from poverty, but it had become a protection to keep people, and particularly children, from falling further in to poverty. Implicitly, the political debate had changed. Liberals were thus forced in to a rearguard position in which they defended the system as a type of stopgap safety net in a period of growing inequality. This protected the programs from deeper cuts in the short term but it signaled a longer-term defeat in that it accelerated the delegitimacy of a welfare policy aimed at economic melioration. After two decades, public patience was running out, and this mood of impatience was perhaps the administration's greatest trump card.

As demonstrated in the abortive attempt at power sharing with the states, the Reagan administration made no serious attempt to restructure institutional arrangements and instead pursued targeted cuts. After making these initial corrections, the administration simply stabilized the welfare system—something detractors and supporters alike were apt to overlook.

From the perspective of Reagan's critics—who implicitly accepted the premises of the Great Society social programs—the Reagan policy was reaction masquerading as reform and uniformly disastrous. To Reagan's conservative supporters—who wanted substantive reform rather than simply slowing the rate of growth in welfare entitlements, who wanted reorganization rather than cosmetic cuts—the Reagan legacy was incomplete. It was incomplete because it rested on no positive vision of what a conservative welfare policy should be. When one has no vision, charges of insensitivity become a barrier to economizing. Congressional Democrats used this as a fallback position and, given Reagan's rather surprising disinterest in the matter, many thoughtful conservatives reluctantly admitted that the Democratic line in the sand was a wise one. Although Reagan may have scaled back the old order, he failed to uproot it. He was like the victorious general who beat the enemy in pitched battle and, with no thought to the subsequent moves, allowed the defeated to retreat and regroup.

Nonetheless, Reagan was most effective in challenging the assumptions on which that welfare system was built. Whereas Nixon and Ford had helped legitimize the Great Society welfare programs, Reagan helped delegitimize and render these programs vulnerable to subsequent budget cuts—cuts that would be necessary in light of persisting deficits that were an ironic legacy of Reagan-era fiscal policy.

It was this policy of delegitimizing Great Society projects aimed at the urban poor, as much as his slashing of select social programs, that Reagan's critics either maligned or supporters lauded. Predictably, one's hostility or sympathy to Reagan's welfare position was almost always on the plane of ideas, or put more dispassionately, in terms of political prejudice. If one was inclined to favor the Great Society, then Reagan-era alterations were Dickensian attempts to pauperize society's weakest and most vulnerable members. If one was inclined against the Great Society, then Reagan's rollback rid the system of policies that were in the long-term interest of the Washington bureaucracy rather than the long-term interest of the taxpayer and, indirectly, the recipient. Though one can quibble about how much or how little Reagan actually did in either tightening eligibility or in cutting requirements, the one lasting effect is precisely in this final delegitimizing of the Great Society experiment. He articulated, and articulated brilliantly, the long-standing grievances many Americans harbored against the post-1960s welfare system.

With an uncanny ability to read the mood of the majority, Reagan expressed a typical American assumption about work that is part myth and part national character. In a society that puts such faith in private initiative and in the power of private interest to forward national growth, it is not surprising that "welfare as a way of life" touches a raw nerve. The principle offends many Americans' sense of the redemptive and almost moral virtue of work, of self-improvement and enterprise. It is no exaggeration to suggest that the "welfare state" subtly contradicts the idea of the rehabilitative possibilities of American society. As with détente, the Great Society "welfare trap" seemed a sellout to America's principles. Welfarism was, for many, an admission of societal failure. Here was the political essence of Reagan's message, one that assuaged Great Society critics and antagonized its demoralized supporters.

The missed opportunity of the Reagan years was that he could not use this position—based on an almost moral revulsion against welfarism—as the basis for reaching out to the disaffected, to those who genuinely wanted to break out of the "welfare trap." As with so many things about Reagan, after the stirring rhetoric, there was a strange passivity in face of the deeper complexities of political life. Outrage against government ineptitude or waste is, by itself, insufficient as a long-term public policy. Consequently, the lack of a substantive policy for pressing problems means that another political generation must attend to the difficult realities or, perhaps worse, another political party may claim credit.

The missed opportunity of the Reagan years was illustrated by President Clinton's co-opting the Reagan rhetoric and perhaps doing so in a more convincing manner. "Workfare not welfare" and not making welfare "a way of life" were appealing messages for a left of center Democrat wanting to move to the political middle. That Clinton did next to nothing on the welfare issue in his first term despite Senator Moynihan's urging kept welfare reform a Republican issue; that Clinton felt compelled to endorse a Republican congressional plan in 1996 despite Moynihan's vigorous opposition also kept it a Republican issue. The astonishing ineptitude of Clinton in seizing the agenda is all the more surprising in that he, unlike Reagan, has had the ability to both demonstrate empathy with the welfare recipient but display a genuine interest in policy detail; that he did almost nothing on an issue that was practically handed to him on a silver platter was astonishing.

It is perhaps fitting that the 1990s welfare debate, which has simmered on and off, was in large measure a function of Reagan-era policies. First, Reagan delegitimized the Great Society and, second, subsequent budgetary pressures further eroded domestic spending. This, better than anything, illustrated the ironic passivity but long-term yield of Reagan reformism: state the principle boldly, make cuts that more conventional politicians would not dare to and let things fall where they may. Never concerned with the policy details of welfare reform, Reagan and his immediate staff simply wanted to purge the system of its latter accretions and purge it they did. It was not so much reform but a cold cut. Unlike Clinton, Reagan succeeded in meeting his objectives and changing the debate and, in politics, successfully cosmetic reform beats inept policy any day.

Cutting Washington Bureaucracy: The Strange Case of HUD

The Reagan policy of trimming, and possibly even abolishing, select government agencies was the third part of the agenda for administrative reform. As with the proposals for the New Federalism, the motives for administrative cuts were both economic and ideological, particularly in the case of those agencies that were created specifically as regulatory ones.

Instead of directly taking on the New Deal, Reagan focused on those programs associated with Lyndon Johnson's Great Society legislation, such as the Department of Housing and Urban Development—even the very name echoed the confident period of social planning. Another one of Reagan's 1980

campaign pledges was to eliminate the agencies established by President
Carter, the Departments of Energy and Education. In the end, the Reagan
administration abolished not a single agency and, in fact, created a new cabinet
level department, that of Veterans Affairs. The administration did, however,
cut the budgets of several agencies and took the axe to specific programs, such
as public service job projects and subsidies to mass transit. Unfortunately, the
zeal the new administration took in pruning the bureaucracy was all too often
offset by a truly astonishing waste and inefficiency, if not outright corruption.
The best example of this was the sorry mess at the Department of Housing and
Urban Development, otherwise known as HUD.

The case of budget cuts at HUD represented a stark example of the costs
entailed in altering the status quo but doing it in a way that was neither
programmatic nor disciplined. A strong, and strongly conservative, case could
be made that a bloated agency such as HUD could only benefit from massive
institutional reordering. Conservatives, such as Jack Kemp, could also argue
that the poor and disadvantaged would benefit more from block grants to local
authorities and tax incentives, such as "enterprise zones," than from an
entrenched bureaucracy in Washington. This was an application of Nixon's
logic about welfare services versus the welfare state, but infused with a faith in
the regenerative powers of the free market. (Kemp would later be HUD
secretary in the Bush administration but was given insufficient political
backing from the White House to implement changes.)   Rhetorically, the
Reagan administration endorsed such positions, but when it came to the details
of reforming HUD, it failed to develop a blueprint for scaling back the agency.

Through budget director David Stockman's initiatives, Reagan did at least
keep his pledges to scale back HUD. As Michael Schaller noted, between 1981
and 1987 the Reagan administration slashed the HUD budget from thirty-three
to fourteen billion dollars and reduced the HUD workforce by 30 percent.[11]
Beyond the massive cuts, the administration neglected the agency from top to
bottom. As HUD secretary, Reagan appointed Sam Pierce, a prominent Wall
Street attorney, who was also the only African American in Reagan's cabinet.
Reagan's lack of attention to HUD affairs was anecdotally revealed in his
failure to recognize Pierce at a White House gathering, in which he referred to
his cabinet secretary as "Mr. Mayor."

For his part, Pierce hardly helped matters. Completely uninvolved in the
workings of the agency, he isolated himself from his staff, remained aloof in his
office and reportedly watched a great deal of television. He soon acquired the
nickname "Silent Sam."   It was widely believed that he was waiting for the
aging Thurgood Marshall to retire or perhaps die so Pierce, a conservative
lawyer with a distinguished professional record, could be appointed to the
"black" seat on the Supreme Court.

Unfortunately, the institutional neglect of the agency seeped down to all levels. In fact, HUD became something of a "dumping ground" for Republican political appointees, many of whom were neither particularly interested nor well qualified in housing or urban issues.[12] Real power in the agency devolved to a group of transient appointees, many of them young and consequently dubbed the "brat pack" by the *Washington Post*. What was particularly surprising was that the White House, which pledged to clean up HUD, allowed this policy drift to happen under its "reformist" watch. At the top of the "brat pack," was the socially well-connected Deborah Gore Dean, whose previous work experience had been confined to working in a Georgetown bar. In time, Dean assumed an astonishing degree of internal control. Led by Dean, who later earned the epithet "Robbin' Hud," Reagan-era political appointees directed building contracts to Republican political allies.

In fact, the Reagan administration presided over the worst case of corruption in the agency's history. Michael Schaller surmised that Pierce allowed several billion dollars to go to contracts directly favoring friends and associates and to those who had made contributions to Republican causes.[13] Lost in this, of course, were the constituencies that HUD was supposed to serve. Had conservatives scrutinized the situation, they might have noticed that the sheer waste and corruption at the agency, not to mention the low morale among its workers, offset the impressive budget cutting. It was hardly a model of administrative reform on which Reagan campaigned—indeed, it was the very mismanagement and self-interest against which he had railed since the 1960s.

Although an extreme example of the administration's sloppy policy, the HUD fiasco was symptomatic of the surprising technical incompetence of many Reagan appointees who operated both without tight controls but with lose, undefined mandates. In its Orwellian office complex in faraway southwest Washington, HUD was truly a bureaucratic backwater for the Reagan entourage. Sadly, HUD mismanagement also reflected the astonishing ethical laxity on the part of administration officials and the inability of the president to discipline his staff and cabinet members. Simply put, Reagan was oblivious to the rampant conflict of interest that sullied members of his own cabinet and inner circle.

Despite deep cuts at programs such as HUD, there was no real radical scaling back of Washington bureaucracy. David Stockman, who was the director of the Office of Management and Budget in the first term, believed that Reagan had neither the will nor the inclination for the radical cutbacks that he had so often espoused. The problem, however, ran deeper. Reagan was still trapped in the assumptions that Washington was a big Sacramento: that government could be scaled back, and substantial savings achieved, by simply pruning the overgrown thicket of executive branch agencies. As Stockman pointed out, these agencies were only the visible tip of the welfare state. Even if they were all cut back substantially—which would have required an act of political will that he soon discovered did not exist in the Reagan White House—the savings would have been relatively small and the difference rather negligible. As Stockman argued, the bulk of the so-called welfare state is, in fact, tied in to discretionary programs perpetuated by Congress and that go to essentially middle-class constituents. As the chapter on budgetary reform will demonstrate, Reagan was not about to touch those parts of the welfare state that were politically popular.

In the end, Reagan's pledge to get the government "off the backs of the people" involved taking government out of the business of subsidizing the poor. Even a "non-Republican" agency such as HUD had Republican constituents and, where there were constituencies, there would be no dramatic cutbacks.

The Reagan Years: Scaling Back the Welfare State?

Campaigning for the presidency, Reagan had made a concrete pledge to increase defense spending and to cut taxes even if his appealing promises to purge government waste and to clean up "the Washington mess" were conveniently vague. Looking at spending priorities, however, one could suggest that Reagan did indeed fulfill his promises of reorienting priorities. In 1980, defense spending amounted to 21 percent of the budget, while social spending on welfare services amounted to 28 percent. By 1987, the figures were entirely reversed.

In defense policy, the Reagan team spent lavishly, without much coordinating vision other than outspending the Soviets; in social policy, the Reagan team cut recklessly, without much of a coordinating plan other than not offending middle-class constituencies. Weinberger and others at Defense spent recklessly in the early years in part to preempt anticipated congressional oversight that would whittle down the huge budgets—congressional oversight that did not come until 1985. By contrast, Stockman and others cut knowing that congressional opposition to spending cuts would emerge; by 1982, the "window" for deep cuts had in fact closed. Anticipating congressional scrutiny, Stockman made significant, though not drastic, cuts in social spending and accomplished part of the Reagan objectives—nowhere near what Stockman wanted, but which should not obscure the substantive accomplishment of the Reagan team. After all, Reagan was the first president since Roosevelt to slow down the growth of government; he was the first chief executive who popularized the idea of shutting government projects down.

Politicians, however, can get carried away with their own rhetoric. Having spent so long in the marketing division of political merchandising, it was perhaps predictable that Reagan oversold his campaign to scale back big government. The truth is that government is not on the people's backs, as Reagan intimated, but rather in their pension check, the local military base or in the funding for highway construction. Reagan had no intention of scaling back the state but only the Great Society entitlement programs that had become a perpetual dole and, as the next chapter will suggest, those programs that regulated business.

In practice, the sweeping Reagan condemnation of big government was perhaps problematic for all but the most stalwart and, indeed, libertarian conservatives. By contrast, the rhetoric against the targeted "welfare state" played in Peoria, and other middle-class constituencies throughout the country. In attacking the "welfare state," Reagan implicitly targeted the most politically vulnerable parts of the rapid expansion of the modern executive branch: programs aimed at social engineering and economic redistribution. He aimed his political sights at those programs that broke with the old "safety net." Reagan thus remained faithful to Roosevelt New Deal prescription even in his rejection of the 1960s innovations that moved beyond the New Deal. As Richard Polenberg argued, the Reagan administration attempted to turn the welfare state back to 1959, not 1939.[14] Reagan, wrote Lou Cannon, took a table knife to the New Deal programs and a cleaver to the Great Society.[15]

As with his studied attacks on cultural permissiveness and his defense of the Vietnam conflict as an honorable affair, Reagan's criticism of the welfare state was an ambitious attack on the political legacy of the 1960s. Although he did not personally dismantle that political legacy, he certainly created the climate for its rollback. It thus does no good to make a tally of Reagan's rather ambiguous accomplishments: the failure to introduce New Federalism, the relatively tame cuts in welfare, the sloppy handling of HUD. For his part, Reagan accomplished his objectives: discredit the "welfare state" so that it cannot be expanded and so that its eventual rollback is a near inevitability.

Nonetheless, a troubling legacy remains. The canny tactics of Reagan's selective assault on big government has also created an ironic disjunction between professed belief and policy. Maintaining the fiction that big government is bad, while slashing only those government programs that dole out funds to the urban poor or those who should be working, creates a type of political fiction, and political fiction carries long-term corrosive effects. Herein lies the intellectual weakness of the Reagan vision of scaling back the state.

One would be tempted to suggest that Reagan's simplicities—the true-believing dogma of the proselytizer—would inevitably give way to a more sophisticated revision, one that consolidates the electoral gains of the 1980s even as it brought more consistency and nuance to the conservative philosophy. That has not happened and does not appear likely. Mesmerized by the Reagan rhetoric, conservatives act as if it would be irresponsible to tamper with Reagan's legacy, however vague.

Ironically, the president known as the great communicator seemed to lack a substantive, conservative vision for scaling back the state; he failed to articulate what could be reduced and what would remain. But the rhetoric continued from the early days—the same programmatic slogans on index cards. Reagan's rhetoric remained part of the Speech—frozen in anecdotes that might have been pitched to Pasadena Rotarians of the 1950s. Statecraft is bigger than such things. Serious, as opposed to sound-bite, reform demands more thought and more discipline. Perhaps this is why political converts so seldom reach the highest rungs and, in truth, there is something even embarrassing about the conversion experience trotted out for public consumption. One wants something more lasting, more substantial. In politics, nothing is as tiresome as the convert who still parrots the old stock phrases, even as the faith has dimmed or the reality of experience proves more difficult than the black and white dichotomies of the true believer. By 1988, if not before, the Speech was starting to wear thin.

Notes

1. Garry Wills, *Nixon Agonistes: The Crisis of the Self-Made Man* (Boston: Houghton Mifflin, 1970), 535.

2. It was at this time that many liberals, who previously saw Congress as an unwanted brake on activist and relatively liberal presidents, began to sound alarms against the "imperial presidency." Their alarms sounded shrill precisely because they had endorsed an activist presidency for so long.

3. Joan Hoff, *Nixon Reconsidered* (New York: Basic Books, 1994), 66.

4. Hoff, *Nixon Reconsidered*, 69.

5. See Dilys M. Hill, "Domestic Policy in an Era of 'Negative Governance,'" in *Reagan Presidency: An Incomplete Revolution?* Dilys M. Hill, Raymond A. Moore, and Phil Williams, eds. (New York: St. Martin's Press, 1990), 169-171.

6. Michael Schaller, *Reckoning with Reagan: America and Its President in the 1980s* (New York: Oxford University Press, 1992), 71.

7. Lou Cannon, *Reagan* (New York: G.P. Putnam's Sons, 1982), 343; see also Hugh Heclo, "Reaganism and the Search for a Public Philosophy," in *Perspectives on the Reagan Years*, John L. Palmer, ed. (Washington, D.C.: Urban Institute Press, 1986), 52.

8. Hoff, *Nixon Reconsidered*, 73.

9. Rowland Evans and Robert D. Novak, *The Reagan Revolution* (New York: E.P. Dutton, 1981), 127; Hill, "Domestic Policy," 161.

10. Hill, "Domestic Policy," 166.

11. Schaller, *Reckoning with Reagan*, 115.

12. Haynes Johnson, *Sleepwalking through History: America in the Reagan Years* (New York: W.W. Norton, 1991), 182.

13. Johnson, *Sleepwalking through History*, 181; Schaller, *Reckoning with Reagan*, 117. The 1995 indictment of former cabinet secretary James Watt had its origins with these scandals at HUD. Watt lied to a congressional panel about phone calls he made to HUD administrators on behalf of businessmen—Watt was paid several hundred thousand dollars for such "calls." Watt, however, was not alone; former Republican National Committee chairman Lee Atwater and former trade representative Carla Hills engaged in similar lobbying efforts. See Johnson, *Sleepwalking through History*, 180.

14. Richard Polenberg, "Roosevelt Revolution, Reagan Counterrevolution," *The Reagan Revolution?* B.B. Kymlicka and Jean V. Matthews, eds. (Chicago, Ill.: Dorsey Press, 1988), 52.

15. Cannon, *Reagan*, 336.

Chapter 10

Regulatory Reform: The Conservative Vision

In the Reagan rhetoric, the welfare state needed to be scaled back because it re-distributed income away from middle-class constituents toward projects that either did not work or actually deepened problems by simply creating newly dependent constituencies. Whether one likes the policy or not, there was a rough sense of justice to the equation: vulnerable groups, after all, are the first to get pruned from the diminishing political pork barrel.

The welfare state, however, was only one part of Reagan's big government equation; the "regulatory state" constituted the other part of the expanded Washington bureaucracy. Government, argued Ronald Reagan, regulated too much, interfered with the natural workings of the economy, and substituted mindless rules and regulations for old-fashioned common sense. This theme, which went back to his GE days, was easy to update in the political climate of the late 1970s when Reagan was running as a citizen-politician bent on reforming a Washington regulatory apparatus that had grown out of control and had become a putative bureaucratic empire of overly zealous administrators, environmentalists and consumer advocates. Regulatory reform, Reagan argued, would unshackle the sluggish U.S. economy of the Carter years, for regulation hurt business and what hurt business, hurt America.

It is perhaps hard to get excited about the details of regulation. They are often arcane, excessively technical and dry—the stuff of lawyers, engineers and accountants. Actually, there is a certain breed that thrives on policy detail but these people tend to be the faceless technicians who work the lonely corridors and fluorescent-lighted offices of second-tier agencies known by unflattering acronyms. Alternatively, they are the highly paid attorneys who operate the

147

back channels and permeable boundaries between the corporate law firms and the Capitol Hill committees and subcommittees where legislation is brokered, finessed and crafted. Dedicated and diligent though they may be, public servants are poor at selling their mission to the general public. For their part, private advocates—the lawyers and the lobbyists—are generally uninterested in raising public consciousness unless it directly serves their clients' interests.

The issues, however, are too important to be left to the experts. For critics of regulatory policy, the rules and regulations that a faraway federal government impose on the citizen are the most tangible reminder of the unwelcome, and even frivolous, intrusion into private affairs. For defenders of the regulatory powers of the state, the situation is just the opposite. It is, in fact, regulatory issues that defenders of "big government" implicitly use to challenge the assumptions of those who want to roll back federal controls and oversight. With much justification, defenders of the status quo argue that if government did not enforce pollution standards, inspect slaughterhouses and mandate safety belts, who would?

Regulation, and by extension, regulatory reform is thus best understood in terms of specific problems that affect one's daily life. Conceptually, regulation can be broken down a number of ways, and one such way is into different categories affecting the environment, a relatively recent concern; public and consumer safety; and the market itself.

The Politics of Regulation and Liberalization: Some General Observations

It is no overstatement to suggest that political ideologies are built around a relatively unified body of beliefs, nor is it wrong to suggest that ideologies of both right and left are built, in large part, around the idea of the market—the sum total of all economic interactions. In the popular imagination, conservatives tend to dislike regulation, and want to liberate the market; liberals, by contrast, tend to like regulation because it softens the worst aspects of the market. This would stand to reason: conservatives emphasize freedom from interference and restriction whereas liberals emphasize a different kind of freedom, that of equalizing opportunity and reducing inequalities.

There is, however, an element of half-truth to this approximate equation, for the arguments about the market actually shift over time. Indeed, politicians of both left and right array themselves differently according to the nature of the perceived problem, the equation of constituencies and the political strategy of what to liberalize and what to regulate. Depending on the nature of the problem, a reform agenda may call for simultaneous market regulation in some areas and market deregulation, what some call liberalization, in other areas.

Though ideologues—such as social democrats or free-market libertarians—argue according to a blueprint for change, political life rarely works according to neat formulae. To assume that it does is to commit the intellectual sin of transposition, that is to abstract from one experience a rule that has an allegedly universal relevance. Ideology is certainly useful but often it is simply a base from which politicians and reformers often deviate and do so quite successfully.

One need only think of the problems associated with the collapse of communism in Eastern Europe to see how the alternately regulating and liberalizing trends of political reform overlap. The dismantling of the overly restrictive command economies under the banner of market liberalization in the 1980s and 1990s illustrated an extreme and long-overdue case for getting the commissar and the central planner "off the backs of the people." To borrow yet another Reaganism, Soviet-type central planning was part of the problem, not the solution. Nonetheless, market liberalization has, in turn, contributed to another set of problems. The subsequent spread of corruption and Mafia-type capitalism that has taken hold in societies that have neither the legal nor regulatory infrastructure necessary for such transactions has demonstrated the need for laws and norms to govern the newly opened markets. Within a space of only a few years, the discourse on reform has thus shifted from market liberalization to the latest reform issue, instigating the "rule of law."

The alternate push for regulation and then subsequent deregulation (or vice versa) tend to follow one another in cycles. This is a simple truism of political life—one phase leads to its own excesses and must be treated with corrective remedies. Social scientists call this the law of unintended consequences. Looking at the politics of regulatory reform—regardless of whether that reform is aimed at either liberalization or regulation—one should ask a few simple questions: what is the problem, who is to be protected, who is to be regulated or deregulated and, most important of all, what are the constituencies that support or oppose the policies in question.

Indeed the question of regulation goes back to the very origins of liberal thought in the middle decades of the eighteenth century. Ideas that were initially popularized by the Scottish moral philosopher Adam Smith—rightly regarded as the founder of modern economic science—became the basis of a loose body of ideas that we have come to know as liberalism. These early advocates of market liberalization urged cutting through the thicket of market regulations that encumbered the economy and protected inefficient producers who, in turn, passed higher prices on to the consumer.

Nonetheless, ideology, like bureaucracy, expands over time and accommodates concerns that were not initially addressed in the beginning phases of the enterprise. By the mid-nineteenth century, thoughtful British liberals such as John Stuart Mill, believed that liberalism would itself have to evolve in order to remain politically relevant. For these critics, simple reliance on the market would not bring maximum liberty simply because there was much the market could not provide. Mill, for example, pointed to the tensions between maximum economic efficiency on one hand and other issues that we might call quality of life issues—sanitation, consumer protection, health and safety—on the other. These issues were not simply "academic," that is divorced form practical affairs, but were the very stuff of daily life. Thoughtful observers in both Britain and America were also troubled by the squalid aspects of industrial life, and it was thus inevitable that a new generation of reformers would publicize the attendant problems and propose corrective remedies.

Having started out as an ideology devoted to removing regulations, liberals began to believe that some regulations were indeed necessary to a civilized society and had to be imposed by the state. This was the political backdrop behind the great age of regulatory reform at the turn of the twentieth century, but the American experience, although growing out of the great tributary of British tradition, had also branched out and thus some explanation is in order.

Regulation and Liberalization in American Politics: Three Centuries

The Spirit of '76?

It is best to begin the story of American regulatory reform, not at the end, but at the beginning—before America was an independent country. For much of the 1700s, the colonial system under Great Britain was one geared to the mother country: the American colonies existed merely to provide raw materials and, in turn, to purchase the finished products of British industry. (The American colonies were also useful in housing Britain's social castaways—religious enthusiasts and paupers.) Although there was a large measure of benign neglect throughout much of the colonial era, the Crown nonetheless regulated trade and commercial interchange to Britain's benefit. Events went from tolerable to quite unbearable: by the 1760s, agents of the Crown tightened regulatory legislation and began to enforce statutes that had long been neglected. Soon colonial agitation was directed against a host of duties—the eighteenth-century form of taxation—and laws that regulated colonial trade with the outside world. The Boston Tea Party, for example, was not only a tax revolt but a protest against increasingly stringent regulatory measures.

One might well assume that the push for colonial independence, which put an end to all royal regulation of "international" trade, consumption and production, would have inaugurated the golden era of laissez-faire economics and free international trade. 1776 was, after all, a big year for freedom: Adam Smith had published his monumental work, *The Wealth of Nations,* and Thomas Jefferson penned the Declaration of Independence. Such comparisons are, however, often misleading and perhaps the work of speech makers who rummage through the attic of history, plundering some rhetorical bric-a-brac for the talk to the Jaycees or the local boosters.

Ultimately, the American push for independence was much less an economic than a political movement. Although American independence severed the old colonial system that had worked to the advantage of British producers and hurt American consumers, after any revolution the old regime creeps back in unpredictable ways. Not surprisingly, the practical men directing the affairs of the new republic wanted tariffs to protect American merchants and to stimulate new industries on American soil. To a large extent, the issue was colored by region and constituency. Representing the northeast and manufacturers, the Caribbean-born New York politician Alexander Hamilton wanted a government that would stimulate the economy and protect infant industries; representing the South and agricultural interests, Jefferson the Virginian wanted a government that regulated lightly.

The Nineteenth Century: Frontiers and Factories

Though his political ambitions were thwarted, Hamilton's ideas eventually won the day by the early nineteenth century. Laissez-faire ideas thus made little impact on the American republic, which pursued a high-tariff policy in the early years of the nineteenth century and used the receipts to finance infrastructure development: the national road, canals and later the railroad. The tariff obstructed foreign goods from entering American territory; it protected the infant industries of New England—industries that did not want to be swamped by cheaper British goods. For the federal government, the tariff was also the chief form of taxation. American manufacturers were foursquare behind such intervention—business supports intervention when it is good for profits. It is thus a mistake to view business as ipso facto opposed to government and vice versa.

If there was one problem about such economic intervention, what could be called neoprotectionism, it was that it lacked a certain intellectual glamour. Old-fashioned mercantilism was never a political theory as much as an accumulated body of policies and practices that worked in the context and the time. It had its weaknesses. For one, it was overly pessimistic about the possibilities of economic growth. Conversely, mercantilism did have a certain pessimistic truth about it: the world was not a fair one, and it was rates of growth in an expanding market, rather than the idea of expansion itself, that counted more in the struggle for economic primacy. Although Adam Smith and the new proponents of liberal economics who excoriated protectionist regulations did so in a systematic fashion, such intellectual systems—even if they do clarify some misconceptions—are often poor guides to policy. For all the talk of freedom from government intervention and regulation, most states in the nineteenth century pursued policies that seemed suspiciously similar to the bad old days of kings and counting houses.

In America, the tariff issue simmered on and off again through much of the nineteenth century. After the Civil War, the newly formed Republican Party tilted toward the industrial and abolitionist northern states and favored manufacturing interests. In the second half of the nineteenth century, the United States, which was under near Republican domination, came to be one of the most protectionist countries in the world; it was also the period of the most rapid industrial development in U.S. history.

In many ways, the tariff was a simple and politically expedient form of market regulation. It was based on a difference between American producers (implicitly good) and foreign producers (implicitly bad); it generated revenue that the government needed; its costs, borne by consumers (implicitly ignorant) were often diffusely spread through the economy (painless) whereas the beneficiaries, producers, tended to be concentrated. Producers were, after all, a self-aware interest group that made political contributions (immediate payoff).

In the last quarter of the nineteenth century, politicians of both parties were reluctant to intervene in domestic disputes. Reaping the benefits of being the party that saved the Union, Republicans had a lock on the White House and were not about to upset business factions that favored tariffs but feared government meddling. Even Democrats, such as Grover Cleveland of New York, could only succeed at the polls by reassuring business that they, too, would not meddle with prosperity. Questions of domestic intervention unsettled this easy equation and tended to pit consumers against producers and small producers against big ones. Politicians rarely like such sharp lines of confrontation: the possibilities for painless negotiation are few and the penalties for mistake, high.

By the late nineteenth century, however, discontent bubbled into the political process and it came from the western states, where the land was flat, the corn golden and the people, mad as hell. Western Populism was loud and belligerent and rightfully so. Simply put, western farmers got the raw end of the gilded age economic bargain. America had pursued free trade in agriculture but, with the opening up of new wheat production in Ukraine and Argentina, the price of wheat fell. Mechanized agriculture had also increased production, further depressing prices. To complicate matters, the woebegone western farmer was forced to purchase expensive farm equipment, that was in fact protected by a tariff and therefore more expensive. If that were not enough, many of the railroads rigged their prices to favor certain big producers and squeezed the little man, who received no such benefit of the "rebate." Controlling railroad collusion thus became a Populist rallying cry.

It was this frothing economic resentment—more complex than simply class envy and far from socialism—that propelled Nebraska's William Jennings Bryan to two Democratic presidential nominations. He lost both times. His base was too slender, too regional, too extreme. With his rich voice and good looks, his lay preacher's style and his unexamined assumptions, Bryan offered too much, too soon. One ironic penalty of reform politics, however, is that one often loses the election but gives the victor a political issue. If the victor is shrewd, he annexes the ideas of his opponents and separates the valid wheat from the controversial chaff; he assuages anxieties in one camp by "feeling their pain," and eases tensions in another camp by not "rocking the boat," and lo and behold, political reform emerges from the firmament.

Regulatory reform was timely in this period, not simply because of this agrarian discontent, but because of problems associated with the growing pains of a young, industrial economy. America's industrial boom in the years after the Civil War, the so-called gilded age, was a time of conspicuous consumption, business mergers and colossal profits. Shipping, steel, oil, coal, railroads blurred with Vanderbilts, Mellons, Carnegies, Rockefellers and Astors, and the other names that roll on in a voluptuous litany of money begetting money.

Just as Americans had settled the frontier, tamed nature and restrained the impulses of lawlessness and violence, so too an increasingly bourgeois America softened the rough edges of the economy: society was becoming genteel. Looked at in retrospect, the robber barons get an unjustifiably bad name: they were the first generation outlaw entrepreneurs who played by the rules of the system—one predicated on an absence of rules other than sheer economic survival. These men were, after all, virtuosos of survival. Such a free-for-all, however, cannot go on indefinitely: even the scoundrels who hit it rich want an element of law and order if only to secure their riches. Soon the sheriff comes to town. The church is set up, the saloon shut down and the bad boys scramble to clean up their act, which not only provides a measure of legitimacy but often freezes others out of the game. So it was in the frontier—so, too, in the U.S. economy as it left the "cowboy" phase and matured. The sheriff became a regulator, and his deputized posse was the regulatory commission. For his part, the ruthless and gutsy merchant, prospector or land speculator who hit it big in the frenzy of the early days could retire knowing that all was safe in the growing frontier town, already acquiring a certain respectability.

The twentieth century, the great age of American regulation, was born. Just as the tariff receded in importance, the question of domestic regulation emerged full blown.

The Twentieth Century: The Three Waves of Regulation

Predictably, it was the two Roosevelts, Theodore and Franklin, who were responsible for two of the three great waves of regulatory reform in the twentieth century.

For his part, Theodore Roosevelt represented his party's "progressive" wing whereas both his predecessor, William McKinley, and his successor, William Howard Taft belonged to the probusiness wing that had been a Republican mainstay since the mid-nineteenth century. A reform-minded New York politician, Roosevelt was the perfect man for the Progressive era. He had spent part of his young manhood out in the badlands of the Dakotas and devoted his early career to fighting police corruption in New York City. Roosevelt had both the sense of civic-mindedness and the political astuteness to push through reforms; he combined the moralistic ardor of the nineteenth-century New England reformer with the political machismo of the straight-talking sheriff. Even though he and President McKinley trounced the western populist Bryan at the polls, Roosevelt, (who ascended to the presidency after the McKinley assassination) also understood the political windfall of reform.

In another sense, international changes shaped Roosevelt's political equation. After all, America was a New World power and just as Roosevelt wanted the nation to take its rightful role as a leading military power in the community of civilized states, he wanted America to resemble other advanced states in the efficient administration of government and the economy. In this period, political discourse was infused with ideas of efficiency and coordination—the state was seen as something of a machine, not that of a machine of corrupt politicians passing out bribes and payoffs, but of a well-run administrative organization. Consequently, the push for regulation became, not only a push to soften the excesses of industrial society, but also to make the state into an efficient organ of political and even social coordination. Like Disraeli in Britain and Bismarck in Germany, Theodore Roosevelt urged this activist statist philosophy from the right of the political spectrum—to rejuvenate the conservative party in an expanding electorate but also to contain the spread of socialism among the lower orders.

Under Theodore Roosevelt, the Republicans issued the most advanced regulatory reforms to date. His administration witnessed new legislation regulating child labor, worker safety, and food quality standards. Such regulation was not simply directed toward workers and consumers, it was directed toward the market as well. The administration put new regulatory teeth into the existing statutes governing interstate commerce; the administration endeavored to splinter the huge trusts, or monopolies, in order to guarantee the efficiency of an open market. In this respect, regulatory reform offered a solution to one of the problems of mature capitalism: the tendency of the efficient to devour competition until competition disappears and, with the costs of entry into the market prohibitively high, the industry eventually becomes a monopoly.

Republican reformism, however, had its limits and the Roosevelt agenda was usurped to some degree by Democrat Woodrow Wilson who later reclaimed Bryan's earlier Populism for the Democratic Party. A compromise choice among party leaders, Wilson was shrewd and tactical; he downplayed both Bryan's regionalism and ideological excess. Indeed, it was during the Wilson administration that Congress implemented many of Bryan's older schemes: the popular vote, rather than state legislatures, would elect U.S. senators, for example. The government also created the Federal Reserve Bank to provide stability to the banking sector—long the scapegoat of angry Populists.

Regulatory reform nonetheless faded from popular enthusiasm during and after America's involvement in the First World War. Popular attention was directed first to mobilization and winning the war, and then to demobilization and enjoying the peace. The progressive agenda was thus replaced by the more cautious but reassuringly predictable probusiness conservatism of Warren Harding, Calvin Coolidge and, for a time, Herbert Hoover. In the easy and abundant years after the First World War, Republicans held fast to a politically expedient party line that did not upset the bubbling prosperity of the Jazz age. Ultimately, the Great Depression of 1929 brought the good times to an abrupt end, and the still unresolved problem of a boom and bust economy ushered in a new cycle of reformist activity. This second wave, associated with the second Roosevelt, set the stage for American politics in the second half of the twentieth century.

In politics, the temporary exhaustion of one party's governing philosophy creates opportunities for the opposite party to craft its message, not so much in terms of a new philosophy, but in terms of both its own constituencies and the other party's fatal contradictions. This was the opportunity for Franklin Roosevelt who was handed the task in a time of a national crisis and, like all great politicians, he rose to the occasion. The drifting Democrat Party was actually the natural party of regulatory reform in these years, for it was less tied to big business, which was always ambivalent about regulation even if it did serve business interests. By 1932, however, businesses and banks were folding; people were out of work; the system seemed to be coming apart. As an emergency corrective, Franklin Roosevelt supervised the creation of a new set of agencies: his administration established the Securities and Exchange Commission to monitor the financial market and create a set of safeguards to prevent another collapse. The administration created the National Recovery Agency—a host of departments that attempted, not so much to end the Depression, but to provide government relief until the economy moved out of the Depression. Roosevelt also introduced a number of new labor laws, which did in fact antagonize business leaders, but which nonetheless placated organized labor, a key Democratic constituency.

Tarred by the brush of Hooverism, Republicans were all but compelled to endorse many of these new regulations and government programs. Politically and even economically, it would have been unwise not to do so. (One of the strengths of conservatism is in endorsing the thrust of liberalism but in tempering its excesses.)

Republicans nevertheless had tactical room for selectively criticizing the thrust of New Deal regulations, even if it were politically taboo to tamper with social security. With the growing affluence after the Second World War and with the easing of "emergency" conditions, it became possible, and even necessary, for Republicans to start to prey upon tensions within the New Deal coalition, much as Roosevelt had divided the Republican coalition in the 1930s. In 1952, Barry Goldwater's rhetorical argument against Truman's Fair Deal was an attempt to sever the unnatural alliances of organized labor and business: Goldwater's ploy was to appeal to small business, which was often squeezed out of the alliance. What Goldwater could do in the 1950s was to link government regulation to an ideology of antibusiness socialism. This had not been possible in the earlier decades when unemployment lines were long, when businesses foreclosed and when the rich were viewed as corpulent plutocrats with top hats and tails, that is, as caricatures straight out of the Monopoly board game. The businessman of the 1940s and 1950s, however, was no caricature: he was the democratic everyman in a flannel suit, the self-reliant taxpayer who took part in the postwar economic boom and who made America great.

Although Goldwater's critique worked with some segments of the electorate, there was nevertheless a natural barrier, for the postwar economic boom made it feasible for businesses to experience economic growth and labor to receive rising wages. Since other industrial economies had been bombed out during the war, there was little international competition. Indeed, American affluence continued unabated through the 1940s and there was no massive recession after the postwar demobilization as many had feared; a modicum of government coordination had prevented the economic bust of 1929 and helped keep a good thing going. It was inevitable then that the Goldwater message played, not to corporate America, but to the fringes: to the small-town Chamber of Commerce types and the traditional Republican constituencies that wanted a choice not an echo at the congressional level. At the presidential level, however, Republicans were content with Ike, who in fact legitimized big government by putting a smiling, reassuring face on it.

It is in the Goldwater rhetorical shadow that we find Reagan in the 1950s—pitching his probusiness, low-tax, minimal regulation line to the GE corporate cadres and then branching out to what he called the "mashed-potato circuit," the probusiness revival meetings. Reagan's antiregulatory theology was always strong in the broad sweep, weak in the details. That was the secret of his success, for the "mashed-potato circuit" was not about the technical virtues or failings of regulation but about big themes—free enterprise, intrusive government and the American way of life interspersed with fetching anecdotes, just enough to entertain and get the audience sufficiently riled. As in his 1930s stint as a radio announcer, Reagan was adept at giving his audience what they wanted to hear. A radio announcer who had invented play by play sport scenes from mere details wired in over the telegraph, Reagan understood that atmosphere was always more important than fidelity to detail.

Reagan's rise to political office in 1966 corresponded to the third wave of regulatory reform. In contrast to the first two waves, the third wave—which involved a deepening commitment to environmental and product safety—lacked the broader political symbolism that gave it staying power. It involved the creation of whole new federal agencies: the Environmental Protection Agency, the Department of Transportation, the Energy Department. Unlike the first wave at the turn of the century, the problems with industry in this third phase were less naked, less obvious for the eye to see. Pollution and product safety simply lacked the immediacy of rancid meat in slaughterhouses, sweatshops, and the exploitation of child labor. Like poverty, modern industrial problems tend to be camouflaged. Unlike the second wave of regulatory reform in the 1930s, there was no crisis of market failure to galvanize another round of regulation; indeed, voters and business interests took the idea of a fine-tuned market for granted and thus were less likely to countenance the idea of a new, third wave of regulations.

In fact, questions of regulation became more overtly politicized—in a negative sense—in the 1960s than had previously been the case in the first and second waves. It was the radicals on the left who had leveled the first charge in the 1960s. Just as they had ridiculed Cold War America as an imperialist power subverting revolution in the developing world, and just as they criticized the "new Mandarins" who flocked to Washington in the Kennedy-Johnson years, radicals turned their sights on the regulatory establishment and its symbiotic relation with the businesses it regulated. Radicals argued that, far from being a means to control the excesses of industrial capitalism, regulation and regulatory agencies were in fact a way for industries to "capture" part of the state apparatus and ensure their economic domination of society. For many radicals, regulation was a sham that perpetuated the dominant status quo. The New Radicals actually had echoed older ideas of late-nineteenth-century western Populists who condemned banks, railroads and the trusts, but there was a crucial difference. The Populists had made a distinction between the small and the big businessman, whereas the New Radicals, to whom all business was slightly bourgeois and thus suspect, made no such distinction. With visions of redistributive social democracy, the New Radicals stigmatized individual wealth creation and thus alienated themselves from the vast majority of Americans, to whom the hypothetical possibility of wealth creation and social mobility is virtually sacrosanct.

On the right, a respectable school of economists, one often associated with the University of Chicago, began to question, not the probusiness dimension to regulation, but instead its economic costs. In short, these economists took the Goldwater-Reagan line about the inordinate costs of regulatory legislation and, as economists are wont to do, they created models and numerical tests. The most notable example was the number devised by Murray Weidenbaum in the early 1970s; the number was a type of Benthamite formula that quantified what many believed was, in the final analysis, beyond calculation. Conservative critics, however, needed no formula to feel that regulation impinged on business. In the broadest sense, the tactical advantage of conservatives who questioned the effects of regulation was that they did not challenge the American vision of wealth creation—indeed, they supported it. In the matter of regulation, those dissenting voices of the right thus had an advantage all but denied to those on the left.

The Politics of Regulation: From Carter to Reagan

Inevitably, dissent from both left and right colored the political debate about regulation in the 1970s—a period of high inflation, creeping energy crises, industrial sluggishness and diminished business confidence. In 1976, Jimmy Carter had won the Democratic primary, and later the White House, by reviving the alliance of organized labor and consumer groups—an alliance that had been put under stress in 1972 when the McGovern wing alienated culturally conservative labor constituencies by drifting too far to the left on social issues. Carter had brought that coalition back to the center, and his presidential initiatives reflected the need to balance the interests of consumers, business, labor and environmentalists. In fact, the campaign for deregulatory reform really began in the Carter years.[1]

In the late 1970s, there were good reasons for the deregulation of certain industries, such as interstate trucking, telephones and commercial airlines.

Much of this was immediately beneficial to both consumers and the most competitive firms. Carter's ambitious policy was, however, subject to stresses when the economy, after improving in the early years of his administration, went into a recession at the worst possible time, just as the 1980 election approached.

With a sagging economy in 1980, challenger Reagan could talk tough—for tough talk was his metier—on the need for deregulation. Skillfully, Reagan and his campaign advisors drove wedges into the Carter coalition by linking the administration to an antibusiness philosophy of government regulation. In the 1980 presidential campaign, Reagan's strident confidence that business needed to be unshackled by meddling bureaucrats seemed appealing to many discontented and confused voters. Too much environmental and product safety regulation, Reagan argued, was bad for both business and workers.

Reagan's position would also have carried much less appeal had the economy been robust and had Carter been perceived as a man capable of controlling the vicissitudes of both foreign and domestic policy. Although swing voters saw Carter as both decent and technically adept, many had lost faith, not in his vision of regulation, but in his capacity for leadership. As in foreign policy, Reagan's biggest asset was that he was not Carter and, in a period of uncertainty and unease, skeptical voters were willing to give him a chance.

Reagan's political argument on regulatory reform was a rough campaign calculation rather than a clear ideological formula. The election, nonetheless, brought to Washington a cadre of political operatives who did have an agenda: Reagan's victory over Carter, they reasoned, was indeed a mandate for radical deregulation. In turn, Reagan and his White House handlers openly endorsed this vision, but they gave a green light to deregulation in the abstract rather than specific marching orders. Most of the appointees tilted considerably toward business interests and, accordingly, tried to overturn those recent accomplishments in both consumer and environmental protection that they believed impinged on business. The mess that many of these crusading deregulators made of their tenure demonstrated the political pitfalls, and indeed the economic costs, of abrogating the trade-off between business and consumer groups in the regulatory balancing act.

The OMB Task Force: The Beginning Phases

The director of the Office of Management and Budget (the OMB) is not usually considered a high-profile position within the White House, yet for David Stockman, Reagan's budget director, the position was an opportunity to put his views on supply-side economics into practice. Stockman's checkered career and his budget-cutting credentials will be examined in the subsequent chapter on budgetary reform, but he is significant here precisely because he was also given an unprecedented degree of power in cutting back governmental regulations that free-market conservatives believed impeded the natural workings of the economy.

Stockman came to office, not through the various agencies where one builds up regulatory experience, tempers enthusiasm and learns to negotiate the thicket of competing interest groups and constituencies, but through the political process. A congressman in the late 1970s, Stockman identified himself with the supply-side partisans in the House. Although supply-siders were most interested in cutting taxes and thereby stimulating growth, they nonetheless saw regulation as a type of tax, as well as an intrusion into the allegedly self-regulating economy. As Reagan's budget director, Stockman viewed his mandate as a rollback of most regulatory legislation and, for him, this was the first phase in his plan to scale back the welfare state. Reagan's benign blessing became Stockman's tactical advantage in the short run: Stockman was thus given a free hand in running the shop. (Over the longer term, however, this short-term advantage led to Stockman's undoing, as will be seen in the subsequent chapter.)

"Avoiding an Economic Dunkirk"—a memo Stockman wrote for the Reagan team in late 1980—called for "regulatory ventilation." It was an ambitious statement of objectives—one of those intellectual blueprints that an enthusiast in the transition team draws up to chart policy. Such tomes are often forgotten or go unread, and do their authors more harm than good, for such intellectual blueprints are more appropriate to policy think tanks than to bureaucracy. Stockman, however, had a persuasive messenger: Jack Kemp, who made a trip to California to present these urgent ideas to the transition team. In a campaign when the candidate had talked rather vaguely about regulatory rollback, Stockman seemed to have a clue of where Reagan at least ought to go. He could turn the pleasing slogans of the "Speech" into effective policy. First offered the Energy Department, Stockman instead expressed his desire for the Budget Office and was eventually offered the post he had sought from the beginning.

While the cumbersome transition team was still sorting out functions, Stockman began by setting up the committee that would eventually begin the process of "regulatory ventilation," that is regulatory rollback. Select committees enable the administrator to bypass the established bureaucracy, which is often committed to certain regulatory practices. To this end, Stockman recruited an OMB bureaucrat from the old regime, James Tizzo, who had worked in the Nixon, Ford and Carter administrations and who possessed both an astonishing knowledge of regulations and the urge to scale them back. He assisted James C. Miller, a conservative economist whom Stockman appointed as head of the newly formed Office of Deregulation, the command center in the campaign for regulatory rollback. The Office of Deregulation reviewed hundreds of laws and, by the time Reagan was sworn into office, they were poised to act. These tactics represented a radical reversal of regulatory policy, in which reformist initiatives had traditionally originated in legislation rather than executive action. Already, the Reagan administration's ambitious tactics raised questions of propriety and, indirectly, prepared the groundwork for later congressional scrutiny: reform requires publicity and the covert nature of backroom committees or administrative juntas usually gives momentum to political opponents.

Prior to Reagan's taking office, Stockman had urged a 17.5 percent cut in all federal funding for regulation.[2] The rationale was simple: if agencies have no money then they were denied powers to regulate.[3] It was similar to the strategy of welfare reform—cut off funding rather than negotiate with the constituencies and interested parties who would invariably try to preserve the status quo. Stockman also wanted to eliminate the Federal Trade Commission, which had been set up to regulate interstate commerce, but George Bush and more cautious voices in the administration urged a slower approach.

Two days after his inauguration, Reagan ordered the creation of a regulatory task force, presumably one that would give political legitimacy to the decisions already drawn up by Miller and Tizzo. The task force was headed by George Bush, the vice presidential figurehead needed to give political clout to what might well be seen as a back-channel operation. Within less than a week, the task force announced the suspension of the "midnight regulations" that outgoing Carter appointees had written into law as a way of either ideologically taunting the incoming Reagan administration or forcing them to dismantle more, and thereby risk further congressional opposition. The new Reagan team did not flinch; it ordered a sixty-day freeze on all regulations and urged the elimination of hundreds of other regulations. By late spring, Vice President Bush had publicly announced that the task force had saved consumers millions of dollars.

As suggested above, the real power on the task force was James C. Miller, who would later succeed Stockman as OMB director. A conservative ideologue and a professional economist, Miller was a longtime critic of government regulation who began to apply the cost-benefit analysis that Murray Weidenbaum had popularized. In the 1970s, both he and Weidenbaum had been affiliated with the American Enterprise Institute—the relatively conservative think tank that also published the journal *Regulation*. Although many economists believed that the Weidenbaum type of cost-benefit calculation was all but impossible, Miller claimed that every regulation was going to be subjected to such analysis. Business interests applauded this push for deregulation; in fact, the U.S. Chamber of Commerce had issued "the terrible twenty," those Commerce Department laws that ostensibly failed the cost-benefit analysis.

Early on, however, Miller attracted congressional scrutiny in part because he refused to reveal his private log of meetings for congressional oversight. This heightened suspicions that Miller was meeting with industry represen-tatives who wanted regulations rescinded and was making changes on their behalf. This was a fair accusation in the political tug-of-war, which always clouded the regulation equation: Republicans accused Democrats of shackling business with frivolous and costly regulations whereas Democrats accused Republicans of being in the pockets of industry. Protecting or dismantling regulations thus often degenerated into stereotype and innuendo.

Within a year, Miller had moved to the Federal Trade Commission, David Stockman had, for reasons addressed in the following chapter, lost much of his ideological luster and many of the supply-siders had left the administration. The heroic phase of deregulation had passed, and the OMB regulatory office fell under the control of Christopher DeMuth—a veteran of the Nixon administration who had later gone on to the University of Chicago Law school and then specialized in regulatory matters. A friend of Stockman, DeMuth had nonetheless expressed reservations in the late 1970s over the feasibility of the Weidenbaum number. Cost-benefit analysis, DeMuth argued, was simply impossible to calculate. Scholarly and less overtly ideological than Miller, DeMuth did not raise congressional fears. The transition from Miller to DeMuth thus demonstrated the end of a stridently ideological phase of regulatory rollback by the administration's second year, but this gets ahead of the narrative—which will next focus on the actual regulatory policies of the Reagan team in several areas.

Notes

1. Haynes Johnson, *Sleepwalking through History: America in the Reagan Years* (New York: W.W. Norton, 1991), 156; Michael Schaller, *Reckoning with Reagan: America and Its President in the 1980s* (New York: Oxford University Press, 1992), 99.

2. Rowland Evans and Robert D. Novak, *The Reagan Revolution* (New York: E.P. Dutton, 1981), 150.

3. George C. Eads and Michael Fix, *Relief or Reform? Reagan's Regulatory Dilemma* (Washington, D.C.: Urban Institute Press, 1984), 9.

Chapter 11

The Reagan Years: One Giant Step Backwards?

It is perhaps easier to look at Reagan-era regulation on a departmental basis rather than in a functional basis, that is, regulation as a matter of either consumer protection or market regulation. Nowhere was this more true than at the Department of Transportation, where Reagan's secretary, Drew Lewis, was involved in issues that touched on questions of both auto safety and the competitiveness of the U.S. auto industry—regulations that alternately favored consumers or favored industry.

Transportation: The Pragmatic Approach to Regulatory Reform

For the Reagan transition team, Lewis, a prominent Pennsylvania Republican, was a natural choice at Transportation.[1] First, he was a Republican loyalist who, as early as 1977, had become an active supporter of Reagan's 1980 nomination and was a crucial power broker in drumming up support in the Northeast. Beyond political loyalty, Lewis had an extensive background in transportation issues, particularly in railroad reorganization in the early 1970s. A Harvard MBA, Lewis' ability was in taking over failing enterprises and returning them to profitability: this colored his subsequent policies on regulatory reform.

As the cabinet secretary with jurisdiction over the air-traffic control system, Lewis urged Reagan to fire the air-traffic controllers when their union,

163

Patco, had gone on strike early in Reagan's first term. More importantly, Lewis demonstrated the political uses of both deregulation in some areas and the imposition of market controls in other areas—a combination that some free market ideologues, such as David Stockman, found not only inconsistent but distasteful.

Questions of auto safety had actually galvanized the consumer movement of the late 1960s and 1970s. Indeed, there are times when a single book can shape a political debate, and Ralph Nader's 1966 treatise *Unsafe at Any Speed* was one such work. It brought the issue of automotive safety to light and created a popular groundswell for new safety regulations; questions of auto safety later merged with questions of air quality and, in turn, led to laws regulating emission standards for the auto industry, thereby demonstrating the overlap between the consumer and the environmental movements.

A pragmatic "can-do" type, Lewis did not need to elaborate cost-benefit analysis of the Weidenbaum "number" to understand that government regulations cut in to corporate profits. As secretary of transportation, he directed the administration's Task Force on the Auto Industry and, in April of 1981, the task force issued a report that listed thirty-four safety and environmental regulations that would be either postponed, reconsidered or abolished altogether.

Lewis's tenure at Transportation, nevertheless, illustrated the ambiguities in imposing an ideological litmus test of free-market ideology on transportation issues. Unlike the supply-siders who tended to view regulation as a tax, Lewis himself urged a four-cent gasoline tax to finance highway construction. Unlike some of the more committed free-market ideologues in the administration, Lewis was also interested in supporting the sagging U.S. auto industry. This, more than anything, revealed the divisions over the question of regulatory reform in the Reagan administration. For some, regulatory reform involved only one thing: scaling back all government involvement whatsoever. For others, regulatory reform was a selective enterprise whereby the state removed perceived burdens on industry but, if conditions called for it, the state could also selectively regulate the market. The former position had the advantage of consistency but was politically questionable; the latter position lacked ideological consistency but was politically feasible and in line with the pragmatic traditions of U.S. policy from the beginning of the Republic.

Along with Commerce Secretary Malcolm Baldrige, Labor Secretary Raymond Donovan, and Trade Representative William Brock, Drew Lewis was active in the effort to curb Japanese auto imports into the United States—an important issue in the late 1970s when the U.S. auto industry, long accustomed to near total dominance in the domestic market, was first feeling the pressure of foreign competition. Unlike the sagging textile industry in the southeast, which was uncompetitive because of low-wage foreign competition, the U.S. auto industry's problems were different. Its chief competition came, not from low-wage countries, but from technologically advanced, high-wage countries such as Japan and Germany. In the updated mercantilistic language of the 1970s and 1980s, it was as if the defeated Axis powers were having their revenge on American industry that had grown stodgy and failed to reinvest in new technologies. The auto industry, many anxious observers argued, was nonetheless too important to be left to the vicissitudes of the market.

In the late 1970s, Congress had decided to bail out the bankrupt Chrysler Corporation and, in effect, finance its corporate restructuring. Then a Michigan congressman, David Stockman had resolutely opposed such government protectionism. The workings of the free market, Stockman and other principled laissez-faire supporters argued, should proceed regardless of social costs; to do otherwise would be to reward inefficiency and, indirectly, penalize the consumer. (By the mid-1980s, Chrysler, under the leadership of former Ford executive Lee Iacocca, had managed to overhaul its management practices and return the company to profitability—something that belied Stockman's assertion that government intervention would only provide incentives for the inefficient. Indeed, the Chrysler case demonstrated the complicated realities of business-government relations.)

Rightly or wrongly, U.S. auto manufacturers argued in the early 1980s that Japanese firms were "dumping" goods, that is selling their products in the U.S. at artificially low prices in order to gain a "bridge-head" in the lucrative U.S. market.[2] On this very point, Lewis made an explicit connection between government regulation and the compensatory need for a government-led strategy to restrict Japanese auto exports into the United States. Washington, Lewis argued, had over-regulated the auto industry by mandating air and safety regulations; now the government had the responsibility for bailing out the industry that it had hobbled in its showdown with the Japanese. This equation echoed Reagan's 1980 campaign rhetoric, particularly his appearance at abandoned factories in Youngstown, Ohio, in 1980. Government regulation, Reagan then declared, had forced the Youngstown plant closures. Although factually incorrect, Reagan's message nonetheless played in Youngstown and, indeed, throughout the delegate rich states of the Rust Belt, which were central to any Republican presidential victory.

It took no leap of the imagination to go from Reagan's casual rhetoric to Lewis' policy. Not all in the administration, however, were enamored. Viewing the world through the prism of the supply-side creed, Stockman viewed Lewis's policy as the first step to a government industrial policy. Stockman was only half right: trade and tariff policy are forms of government intervention that, depending on the circumstances, can either forward or impede the liberalization of international trade. Lewis and his supporters could thus argue that they had to take measures as retaliation against Japanese "mercantilist" policies and that this could be a corrective step toward freer trade in both countries.

Stockman, Treasury Secretary Don Regan and Chief Economist Murray Weidenbaum all disagreed with Lewis's approach and opposed what they viewed as outright protectionism. Politically more attuned than he perhaps let on, Reagan implicitly sided with Lewis and those who urged import controls. Eventually White House Counselor Ed Meese brokered a compromise position between the White House factions and, on the basis of this, U.S. Ambassador to Tokyo, former Wyoming senator Mike Mansfield, negotiated a deal with the Japanese government. In the deal, the Japanese accepted a "voluntary" agreement to limit their U.S.-bound auto exports to 1.68 million vehicles per year.[3]

Accustomed to reading popular currents and putting pragmatic compromises above ideological formulae, astute politicians understand the commonsense middle ground between excessive government intervention that stifles private initiative and an unfettered economy that may be economically efficient in the long run but socially unpredictable in the short run. Ardent free-market conservatives deride this fine-tuning and selective intervention as "welfare capitalism," but the governors of Illinois, Michigan and Ohio who lobbied on behalf of the Lewis proposals thought otherwise. (Indeed, it was widely believed that Lewis was using his Washington experience as an interlude before an anticipated Pennsylvania Senate race.) Both Lewis and the midwestern governors made an argument for using trade policy to protect an industry vital to the nation's economy.

Barely disguising his intellectual disdain, David Stockman described this policy as "an attempt to impose political solutions on economic problems, and as such was reactionary. Industries rise and fall, and in doing so bring about growth, technological advance, and rising living standards.... But the politician is by nature opposed to the cycle of creation and destruction of industry. He wants everything to be level, smooth and unchanging."[4] While politicians cannot bail out whole industries that run counter to the nation's comparative advantage, politicians who do nothing in the face of Stockman's "cycle of creation and destruction" risk being put out of office and rightly so. Indeed, the politician must ease the costs of short-term dislocations, not to impede longer-term economic transitions, but to facilitate them.

One could suggest that Lewis's policies at Transportation illustrated the pragmatic side of regulatory reform. Far more than the Weidenbaum "cost-benefit analysis," Lewis's approach rested on the calculations that most politicians must make. Lewis made a calculation that consumer and safety regulations could be shelved in the interest of keeping prices down, which helped profits in a troubled industry that was central to the nation's economy: given the political climate, freezing environmental and safety regulation to ostensibly help the sagging economy was an acceptable trade-off.

The Lewis approach, however, differed sharply from Reagan administration environmental policies—ones in which corporate profit and, indirectly, worker security did not equate with a perceived national interest. If Lewis' tenure at Transportation demonstrated the political possibilities of deregulation, the administration's environmental policy illustrated the political pitfalls of deregulatory jihad under the banner of ideology.

The Politics of Regulation: Environmental and Energy Policy

Whereas questions of auto safety were novel to the 1960s, environmental concerns dated back to the end of the nineteenth century. It is almost a cliche to note that Teddy Roosevelt, who gave his name to the "Teddy Bear" for a bear cub he rescued, was the first environmentalist chief executive. Roosevelt was indeed a conservationist—fitting for a man who spent much of his time outdoors—but Roosevelt also reflected the late Victorian romantic view of the frontier. The early conservation movement had focused on the preservation of America's natural splendors and the protection of virgin territory from the ravages of commercial exploitation and development. In this sense, the preservation movement was an integral part of the progressive agenda for containing and, where possible, rectifying the worst aspects of industrialization.

True to form, the second great wave of environmental legislation occurred during Franklin Roosevelt's administration. The depredations of environmental erosion had led to the so-called dust bowl that intensified the Great Depression of the 1930s. As a corrective, Roosevelt established the Civilian Conservation Corps and a number of programs for controlling soil erosion; environmental controls thus had direct economic implications. Franklin Roosevelt's environmental legacy was, however, ambiguous. His administration presided over the construction of gigantic irrigation projects and dams, such as the Tennessee Valley Authority and the Hoover Dam, which facilitated economic development but, indirectly, led to a host of environmental changes. As in Stalin's Soviet Union, these heroic engineering projects, the new concrete cathedrals, seemed to be the wave of the future in New Deal America. These works projects brought electricity to southern and western consumers and water to western farmers—all part of the New Deal coalition.

During the Eisenhower years, environmental concerns were not at the top of the national agenda. This was an age of atom splitting, of synthetics and automotive culture. Diseases were controlled with new medicines and crops with new pesticides; a host of consumer products simplified life and created an affluence unthinkable only a generation before. Even leisure, which Americans enjoyed more abundantly than before, was colored by technology: the car became a pastime. Not only were there new highways, but there were drive-in theaters and drive-in restaurants, and when people visited nature, it was with a streamlined silver camper hitched to the back of their automobile. Both science and consumer goods seemed to hold forth promise of a better and a safer life.

By the 1960s, however, environmental concerns once again emerged in the popular consciousness and, again, a single book was instrumental in shaping the debate. Rachel Carson's influential 1962 book *Silent Spring*, which explored the toxic effects of man-made pollutants on the environment, inspired the modern environmental movement. Environmentalists joined with consumer advocates and urged that government hold industry accountable, not only for the quality and safety of its products, but for emissions and pollutants.

The third wave of environmental regulation corresponded to the years of Nixon's presidency. In 1970, the Environmental Protection Agency was established to oversee congressionally mandated environmental legislation (i.e., the 1970 Clear Air Act and the 1972 Clean Water Act). An advisory commission had, in fact, urged that the Executive branch combine the Department of Interior with other relevant environmental departments and, in effect, create a superagency. Feeling that then secretary of the interior Walter Hickel was not up to the administrative tasks, Nixon instead created a separate cabinet department.

It was also in this era that the issue of pollution entered the mainstream of popular culture. In a public service television advertisement of the era, a Native American in headdress paddled his canoe through a backwoods river only to stumble out of this pristine wilderness onto a busy highway where trash was tossed indiscriminately at his feet from a passing car. Whether conscious or not, the commercial brought together a number of political themes of the era—ethnic chic, Roosevelt frontier, Naderism, green politics and even a touch of the Burt Reynolds film *Deliverance*—and left the viewer looking at the present mess through the eyes of a "first American." The eco-Indian's tear was one of lament, not for the vanishing frontier, but for America the Beautiful that had become polluted and destroyed. As an advertisement, it was brilliant.

The Energy Interlude

Environmental regulation was not simply aimed at environmental degradation but also at preserving nonrenewable resources, most typically oil. This issue had been rudely thrust on the American public during the "oil shocks" of the early 1970s, when members of the Oil Producing and Exporting Countries (OPEC) issued an oil embargo in retaliation for U.S. support of Israel during the 1973 Arab-Israeli war. The stereotype of the rich oil sheik dictating to the American consumer—not one to question his high consumption of fuel or his low-mileage car—filtered into the popular imagination. Implicitly, the environmental question became a consumer issue and would later become the basis of Carter's energy policy, in which he declared national self-sufficiency in energy resources to be the moral equivalent of war.

Early in 1977, President Carter and his political advisors sensed that developing a national energy policy to counter the worldwide energy crisis could prove politically popular with consumers. To this end, Carter directed his energy advisor and former secretary of defense in the Ford administration, James Schlesinger, to draw up a plan. (Schlesinger's appointment incidentally demonstrated the national security dimensions of energy policy.) As with President Clinton's failed health reform program some two decades later, Carter's energy policy was drawn up in relative secrecy and without the consultation of powerful political allies on the Hill. Even members of Carter's staff complained that Schlesinger had failed to consult them. Moreover, Carter proved politically inept in the legislative process, taking an almost Wilsonian rhetorical high ground rather than bargaining with powerful Democratic committee chairmen in both the House and Senate.

In the fall of 1977, congress had created the new Department of Energy by consolidating a preexisting nuclear regulatory commission with a patchwork of other agencies. Although Carter's energy legislation passed both houses of Congress eighteen months after the initial proposal, the legislation had been gutted. After auspicious beginnings, Carter had failed to capture the popular political imagination. (In final form, the energy legislation deregulated the natural gas industry, created a standard pricing system for intra- and interstate gas, and established tax credits for energy conservation.) Nonetheless, it seemed too much the product of Carter's technocratic style. Indeed, his comparison of national self-sufficiency to the moral equivalency of war—a clumsy rephrasing of William James's wording—was doubly unfortunate: waiting in line for gas seemed slightly different from sending U.S. boys to the jungles of Vietnam. Though he endeavored to satisfy the various parts of his coalition, such as consumers and environmentalists, through energy legislation, Carter nonetheless tested the patience of his political allies and gave the opposition an easy target.

Put bluntly, Carter's technocratic streak contrasted unfavorably with Reagan's confident certainties that Washington bureaucrats should not be in the business of regulating either energy consumption or industry. In one push, Carter could be linked to intrusive government, excessive regulations and somehow imposing limits on future growth. In 1980, Reagan had in fact promised to abolish the Carter-era Department of Energy.

Cleaning Up the EPA? The Gorsuch Rollback

In 1980, Reagan had also effectively campaigned against the then prevailing trend in federal environmental policy. In Reagan's campaign rhetoric, regulators and environmentalists had become "zealots" just as consumer advocates had somehow become "Naderites." This was a shrewd way to emphasize the social cleavages between lower middle-class constituents who were concerned with job security more than the environment. It was an updating of the old-fashioned criticism of progressive reformers as preachy elitists, aloof from the cultural concerns of the average worker—the very types whose "Americanness" was easy to belittle and who made "liberals" such an anathema group to some voters in the 1970s and 1980s. Cleverly, Reagan's rhetoric linked environmental and consumer programs to the New Left, with its distrust of corporate America and the profit motive.

These tactics nonetheless opened up a host of problems for Reagan. For one, it appeared that he truly believed that most environmental problems were fictitious. He was, in fact, quoted in the 1980 campaign as saying that trees caused pollution. His distressed campaign handlers had adequately "goof-proofed" (their term) him on foreign policy and economic issues but apparently not on environmental policy. More importantly, Reagan argued that corporate America could do a better job in monitoring environmental standards than government regulatory agencies—a political position that created later political headaches for the administration.

As governor of California, Reagan's two terms had actually demonstrated an astute environmental policy—one that had been, predictably, developed by his capable staff.[5] In Sacramento, Reagan's Natural Resources Office was headed by Norman Livermore, a conservative with strong ties to the Sierra Club. Livermore proved successful in balancing the interests of both conservationists and business and won plaudits from both sides of the political spectrum. (It was under Governor Reagan that the Muir Woods, the giant redwood forest north of San Francisco, was established as a state park.)

As a presidential candidate, however, Reagan became particularly vulnerable to those who saw environmental regulation as unwelcome government intrusion into the marketplace and even antibusiness. In this, Reagan had come to be influenced by the conservative Colorado businessman, Joseph Coors, scion of the Coors brewing fortune. Coors had been one of the chief financial backers of the Heritage Foundation in Washington, D.C., a conservative think tank established as an alternative to the center-left Brookings Institute, which had been prominent in the 1960s and 1970s: Coors had also been a major campaign contributor to Reagan's 1976 primary campaign. Ultimately, it was through Coors that members of what critics called the "Colorado Mafia"—James Watt and Ann Gorsuch—came into the Reagan orbit. Indeed, Watt and Gorsuch had been part of the self-styled "sagebrush rebellion," a movement of far-western conservatives who had opposed federal regulations governing strip-mining, timber cutting and toxic waste disposal.

Eventually, the administration chose Ann Gorsuch (who later married William Burford, the Reagan administration's head of the Bureau of Land Management) to run the Environmental Protection Agency, which enforced air and water standards. Among the EPA's chief responsibilities was overseeing the Superfund, the congressional mandate to clean up several thousand toxic waste sites. Indeed, the Superfund legislation was itself a political response to a number of publicized toxic waste scandals, the most notable being the notoriously contaminated Love Canal in upstate New York.

In many ways, Gorsuch was an odd and even provocative choice to head an agency with this mandate. She was a dark-horse candidate, but the transition team had particular trouble in finding a Republican with sufficient knowledge of environmental issues and who could also bring a degree of diversity (i.e., a woman) to the cabinet. A Colorado Republican loyalist, Gorsuch had a history of environmental involvement, but her past was guaranteed to stir up concerns on Capitol Hill.

Like Watt, Gorsuch was a Wyoming native but her family had later moved to Colorado, a state that experienced a postwar economic boom. In the 1970s, questions of environmental pollution were particularly pronounced in the Denver region: with its high altitudes and thin air, auto pollution had given Denver smog as bad, if not worse, than Los Angeles. As a response, many Coloradans pushed a "slow-growth" agenda. In a related policy, Denver mayor and later governor, Richard Lamm led the campaign to block a Colorado bid for the 1976 winter Olympics. "Don't Californicate Colorado," was the motto of those who successfully blocked the project—one that business interests and developers had favored. Instead of directly taking on antigrowth Coloradans, conservatives focused on faraway Washington, and specifically on the EPA, which had taken a firm line on the enforcement of air and water regulations in the late 1970s.

Entering the Colorado legislature in 1976, Gorsuch had pursued a consistent antiregulatory line and had become associated with a group of antiregulatory conservatives who called one another the "crazies." It was Gorsuch who had, in fact, helped engineer the advancement of William Burford, whom she later married, to be the speaker of the state legislature. By 1980, however, she had decided not to seek re-election, in part because she had angered women legislators by suggesting that they were weak to rely on feminism. This was Gorsuch's style: confrontational and blunt. She was no consensus builder and this would later contribute to her political unraveling in Washington.[6]

While in the Colorado legislature, Gorsuch had advocated transferring environmental decision-making to the states themselves—a policy widely seen as a type of federalism in the service of weakening environmental legislation. Critics of such environmental "federalism" argued that clean water and air could not be cordoned off between states, and this made the federal government a necessary broker between states in ways that were perhaps not true in education or welfare policy. For many critics, the Gorsuch appointment was a blatant case of antireform reaction adopting the mantle of reform. It was reminiscent of the way arms control opponents, such as Richard Perle and John Lehman, used executive branch arms control agencies to subvert congressional mandates. For many, this amounted to putting the fox in charge of the regulatory hen house.

As EPA secretary, Gorsuch saw her mission in light of Reagan's declaratory statement that federal regulations were overly restrictive; indeed, one of the reasons that the then relatively unknown Gorsuch clicked with the White House was her willingness to be a team player. When Stockman asked if she thought the agency could be cut by half, she immediately agreed and thus won Stockman's initial approval.

Gorsuch, however, never really had the chance to take control of the agency. From the Budget Office, Stockman had already slashed the EPA budget by 12 percent. Moreover, congress did not confirm Gorsuch's nomination until May, by which time, the ambitious phase of deregulation associated with Stockman and Miller had already kicked in and inevitably raised congressional scrutiny about both the speed and wisdom of regulatory rollback. After her confirmation, Gorsuch's situation hardly improved. At the backroom office of deregulation, Miller had been secretive, and many viewed this secrecy as concealing cozy relations with industry; Gorsuch, by contrast, headed a cabinet-level agency and thus her secretive ways created internal problems through the EPA. Indeed, Gorsuch began with an adversarial stance against career bureaucrats whom she saw as protecting the tradition of environmental legislation. For Gorsuch, President Reagan's mandate implied, if not dismantling the agency, at least hollowing it out from within. Following Watt's advice, she isolated herself from the staff and followed Watt's premise that it is always easier to fire those whom you don't know.[7] (Prior to her nomination, Gorsuch had actually made her office in Watt's Interior Department.)

By the summer of 1981, Gorsuch was already under attack. If one treats one's staff in an adversarial manner, disloyalty and leaks can be expected. Soon, a draft outlining the EPA's Clean Air Law amendments was leaked to Democratic representative Henry Waxman of California; the draft demonstrated that the administration was trying to gut the laws through amendments widely viewed as highly favorable to industry. This gave congressional opponents of the administration the political ammunition they needed. By autumn of 1981, the trickle of leaks had turned into a flood. Later documents revealed that Gorsuch wanted a 20 percent cut in the EPA budget that had already been cut by 12 percent by David Stockman. This, however, was not the end of the matter. Other documents showed that Gorsuch intended to cut the EPA career bureaucracy by 50 percent. Just prior to these revelations, the number three man at the EPA, a Reagan appointee, resigned in protest against Gorsuch's leadership.

As secretary, Gorsuch had made a number of changes. Not only did she apply the Weidenbaum strategy of cost-benefit analysis, but she also made the regulatory process more cumbersome by calling for more analysis by more experts. The ironic upshot was not less regulation, but more—precisely to make it prohibitively difficult for government to regulate. This approach was almost comical: exaggerate the requirements to subvert the mission. Even congressional Republicans, such as Vermont's senator Stafford, were losing patience with her. It became clear that she was, in effect, undercutting the congressionally mandated Superfund and tacitly siding with corporations that were supposed to be monitored. In fact, after a year in office, she had only dealt with a handful of the several thousand toxic waste sites that were identified in the Superfund legislation.

The problem of deliberate bureaucratic foot-dragging and even subversion was driven home in the curious case of Rita Lavelle.[8] A Meese protege who had previously worked for a California firm with a notorious record for dumping toxic waste, Lavelle had actually been given the administration job of supervising toxic waste regulation at the EPA. In 1981, she was compelled to resign after a secret memo was leaked—a memo in which she alleged that senior EPA employees had alienated industry. This was going too far. Alienation was not the point of legislation; protection was. Predictably, Lavelle's subsequent resignation garnered more attention for her embattled supervisor, Gorsuch.

By 1983, Chief of Staff James Baker understood that Gorsuch had made a mess of things at EPA; her penchant for secrecy and her coziness with industry had not only alarmed environmental groups but drew bipartisan congressional condemnation. Moreover, Reagan pollster Richard Wirthlin was concerned that environmental issues could hurt the president in his 1984 re-election campaign. Baker wanted Gorsuch out. Unfortunately, it took a call from the president to budge Gorsuch from her office; she was not going and indeed faced congressional inquiries. Never good at the firing game, Reagan mishandled the call and fumbled his lines. In the end, Gorsuch was pushed from office and became a fall gal for the administration's botched deregulatory policy at the EPA.

She was replaced by William Ruckleshouse, a respected attorney who had served as EPA secretary in the Nixon administration. By 1985, Ruckleshouse himself quietly resigned his EPA cabinet post in frustration. (As with "silent Sam" Pierce, Reagan failed to recognize his own cabinet secretary and confused Ruckleshouse with Ford protege, Donald Rumsfeld.)

The publicity from the Gorsuch tenure had, in effect, brought about the scrutiny that made any sweeping repeal of environmental regulation all but impossible. With a strange symmetry, the same failed regulatory policy took place at the Interior Department.

Interior: Watt Kind of Reform?

The second prong of the Reagan administration environmental deregulatory campaign emerged in James Watt's Interior Department. He was, in fact, the second choice for the transition team, which wanted a western politician to head the department. When Wyoming senator Clifford Hansen declined the position, the choice fell to Watt—the recommendation of Reagan crony and confidante Nevada senator Paul Laxalt.

Located behind the Federal Reserve Bank in northwest Washington and housed in a 1930s era, neo-Pharaonic structure, the Interior Department does not constitute one of the "power" agencies to most Beltway insiders. Unlike most countries, where the Interior Ministry deals with internal order and security, that is, either courts or police, the U.S. Interior Ministry deals with territorial questions. Since the federal government owns vast tracts of land in Alaska, the Far West and the Rocky Mountain states, the Interior Department has a specific regional importance. Not only does it administer the national park system but it leases out its sizable domain to ranchers, farmers and, most importantly, to corporate mining and timber interests.

Watt had been a long-standing proponent of the policy by which the federal government would sell its land rights to allow oil and mineral exploitation. In contrast to Reagan, who was unwilling to specify his beliefs because they were essentially undeveloped, Watt had a clear blueprint. In contrast to Gorsuch's penchant for secrecy, Watt was a crusader for deregulation and proud of it. That was the problem. A genuine member of the Religious Right, probably the only member in Reagan's cabinet,[9] Watt's push for deregulation had something of a revivalist mission to it. From the start, however, he became mired in political controversy and became a liability for the White House.

A Wyoming native, Watt was in many ways a creature of the Washington bureaucracy and a skilled graduate of the very regulatory apparatus that he wanted to dismantle. In this sense, he illustrated the thesis that, at a certain point, those representing special interests eventually "capture" the regulatory agency and make it a tool of those to be regulated. This was a variation of the radical argument of the 1960s, but more sophisticated critics put forth a different interpretation: agencies, they argued, have life cycles, that is they tend to be idealistic and unfocused in the early phase, focused and bureaucratic as the agency matures and, after the original mandate changes or is forgotten, become institutions for the regulated. Although there are problems with this thesis, Watt's career in the Interior Department bureaucracy nonetheless illustrated the possibilities for both career punching and the blurred lines between regulator and regulated.

The Wyoming license plate carries the silhouetted image of a broncobuster, but there was little of the cowboy in James Watt, who had come from the isolated, eastern part of the state. Indeed, it is hard to imagine him as anything but a corporate lawyer. With his glasses, receding hairline and wan, mirthless smile, Watt actually seemed to personify the faceless Washington staffer in the revolving door between government and industry.

After finishing law school (first in his class) in 1962, Watt moved to Washington where he worked as a legislative assistant to Wyoming senator Milward Simpson, then as a lobbyist for the chamber of commerce on land and water issues and, finally, as an undersecretary at Interior during the Nixon administration. Watt's job at Interior was to coach Nixon's secretary, former Alaska governor Walter Hickel, on the oil and gas industry. Over time, Watt grew to disdain Hickel, a developer who, in office, gained a newfound respect for environmental protection.[10] There were two ways of looking at Hickel's change of heart. Those favorable to Hickel's later position could argue that the mandate of the agency has a way of changing the appointee and forcing a broader perspective; alternately, critics could argue that he was captured by the career civil service and became part of the interest-group bureaucracy. Contemptuous of Hickel's conversion, Watt as secretary of the interior, claimed he did not intend to be "Hickelized."

After Carter's 1976 election, Watt became the director of the Denver-based Mountain States' Legal Defense Fund, which lobbied on behalf of corporations against environmental regulation. It was significant that the fund received considerable financial backing, not only from Joseph Coors,[11] but also from timber and energy interests. As director, Watt's mission was to outmaneuver the Carter administration on water rights, pollution controls and occupational safety legislation. At the Interior Department, Carter had appointed former Idaho governor Cecil Andrus whose task was to balance the administration's generally probusiness policy with environmental and consumer concerns. The Andrus policy resembled Reagan's Sacramento tenure in which "Ike" Livermore tried to find the middle ground between business and conservation interests, but federal policy is complicated by heightened regional politics in ways that are not true at the state level.

The middle ground was really not what Watt and his corporate sponsors wanted, and the argument that he and others like him used to oppose the Interior Department in the late 1970s was a clever one. In effect, they tapped into regional resentment against, not only Washington, but against the East. This position had its roots in the older populistic traditions where the East Coast Establishment meant the big, and often collusive, financial interests that hurt the small farmer. Populistic anger had been directed against the big consortia, the trusts, the railroads. Indeed, late-nineteenth-century Populists had argued that the federal government, which should have been an "honest broker," was often in the pockets of the moneyed interests. Watt took those arguments, reversed them, and translated them into the political context of the 1970s, where it was a federal bureaucracy, not the big corporations, that impinged on the westerner. The bureaucracy was captured, not by big business, but by environmental zealots who wanted the West to remain pristine but economically undeveloped. The irony was that Watt, subsidized by mining, timber and oil interests, used arguments that were originally antibusiness and reversed them. It was a defense of corporate prerogative masquerading as a type of regionalism—that the far west and the Rocky Mountain states could not be treated as if they were a colony of Washington bureaucrats.[12]

Moreover, Watt was a fundamentalist Christian whose particular religious doctrine colored many of his policies: the Lord, Watt believed, gave man stewardship over oil and mineral rights.[13] Predictably Watt's sanctimonious style rubbed many the wrong way precisely because he was so bureaucratically grasping and the veteran of a number of purges. An antienvironment, prodevelopment secretary of the interior was not only slightly ludicrous but it was a politically suicidal choice for the White House. It was one thing for Reagan to suggest that trees caused pollution, but quite another to have James Watt as cabinet secretary announcing plans to allow strip mining and oil exploration on federally owned land, all the while declaring that it was the Lord's work.

In an action certain to raise alarm among environmentalists, Watt's first act as secretary was to open up part of the California coast—four basins in northern California near the Big Sur region and one in the south-central coast—to offshore oil drilling. The federal charter that farmed out the subsidies to mine and timber on federally owned land was due to expire in 1983 and needed to be renegotiated. Oil drilling, however, had never been allowed, and in this sense, Watt began with an explosive if not confrontational, issue. It was almost a form of political antagonism akin to Ann Gorsuch chain-smoking Marlboros at the meeting on carcinogens. It worked. Not only did California governor Jerry Brown oppose the Watt plan, but so did the California Republican Party, which saw the controversial Watt as a total vote-loser for conservatives.

In other regions, Watt tried to expand private mining in lands abutting Wyoming's Yellowstone Park in Wyoming and Arizona's Grand Canyon. Predictably, key republicans from these states opposed Watt's plans: from Wyoming—former White House chief of staff and then representative Dick Cheney and the state's two senators, one of whom was Alan Simpson, the son of Watt's first boss; from Arizona—Representative Manuel Lujan who sat on the House Interior Committee and would subsequently be President Bush's interior secretary also opposed Watt. Such bipartisan, congressional opposition, while intriguing in itself and a perfect demonstration of Watt's political clumsiness, also obscured the question of Watt's regulatory reform. The issues in question had moved from ones of removing federally imposed restrictions, in keeping with laissez-faire assumptions, to facilitating corporate opportunities, a type of welfare capitalism. As with the blurring of corporate interest and national security policy in defense contracting, Watt's environmental policies illustrated the similarly blurred possibilities between corporate profit and public policy but under the rubric of dismantling past Interior Department practices.

In trying to open up federally owned land for private exploitation, Watt had built on precedent but he had taken it to unprecedented lengths. In other areas, however, Watt reversed precedent. If the question of oil exploration and strip-mining demonstrated pecuniary interests masquerading behind the mantle of reform, the issue of water rights demonstrated even more sharply the rather dubious nature of Reagan-era reforms at the Interior Department.

Going back to the 1970s, one of Watt's biggest cases as head of the Rocky Mountain Defense Fund had been directed against the EPA on the issue of water rights—negligible in the East but vastly important in the West. Water rights had enabled cities such as Los Angeles and Phoenix to expand. Putting aside water projects that facilitated urban settlement—projects that were often municipally funded—one of the central problems with federal water projects that aimed to encourage agriculture or settlement is that they often outlive their original intent and become an entitlement program to wealthy ranchers and farmers. Depending on one's perspective, the federal water subsidy policies became a type of welfare capitalism for agribusiness or a type of dependency where the farmer grew "addicted" to a government subsidy much as the welfare recipient had.

In response to this problem, Carter's interior secretary Cecil Andrus had introduced a form of means-testing to determine the feasibility of continuing federal water projects. (In effect, the Carter-era EPA pursued the policy that almost all Reagan appointees urged, in principle, as a means for dismantling regulatory encumbrances.) In the late 1970s, however, the idea of means-testing for water rights antagonized many and, indeed, James Watt challenged the Carter EPA on this very issue. This was interesting: Watt maintained that their inalienable rights as westerners were denied by the federal government's means-testing its water subsidies. In the subversion of logic that often hides behind ideological shibboleths, defending water subsidies became a matter of regional freedom from government intervention. As secretary, Watt backed off the means-testing plan and eventually astutely used water rights as a type of pork-barrel appropriation, which bought support in the West for his policies. Clearly, this demonstrated a large measure of hypocrisy in the Reagan administration: when means-testing meant rescinding regulation that impinged on business it was implicitly good. When means-testing meant scaling back veritable entitlement programs to powerful business constituents, it was implicitly bad and labeled "excessive regulation."

In terms of his stated objectives, Watt achieved relatively little. Congress blocked almost all attempts to open up vast tracts of federal land to mining and oil exploration and, conversely, Congress pushed for the creation of even more federal parkland. Moreover, Watt galvanized the environmental movement. Sierra Club membership rose exponentially and, in terms of environmental consciousness, America was perhaps better off for Watt's abortive policies.

It was doubly interesting how the political rhetoric in these years swung away from the "Naderite" label and the charge of "environmental extremists." In time, Watt became the issue, the extremist, and congressional Republicans deserted the president in droves on environmental issues. Here was the crux: with an almost crusading zeal, Watt used the rhetoric of reform to dismantle the regulatory apparatus in the interests of corporate profit. This hardly evoked images of rugged ranchers and homesteaders—the political symbols of the sagebrush rebellion. Indeed, Watt became an almost Dickensian personification of the rollback of conservation laws; he gave deregulation an unjustifiably bad name. Even the oil industry executives felt that he was hurting, rather than helping, them.

Watt soon came to feel marginalized in the cabinet. As with Gorsuch, White House handlers such as Jim Baker wanted Watt out of sight and out of Washington. With her instinctive desire to protect her husband, even Nancy Reagan took on James Watt. When Watt castigated the Beach Boys as inappropriate family material for the annual Fourth of July concert on the Mall, Nancy Reagan came to their defense and the president agreed. (Watt believed that Wayne Newton, Las Vegas lounge performer and contributor to conservative causes, was more wholesome family entertainment for the Mall.) With Gorsuch gone in the spring of 1983, Watt continued to hang on, albeit tenuously. Fortunately for the White House, it got its opportunity. When asked in the fall of 1983 about his record on affirmative action, Watt defended it by saying that one of his committees was indeed integrated because it contained a Jew, a black and a cripple.[14] His misstatement, which echoed Ford agriculture secretary Earl Butz's equally tactless gaffe, was simply a convenient excuse for an anxious White House to force him from office.

Nevertheless, it suggested something peculiar about an administration if one of the few men with the conviction and intellectual discipline to pursue a tight strategy—which the president presumably endorsed—was progressively eased out of policy circles by the White House handlers. For the White House, however, Watt's problem was tactical; there was never a repudiation of his policies. In the late 1980s, Reagan was still defending Watt, but Reagan never troubled himself to figure what regulation meant beyond a few catchy anecdotes. Regulatory reform was yet another area where Reagan's intellectual laziness could not be compensated by coaching and cue cards.

In the end, the ideological confrontationalism of both Watt and Gorsuch brought about direct opposition and contributed to their demise. After them, the Reagan White House all but abandoned its effort to undo environmental regulation. At Interior, Watt was replaced by Judge William Clark, who had worked with Reagan in Sacramento and had brought a measure of political damage control to the department, much as he had at the National Security Council in the wake of Richard Allen's resignation.

The Savings and Loan Debacle: Deregulating the Thrift Industry

Perhaps the most troubling aspect of the administration's regulatory record was in the thrift industry debacle of the 1980s, when scores of savings and loan institutions eventually went bankrupt leaving the taxpayer to foot the bill.

Banking regulation is a function of one of two opposites: either banks are efficient and tend to aggregate economic power or they are inefficient and tend to create problems for the economy. The first problem, the fear of inordinate centralization of economic power, is as old as the Republic itself. For this reason, American banks have had state charters and were, until recent times, prohibited from interstate commerce: the American banking structure thus resembled the American political system in its "federal" and decentralized structure. Political arguments against banks were revived in the late nineteenth century when agrarian Populists charged that banks and railroads colluded: the bank charged high rates to loan the farmer money, just as the railroads gouged him with high prices. It was small wonder that old rural prejudices against bankers as usurers persisted.

On the other hand, banks themselves were often rickety institutions prone to bank runs and financial scares, and this was the opposite problem. In the twentieth century, the phases of banking regulation roughly approximated the three waves of environmental legislation: it was, however, the problem of rickety structures that motivated the various reforms. In the first phase, legislation created the Federal Reserve Bank (in 1913), which added a measure of institutional responsibility to the banking system by setting reserve requirements. The second phase of banking regulation, during the administration of Franklin Roosevelt, was a direct response to catastrophic bank failure in the Great Depression. Roosevelt not only closed the banks in a celebrated bank holiday but helped push through legislation that insured banking deposits. In effect, Roosevelt helped to minimize the element of panic that could send a chain reaction through the banking system. As the French financial reformer Jacques Necker had argued in the late-eighteenth-century, reformers must understand the psychology of panic: if the populace had, for example, a phobia of grain shortages, then reform should accommodate irrational prejudices and work from there. In the same way, banking reform added a measure of public confidence necessary for the market and thereby minimized the threat of panic.

If the third phase of serious environmental reform corresponded to the Nixon administration, and perhaps led in to the Carter years, the third phase of banking reform could be located in the late Carter years and then into Reagan's tenure. This phase of banking reform was directly connected to the inefficiencies of the market and specifically the savings and loan institutions, commonly known as the thrift institutions. The original impetus for deregulating the thrifts came from the Democratic controlled congress rather than the White House. Although thrift deregulation predated Reagan's presidency, his administration's overall ideology of deregulation nonetheless accelerated this trend and removed traditional restraints precisely at a time when they were perhaps needed most.

By the 1970s, fluctuating interest rates and a changing market had made the old savings and loans, those locally based lending institutions that could not vary their interest rates, increasingly obsolete. As Reagan biographer Lou Cannon suggested, the thrifts were a throwback to a time when local small-town banks existed for the purpose of financing home mortgages; they were like the local bank run by the fictional do-gooder George Bailey—played by Reagan friend, actor Jimmy Stewart—in Frank Capra's film *It's a Wonderful Life*.[15] Though romanticized by Capra, local thrifts had played a significant role in helping several generations of Americans own their own homes. That market niche, however, had disappeared as the economy changed and as larger, regional banks increasingly came to perform functions once exclusively handled by the local thrifts.

In the 1970s, lobbyists for the thrifts had subsequently pressed for deregulation of their industry so that the small banks might compete with the big commercial ones. Those lobbyists had made substantial campaign contributions to a number of congressmen, including California Democratic senator Alan Cranston and Rhode Island Republican congressman Ferdinand St. Germain, both of whom sponsored deregulatory legislation favorable to the thrifts.[16]

Essentially, the deregulatory legislation of the early 1980s, such as the Garn-St. Germain Bill, did three things: (1) it removed the ceiling on the interest rate that savings and loans could offer; (2) it lowered the amount of required reserves; and (3) it expanded the amount of federal deposit insurance from forty to one hundred thousand dollars. Such deregulation was intended to stimulate an increasingly uncompetitive sector of the financial industry, but perversely, it had the effect of compounding some of that industry's long-running problems. Lowering the reserve requirement, for example, made those financially shaky thrifts even more precarious. The deeper problem was that the federal government assumed huge financial risks; raising the level of federal insurance made the taxpayer liable for costs incurred in an industry where many banks were already in a financially precarious position.

Deregulation of the thrift industry nonetheless had strong support within the Reagan White House, particularly from Treasury Secretary Donald Regan, who had previously been head of Merrill Lynch and who saw deregulation of the thrifts as a way of saving a "sick industry."[17] Indeed, Regan had prospered at Merrill Lynch by pushing the firm in to new types of financial services: for Reagan, moving beyond the self-imposed boundaries of the old financial marketplace was the wave of the future. In the larger sense, the new deregulatory laws corresponded to the overall campaign pledge of Reagan that excessive and often needless regulation stifled industry and passed higher prices on to consumers. Liberalizing legislation corresponded to President Reagan's stated belief that, in most instances, business could, and should, regulate its own affairs and did not need Washington's direction.

This argument was echoed by the administration's appointee at the Federal Home Loan Bank Board, Richard Pratt. A Utah native, the boyish-looking Pratt was not only an academic expert in domestic banking but had himself been chief economist for the U.S. Savings and Loan League. As with Watt, Pratt's appointment demonstrated the idea of probusiness groups infiltrating the regulatory apparatus, particularly one that had already been in existence for more than a generation and had lost much the regulatory zeal characteristic of a new agency. (In fairness to Pratt, a onetime champion wrestler and a former Mormon missionary to New Zealand, he probably had more in common with

Jimmy Stewart's George Bailey than he did to James Watt.) Pratt was also the choice of Utah senator Jake Garn, a cosponsor of the 1980 Garn-St.Germain bill.

The trouble that Pratt faced was that the industry was failing in the early 1980s: too many thrifts were money losing propositions. As a way out of these difficulties, Pratt urged that the competitive thrifts merge, but this raised a problem—it contradicted a number of state charters. In order to deal with this, the administration issued federal charters that overrode the state charters: an odd action given the administration's professed adherence to state's rights and opposition to federal meddling.

Deregulation often requires corresponding supervision in other areas but, as in environmental policy, the administration viewed deregulation as a veritable suspension of supervision. Over the objections of many smaller thrifts, the administration pursued an ambitious policy of deepening deregulation. In 1982, the administration relaxed older restrictions that mandated each thrift to have, on its board, four hundred trustees from the local community. The new law allowed thrifts to be dominated by lone entrepreneurs, and here was the beginning of the deluge. This new deregulation thus released the conservative restraints that had linked savings and loan institutions to the communities they served and, consequently, opened the door for swashbuckling businessmen, such as Arizona businessman Charles Keating, who in turn had made Senate campaign contributions totaling three million dollars.[18] Many of the thrift institutions eventually became tied up in questionable real estate loans, particularly in the Southwest, that were recklessly made in full knowledge that government insurance could cover losses.

Even by 1982, trends were looking ominous. By this time Pratt had left his position and joined Treasury Secretary Don Regan's old firm, Merrill Lynch. At the Bank Board, Pratt was replaced by Edwin Gray, who had served Governor Reagan in a minor capacity in the Sacramento days and who also had worked for a San Diego thrift. Everyone assumed that Gray would be a mouthpiece for the industry, but Gray soon saw the need to put brakes on the rush for deregulation. In fact, Gray's own bank examiners were urging a measure of reregulation and warning of the perils of risky financial practices taken in full knowledge that the federal government would assume risks. Gray requested more bank examiners but was rebuffed by the White House. Treasury Secretary Regan accused Gray of being a "re-regulator." Having risen to the highest level at Merrill Lynch by expanding the old brokerage house into real estate and other financial services, Regan was hostile to the idea of imposing new controls. He wanted Gray's resignation.

The upshot was a monumental unwillingness on the part of the White House to acknowledge the problem, even as it progressively deepened. This reluctance continued when James Baker replaced Don Regan at the Treasury Department in 1986, and Regan replaced Baker as chief of staff. Unlike Baker, a master of conciliation and maneuver but also an astute judge of the political temper in Washington, Regan was something of a bully who ruled by intimidation. Soon the administration was caught up in the Iran-Contra fiasco; the savings and loan crisis, brought on by reckless deregulation, was thus obscured from debate.

In a deeper sense, the bipartisan nature of the savings and loan debacle neutralized it as a campaign issue for the Democrats. Democratic House whip Tony Coelho of California had himself benefited from a one hundred thousand-dollar deal engineered by his friend, junk-bond dealer Michael Milliken, who eventually went to prison for financial irregularities. Coelho had learned how to rake in the "soft money"—the corporate contributions for "party building" purposes—that flowed to Democrats who controlled the House. (After leaving congress, Coelho went to work on Wall Street.) Though he fell from office because of illegal campaign contributions masquerading as a book deal, Democratic House Speaker Jim Wright of Texas was himself tainted by his associations with savings and loans. Three of the "Keating five" were Democratic senators, and included Don Reigle of Michigan who was head of the Senate Banking and Finance Committee and Alan Cranston, who had been conspicuous in the early move for thrift deregulation. (The other three were John Glenn of Ohio, Dennis DiConcini and John McCain, both of Arizona.)

This, of course, obscures the enormous costs that have accrued as a result of thrift deregulation. It has been estimated that, had the Reagan White House acted to contain the costs in 1982, cleaning up the savings and loan mess might have cost only twenty-five billion dollars. To do so, however, would have been to admit a mistake, and mistakes give the opposition an opening in upcoming elections. By 1984, estimated costs rose to one hundred billion dollars, but the White House still refused to acknowledge a problem. It was "morning again in America," and it might have given Democratic challenger Walter Mondale ammunition to assail Reagan on the financial costs of heroic deregulation.

The real costs only emerged with clarity during the Bush administration, with Reagan back in California, Chief of Staff Don Regan disgraced in the wake of the Iran-Contra fiasco and James A. Baker safely ensconced at the State Department. In these years, President Bush's son, Neil, was brought before a congressional committee and questioned about his ties to a Colorado savings and loan. Eventually, Republicans got their revenge in the Whitewater saga, which yielded no illegalities, but certainly illustrated the crassest of conflicts of interest on the part of both Clintons—something that has successfully tarnished their claim to the reform mantle and perhaps sealed Clinton's reputation as a shrewd politician with his hand in the Ozark money trough. The ongoing partisan nature of the attacks—perhaps too tempting for either party to resist—clouded the staggering long-term costs of the savings and loan fiasco that took place in the Reagan years. By 1989, the costs borne by the taxpayers were estimated at approximately five hundred billion dollars[19] and many believed this was on the low side.

The savings and loan debacle offered no better example of the intellectual and policy poverty of the pell-mell push for deregulation. Instead of spurring business growth, the thrift deregulation set off a chain reaction of bad loans that will take a generation to pay off. Those willing to absolve the Reagan administration can suggest, with much justification, that the root of the problem was in Franklin Roosevelt's legislation, which insured both healthy and unhealthy banks and, later, with a Democratically controlled congress that made a precarious system often worse. Nonetheless, the Reagan administration, which ran those regulatory agencies, had the ultimate responsibility to carry out mandate of oversight. It failed and, for ideological reasons and questions of pure expediency, failed extravagantly. Far more than the HUD scandal or the subversion of environmental regulation at the EPA or Interior, the Savings and Loan crisis of the 1980s will stand as testimony to the abject failure of regulatory policy under Ronald Reagan. Congress eventually managed to contain the deregulatory ambitions of Gorsuch and Watt, but Congress failed completely to halt the effects of thrift deregulation and the costs will be ours, if not forever, at least for a generation.

History is full of ironies. It was ironic that the most ardent proponents of thrift deregulation in these years were often ideologically inclined bureaucrats and those who urged caution and even "re-regulation" were industry insiders and businessmen themselves.[20] (In this sense, the symbiotic relation between industry and regulators could serve as a conservative restraint.) The greatest irony was that Reagan presided over an administration that, in its ideological zeal, created a climate that destroyed the deregulatory momentum created by Carter. The administration that pledged to cut government waste had, according to biographer Lou Cannon, created the most expensive scandal in U.S. history.[21] By 1991, 600 of the 2,500 thrift institutions had failed, and half of the balance was heading toward bankruptcy.[22] Even in the late 1990s, there is an air of unreality about the staggering losses, which Robert Schaller described as the "biggest bank job ever."[23]

Reagan-Era Regulatory Reform: Promise and Policy

Reagan's message of regulatory reform was neither detailed nor even specific, and perhaps this accounted for its superficial appeal in the 1980 election. Essentially, Reagan's position on regulatory reform was vague and rested on politically appealing but also vacuous comments about the intrusive role of government but also on his stock anecdotes of government stupidity. In the broadest sense, regulatory reform could be the basis of a number of policy options, from liberalizing and abolishing regulatory legislation to downsizing, if not dismantling, government agencies—agencies whose very existence was predicated on regulating the economy, the environment and the housing sector. Reagan biographer Lou Cannon noted that Reagan was personally uninvolved and even uninterested in the technical details of regulatory reform.[24] He made no intellectual distinctions between necessary and unnecessary regulation, such as the outdated regulations on the airlines industry that in fact dated from the 1930s.[25]

Unlike Carter policy makers—who struggled to balance the interests of consumers with those of business—deregulatory activists in the Reagan administration rejected the political balance and allowed the question of liberalization to become a cover for rolling back legislation that impinged on business. In the process many of the earlier restraints were cast aside. The administration's policy was characterized, not by an overarching strategy, but by a random and scattered approach—one that was often driven by cabinet members who were given wide leeway and were only later blocked by congressional oversight. Ironically, the conservative ideologues in the Executive branch helped to slow down the push for deregulation by stridently politicizing it and by tying it so blatantly to corporate interest. That, it must be said, was the real Reagan legacy in regulatory reform: it was one giant step backwards.

Notes

1. In the 1976 race for the Republican primary, Lewis had been considered crucial in keeping the state's sizable bloc of delegates loyal to the Ford camp, despite the active wooing of the Reagan team. At the urging of campaign manager John Sears, Reagan announced that Richard Schweiker of Pennsylvania would be his proposed running mate—a move made to win over Lewis. It failed.

2. Although much of this was the malingering of swollen industrial bureaucracies that had lost "competitive edge" in a market that had been too safe for too long, there was some truth to the charge of Japan's export strategy. The Japanese firms were aiming at the "beachhead effect"—the company, often assisted by government export-oriented policies, gains a share in the targeted market through artificially low prices and thereby creates brand loyalty, if not customer dependency.

3. David Stockman, *The Triumph of Politics: The Inside Story of the Reagan Revolution* (New York: Harper and Row, 1986; Avon Paperback Edition, 1987), 172.

4. Stockman, *Triumph of Politics*, 171.

5. Lou Cannon, *President Reagan: The Role of a Lifetime* (New York: Simon and Schuster, 1991), 530.

6. Indeed, there was something provocative about Gorsuch's manner. When being briefed on the environmental impact of carcinogens, for example, she chain-smoked Marlboros. Such behavior may win grudging respect in a club of trail lawyers, whose business is to demoralize or antagonize adversaries, but it gains one no friends in Washington, where deliberate provocation creates bad blood and undermines reputations.

7. Jonathan Lash, *A Season of Spoils: The Reagan Administration's Attack on the Environment* (New York: Pantheon, 1984), 18.

8. On Gorsuch and Lavelle, see Haynes Johnson, *Sleepwalking through History: America in the Reagan Years* (New York: W.W. Norton, 1991), 170.

9. Michael Schaller, *Reckoning with Reagan: America and Its President in the 1980s* (New York: Oxford University Press, 1992), 40.

10. Cannon, *The Role of a Lifetime*, 531.

11. Schaller, *Reckoning with Reagan*, 100.

12. One of the many political uses of ideology is that it can be manipulated and altered for a variety of purposes. Ironically, Watt also updated arguments that black writers had explored in the 1960s—that the ghetto was, in fact, an economic colony of white, mainstream society. In keeping with national liberation movements throughout the developing world, the colonized needed to assert their economic and cultural independence.

13. Wives of Watt's subordinates had wondered if their husbands' careers might be hurt if they did not attend Mrs. Watt's prayer meetings. In the 1970s, Watt once got down on his knees to pray with someone he was about to fire from his staff.

14. Schaller, *Reckoning with Reagan*, 102.

15. Cannon, *The Role of a Lifetime*, 826.

16. Schaller, *Reckoning with Reagan*, 109.

17. Cannon, *The Role of a Lifetime*, 826.

18. Schaller, *Reckoning with Reagan*, 111-114.

19. Schaller, *Reckoning with Reagan*, 115.

20. Gray, William Seidemann, and John Shad at the Securities and Exchange Commission were all examples of businessmen who urged restraint in the face of ideologically driven deregulation and its excesses.

21. Cannon, *The Role of a Lifetime*, 824.

22. Schaller, *Reckoning with Reagan*, 115.

23. Schaller, *Reckoning with Reagan*, 108.

24. Cannon, *The Role of a Lifetime*, 821.

25. Schaller, *Reckoning with Reagan*, 99.

Chapter 12

Fiscal Reform: The Conservative Vision

In his 1980 presidential campaign, Reagan combined two traditionally conservative messages: the economic waste of an overgrown federal bureaucracy on one hand and a type of moral disapproval of deficit spending on the other. In one simple push, Reagan promised to use the evil of the Carter-era budget deficit and the accumulating national debt as part of a campaign, not just to rein in the slow and steady increase in government spending, but to lighten the tax burden. The real novelty of Reagan's message was the sequence. Rather than balancing the books and only then providing tax relief, as he had done in Sacramento, Reagan proposed pursuing the two policies simultaneously.

To this equation, Reagan added a simple but highly disputed premise: he promised that lowering federal taxes would unleash such economic productivity that government revenues would rise sharply and, combined with the massive savings he promised to introduce, the federal budget would soon be balanced and the national debt whittled down.

The Politics of Taxation: Left and Right

Politics is waged, not only in terms of political principle, but also in terms of the distribution of goods. Inevitably, both liberals and conservatives appeal to competing conceptions of economic, and indeed, political self-interest. Faithful to the idea of taxation as a type of social policy, liberals have tended to countenance high taxes for the services it could provide and, more often than not, to favor cutbacks in military spending, if any expenditure cuts were to be made. Adhering to the idea that lower taxes stimulate economic growth and high taxes retard it, conservatives have tended to favor cutbacks in nonmilitary domestic spending as a way of keeping government spending within limits.

Democrats often decry Republican tax policies as favoring the wealthy, but the deeper truth is that the American tax code has always favored the wealthy; indeed, most segments of American society are hostile to the idea of higher taxes. These are predictable assumptions in a society of relative abundance and social mobility, where the idea of wealth creation is almost sacrosanct and where socially egalitarian ideas do not extend to tax policies aimed at explicit economic equalization. Fairness in the tax code is one thing; social leveling by taxing earned income is, however, an altogether different matter.

It is predictable that periods of tax relief are periods that follow ones of unusually high tax rates. In the 1920s, for example, Republican Secretary of the Treasury Andrew Mellon pursued a type of tax relief—a predictable recoil against the high rates of the Wilson administration that had supervised the massive national mobilization during World War I. The 1920s were, in fact, years of widespread experimentation with different types of taxation. Increasingly, the federal government pursued income and business taxes instead of the old tariff—a tax borne by consumers—as the main source of its revenue, whereas state and local government relied on sales and property taxes, respectively.

The premise, of course, is that governments tend to balance receipts and expenditures, that is, they do not simply print money. Although debasing coinage, that is, printing more money to cover expenditures, was a time honored tradition for old regime governments, it was also highly inflationary and often did more economic harm than good, and hurting the economy meant lowering tax receipts. Deficit spending, by contrast, has had a more respectable tradition, even if had been open to some of the same abuses.

In one sense, there is nothing inherently wrong with running a deficit: wartime finance, investment in public works and infrastructure, or even refinancing to pay off the debt at favorable rates, are all justifiable reasons for running continued deficits. In another sense, however, continued deficit spending without compensating returns to investment is a problem that haunts all mismanaged governments. Consequently, balancing the books, or even bringing some modicum of discipline to runaway expenditure, has often been the first goal of all political reformers. It is not only a matter of efficiency but of justice, for in governance few things are more unjust than saddling future generations with the debts of the present free-spenders. Ultimately, the reform of both undisciplined spending habits and attendant institutional arrangement carries practical but also moral implications.

The Politics of Deficit Spending in American History

In recent American history, federal deficits have been a popular issue for aspiring presidential candidates. Before he discovered he was a Keynesian liberal, Franklin Roosevelt campaigned to balance Herbert Hoover's budget deficit. In keeping with his larger message of restraint after Watergate, conservative Democrat Jimmy Carter campaigned in 1976 against Ford's deficit.[1] By 1980, even the ideologically unpredictable Jerry Brown, Ronald Reagan's Democratic successor as governor of California, was calling for a balanced budget amendment to the U.S. Constitution. Each one of these candidates took positions that were perhaps more opportunistic than ideological: it would have been politically foolish for opponents not to attack the Hoover, Ford or Carter deficit.

Deficit spending, however, goes back to the earliest days of the Republic, which was saddled with a national debt incurred by the War of Independence. Inevitably, the question of how to manage the debt colored political differences between the two great parties of the early Republic: the Federalists and the anti-Federalists.

Articulating the Federalist position, Alexander Hamilton—who was also the Republic's first secretary of the treasury—believed that national debt was not altogether bad. National, or public, debt meant that citizens had a stake in their own government. Hamilton further reasoned that government, like business, had to borrow to invest in infrastructure, national defense and to provide the things that all citizens expect from the state. For Hamilton, the question of debt thus depended on how the debt was managed and what purposes it served. These were predictable ideas for Federalists, who favored a strong central government at the expense of the states and who represented business and banking interests in the Northeast.

By contrast, the anti-Federalists, represented by Jefferson, took a different view of public debt. Speaking for the small farmer, not the banker and industrialist, Jefferson believed that the debt saddled future generations and impinged on political freedom. Voicing the concerns of the southern colonies that wanted a loose confederation, rather than a strong central state, Jefferson believed debt was not only a financial encumbrance, but it facilitated the expansion of a larger, and implicitly, more intrusive federal government.[2]

The federal government eventually managed to pay off the inherited wartime debt by the astute use of the tariff, which both protected manufacturers but also taxed consumers. This set the pattern for U.S. fiscal policy for much of the nineteenth century: the federal government could manage its expenditures—still relatively modest compared to twentieth-century spending patterns—without recourse to deficit spending. The situation remained much the same until the twentieth century: a century that witnessed the rapid expansion of both government involvement in the economy and the concomitant expansion of presidential power. In the twentieth century, new forms of taxation, such as the federal income tax, eventually replaced the tariff as a main source of federal revenue.

The Great Depression of the 1930s, however, raised problems that neither Hamilton nor Jefferson had to face, namely the sharp downturns in the business cycle. In classical economics, the business cycle was supposed to be self-correcting, but self-correction seemed like a harsh name for letting economic dislocation work its way through the system.[3] Indeed, international actions taken to confine the 1930s economic problem backfired and only deepened the economic crisis, which soon took on worldwide dimensions.

The Depression nonetheless stimulated a new line of thinking about the persistence of business cycles and foreshadowed what has been called Keynesian or "demand" management. Challenging the orthodox economic notion that supply rises to meet economic demand, Cambridge economist John Maynard Keynes suggested that underconsumption, and alternately over-production, was a driving force behind the economic collapse of the 1930s. Keynes thus highlighted what was called "the paradox of thrift"—a new twist to the age-old policy of deficit spending in times of crisis. Keynes suggested that the way to cure a depression was for the government to prime the economic pump, that is, by increasing expenditures on goods and services. This, Keynes argued, carried a "multiplier effect" in which federal spending would in turn stimulate consumer spending and business profits.

This was relevant for budgetary reform in that Keynes gave old-fashioned deficit spending a new intellectual respectability. The problem, however, was that Keynesian policies did not cure the economic downturn of the 1930s. Only when World War II started could the U.S. government devote enough funds for industrial mobilization needed to make the multiplier effect truly meaningful. (Any seventeenth-century mercantilist could have predicted that overseas war was good for a sagging economy, but in the modern age, such truisms need to have larger intellectual rationalizations.)

By the early 1960s, a new wave of Keynesian economists came to Washington. At this time, demand management that could cure the business cycle became linked to a subtle change in social policy in which government services expanded beyond the traditional ideas of the social safety net and construction of public works, to novel ideas of social melioration. (This departure made it increasingly easier for conservatives to attack, not only deficit spending, but also big government.) It would be wrong to suggest that the 1960s were years of persistent deficit spending; by and large, they were not. What is important, however, was that by the 1960s, older ideas of laissez-faire non-intervention in the economy were still viewed as outmoded and rather old-fashioned. All but the most conservative, endorsed government intervention in managing and fine-tuning the nation's economy. In absence of deficits to criticize, Republicans may have tactically railed against tax and spend policies or pointed with alarm to rising expenditures, but few went so far as to challenge the premises of modern economic policy. Even Nixon by the early 1970s confessed, "we are all Keynesians now."

Although he had always talked about business values, Nixon acted like a dirigiste planner. The last of the big spending presidents, Nixon illustrated and perhaps caricatured the increasingly blurred lines between Democrats and Republicans in deficit spending, perhaps because he pursued his "Keynesian policies" as a way of tactically outflanking the Democrats; consequently, his policies lacked conviction but also alienated many of the Republican right. In some senses, Nixon was not truly representative of his party's conservative, ideological wing. Reagan, by contrast, appeared as somehow above this tactical politics and even cynical positioning. Reagan represented the gut convictions of the party faithful—those who saw Nixon as selling out to the ways of Washington.

Ronald Reagan: Mainstream Conservative or Fringe Right?

Up until his 1980 bid for the presidency, Reagan was in the mainstream of conservative opposition to big government, high taxes and federal deficits. During his 1980 campaign he was still an opponent of big government, high taxes and continued deficits but he also advocated massive cuts in personal and business taxes as a way to stimulate economic productivity. This was curious. Conservative Republicans traditionally did not see tax cuts as a step toward fiscal discipline necessary to redress deficits. It was this, not the rollback of the Great Society nor the vaunted military buildup, that was the real story of the "Reagan redirection."

"The Reagan Revolution" in fiscal policy is the story of Reagan's strange diversion away from traditional fiscal orthodoxy into a type of economic gimmickry that was popular for a time and then quietly dissipated. Whereas previous chapters have focused on the efforts of Reagan to create a wedge within Carter's fragmenting coalition, the story of Reagan and fiscal discipline is almost exclusively one of intracoalition differences. In short, it is the story of the rise and fall of supply-side doctrine, something of a conservative heresy.

Traditionally, Republican opposition to expanded federal programs had been synonymous with fiscal conservatism: when government spending seemed to work, as it did in the easy years after the Second World War and in the 1950s, Republicans were in many ways denied a political issue with which to challenge Democrats. In these years, they were predictably strongest on issues of national security, and were forced to tacitly endorse big government. Those Republicans who did rally against big deficits seemed like old-fashioned naysayers—small town Rotarians who preferred the harsh medicine of boom and bust cycles to prudent "scientific" management. In short, they seemed a throwback to an earlier, vaguely premodern age. It was Keynes, not Herbert Spencer nor Andrew Carnegie, who captured the temper of the times.

Consequently, Republican political tactics involved endorsing the status quo but suggesting that they, with a concern for the taxpayer's dollar, could manage things better than "tax and spend" Democrats. This was in the pragmatic tradition of conservatism: co-opt liberal ideas but tone them down and make them work. When, in later years, House Republican Newt Gingrich of Georgia chided Kansas senator Robert Dole for being "a tax-collector for the welfare state," Gingrich (and other ideological enthusiasts) perhaps failed to appreciate the practical compromises that an earlier generation of Republicans had been compelled to make.

Nonetheless, there was a fringe of the Republican coalition in the 1950s that was unwilling to countenance, not only the welfare state, but also rising federal expenditures. Although they may not have criticized deficit spending in the Eisenhower years, they nonetheless attacked the idea of progressively rising costs—that more government was somehow better.

Predictably, these arguments intensified when Democrats were in office, but the arguments still had to be carefully crafted: when Republicans strayed too far from pragmatic accommodation, they got into trouble. Barry Goldwater in 1964, for example, ran afoul of mainstream voters partly because he appeared too eager to undo the postwar economic policies. In fact, Garry Wills noted that in order to make their candidate more intellectually respectable, Goldwater's campaign handlers encouraged him to be coached by free-market economists such as Milton Friedman.[4] It was part of the deliberate strategy to (in the words of his campaign handlers) "de-kook" Goldwater.[5] Goldwater was particularly hard to coach. Having questioned the viability of the TVA—in Tennessee of all places, he proved to be his own worst enemy. Some of Goldwater's handlers in 1964 were actually anxious about Ronald Reagan's televised speech precisely because they feared Reagan might raise voter anxieties about Goldwater's rolling back social security payments.

For many, the radical economic individualism of Goldwater and Reagan seemed quaint and even simplistically old-fashioned in 1964. By the 1970s, however, Nixon's lifting of wage and price controls coupled with the OPEC oil shocks released pent-up inflationary pressures. "Stagflation," that curious combination of inflation and industrial stagnation, persisted throughout the Ford years. Government spending, it seemed, could cure the worst excesses of boom and bust like the depression of the 1930s but could not shake off the slow economic wasting disease of the 1970s.

By this time, Keynesian deficit spending came under attack from all quarters. Throughout the European social democratic countries, critics noted that the costs of the postwar welfare state were increasing faster than the rate of economic growth. Accordingly, many in policy circles reappraised the overly optimistic assumptions of what activist government could both accomplish and sustain. Conservative economic ideas had slowly begun to reemerge after their long intellectual dormancy: in the United States, classical, free-market and libertarian economics, which had been associated with the University of Chicago, experienced something of a revival. In the intellectual oscillation of ideas, conservative economic doctrine became fashionable again.

One could certainly criticize all the trappings of Keynesian economics and deficit spending without couching the criticism in ideological terms; indeed, to dispense with "highfalutin'" theories simplified matters. It was much easier to speak from old-fashioned common sense—a tactic that Goldwater had tried but failed. Goldwater's problem in 1964 was not of content but of degree: he got carried away. Goldwater appeared to be the crusty conservative who threatened to cut everyone out of the will. Reagan, by contrast, appeared to be the reassuring conservative who understood our mistakes but told us that a little economic pain was in our own best interest. This was the right touch: prudent conservatives need only probe public reservations and suggest better alternatives without being too specific.

It was no surprise that Reagan—faithful to the Republican line and always an opponent of big government and high taxes—should advocate fiscal restraint and budgetary tightening. In many ways, he was a "castor-oil conservative," one who believed that federal deficits could be cut back only with a degree of painful restraint. Economist Herb Stein noted that in 1976 Reagan was telling friends that he feared the economy was in for a fearful recession as a result of federal deficits and overspending, what Reagan termed the "binge" of the Great Society. Large government expenditures, Reagan believed, might have been necessary in wartime and in periods of economic crisis, but in more normal times, large expenditures became a prescription for higher taxes and running budget deficits that had been given an unfortunate legitimacy by Keynesian fiscal theory.

In his 1976 primary challenge to President Ford, Reagan had tried to position himself on the Republican right and, accordingly, to portray Ford as a crypto-liberal who favored détente and who endorsed deficit spending. Reagan had tapped into a vein of conservative discontent when he attacked Ford's fifty-one-billion-dollar federal deficit.[6] As a corrective, candidate Reagan later proposed ninety billion dollars in expenditure reduction, though he conveniently failed to specify where such cuts could be made.[7] Reagan's strength was never in the details but in his conviction that government had overspent and that a final reckoning was inevitable. Nonetheless, many Republicans believed that the "ninety billion" speech might have cost Reagan the 1976 nomination since it raised doubts about his economic stewardship. The arbitrary equation raised concerns that Reagan lacked the government experience and maturity necessary to reassure markets. In 1976, Reagan actually seemed to have Goldwater's old problem of appearing like a radical fiscal conservative who might do more harm than good. As Lou Cannon noted, Reagan's use of the term "binge" had important connotations for one who was also the child of an alcoholic. Binge connoted a type of dependency that could only be cured by painful and disciplined withdrawal from the addiction, in this case an addiction to social spending on credit. It was the old-time religion of Republican belt-tightening; the trouble, however, was that it seemed erratic and raised apprehension among business leaders who wanted a probusiness line but nothing too, terribly radical. Even if the principle of fiscal discipline were solid, Reagan's ninety billion dollar cure for the common binge was the type of force-fed medicine that might kill the patient. Ford proved reassuring to the Business Roundtable and Chamber of Commerce types; even Goldwater endorsed Ford in 1976.

One might ask a further question, namely, why were budget deficits so important as a political issue in these years? Indeed, the Reagan administration discreetly learned to live with huge deficits in the 1980s, which suggests a possible lack of commitment to the cause of deficit reduction. One immediate reason for this urgency was the stubborn inflation that reappeared in the late 1970s—an inflation that many believed was somehow linked to federal budget deficits.

A fiscal conservative, Carter had initially campaigned to bring down the federal budget deficit. In order to reassure Wall Street, he had appointed the centrist economist Charles Shulz to be his chief economist and Bendix chief Michael Blumenthal to be treasury secretary. Carter had managed to bring down both the budget deficit and the rate of inflation, but inflation shot up right before the 1980 election. Not only did the Iranian Revolution of 1979 jack up oil prices, but Federal Reserve Chairman Paul Volker, himself a Carter appointee, pursued a harsh anti-inflation policy that contributed to high rates of unemployment. This damaged Carter's reelection prospects, particularly when labor, not business, was a key Democratic constituency. Labor, of course, was not enamored by anti-inflation policies that created unemployment. In effect, Carter, and the Federal Reserve chairman that he appointed, had pursued the budgetary belt-tightening that Reagan and most conservative Republicans had favored. Ironically, Carter seemed like a pseudo-Republican, although one with all the economic liabilities that went with the "castor-oil" approach.

Reagan, however, had moved away from that traditional Republican line and now attacked Carter from an altogether different, and even rather quixotic, angle. Reagan became a spokesman for the supply-siders: a most curious vision of budgetary reform.

Ronald Reagan as a Supply-Side Convert

Given the binge diagnosis, one might well ask what transformed the "castor-oil" Reagan of 1976 to the Reagan of the 1980 campaign who promised, not belt-tightening, but a painless policy of tax cuts, budget cutting and expanded defense spending—in short an economic version of nirvana. The answer could be found in the rise of supply-side doctrine.

Supply-side economics was a heretical offshoot of traditional fiscal conservatism, but like all heresies it caricatured the original creed. Supply-side proponents—economist Arthur Laffer, the creator of the overblown "Laffer Curve" and economic publicists such as George Gilder and Jude Wanniski—were outside the mainstream of both the economics profession and the Republican Party.[8] Garry Wills even went so far as to describe Laffer as an "academic showman,"[9] which was perhaps a bit harsh since showmanship and even flamboyance is a necessary part of heresy. Supply-side doctrine was nevertheless given a certain intellectual respectability by *Wall Street Journal* editorial writer William Bartlett, who later went on to a second career as a Clinton critic during the early stages of the Whitewater saga.

Supply-side doctrine began with a premise, accepted by all economists, that government tax rates can be so excessive as to bring in shrinking revenues. All politicians, provided they have any common sense, understand that the sovereign does not kill the goose that lays the proverbial golden egg. Taking this truism, supply-siders reasoned that the opposite was equally valid: if government could cut taxes sufficiently, then the economy would expand and if the economy expanded then government would collect more revenue and, ideally, balance the budget. Here, supply-siders got carried away: they took a common assumption, that tax relief could have a stimulative effect, and used it as a basis for solving all economic problems. It was the slippery slope argument in reverse; it was, to push metaphors, the slippery ladder—an inch of economic good leads to a mile of salvation. In providing tax relief as a means for balancing the budget, supply-siders were in effect challenging traditional Republican caution and throwing it to the winds. Conservative economist Herb Stein politely called it "the economics of joy."

One need not be an economist to understand that the trouble with supply-side claims was that their forecasts were wildly extravagant. With its casual promises and inflated optimism, it was also not suprising that supply-side doctrine caught on with a younger generation of House Republicans, who tended to be less cautious and more controversial than their older Senate colleagues. One of the enthusiasts was New York representative Jack Kemp,[10] something of a unique force within Republican politics and who would later become Bob Dole's improbable running mate in the 1996 presidential campaign.

As with Reagan, Kemp was a Republican who began his career as a Democrat. The facts of Kemp's football career are well known; what is less well known was that Kemp was an off-season legislative aide to Reagan in 1960s Sacramento. Eventually Kemp was traded from Los Angeles to Buffalo and, after retiring from pro football, ran for Congress, representing a suburban, blue-collar district outside the city.

The son of a southern California Christian Scientist and self-made trucking entrepreneur, Kemp had, by the 1970s, become a walking, talking apostle of economic opportunity. Mary Baker Eddy's theological certainties had metamorphosed into the gospel of wealth creation and economic positive thinking: the old-fashioned castor-oil Calvinism was not for him. With a gift for political advertising, Kemp's vision of national renewal was not for the Great Society but for "the opportunity society." Even more than Reagan, Kemp had a sense of the unlimited possibilities of economic growth and what it could mean for tens of thousands of American families. (Both Reagan and Kemp also shared some rather eccentric ideas about the gold standard.)

There were, however, important differences between the two men. Reagan's father had failed in owning his own business, whereas Kemp's had succeeded. In the film industry and then in Pacific Palisades, where GE had outfitted his home with the latest electronic gadgetry, Reagan had moved far from his working-class roots. Reagan talked of opportunity but lived an isolated and, in many ways, artificial world bankrolled by other self-made millionaires. Though an entertainer-athlete, Kemp's experience was less isolating. In the racially integrated world of professional football and then representing a blue-collar district outside of Buffalo, he was a sincere champion of inclusion and, for Kemp, economic growth was the engine of inclusion.

In supply-side theology, Kemp had discovered something that satisfied an emotional search. It also gave him a doctrine by which to challenge both the Democratic majority in the House and the Republican old guard. In the House, he allied himself with other junior representatives, such as Newt Gingrich of Georgia and Trent Lott of Mississippi who chafed under the old regime of minority status. As with the proselytizing Barry Goldwater in the 1950s, these Young Turks had one undeniable point in their favor: through habits of ideological submission, minority parties often perpetuate their own second-class status by accepting the status quo as easy and predictable. Submission, many believe, can only be broken by returning to the old-time religion, by doctrinal revivalism and by jolting the congregation out of its complacent ways. When he spoke of "empowerment," Kemp was also describing a rising new conservative movement shorn of its old habits.

In 1977, Kemp jointly sponsored the Kemp-Roth Bill to lower the tax rates by 30 percent. For House Republicans, Kemp-Roth was meant to be an attractive alternative to older "castor-oil" economics, which may have played to the Chamber of Commerce crowd but hardly generated enthusiasm in the electorate. In doing so, some Republicans felt they could overcome the politically unappealing image of naysayer and offer a vision as optimistic and compelling as Keynesian deficit spending had been in its heyday.

Though not part of the original supply-side sect, Ronald Reagan gradually positioned himself to a point where he annexed their ideas. Inevitably, there was a purely tactical dimension to Reagan's positioning. As the 1980 election approached, Reagan and his advisors began the strategy against Carter, but first Reagan had to win the Republican nomination. In this, Reagan had two disadvantages. First, he was approaching seventy, and age became a factor. Second, Reagan had competition on the right—competition from the young and healthy Kemp, a new kind of conservative. Even if some of his ideas were a bit odd, Kemp had the looks and upbeat energy of a coming man: he was conservative without being overtly right wing.

Eventually, Reagan's campaign manager John Sears—who had also urged Reagan to challenge Ford in the 1976 primaries—persuaded Reagan to co-opt the Kemp message. In doing so, Sears hoped to keep Kemp from entering the 1980 Republican primaries. Sears' shrewd strategy was to get Kemp aboard the Reagan camp, even going so far as to have Kemp tour with Reagan. (One suspects that Kemp was being lured with the tacit promise of, not only wider audiences, but perhaps even a shot at the vice presidency.)

Borrowing supply-side assumptions was useful not only to neutralize Kemp but to plug in to another trend. Indeed, supply-side doctrine put an intellectual gloss on a larger movement that was sweeping the country, tax relief, a movement that originated in Reagan's own state of California. Reagan himself had tried to get on the tax cut bandwagon in the early 1970s, but the time was not right. By 1978, however, California voters endorsed Proposition Thirteen, the Jarvis-Gann Amendment that lowered state property taxes. In an age when everyone demanded his or her rights, it was perhaps predictable that many would clamor for "taxpayer's rights." Keeping tax rates low had always been a standard Republican rallying cry but lowering them, particularly with deficits, was a new and, to some, a dangerous policy.

It would be wrong to suggest that Reagan simply annexed supply-side ideas: he was actually himself converted. Indeed, Reagan was always susceptible to advisors who had a facility with anecdotes, and this was particularly true in economic policy. Supply-side doctrine converged completely with his own Hollywood experience: when he had moved into a higher tax bracket, it did not pay for him to make more than four films a year. (The problem with this anecdote was that a film actor is something of an entrepreneur who operates on an atypical schedule and salary.) For Reagan, supply-side was not the arid and often dreary economics known as the "dismal science," but rather the promise of boundless opportunity, the American dream itself. Reagan had, in fact, majored in economics at Eureka College all those years ago, but the Eureka brand of economics was one shot through with the social issues that had been so dear to the Disciples' progressive creed. Like Kemp, Reagan's old-time religion blended in to the happy certainties of the supply-side promise. The religion of the "joyous soul" turned to economics—it was Norman Vincent Peal with a stock portfolio.

Nonetheless, the merits of supply-side economics were not shared throughout the Reagan camp. Most mainstream advisors in the campaign, such as Murray Weidenbaum, William Niskanen and Martin Anderson, saw the question of personal tax cuts as an unwanted diversion from Reagan's promise to rein in federal spending. Most of Reagan's economic advisors were defenders of the "castor-oil" approach who saw supply-side ideas as snake oil if not outright quackery. Precisely because they saw these projections as hopelessly unrealistic, these economists urged that supply-side promises be toned down. For them, supply-side economics was the kind of funny money theories that right-wing populists from the hinterland always cooked up and which always made Wall Street nervous.

Predictably, the Reagan economic package—laced with supply-side precepts—became an issue early in the 1980 Republican primaries. It was telling that most business leaders had supported former Texas governor and Nixon treasury secretary John Connally or Connally's fellow Texan, former Republican National Committee chairman, George Bush. In a phrase that he would eventually live to regret, Bush even went so far as to call supply-side doctrine "voodoo economics." Nonetheless, neither Bush nor Connally had a base of support within the Republican right. After a surprise loss to Bush in the Iowa primary, Reagan rebounded in the New Hampshire primary: a strong antitax state. Having subsequently won the Republican nomination, Reagan softened much of the supply-side rhetoric—part of the predictable move to the center before the general election. Indeed, most of Reagan's mainstream economic advisors assumed that his supply-side promises were the type of ephemeral campaign pledges characteristic of American presidential politics, in which candidates promise far more than they can possibly deliver.

To risk repetition, one should not look for too much ideology in a presidential campaign that is, after all, a patching together of promises aimed at a broad coalition of different groups. To disaffected voters, tired of taxes and alienated by the excesses of the "welfare state," Reagan promised tax relief. To those same voters, who liked certain parts of the welfare state, he did not threaten massive spending cuts of the ninety-billion variety. To Wall Street, Reagan promised both corporate tax cuts to stimulate the economy and a probusiness deregulatory policy. To deficit hawks, he was a conservative Republican with a reputation for fiscal discipline.

Ronald Reagan was thus all things to all people in the center-right of the political spectrum: compromises, and even conflict, between the promises were thus secondary. For many voters, including many Democratic swing voters, Reagan's strength was that he was not Carter, who seemed unable to rein in inflation and inspire business confidence.

David Stockman and "The Reagan Redirection": The Long and Winding Road

Budget directors are usually the faceless figures in the White House but David Stockman broke that tradition. By his very presence in the administration policy debates, he demonstrated the prominence of supply-side economic doctrine in the so-called Reagan redirection—a redirection that Reagan was in no position to implement as Stockman later argued in his acerbic but informative memoirs.

It is hard to know what to make of Stockman. As Lou Cannon suggested, he was prone to intellectual exhibitionism and probably overstated his own importance within the political process; he was thus the victim of his own rhetorical overstatement. He was, however, crucial for the narrative of budgetary reform for he was involved in almost every aspect of policy and, in the early days of the Reagan administration, budget priorities drove policy. In addition, Stockman seemed to be one of the few people in the White House who was prepared to take candidate Reagan at his word and accordingly shape a coherent policy initiative. In taking the often jumbled campaign messages and crafting policy, Stockman perhaps misread the Reagan reform platform, which was primarily a means for winning office and, then, only the roughest of policy guides.

Indeed, Stockman's experience in the 1970s demonstrated, not only the pitfalls of radical reform, but the rather thin reformist credentials of President Reagan. Stockman's tenure thus demonstrated the danger of a hands-off politician willing to delegate nearly everything to subordinates who often operated according to their own interpretations of what the chief executive stood for. In some senses, the same technical problems that marred Reagan's defense and regulatory policy reappeared in budget policy.

A Michigan native, Stockman had entered politics from the hard left and his path to Washington was a circuitous one. His parents were rural conservatives in southwestern Michigan who raised their five children in the disciplined and ordered world of the family fruit farm in Scottdale, Michigan, where Stockman's maternal grandfather had been a local Republican politician.

It was at Michigan State that Stockman got caught up in the political enthusiasms of the 1960s. Recoiling from the ordered, and rather conservative Republicanism of Scottdale, Stockman absorbed the intellectual arguments of the religious left and participated in the civil rights and, later, the antiwar movements. It was a time when reform seemed timid, old-fashioned and even "political" in the pejorative sense—remaking society was the more immediate challenge.

In order to dodge the Vietnam draft, Stockman entered Harvard Divinity School. At Harvard, however, he was more interested in policy courses at the Kennedy School of Government than courses on Reinhold Niebuhr at the Divinity school. Indeed, Stockman had always sought out influential mentors and he soon entered the orbit of Professors James Q. Wilson, Nathan Glazer and Daniel P. Moynihan. Moynihan, in particular, had gained prominence in the 1960s and early 1970s for his trenchant critiques of the New Left and its almost nihilistic excesses. Soon, Stockman became a live-in baby-sitter at the Moynihan household; one wonders what influence Moynihan, with his skeptical view of campus radicalism and his appreciation for the intellectual corruptions that often come from trying to do the impossible, had on Stockman. Like Niebuhr in an earlier generation, Moynihan was a liberal who critiqued liberal assumptions in order to strengthen them. Stockman, however, was never really a liberal; he had gone from adolescent conservative to campus radical and, in mellowing, slowly drifted back to an intellectual conservatism, the doctrine of the marketplace.

Through Moynihan, and a number of intervening connections, Stockman had come to the attention of Illinois congressman John Anderson, who was looking for an energetic person to work on budgetary issues for a House Republican caucus. In 1970, Stockman began what would be a ten-year career in the House of Representatives.

In the early years, Stockman labored in the dreary and often thankless back warrens of the legislative universe, putting in long hours on arcane and unglamorous budgetary issues, which he soon came to master. A workaholic focused on technical issues, he became a congressional apparatchik and put his radical student days behind him. A congressional staffer was not the archetypal job for a young person in the early 1970s: it was a place where one punched a metaphorical clock before law school or lobbying or heading back to the home district to run for office. Stockman, however, worked his way through the legislative machine: an ambitious young man from the heartland in a world of middle-aged power brokers. Even the grueling hours that army officer Al Haig put in for NSC advisor Kissinger carried a certain national security chic and the cachet of the White House; by contrast, being a congressional staffer for a minority party caucus was a life of emotional dreariness for all but the most ambitious and driven.

In 1972, the year of Nixon's reelection, Stockman became head of the House Republican Budget Caucus. In 1975, the intellectually prominent Irving Kristol helped him get published in the pages of *Public Interest* and this broadened Stockman's appeal as a rising Hill staffer. His article, on the "public pork barrel," contained nothing particularly original but did demonstrate an intellectual ambition untypical of Hill staffers who tend to be interested in process rather than larger ideas. The article also demonstrated the importance of being plugged into the growing "neoconservative" intellectual milieu.

In the wake of Watergate, Stockman decided to run for elective office in his own right. By 1976, he eventually entered Congress, representing his solidly Republican home district in Michigan, and it was in the House that Stockman entered the political debate about supply-side tax cuts.[11] As a Republican on the Commerce Committee, he began challenging both the Republican and Democratic old guard, chiding them for their support of the allegedly bloated welfare state. Along with Newt Gingrich, Trent Lott and then Democrat Phil Gramm, Stockman joined the generational assault on the tax and spend habits that congressmen of both parties had perpetuated. While Kemp supported the crusade for a personal tax-cut enshrined Kemp-Roth Bill, Stockman and Gramm proposed parallel legislation to cut back the spending programs that every congressman bemoaned but that none seemed prepared to truly eliminate.

This highlighted a subtle difference between Stockman and the supply-siders, who were concerned chiefly with tax cuts to stimulate economic growth and were relatively unconcerned with big government or deficits, which they believed would be solved by rapid economic growth. Stockman's goal, by contrast, was to roll back the regulatory state and to do this required more than simply intellectually denying it—as the supply-siders had—or by railing against welfare queens and self-interested bureaucrats—the Reagan approach— but by actually taking on farm supports, tariffs, middle-class entitlements and the hundreds of other discretionary programs that congressmen of both parties negotiated into their unwieldy congressional appropriation bills. For Stockman, the supply-side tax cut was merely the political cover for making these radical cuts politically palatable. As every reformer knows, he who takes with one hand must give with another in order to neutralize opposition. In a related sense, Stockman appreciated a second advantage of a tax cut: it would erode revenue, which, in turn, would force Congress to make either politically painful cuts or risk exploding the deficit. For Stockman, tax cuts became a means, not for the opportunity society, but for taking congressional hands out of the "political pork barrel." (There were two hidden premises in Stockman's equation: (1) that Congress and the president would not countenance higher taxes, which was correct, and (2) that they would not allow an exploding deficit, which turned out to be dead wrong.)

Through Jack Kemp, whom he described as his "intellectual guru," Stockman entered the Reagan camp. By mid-1980, Stockman, who had expressed initial reservations about Reagan, felt that Kemp and the other supply-siders had converted Reagan to the cause—that Reagan was the candidate who could popularize their doctrine. Although he expressed reservations about the "Bible" and the "gun" factions in the right wing, Stockman viewed Reagan as the candidate who could put an end to the political "free lunch."

In time, Stockman became not simply an appendage to Kemp—who perhaps had his political liabilities—but indeed a player in his own right within the Reagan entourage. Stockman's big break came prior to the presidential debates. His old boss, Republican congressman John Anderson, was mounting an improbable third-party candidacy; the Reagan campaign soon recruited Stockman to impersonate Anderson in a mock debate, as preparation for the televised event. In his memoir, Stockman argued that the mock debate revealed Ronald Reagan's limited intellectual grasp of the issues, but for Stockman it was too late for any reservations. Instead, he hinted that they, the supply-siders, had to create a supply-sider candidate ex nihilo.

This highlighted a recurring tension in the Stockman memoir: belittling Reagan for his intellectual limitations and suggesting that his politics were often the product of handlers and rehearsals rather than genuine convictions. Stockman was probably half-right in his assessment but, in light of this, one wonders why he did not accordingly later scale back the vastly ambitious legislative agenda. Stockman, however, had an intimation that, in the debates, Reagan's easygoing manner would work well against John Anderson's cocksure intelligence and Carter's rhetorical ineptitude. Reagan was, after all, a seasoned performer who, though coached and protected, had nevertheless been on the campaign trail for nearly two years.

In the weeks after Reagan's November 1980 victory, the transition team began the appointment process. When Reagan's economic advisors met in California, Jack Kemp briefed them with a thirty-page treatise, "Avoiding an

Economic Dunkirk," a treatise that Stockman himself had written. The title captured the self-generated sense of urgency that Stockman, and all ideologues, use to their short-term advantage but often long-term detriment. It was predictable that the transition team invited Kemp to give his sermon. Kemp, they perhaps reasoned, did not need a position in the new administration: he simply needed an adoring audience. Instead, the transition team made its offer to Stockman, who had congressional experience and who was connected to the supply-side faction that needed some payoff. Perhaps some in the Reagan entourage simply thought Stockman was smarter than Kemp, whose economic religion always got carried away; perhaps others thought Kemp's name on the political marquee might take away some luster from the top billing in the act. The transition team members well understood that Ronald Reagan was the only leading man.

Initially offered the Department of Energy, Stockman voiced his desire to be head of the OMB, which had been Weinberger's old job under Nixon. With support from Kemp and the supply-siders, and with publicity from conservative journalist Bob Novak's column, Stockman was eventually offered the position he sought.

On December 19, 1980, Stockman then wrote a memo to both Baker and Meese outlining a blueprint for action—ostensibly echoing the Economic Dunkirk memo—and both implicitly agreed to it.[12] (This contrasted to their later refusal to sign off on Al Haig's blueprint for policy redirection at State.) In Stockman's overblown phraseology, the revolution had begun.

Before Reagan took office in January of 1981, Stockman had already begun his work. In his 1985 book, Stockman hinted at the disorganization of the transition team, which was headed by the notoriously undisciplined Ed Meese. Indeed, the economic literacy of the White House staff was not high. Meese, Stockman suggested, mistook Washington for an overgrown Sacramento and was wholly new to the idea of multiyear budgeting. Considerably more savvy, White House Chief of Staff Baker was both politically cautious but also surprisingly uninformed about policy details.[13] Stockman, however, developed a close working relationship with Baker. Keenly aware that many of the Californians saw him as insufficiently conservative, Baker had to swallow much of his skepticism over supply-side doctrine and, consequently, gave Stockman free reign.

Indeed, Stockman realized that few within Reagan's California entourage were prepared, in terms of technical knowledge, to oversee the details of Reagan's promises—tax cuts, increased defense spending, anti-inflationary monetary policy and a balanced budget—which Stockman claimed were taken as an "a priori."[14] Although Stockman noted that these promises were riddled with contradictions, he nonetheless pushed ahead with his "Grand Doctrine"—his term—for dismantling the welfare state.

Although Stockman was naive to think that his views were widely shared in the White House, he was nonetheless crucial in the initial stages of drawing up budgets. Chief economic advisor, Murray Weidenbaum, was not even appointed until January, at which point much of the groundwork in fiscal policy had already been laid.[15] Moreover, the transition team had appointed Donald Regan at Treasury. Head of Merrill Lynch, Regan was the recommendation of campaign treasurer and designate CIA head, William Casey. (Regan was, in fact, the third choice after former Nixon and Ford treasury secretary, William Simon, and Wall Street financier, Walter Wriston.) New to Washington, Regan had claimed he needed "time to get up to speed." To complicate matters, he believed that his task was to execute rather than develop policy, and for these reasons, the man central to any economic strategy was absent at the critical, early stages of policy formation. Consequently, even more responsibility fell to budget director Stockman, who was poised to take yet another improbable turn in his long and winding journey.

Notes

1. Lou Cannon, *President Reagan: The Role of a Lifetime* (New York: Simon and Schuster, 1991), 235.

2. Having served as ambassador to France, Jefferson saw how the debt could metastasize. Indeed, the mountain of Crown debt and the erratic attempts to rein it in during the 1780s contributed to the revolutionary spasm that toppled the Bourbon monarchy in 1792 and led to the Reign of Terror. For Jefferson, debt was dangerous because it corroded the credibility of a regime.

For Hamilton, the problem was not the debt but how it was managed or mismanaged. France's problem was not simply debt—which was proportionately smaller than Great Britain's—but the notoriously lax and incoherent bookkeeping methods of the French monarchy.

3. From the perspective of classical economics, the massive immigration of famished peasants during the Irish Potato Famine of the 1840s was a form of market self-correction. In a world where fortunes fluctuate, it is almost impossible to argue against this type of self-correction. John Maynard Keynes was thus right when he argued that in the long run, we are all dead. Death, however, is not a terribly helpful policy solution for famished or plague-stricken peasants who may want more than events to take their course, that is, death.

4. Garry Wills, *Nixon Agonistes: The Crisis of the Self-Made Man* (Boston: Houghton Mifflin, 1970), 553.

5. Wills, *Nixon Agonistes*, 253.

6. Stephen E. Ambrose, *Nixon.* Vol. 3, *Ruin and Recovery*, (New York: Simon and Schuster, 1991), 596.

7. Herbert Stein, *Presidential Economics: The Making of Economic Policy from Roosevelt to Clinton*, third revised edition, (Washington, D.C.: American Enterprise Institute for Public Policy Research, 1994), 255.

8. Michael Schaller, *Reckoning with Reagan: America and Its President in the 1980s* (New York: Oxford University Press, 1992), 26; see also, Haynes Johnson, *Sleepwalking through History: America in the 1980s* (New York: W.W. Norton, 1991), 103.

9. Garry Wills, *Reagan's America: Innocents at Home* (Garden City, N.Y.: Doubleday, 1987), 364.

10. Cannon, *The Role of a Lifetime*, 236; Wills, *Reagan's American*, 365; Herbert Stein, *Presidential Economics*, 249.

11. Cannon, *The Role of a Lifetime*, 236-238.

12. David Stockman, *The Triumph of Politics: The Inside Story of the Reagan Revolution* (New York: Harper and Row, 1986; Avon Paperback Edition, 1987), 83.

13. Stockman, *Triumph of Politics*, 91.

14. Stockman, *Triumph of Politics*, 90.

15. Stockman, *Triumph of Politics*, 104.

Chapter 13

The Reagan Years: Balancing the Books?

Having never served in a White House, Stockman was in some ways unprepared, not for the task of budget director—but for that of being a budget director with a free hand in policy initiatives. There would have been no problem if these initiatives had been of a business as usual variety, but they were not. Reagan had made rather extravagant 1980 campaign promises—supply-side tax cuts, an increase in military spending, and concerted budget cuts—and this type of radical change requires a greater measure of competence than simply maintaining precedent with occasional fine-tuning along the way.

Realizing that the OMB staff would have to do much of the work in translating Reagan campaign promise into economic policy, Stockman had assumed a progressively larger role in policy formation.[1] In order to push through the cuts in domestic spending needed to accompany the supply-side tax cuts and a balanced budget, Stockman also pressed Meese to create, by late January, a special Budget Working Group that consisted of committed budget cutters such as Commerce Secretary Bill Brock, Martin Anderson, Murray Weidenbaum as well as Donald Regan. (According to Stockman, Regan did not seem to be committed to anything in particular other than promoting himself; Stockman called him an "ideological neuter.") The strategy of the group was to push through budget cuts before cabinet secretaries could resist the erosion of their budgetary prerogative.[2] By the first week of February, they had achieved a projected savings of twenty-six billion dollars for fiscal year 1982 and forty-seven billion dollars for 1984.[3]

By the first week of February, the OMB budget estimates came in. These estimates factored in the Kemp-Roth 30 percent tax cut, related business tax cuts and increased defense budgets, coupled to the inflation rate and, accordingly, projected a one hundred and thirty billion dollar deficit.[4] What is puzzling to the outside observer is that the White House handlers did not immediately back off tax cuts and reassess the economic package. For his part, Stockman suggested that they should have reassessed their plans at that juncture but there is something slightly disingenuous about his ex post facto reassessment. Instead, the administration moved the targeted balanced budget date until 1984. Despite growing reservations, Stockman pushed ahead with a bold strategy of massive expenditure cuts and belittled those who raised any doubts as being part of the "regulatory state," "Naderites" or part of the "Second Republic." (For Stockman, political criticism often veered into a form of ideological name-calling.)

Stockman also finessed the problem by proposing a hypothetical category of future savings that would be named later. What he did not tell the cabinet was that his "plan" involved eliminating social security entitlements. Nonetheless, it was astonishing that the "mysterious" savings that would cover the budget deficit was not discussed, and the president's economic plan changed accordingly. It was a testament to Stockman's rather manipulative tactics but even more to the utter policy gullibility, in not unreality, of the White House staff. Oblivious, Reagan maintained a naive trust that it would be worked out. "He was," noted Stockman, "taking my plan on faith alone, having no reason to suspect that the numbers wouldn't add up."[5]

On February 18, 1981, Reagan outlined to Congress his bold, economic agenda—one that cobbled together his campaign promises and that had been the basis of Stockman's hectic budget cutting initiatives. Striking a note of urgency, Reagan promised, not major cuts in expenditure, but slowing the rate of budgetary growth, eliminating needless regulation, reducing the income tax rate by 30 percent over three years to stimulate the economy, as well as a tight monetary policy to rein in inflation.

In 1981, the White House had pursued what Samuel Huntington called the "blitzkrieg" approach—a bold reformist agenda implemented in a flurry of activity. This policy is most suitable in a crisis, such as in Franklin Roosevelt's first hundred days, or when the opposition can undermine the agenda either by blocking it or by slowly co-opting and gutting it. It was this—congressional opposition to tax cuts but even more the problem of congressional appropriations smuggled in to any "reform" legislation—that Stockman had feared. Stockman's own view of White House policy was even more grandiose; fearing that Congress would not countenance his bold dismantling of the "welfare state," he assumed that Congress needed to be a rubber stamp for the revolution. As he admitted, he was naive about the degree to which Congress would comply.

The real problem with the blitzkrieg approach to reform, however, is that it compounds miscalculation and makes a policy of trial and error adjustment exceedingly difficult over time. The choices need to be clear, the risks known, the alternatives measured: there is no room for wavering and second-guessing. A reformer cannot pursue the blitzkrieg approach and say afterwards that he "goofed," to borrow Reagan's handy phrase. To do so is to appear politically incompetent and only the best and the luckiest of politicians can back away from botched reform and make a second go of things.

One is tempted to think that there was a strong element of fantasy in Stockman's "Grand Doctrine" for changing the way that the "Second Republic" worked. Nonetheless, many in the administration, including Baker, endorsed Stockman's plan not only for massive regulatory rollback but for enough cuts in nonmilitary domestic spending necessary to cover the massive tax cuts that Reagan had promised. Everyone in the administration seemed to look to Stockman as the ultimate budget expert, but he had begun, even as of February 1981, to realize that the projected budget numbers would simply not add up, which led to the desperate search for forty-four billion dollars in further cuts needed to close the gap. To repeat, the cumulative effect of the tax cut, massively increased defense expenditure, relatively limited cuts in domestic spending and budget projections adjusted because of inflation created a far bigger budget deficit than anyone could possibly have imagined.

None of this would have been fatal had the administration, in the early days of budget negotiations, explicitly decided to forgo the blitzkrieg approach and follow the type of incremental reform that Huntington called "Fabian" or "branch" reform. In fact, the "branch" approach is, with the exception of crisis conditions, really the only type of approach to follow in the budget negotiations between leaders of the legislature's two houses and agents of the executive branch. The tricornered bargaining that goes in to crafting a federal budget may seem cumbersome but it also evolves out of the system of separation of powers, in which the executive proposes budgetary guidelines even as Congress has the ultimate power of the purse.

Although 1981 was a time of stunning legislative accomplishment for President Reagan, these triumphs obscured the deeper structural problems underlying the White House strategy for fiscal reform. To grasp the internal contradictions, one has to look at the effort to cut expenditure on one hand and raise revenue on the other but, first, the question of controlling expenditure.

Year One of the Redirection: The Illusory Expenditure Cuts

President Reagan's justification for the tax cuts were twofold: one, the supply-side assumption, discounted by both Wall Street and many Reagan insiders themselves, that massive tax cuts would bring in more revenue and, two, the assumption that Reagan was going to make bold across the board cuts in domestic spending.

Campaigning for governor in 1966, Reagan had pledged to eliminate government waste and abuse and bring fiscal order to the state coffers left in disarray by the allegedly fiscally irresponsible Pat Brown. Immediately after taking office, Reagan had made 10 percent across the board cuts—an uneconomical way to cut state expenditure precisely because all government programs are not equal. In fact, governor-elect Reagan had trouble even getting a budget chief and it was not until the ideologically suspect Caspar Weinberger came to Sacramento that the fiscal mess was cleaned up and some degree of order imposed. This foreshadowed Reagan's experience in Washington, to the extent that ideological enthusiasts made a mess of economic policy in the first year and left the more traditional and technically competent centrists to supervise the damage control.

Despite this sobering experience at the state level, Reagan's attitude to federal expenditure was much the same: cutting government waste would solve the deficit problem inherited from Carter. Reagan, whom Stockman portrayed as a benign but disinterested executive, had encouraged Stockman: "Keep bringing your black books, Dave," urged Reagan. Stockman, however, implied that Reagan—who was fixated on a few anecdotes such as cutting bureaucratic waste and trimming the welfare rolls—lacked all political will to make the real cuts as his campaign rhetoric suggested.

Although Reagan may have seen himself as a heroic budget cutter, one need only tally up the 1981-1982 budget projections to grasp that Reagan's self-perception and political reputation as a cost-cutter were both vastly overblown. Even by March—only three months in to the new administration—Stockman sensed that the "glory days of the [budget] cutting room were over."[6] Three further points are essential to grasp.

First, the White House in effect took seven politically popular programs off the political cutting block: social security; Medicare; veteran's benefits; Head Start; Supplemental Security Income for the poor, disabled and elderly; and summer jobs for urban youth, along with low income student lunches; and veteran's disability benefits—seven programs, protected from any cuts whatsoever, that amounted to 40 percent of the federal budget. Stockman intimated in his memoir that this "hands-off" policy was not so much a deliberate choice but had been inadvertently forced on the White House by policy ineptitude (on the part of Meese) compounded by a subsequent media leak. Regardless of how it was handled, blocking off these programs reflected an overall reluctance to make deep spending cuts as the Reagan rhetoric had suggested.

Second, Reagan did not simply raise defense spending—he raised it exponentially, in fact doubling the rate of growth promised during the 1980 campaign. In the matter of the military buildup, the administration deficit hawks were unable to achieve the slower rate of growth in military spending that would have fulfilled Reagan's campaign promises but also preserved a modicum of budgetary restraint.

On the bloated defense budgets, the administration had been internally divided with Stockman, Baker, Meese, Deaver and most of the economists favoring a slower growth projection while Weinberger, backed by Haig, lobbied heavily for the higher spending proposal. The astonishing thing was not only the dogged determination of Weinberger in pushing departmental prerogative over White House economic policy, but the degree that he was able to manipulate Reagan, who had little grasp of military or budgetary details. Weinberger had argued that national defense was not a budgetary issue but he also played on Ronald Reagan's anticommunist instincts and even gullibility. National security and fiscal responsibility thus became incompatible goals, though they need not have. Weinberger thus preserved the huge budget increases that Stockman maintained had originated from a simple calculation mistake early in 1981 but which Weinberger fought to preserve.

It was predictable that the policy of massive defense increases would damage Reagan's credibility as a serious budget-cutter. For this reason, economic advisor Martin Anderson had shrewdly urged, as early as January of 1981, that there had to be at least symbolic cuts at the Pentagon, in order to underscore the administration's credibility to make hard, rather than cosmetic, cuts in other areas. The symbolic gestures were, however, too small to be of any value. The growing perception of swollen Pentagon budgets inevitably altered the budgetary negotiations between the White House and Congress. Fearing that massive domestic spending cuts would hurt their reelection chances, congressional Republicans later balked at deep budget cuts when they understood that Weinberger had in fact received everything he wanted. In addition, congressional Democrats could also block cuts in social spending by charging that cuts had to be made across the board.

Third, Reagan, in his first year of office, resisted congressional attempts to restructure entitlement programs and it was here, in social security, not in government waste or transfer payments to the underclass, that the truly expanding costs of the welfare state lay.

The question of entitlements was raised in the early months of 1981 when a group of senators, led by Republican Pete Domenici of New Mexico, proposed a plan to halt the growth of entitlements—the single largest area of budgetary growth.[7] Domenici was soon joined by Bob Dole of Kansas and Democrat Ernest Hollings of South Carolina, who had actually made similar proposals during the Carter era. Both Domenici and Dole were part of the new Republican majority in the Senate and interpreted Reagan's victory as a mandate for a radical reversal in spending patterns. They wanted the president to use his political clout to expunge the cost of living adjustments (COLAs) built into entitlements—a policy that had originated only in the early 1970s.[8] In short, a bipartisan group of senators was signaling its willingness to work with a newly elected president who allegedly came to Washington to bring fiscal solvency to the federal government.

The senators, however, soon realized that President Reagan had no intention of running into a political fight that jeopardized his popularity nor of initiating reforms to tackle entitlement spending. Slashing HUD and AFDC was relatively easy, but trimming cost of living adjustments created friction with the middle-class voters that Reagan courted in 1980 and needed for 1984. Ultimately, Chief of Staff Jim Baker was instrumental in blocking any plan for "tampering" with social security.[9] There were several reasons for this. Politically savvy and personally responsible for much of the president's success on the Hill, Baker was also instinctively cautious. He was not one for making bold moves nor for seizing the initiative. Perhaps Jim Baker's own insecurity with the right wing of the Republican Party made him cautious about risking Reagan's political standing. Indeed, the charge of tampering with social security was to Democrats what the welfare queen and mandatory bussing were to Republicans—a perfect issue to trump the other side. A third plausible reason for Baker's caution was timing: in early 1981, few could have fully appreciated the exploding deficits of the 1980s.

It is impossible to know if the president could have used the 1981 occasion to "educate" the public. By temperament and by inclination, Ronald Reagan was not the man to educate people. The Republican senators were nonetheless troubled, not by Chief of Staff Baker's stance, but by Reagan's rather simplistic understanding of the fiscal problem. As Cannon noted, despite his gubernatorial experience, Reagan never really understood the budgetary process:[10] beyond his strong convictions, he always left the details of government to others. Realizing that they themselves owed their Senate majority to Reagan's presidential coattails, Dole and Domenici had no choice but to go along with the genial and popular chief executive.

Reagan's early resistance to social security reform—a policy practically handed to him by a bipartisan group of Senate leaders—illustrated the weaknesses in the White House vision for fiscal reform. Ironically, Reagan probably would have received widespread support had he formulated an across the board deficit spending plan that "saved social security" and that cut all groups proportionately.

One wonders where David Stockman was in all of this, for after all, he was committed to reforming government spending patterns and the built-in system of welfare entitlements. In a puzzling move, Stockman actually helped convince Reagan against the senators' plan. What Stockman, however, did not tell Reagan or any one else, was that he intended a more radical plan for taking on the social security system and for using the savings as the way to cover the forty-four billion dollar gap already alluded to. This was the origin of the abortive Reagan plan of May 1981—just after the Senate proposal—to push for reform of the social security system by penalizing those who took early retirement via a harsh, and in many ways, unfair penalty levied immediately rather than in the remote future as with most social security adjustments. In effect, it was a reform of the social security system on the backs of those who had played by the rules and were being subsequently penalized: a type of retroactive punishment.

Mystified by Stockman's deliberately opaque presentation, Reagan endorsed what he did not understand. Stockman, along with Martin Anderson and Health and Human Services Secretary Richard Schweiker, who incidentally had the plan forced on him, were all naive to think this approach could withstand congressional scrutiny. Democrats rightly pounced on the plan and soon Republican senators themselves rejected the idea in a unanimous vote.

The abortive and ill-conceived social security reform was the final conclusive link in Reagan's failure to reform federal spending patterns. After rejecting a sensible bipartisan alternative, the White House went for a highly questionable proposal that had not been "market-tested" in Congress, that the president did not even grasp, and that violated almost any standard of fairness on which reform depends. Large generalities are often read into small defeats: Reagan never again really recovered the budget cutting initiative nor the reputation of making fair and technically bold cuts. The Reagan fiscal revolution—inchoate and conceptually unformed as it was—was effectively over by late spring of 1981.

What was left, instead, was to make the further cuts that the White House needed to justify its vision of 30 percent tax cuts. In putting built-in entitlements off the cutting-room table, the White House and Congress could only go after the discretionary spending programs that emerged out of the Great Society programs—but as Stockman would have described it this was the "nickel and dime" type of savings that only dented the growing budget deficit.

By late June, the Democratic controlled House of Representatives had passed a second spending reduction package known as the Gramm-Latta Bill. Congressional passage was a triumph of the alliance between the White House, the minority Republicans and the conservative Democrats, known as the Boll Weevils. White House success was made possible, however, only by (1) a frantic bout of last-minute bargaining that diluted savings and (2) a tactical mistake by the House Democratic leadership that denied an up or down vote in an effort to drive a wedge between the White House and the Boll Weevils. The Democratic plan backfired.[11] For all the White House triumphantalism about the legislative maneuver, the success also obscured the fact that the bill only guaranteed sixteen billion dollars in spending cuts with promises of twice that much in the future—hardly enough to cover the projected deficit of more than two hundred and fifty billion dollars projected over the coming years.[12]

Despite significant cuts in spending—the first time that Congress and the White House had played the "politics of subtraction"—the magnitude of the impending deficit had completely overshadowed the symbolic changes in Washington's spending pattern.

Year One of the Redirection:
Cutting Taxes as a Revolutionary Gesture

Complicating the whole issue of deficits and expenditure cuts in the spring of 1981 was the question of the supply-side tax cuts—the veritable centerpiece of the Reagan Economic Recovery Program of February 1981. Although some White House staff members had an early fear that the projected budgetary numbers would not add up, there seemed to be an air of unreality throughout the White House, as if they had all decided to forgo root-canal economics and had gone on supply-side laughing gas. Just as Reagan, the gut anticommunist, backed the largest increase in defense expenditure that was politically possible, Reagan, the convert to the supply-side creed, pushed the largest tax cut possible, the Kemp-Roth plan. Tax reduction had converged with his own experience, and he firmly resisted any attempt to renege on this campaign promise.

To compound matters, Treasury Secretary Donald Regan sensed that he could gain points with the president by adopting the supply-side mantra and becoming a loud, if not bombastic, supporter of Kemp-Roth. Regan, whose political ambition perhaps outweighed his policy instincts, was in turn advised by two supply-siders at Treasury, Paul Craig Roberts and Norman Ture.

On the other hand, supply-side skeptics lacked political clout. Jim Baker and his budgetary lieutenant Richard Darman could not oppose tax cuts in large part because they were politically suspect with the Republican right wing.

Although White House Counselor Ed Meese sensed mounting fiscal problems, he also lacked the budgetary skills and administrative savvy necessary to persuade Reagan to pursue a smaller tax cut if not back off the pledge altogether. Even in his own memoirs, Stockman's own position on tax cuts seems highly ambiguous and even inconsistent. He leads the reader to infer that he pushed the tax cut idea long after he knew the budget would not add up and that Congress and many in the White House would not countenance big expenditure cuts. Stockman suggested that he intended to use the threat of exploding deficits to push both parties to make further cuts and thus intimates that he treated tax cuts as a type of fiscal brinkmanship—if so, an extraordinarily irresponsible position. The reader of Stockman's book is left wondering if he were either dishonest, and thus rewriting history to absolve his own errors, or simply astonishingly naive. Either way, Stockman was guilty of very poor political judgment.

Although Kemp-Roth had caught on among a group of House Republicans that clustered around Kemp, its congressional supporters were in the definite minority—in fact it would seem most in Congress were firm opponents. Both the Democratic Boll Weevils and most Republican senators were fiscal conservatives who favored a balanced budget but who saw tax cuts as a regression from traditional fiscal discipline. For Stockman, these were the very people who wanted spending cuts precisely so they could preserve, not dismantle, their favorite spending programs. By contrast, these fiscal conservatives were more disposed to business tax cuts, as embodied in depreciation cuts sponsored by congressman Barnard Conable—eventually part of the Reagan tax relief package written in to law in August of 1981. Deriding these fiscal conservatives, such as Pete Domenici of New Mexico, as "Hooverites," Stockman even went so far as urging the *Wall Street Journal* writer and ardent supply-side advocate William Bartlett to label the New Mexico senator John Maynard Domenici in one of his columns. (Again, Stockman's resort to unnecessary name-calling was utterly puzzling.)

For a variety of reasons, many fiscally conservative senators buckled and eventually endorsed the combined spending and tax package that the White House favored. This was no surprise. In the spring of 1981, Republican members were like lemmings who were prepared, perhaps against their better judgment, to follow their presidential leader. For Republicans, there was an element of campaign euphoria that caused them to suspend their skepticism built on long years of experience. Reagan was, after all, the great budget-cutter and this added credibility to his pledge for tax cuts in the context of a balanced budget.

The deeper contest, however, was in the Democratically controlled House, where the White House struggled to play off the conservative Boll Weevils against their more liberal leaders. For the Boll Weevils, there was an element of survival in the new political equation; they needed to distance themselves from the liberal Democratic wing of the party, particularly if they were to win reelection in their southern districts—districts that had supported Reagan and had soundly repudiated Carter in 1980. The same held true for mainline Democrats, who were well aware of Reagan's popularity and needed to put forth their own tax relief plan—one which called for a 10 percent reduction in one year as opposed to the 30 percent, spread through three years, embodied in the supply-side Kemp-Roth plan. Even Stockman, who seemed an increasingly ambiguous defender of the supply-side theology, suggested in his 1985 book that the Democratic plan was significantly better than the Kemp-Roth proposal that eventually passed.

Nonetheless, the White House managed to outmaneuver the Democratic tax experts, such as Leon Panetta of California and House banking chairman Jim Jones of Oklahoma. Panetta and Jones may have endorsed the better plan, but Reagan was emotionally committed to Kemp-Roth and refused all White House advice to negotiate with congressional Democrats. Tax relief was perhaps one of the few issues that Reagan stubbornly held on to in the face of contrary advice. His stubbornness paid off, and his rapid recovery from the Hinkley assassination attempt in the spring of 1981 created a groundswell of popular support: Baker and legislative advisor Max Friedendorf used the outpouring of sympathy for the recovering chief executive as leverage in their ongoing dealings with reluctant congressmen.

Despite being fiscal conservatives who looked askance at supply-side tax cuts, Boll Weevils panicked and abandoned their leadership in favor of the White House plan. By July of 1981, both houses of Congress passed substantial tax cuts that came close to resembling the original Kemp-Roth package. On August 13, President Reagan then signed the Economic Recovery Act of 1981, which spread a 25 percent income tax cut over three years: 5 percent by October of 1981 and then a further 10 percent in both July of 1982 and 1983. The Recovery Act not only reduced the top rate from 70 to 50 percent but also included a number of other tax exemptions; in fact, the package contained tax cuts for both individuals and businesses. In order to garner congressional support, the act also provided tax breaks for oil producers but more importantly significant depreciation for capital equipment.

At the time, commentators were favorably contrasting Reagan's tax policy to Carter's failed legislative proposals, notably the Energy program that took a year and a half to pass through both houses of congress. Reagan, it seemed, had managed to break out of Washington gridlock in a masterly legislative maneuver. The trouble, however, was in the details: Congress capitulated, against its better judgment, to a plan that was built on shifting sand, that would aggravate the deficit and that would make subsequent tax increases in other areas necessary even as early as 1982.

The Grieder Episode

By the summer of 1981, Stockman had himself come to realize the numbers of the Reagan budget would not add up and that the earlier promises of deficit reduction and tax increases were themselves wildly inflated. By autumn of that year, he was in a rear-guard action to undo the effects of the tax cut. At that time, Ronald Reagan had become the first chief executive to preside over a federal deficit in the triple billion digits. By October of 1981, the national debt reached the trillion-dollar mark for the first time in U.S. history.

In one of the stranger episodes of the Reagan administration, Stockman had, over the course of 1981, allowed himself to be interviewed by Washington journalist William Grieder, who had made it clear to Stockman that the conversations would be the basis of published articles.[13] In his progressive disillusionment, Stockman confessed not only to "doctored projections,"[14] but to grave misgivings about the administration's policy. These confessions became part of an *Atlantic* article that appeared in November of 1981. It was a troubling admission from the president's own budget director. Stockman had probably intended to use Grieder as a mouthpiece in Stockman's own confrontation with those unwilling to make difficult cuts, perhaps even with the president himself. He probably also believed that the article would vindicate him and force the debate in his direction, for Stockman had initially viewed the supply-side driven tax relief as necessary to make drastic cuts in expenditure palatable to the American public, but he had also come to see supply-side doctrine as something of a charade that insulated Reagan from having to make hard choices.

Ultimately, the Greider article exposed the inconsistencies in the administration's fiscal strategy, which seemed increasingly like a nonstrategy. The public was led to believe that Stockman was severely reprimanded by the president: the alleged "woodshed episode." While Stockman did, in fact, submit his resignation, Reagan did not accept it. Always anxious for harmony in his official "family," he barely admonished Stockman. Moreover, Chief of Staff Jim Baker, who was dubious about the supply-side scenario, tacitly supported Stockman. The outcome of the whole episode was that Reagan came across as something less than the deficit hawk that he was portrayed to be. Whatever he may have said in the campaign, it was increasingly clear that he had no real policy commitment to restrain, let alone balance, the budget.

Supply-side promises had, by degrees, been exposed as unrealistic. Indeed, Stockman's confession was the final conclusive evidence that supply-side theology was, at bottom, a dubious proposition. Not only were tax cuts not bringing in revenue that its advocates had promised, but the economy was in a tailspin. By 1982, most of the supply-siders themselves had left the administration[15] and though Stockman remained until 1985, one has to feel that he served Reagan in order to undo the effects of what he initially had helped promote. Indeed, relations between Stockman and the supply-siders cooled considerably, and Stockman's descriptions of the central characters took on a note of sarcasm that is often the mark of disillusioned intellectuals. Increasingly, Stockman adopted fiscally conservative and cautious positions advocated by Jim Baker's economic advisor, Richard Darman, who later went on to serve as Budget chief in the Bush White House.

After the Revolution: The Politics of Tax and Spend

Personnel changes shifted toward a return to traditional Republican fiscal conservatism even as the administration had to handle the political mess that emerged from its contradictory economic policies. The administration policies yielded a number of casualties. By 1982, the fiscal conservative Martin Anderson resigned, perhaps in protest and frustration. Though not a supply-sider, White House economic advisor Murray Weidenbaum resigned in 1982 and the inference was that he was being made the scapegoat for the admin-istration's botched fiscal policy. He was replaced by the conservative, Harvard economist Martin Feldstein who subsequently urged Reagan to think about raising taxes.

To compound matters, congressional Republicans were hit hard in the 1982 elections. In the House, Democrats won enough seats to break the alliance between the Boll Weevils and the White House—an alliance that was already under stress because of the downturn in the economy, then experiencing the deepest recession since the 1930s.

Construing his mandate to be one of curtailing the stubborn inflation of the 1970s, Federal Reserve chief, and Carter appointee, Paul Volker had pursued a "monetarist" approach that tightened the flow of money in the economy, which in turn provoked a recession and high unemployment. Understanding next to nothing about the fundamentals of the Federal Reserve Bank, Reagan expressly supported Volker—appointed for a fixed term but still susceptible to a large measure of political pressure—at a time when White House handlers and congressional Republicans alike urged that Reagan publicly condemn the Fed. For his part, Reagan completely accepted Volker's explanation that the harsh monetarist medicine was necessary to cure the inflation, a legacy of government spending habits from the 1960s and 1970s. In his unwavering support for

Volker and in his optimism that these policies would lead to a recovery, Reagan had, in part, returned to his older economic belief in the "castor-oil" approach.

The trouble, of course, was that Reagan failed to appreciate, or he rationalized away, the discrepancy between Volker's harsh Calvinistic theology of pain after economic excess and the supply-side gimmickry that was as much binge as government entitlement programs were. This underscored the contradictory, and even strange, inconsistency in Reagan's economic prescription: the good he did in supporting Volker when few in policy circles would was largely offset by his ignorance of, or disregard for, the fiscal damage done by his deep tax cuts in a noninflationary economy.

Nonetheless, the administration's economic team and Congress had to do something to control the runaway expenditure, which was making Wall Street nervous. By this time, Secretary of State George Shultz, who had been both budget director and treasury secretary under Nixon, joined Feldstein in urging the president to think of raising taxes. Just as Reagan eventually endorsed détente in all but name, he also implicitly came to endorse the "tax and spend" policies that he had made a career in condemning. In many ways, however, Reagan's tax policies had always been concealed. In Sacramento, for example, his administration had raised income taxes but, with subsequent surpluses, it had also provided tax rebates in the early 1970s—a maneuver that sealed Reagan's reputation as a "tax-cutter." In a more exaggerated way, President Reagan had pushed through massive personal and business tax cuts in 1981 but then simply shifted the tax burden in subsequent years; indeed, the administration was adroit in pursuing concealed tax increases. In 1982, the Reagan administration endorsed sin taxes on both alcohol and tobacco.[16] In 1983, it approved a bipartisan tax increase that had already been scheduled.[17] At the urging of a bipartisan committee, which could take the blame, the administration also raised payroll taxes in two installments and taxed high-end social security recipients—a policy Reagan signed in to law in April of 1983.[18]

Given that the administration issued new taxes to compensate for the budget-busting effects of Kemp-Roth, one wonders why the deficit did not go down. Indeed, in no time during the Reagan years did the deficit drop under one hundred billion dollars and for much of this time, it hovered around the two-hundred-billion-dollar mark.

Opponents of Reagan's policy point to the contradictions between cutting taxes and raising defense expenditure as a means to balance the budget. In principle, however, there is nothing incompatible in bringing down expend-itures in one category, raising it in another, and subsequently balancing the books. The trouble, however, is in the hypothetical nature of the balancing: it requires coordination, political finesse and the capacity to take on powerful vested interests. It also depends on timing. Indeed, what really exploded the deficits, was not the Reagan budget but the implications of the anti-inflationary policies of the 1980s. Whereas inflation creates bracket creep, which inevitably produces more in tax receipts, recessions and anti-inflation policies such as Federal Reserve Chief Volker's approach reverse bracket creep, decrease tax receipts and thus force budget deficits upward. (As Stockman suggested, the administration had two tax cuts: the Kemp-Roth plan and the anti-inflation polices of Paul Volker.) Even if the Reagan White House had done nothing different from the outgoing Carter administration, deficits would have risen considerably as the price for curing inflation. The trouble was that few in the administration, not least among them Ronald Reagan, understood the details of budgetary math. For Reagan, federal deficits were simply a legacy of his predecessor and the spending patterns of a Democratic Congress. His fiscal policy further compounded a bad situation.

Fortunately for Reagan's reelection chances, the economy started to rebound from the long recessionary slump that dated from the Carter years. Volker's tight money policies started to show results and inflation, which had been in the double digits at the end of the Carter years, had fallen drastically. By the second half of 1983, the U.S. economy began a sustained economic recovery that lasted throughout the 1980s. In one sense, the whole discourse on the economy changed after 1983. Inflation no longer seemed linked to federal budget deficits as it was in the 1970s—the heyday of the notorious stagflation. In official policy circles and in congress, a larger federal deficit became an accepted fact of life. Economist Herb Stein noted that everyone disapproved of it, yet in the end nobody was willing to do anything about it, except perhaps watch it grow. In his 1982 State of the Union address, Reagan proposed a balanced budget amendment but it was, as Lou Cannon noted, a "throwaway line." For Reagan, the balanced budget amendment was like the school prayer amendment, a tactical ploy to prove his emotional commitment to the cause even as his policies suggested no commitment whatsoever.

In specific matters such as blocking aggressive deregulation, congressional Democrats used their powers to stop the administration, but in dealing with the expanding deficit, Democrats seemed devoid of ideas.[19] Paradoxically, Reagan's own presidency made complacency on the deficit acceptable, for if Reagan, the alleged budget cutter par excellence, could not restrain government costs who could?

Reagan, who was for so many years a Roosevelt liberal, became a Keynesian spender in Republican clothing; it was the Democratic candidate Walter Mondale who, in 1984, sounded like a "castor-oil" conservative and warned of tax hikes and mounting national debt. Reagan's 1984 electoral landslide was not necessarily an endorsement of his deficit, but perhaps a repudiation of his opponent, still linked to Carter's failed presidency.

Considerably to the left of the fiscally conservative Carter, Mondale had been a protege of fellow Minnesota senator, Hubert Humphrey. Mondale, however, lacked his mentor's buoyant energy. For Republicans, Mondale was also the dream-opponent who, in one link, could be subtly linked to the big-spending years of LBJ and Jimmy Carter "malaise."

Mondale's pledge to fiscal conservatism was also politically unconvincing. It seemed like Carter's newfound hawkishness as the 1980 election approached: a last minute conversion that had neither resonance with party activists nor in the broader electorate.

In the context of the 1980s, social liberalism and fiscal conservatism was not the winning message that it would be in the 1990s for Bill Clinton, who would reap the benefits of three previous Democratic losses and thus bring his chastened party to the center and do it convincingly. What was, however, curious about the 1984 and 1988 elections was that Republicans could evade the charge of fiscal irresponsibility and, conversely, pin the charge on the Democrats. Reagan managed to blame irresponsible spending on the Democratically controlled Congress, even though Republicans were the Senate majority until 1986. In the end, Reagan's ultimate advantage was the economic recovery—the natural upswing in a business cycle, stimulated by old-fashioned Keynesian investment in the form of defense contracts, and, of course, massive borrowing in both public and private sectors. The origin, and the effect, of the Reagan economic recovery is debatable—and there are good reasons to see it as shallow and fraught with problems—but it nonetheless helped Reagan ride a crest of popular support in 1984.

Other than the Stockman episode, in which the motives and personality of the messenger (Stockman himself) overwhelmed the message, the debate on the long-term economic effects of the budget seemed strangely ephemeral. After Stockman left the White House for Wall Street in 1985, he was replaced by William Miller who had been head of the regulatory office in 1981 and then the Federal Trade Commission. The appointment of the relatively low-profile Miller further demonstrated that the head of OMB would not play a key role in Reagan's second term as had been the case in the first year.

By contrast, the Treasury Department emerged as crucial to this later phase of White House economic policy, particularly on the issue of tax reform.

In a speech to Congress in early 1984, Reagan pledged to restructure and simplify the tax code. For political reasons, Chief of Staff Baker had urged Reagan to postpone tax reform until after the election. Increasingly, Treasury Secretary Regan fixed on tax reform, sensing an issue that could raise his political profile and help him curry favor with the president. While at Merrill Lynch, Don Regan had made his name by promoting bold ideas of restructuring, many of which originated with his staff but which he usurped and claimed as his own. In his support for supply-side tax cuts and, later, for tax reform, Regan proved adroit at bandwaggoning on issues that raised his political profile in Washington. He also had an unerring ability to push Ronald Reagan's antitax buttons and, like Weinberger, a gift for folksy anecdotes that Reagan loved.

After Treasury Department bureaucrats drew up a first tax plan and after White House advisors further modified it, the administration eventually came up with its plan—one that could correspond to a preexisting legislation that Democratic representative Richard Gephardt of Missouri and Democratic senator Bill Bradley of New Jersey had initially proposed in 1982.

Chief of Staff Jim Baker and Treasury Secretary Don Regan switched jobs in 1986. The quixotic move proved disastrous at the White House, which floundered after the "troika" disbanded, but nevertheless facilitated passage of the tax reform bill. Although Don Regan was a master of popularizing, if not stealing, technical ideas drawn up by subordinates, he lacked political savvy and the capacity to negotiate; Baker, by contrast, lacked confidence in policy details but was an expert negotiator. By coincidence, both men were at the Treasury Department when different skills were required in the transition from policy formation to that of garnering congressional support.

By 1986, the Reagan White House helped negotiate the Bradley-Gephardt tax reform code,[20] which reduced the marginal rates and made the tax burden more equitable and progressive. Tax policy, directed first by Regan and then his replacement, Jim Baker, was thus the crowning domestic accom-plishment of Reagan's second term.

For a number of reasons, however, Ronald Reagan never received complete credit for this legislative accomplishment. Running budget defi-cits—which many had learned to ignore but which also seemed to contradict traditional conservative principle—somehow tainted his administration. The 1986 tax reform was still overshadowed by 1981 tax cut polices that many viewed as contributing to the deficits in the first place. It was as if Reagan never recovered his reputation that the Greider interview had tarnished and even exposed: while a politician may enjoy triumphs of technical legislation, once his convictions have been exposed as weaker than many thought, it is as if part of his charisma disappears. In the broader sense, the average voter cannot get excited by the technical, incremental developments that go in to fine-tuning the political process and that are named after sponsoring congressmen. Compared to the hype and euphoric promise of the 1981 economic recovery program, it seemed as if Reagan's major domestic accomplishment was simply a sensible, but perhaps belated, correction rather than a fundamental change in the way Washington worked.

By 1986, the Democrats also regained the Senate after a six-year hiatus, and many viewed the political realignment in the upper chamber as a negative verdict on Reagan's fiscal policies. Events soon deteriorated for the administration, for Donald Regan proved unequal to the task of running the White House and failed to realize how the "troika" had minimized Reagan's administrative weaknesses while also conserving his assets. Soon, the details of the Iran-Contra episode emerged and gave further evidence to the political and policy costs of failed presidential oversight. In this sense, economic issues moved off center stage, further denying Reagan the applause for tax reform.

Auditing the Reagan Budgets: The Failure of Fiscal Reformism

It was perhaps in the area of budgetary reform that the inadequacies and contradictions of Reagan's reformist agenda were most evident. Arriving at the White House with the aura of heroic budget cutting, Reagan's ultimate legacy was staggering deficits—deficits that were fundamentally wasteful because there was no national emergency, as in depression or war, nor did they lead to investment in the nation's long-term productivity, as was the case in the late nineteenth century. Whereas the administration's abortive attempt at regulatory reform demonstrated the absence of presidential vision and an excess of zeal by freelancing subordinates, the administration's failed attempt at fiscal discipline demonstrated, not simply an uncoordinated administration, but an absence of fiscal strategy beyond Reagan's bedrock conviction that taxes had to be cut.

The irony of recent history was that Reagan, who cemented so many of the Republican's deepest electoral gains, achieved his political success by doing damage to the traditional Republican credo of prudent fiscal management. In a reversal of roles, Reagan proved as much, if not more, a deficit spender as any Democrat in recent memory. As Lou Cannon suggested, he was a "guns and butter" president[21] who also tripled the size of the federal budget deficit.[22] Having criticized the Great Society as a "binge"[23] Reagan wound up by presiding over an equally large, if not larger, one. The costs of the savings and loan fiasco—an indirect result of Reagan-era deregulatory policy—further compounded the national debt.

When so many political judgments are based on nuance, the colossal deficits and mounting national debt add concrete evidence to the abject policy failure of Reagan-era fiscal policy. No historian of the future will be able to pass judgment on his presidency without taking note of the utter abandonment of principles he had preached for nearly two decades. The end of the Cold War and exponentially rising public debt will surely be the captions of choice for future historians.

It is perhaps predictable that the conventional wisdom always leaves out some surprising twists and legacies—some of which may be comforting to fiscal conservatives, some of which may be unsettling.

The first point is the degree to which many Americans separated their favorable feelings for Reagan the man from policies that plainly contradicted his professed aims. Of course, voters calculate their preferences on a congeries of issues, not least of which is the state of the economy, but it would seem that many voters endorsed Reagan's declaratory commitment to fiscal conservatism even as they lamented his own administration's fiscal lack of discipline. Reagan's successes were always on the plane of ideas: he was strangely indifferent to, and even ignorant of, the execution of policy. Still, it is almost baffling that Reagan popularized the idea of fiscal conservatism even as his supply-side tax cuts and exploding deficits made mockery of his pledges.

If there is one partial clue to this ambiguity it might be in the way that Reagan managed to deflect criticism by blaming Congress and this constitutes a second important legacy: the public still has a tendency to blame fiscal matters on Congress and a tendency to exonerate the president. It was ironic that Reagan, by eroding public trust in Congress, left a subtly poisonous political legacy for his party once it assumed control of both congressional chambers in the 1990s.

In a curious way, Reagan both facilitated and inhibited the success of conservative fiscal assumptions, but in ways that one might not appreciate at first glance. One of the paradoxes of Reagan's failed fiscal policy was that it saddled his successors with astonishing deficits and a mounting debt. This crippled Republican George Bush, who vacillated between a forced conversion to low taxes and the political necessity of solving deficits that approximated three hundred billion dollars in his administration. Coupled to military demobilization in the wake of the Cold War and a "build-down" in defense budgets, George Bush seemed a Cold War throwback unprepared to manage an increasingly post-Cold War economy. In the longer term, however, changing international conditions and the legacy of persistent deficits only intensified the need for prudent fiscal management of the nation's expenditures. The curious combination of Reagan's political successes and fiscal failures thus pushed politicians of both parties who cared about their political survival to scale back expenditure without overtly raising taxes. Regardless of which party received credit, this represented a clear triumph of the conservative values and ideals that Reagan had preached since the 1950s.

In a less triumphant sense, however, Reagan's message represented a striking intellectual defeat for fiscal conservatives, in that Reagan helped divert his party away from the notion of keeping tax rates low toward a kind of tax cut gimmickry that seems anything but conservative. There are many on the right who still see Reagan's triumph as that of the Kemp-Roth supply-side tax cuts—cuts that were subsequently concealed by tax increases in other areas. Politicians, like generals, often learn the wrong lessons from the last war. Remembering the glory days of Reagan's early presidency, many sensible conservatives still see tax cuts as the ticket to electoral salvation. They seem to lose their traditional scruples by announcing unbecoming pledges for tax relief and promise, often unconvincingly, that the combination can balance budgets and reduce the debt. In doing this, conservatives lose the moral superiority that had sustained fiscal conservatives in the lonely but perhaps more heroic days of Senator Robert Taft: that there is no free lunch and that the costs of overspending now—and not whittling down the debt—will always be borne by future generations.

Nonetheless, the larger failure of Reagan's vision of fiscal reform runs far deeper, and it is a moral objection as much as a fiscal one. The strength of conservative principle comes not only in the bookkeeping assumptions of balancing debits and credits—in "economy" and a concern for long-term costs of progressively expanding government—but in the moral imperative of living within one's means. At bottom, the conservative outrage against Keynesian economics was not an intellectual argument but an emotional one—that in public life, as in private or business finances, debt is acceptable only if it leads to fundamental improvement for the future. The strength of conservative principle is less in a free-market philosophy shot through with undeveloped libertarian assumptions, but in the persistence of a quasi-Calvinistic assumption about virtue, savings and generational sacrifice.

Here, then, was the greatest failure of Ronald Reagan: his policy was a consumption- not an investment-based fiscal policy. It amounted to borrowing now from foreign creditors and saddling a future generation with the subsequent debt and, in the end, Reagan proved no different from a generation of politicians whom he condemned. His eight years were a triumph of politics but an abject failure of reform in the spending patterns of the Republic: he took a forty-billion-dollar deficit and managed, by default and neglect, to increase it approximately five times. In fiscal reform, unlike so many other aspects of the reform enterprise, numbers do indeed speak louder than words.

Notes

1. David Stockman, *The Triumph of Politics: The Inside Story of the Reagan Revolution* (New York: Harper and Row, 1986; Avon Paperback Edition, 1987), 98.
2. Stockman, *Triumph of Politics*, 123.
3. Stockman, *Triumph of Politics*, 130.
4. Stockman, *Triumph of Politics*, 133.

5. Stockman, *Triumph of Politics*, 141.

6. Stockman, *Triumph of Politics*, 148.

7. On entitlements, see Michael Schaller, *Reckoning with Reagan: America and Its President in the 1980s* (New York: Oxford University Press, 1992), 45.

8. Contemplating a bid for the Democratic presidential nomination, House Ways and Means Committee chairman Wilbur Mills of Ohio initiated cost of living allowances. Mills, however, did so with the blessing of the Nixon White House. In retrospect, Nixon later regretted this tacit endorsement. See Lou Cannon, *President Reagan: The Role of a Lifetime* (New York: Simon and Schuster, 1991), 242; Joan Hoff, *Nixon Reconsidered* (New York: Basic Books, 1994), 135.

9. Cannon, *The Role of a Lifetime*, 244, 262.

10. Cannon, *The Role of a Lifetime*, 154.

11. Stockman, *Triumph of Politics*, 237.

12. Stockman, *Triumph of Politics*, 242.

13. Cannon, *The Role of a Lifetime*, 232.

14. Garry Wills, *Reagan's America: Innocents at Home* (Garden City, N.Y.: Doubleday, 1987), 336-338.

15. Herbert Stein, *Presidential Economics: The Making of Economic Policy from Roosevelt to Clinton* (Washington, D.C.: American Enterprise Institute for Public Policy Research, 1994), 278.

16. Schaller, *Reckoning with Reagan*, 47.

17. Stein, *Presidential Economics*, 278.

18. Cannon, *The Role of a Lifetime*, 252.

19. Instead of fashioning a coordinated economic policy, Democrats fragmented and some became fixated on chimerical ideas of "industrial policy." Democrats should have focused on the role of deficits in reducing America's economic productivity, which has remained low despite the superficial economic recovery of the 1980s.

20. Schaller, *Reckoning with Reagan*, 51, 64.

21. Cannon, *The Role of a Lifetime*, 279.

22. Cannon, *The Role of a Lifetime*, 21; Schaller, *Reckoning with Reagan*, 70.

23. Cannon, *The Role of a Lifetime*, 270.

Chapter 14

The Moral Dimensions of Reform:
The Conservative Vision

The American doctrine of separation of church and state does not mean that religion is banished from public life, but rather that the state supports no established religion. Indeed, the alternating themes of religious liberty and religious conformity were central to the story of British settlement of the Atlantic colonies in the seventeenth and eighteenth centuries. Toward the end of the eighteenth century, however, a number of Anglo-American constitutional writers had urged a separation of church from state based on frank acknowledgement of the sectarian pluralism of Anglo-American society. Perhaps because of this disestablishment, religion has permeated American society in generic rather than purely sectarian ways. The Declaration of Independence, for example, makes express reference to the Creator; the coins and paper money of the Republic pledge trust in God; the most beloved patriotic anthems are laced with religious themes. Accordingly, some of Ronald Reagan's most stirring rhetoric embodied the ideas of both the providential nature of American society and of the covenant between the past and present generations.

In a democratic system, the politics of reform always involves a type of bargaining, whereby one brings change but change modified through a complicated process of electoral and legislative negotiating. The same is true in the moral dimensions of reform. Strictly speaking we are not discussing the reform of morals—which are out of the range of political institutions—but of the moral and moralistic implications of public policy choices. In a democratic society, this is an issue that is always present but awkwardly addressed and indeed often ignored. Although our political vocabulary is rich with moralistic themes, our political analysts and professional commentators often stumble in this area. In a perverse way, this vagueness also hints at the "compromised" character of "values questions" in the reform process.

First, many reforms that we think of as political have their origins with religious groups. In all societies, religion performs a para-political function. One might go so far as to suggest that, in a democratic society, religion is at the heart of all great social reform movements that begin outside the political process. Religiously motivated reformers in the nineteenth century, for example, wanted to abolish the slave trade and slavery altogether. At the turn of this century, religiously minded reformers urged the social gospel and an activist government that would address issues of poverty and squalor, which were viewed as corrosive to a healthy moral life. Religious minded reformers were also active in prison reform, temperance, civil rights and even opposition to specific wars.

Predictably, the intriguing questions of public life, in which private morals invariably spill over in to debate about the good and just society, are not ones of doctrine or dogma but ones about the ways particular policies foster or inhibit the nation's spiritual health. Abolition, capital punishment, pacifism, temperance, civil rights or the more recent issue of abortion or school prayer have all been political issues on the agenda of social reformers who put moral concerns at the top of their agenda. Of course, one man's moral concern becomes another man's violated liberty, and therein lies the controversy and rival value judgments that always surround reform politics.

Second, politicians often later endorse these para-political, religiously based initiatives but negotiate them through the legislative process by diluting them and by making them palatable to other groups. Consequently, politicians tend to affirm the latent religious values of a society in a generic way that satisfies the majority without alienating minorities. Typically, legislators and candidates who clamor for office on the basis of change are often the professional politicians who bandwagon on popular movements after the missionary foot soldiers of reform have labored and prepared the work, raised consciousness and forged coalitions that press for action. Although the politician claims credit for work that others have done, he nonetheless validates the religiously inspired movement. His calculation validates the moralistic reform movement even as he waters it down. Such opportunism is, in fact, the ultimate form of democratic compromise—signing on to something and then claiming credit. Objective historians and partisans alike are rarely fooled by such tactical conversions: they recognize them for what they are—part of the necessary business of political life.

Politicians thus articulate both the values of the majority and highlight moral themes that play out in the public realm. The president, for example, is not a moral legislator; he is, however, a "moralist in chief" whose task is that of a generalized moral articulation. Though the occupant's credibility and credentials count, it is the office itself that lends this charisma. It is for this reason that presidential campaigns—and the perennial but also vague claim for moral renewal—are so important in American politics. Politicians, reform-minded or otherwise, almost always make symbolic moral gestures to legitimize their policies. The moral dimensions of public policy need only touch on vague questions of the "health" of society: the generic promise of reformism, like revivalism in religion, is in and of itself a cathartic response to perceived drift.

The result is a type of dialectic whereby one group proposes specific policies, politicians co-opt, and the final consequence is something that falls short of the original objectives but that nonetheless changes the policy debate. In this sense, the politics of moralistic reform involves a series of compromises, a dialogue in which real changes emerge even if they lack the transforming power that enthusiasts had originally desired. Religiously minded groups—which have a focus that often transcends purely temporal concerns—often fail to appreciate the bargaining necessary in a democracy. Even when not pursuing overtly denominational concerns, such enthusiasms threaten to erode the wall between church and state and push sympathetic allies into the opposition camp. In fact, groups that wage a moral crusade in the political arena often do so at their own risk, for the price is not a corruption of judgment but of something worse: disillusionment and a sense of powerlessness. This was particularly true in the 1920s—a period that is interesting in that it illuminated some of the main trends, latent or overt, that color contemporary American politics.

The Politics of American Religion: Shifting Alliances in the Twentieth Century

Labels often confuse as much as they clarify. Religious Right, Christian Right, New Right—all these overlapping labels refer to the coalition of religious and cultural conservatives who were central to Reagan's presidential victory in 1980. The roots of the contemporary religious right lie in the complicated alignments of American politics, which is in large part dominated by religion, ethnicity and geography. At the presidential level, American politics can be seen in terms of large voting blocks forged into a winning coalition.

For their part, "fundamentalists" represent a form of Protestant Christianity strongly colored by the realities of the frontier and a communitarian ethos that permeated the Deep South—which had been hinterland in the eighteenth and early nineteenth centuries—the middle and the Far West.[1] One thing that religion—provided by the itinerant circuit riders—did provide was a sense of community to those on the geographic fringes of newly settled territories. Although American popular mythology extols the rugged individual on the range, the reality was quite the opposite: communities, not atomistic individuals, survived in the lonely and often desolate frontier, with its vicissitudes and crop failures, with its awesome and almost biblical bleakness. The history of the West is thus bound to the history of organized religion—the Baptists, Methodists, the Disciples of Christ or the Christian offshoot, the Mormons. Like the Hebrews before they got to the Promised Land, or like the early church fathers in the hinterland, the fundamentalist believes that man is tested and put through trials that force him back on an elemental, pristine faith. His religion is not given over to ritual or nuanced speculation but to judgment, moralism and the equality of believers before the awesome power of the Almighty. The historian Richard Hofstadter described fundamentalism as a religious and even political style—Manichean, dualistic and self-consciously righteous—as much as a theological doctrine.

Contemporary observers are inclined to view the judgmental, scriptural literalness of fundamentalists in terms of conservative politics. In the last quarter of the twentieth century, fundamentalists have indeed voiced opinions that are generally thought to be conservative. It is equally true, however, that modern American conservatives have usurped a political vocabulary and an agenda long associated with a western populism that had been dear to the hearts of most fundamentalists—a populism that in many ways defies the contemporary categories of left and right. Early in this century, for example, fundamentalists tended to be agrarian, isolationist, elitist, anti-Semitic and they often favored government intervention in the economy as a means for controlling big business. Actually, for much of the twentieth century, southern and even western fundamentalists were securely in the Democratic camp.[2] Nebraska's William Jennings Bryan, who represented the Democrats at the presidential level in both 1896 and 1900, appealed to his fundamentalist base by making skillful use of biblical and religious imagery. Although the "great commoner," as he was known, never won the presidency, he articulated the economic and cultural grievances of these western and southern farmers and small town merchants.

Less that two decades after Bryan's "Cross of Gold" speech, Woodrow Wilson, the son of a southern Presbyterian divine, captured the White House in 1912. (He beat both Republican nominees William Howard Taft and third party candidate Theodore Roosevelt.) Wilson echoed Bryan's moralistic impulse, though perhaps not his charisma. A southerner who had become a reform-minded governor of New Jersey and who was a compromise choice at the 1912 Democratic convention, Wilson demonstrated the type of regional and, even cultural, bargaining and compromise necessary on the road to the White House. A Princeton-educated semi-Populist, Wilson was free of Bryan's homespun liabilities, which did not play in the East, either among conservative business groups or Roman Catholics.

After Franklin Roosevelt, four of the five successful Democratic presidential candidates—Truman, Johnson, Carter and Clinton—have been southerners from "low" Protestant denominations. In fact, Clinton's national victory in 1992 and 1996 was a triumph, not of old-fashioned liberalism, but of his capacity to speak in traditional and even moralistic terms more convincingly than either the "high" and emotionally aloof Episcopalian George Bush or the stoic but tight-lipped Methodist Bob Dole.[3]

The fundamentalist style, however, had to be softened and modified for the simple reason that too much of it rocked the Democratic Party boat. Indeed, part of the code of American politics rests on the appeal to coalitions by crafting a generic message that meets specific needs but that does not appear overtly tied to one group or sectional interest. Historically, the Democratic Party rested on a coalition of these southern, rural Protestants and more urban Roman Catholics in the northeast. When fundamentalists became too politicized around values questions, it demonstrated the political tensions, not only within the Democratic Party, but also within the country as a whole.

The 1920s are not generally thought of as a period of political reform but it was during this period that fundamentalists flexed their political muscle and did so quite effectively. This offensive represented a recoil against earlier political reforms and ran parallel to a growing intellectual conservatism within the broad American religious establishment. In another sense, however, the fundamentalist reaction was also directed against a growing pluralism and even flux within American society itself. Historians differ about both the motives and the particular timing of fundamentalist agitation. It would, however, seem that three trends pushed fundamentalists and other groups in to an assertive political posture.

One trend was the growing prestige of science in intellectual life. Fundamentalists, conservative Roman Catholics and conservative Jews all faced competition from scientific theories, such as Darwinian evolution, that ran counter to biblical doctrines of Creationism. Presiding over an autonomous educational system, Roman Catholic authorities could contain the debate within their own domain. For their part, Jews were too few in number to constitute a national interest group that could affect debates about public education. Having no such parallel educational movement at the primary or secondary level and constituting an absolute majority in parts of the country, fundamentalists thus waged their denominational battles in the public-supported state-run institutions.

The fundamentalist offensive against evolutionism that crystallized in the Scopes Monkey Trial of 1925 ran parallel to a wider campaign against theological liberalism, so-called theological modernism within the Christian community.[4] Fundamentalists wanted to put an end to the easy theological interpretation and then fashionable political activism and instead reemphasize scripture. Their position mirrored that of conservative Roman Catholics and Jews in reasserting "orthodox" interpretations of the faith and checking theological liberalism of the previous generation. The Vatican, for example, had strongly rejected Americanism—the idea that the American Roman Catholic community had a particular commitment to ecumenical policies and thus a special autonomy from strict Papal authority. In blocking "Americanism," the Vatican had reasserted a doctrinally conservative line that would last until Vatican Council II in the 1960s.

In a broader and perhaps more subtle sense, fundamentalists were perplexed by the moral drift of society. It is hard to fully grasp in retrospect, but the 1920s marked a decisive break in American history. It was not only the period when urban Americans became the majority for the first time but when new ways of life—urban and consumerist—became the established patterns in popular culture. It was not so much social composition—although that was indeed important—but the growing secularization of public life that threatened fundamentalists.

Of all groups, these changes affected fundamentalists most sharply. Far more than Jews or Roman Catholics—who were compelled to assimilate into an American society already shaped by the religious assumptions of the Protestant majority—fundamentalists felt that their pristine, rural, pious America was under threat. Of course, such a society never existed but, as with all social images, it remained a powerful ideal. In the second and third decades of the twentieth century then, fundamentalists pursued two policies—nativism and temperance—to contain the perceived moral contamination of American society. While both policies were not doctrinal or denominational in the strictest sense, each demonstrated how questions of public morality could prove politically divisive.

First, 1920s nativism led to legislative reforms restricting immigration. Historians have suggested that anti-immigration sentiment was a last-gasp protest of rural America against an increasingly urbanized society. Other historians, however, have maintained that the push to restrict immigration illustrated a general fear of foreign subversive behavior, a fear that led to the famous "Palmer raids," and the Sacco-Vanzetti trial. This paranoia was perhaps an understandable reaction to turn of the century International Anarchism, but also the triumph of Soviet Bolshevism after the First World War; it was predictable that immigrants were seen as carriers of ideological subversion. In addition, 1920s nativism ran parallel to a new mood of isolationism after both the First World War and President Wilson's abortive, and tactically inept, push for U.S. involvement in the League of Nations.

It was also predictable that anti-immigration sentiment bled in to suspicion of immigrant groups: recently arrived Roman Catholic and Jews from southern and eastern Europe.[5] For the fundamentalist block, restricting immigration did not mean propagating the gospel from Congress or the White House; it did, however, imply keeping allegedly alien and somehow un-American religious practices (i.e., Popery or Jewish finance) away from these shores. It was thus a defensive type of reform that had a quasi-denominational undercurrent. There was also a darker side to 1920s nativsim. The Ku Klux Klan, for example, had its highest membership in these years and reached a certain level of respectability, marching even on to the grounds of the U.S. capitol. (A sexual scandal that implicated their Indiana-based leader subsequently caused membership to rapidly dwindle.)

The push for temperance was the second part of the fundamentalist reform project. Prohibition, in which "dry" reformers outlawed alcohol, was a direct manifestation of fundamentalists flexing their intraparty political muscle and thereby indirectly weakening the Democratic coalition. Although temperance has no literal basis in Judeo-Christian, as opposed to Muslim, scripture, it came to be associated as part of the cultural ethos of southern and midwestern fundamentalists. Within rural society, it took on a pseudo-confessional coloring since "rum" was subtly linked to "Romanism."[6] The schism played out even in Reagan's own family: Jack, the flamboyant roustabout drank with his cronies at the Knights of Columbus Hall and spent his life constantly battling the bottle whereas the pious and patient Nelle was a temperance crusader in an evangelical, temperance church.[7]

Inevitably, the push for prohibition brought about the speakeasy, the culture of illicit but dangerously exciting boozing, and the infiltration of organized crime into bootlegging. If anything, the moral fervor of the fundamentalists inaugurated a new period of moral laxity in the 1920s when hemlines shortened and consumption was the rage. Even the newly popularized Jazz carried an uninhibited and even vaguely sexual connotation. In the Manichean conflict between moral rectitude and perceived moral drift, the fundamentalist may have won the battle but they surely lost the war. Not surprisingly, fundamentalists retreated after the 1920s. Disillusioned, many hard-core fundamentalists simply withdrew from the public arena and pursued a self-conscious policy of separatism from the morally contaminated wider society.

Most immediately, the consequences of both nativism and temperance led to heightened tensions between fundamentalists and other parts of the Democratic coalition. The rise of New York's governor Al Smith, himself a Roman Catholic, as the Democratic presidential candidate in 1928 further widened schisms, even as Smith helped break the Republican electoral hold in the increasingly urbanized Northeast. Inevitably, conditions of the 1920s, a period of peace and prosperity, gave Republicans all three presidential elections in the years between the Wilson and Roosevelt administrations.

By 1932, Franklin Roosevelt, the Democratic vice presidential candidate of 1920 and Smith's fellow New Yorker, had managed to cobble together a winning Democratic coalition that lasted for more than a generation.[8] Nevertheless, Roosevelt probably could not have done so had the economic crisis of the 1930s not given a new lease on life to the fragmenting Democratic coalition. Economic survival, rather than moralistic qualms about conspicuous consumption, became the dominating political issue. Economically hard pressed during the Great Depression, westerners and southerners put aside cultural politics in favor of New Deal programs. The government repealed prohibition in 1933. With the endemic unemployment of the Great Depression, restricting immigration took on an economic, rather than an ethnic and thus confessional, dimension. The two issues that had divided fundamentalists from other groups thus disappeared from the political agenda.

After the Second World War, international, rather than purely domestic concerns, colored coalition politics. New political realities not only subsumed confessional differences but even created channels for political alliance. During the Cold War, for example, both rural fundamentalists and urban Roman Catholics enthusiastically supported the Cold War crusade against an atheistic Marxist-Leninism, the so-called Godless communism.[9]

In surveying the role of religious groups in the political process throughout the twentieth century, the dislocating and implosive role of the fundamentalists in the 1920s was perhaps the exception rather than the rule. In a pluralistic society, in which no one denomination predominates and never has even in colonial days, questions of public morality that echo too much of a partisan enthusiasm often become politically divisive. To acknowledge this does not imply that moral concerns have no role in political decisions; they do. Politicians, however, must articulate moral concerns in ways that can appeal to specific interest groups without alienating other blocks of voters. Consequently, generic "values questions" tend to take on an increasing importance. As such, the idea of civil religion—in which the flag, the constitution and the pledge of allegiance take on a pseudo-sacred character and in which American history itself takes on a quasi-providential purpose—becomes a kind of safe "code" for endorsing such values without being overtly specific.

The Moral Dimensions of Politics: The Culture Wars

In contemporary language, issues of public order, and even public morality, tend to be subsumed under the rubric of "values." This has the benefit of being a safe and even generic way of tapping into religious and communitarian values without offending particular groups.

American voters want their political leaders, and particularly their presidents, to espouse traditional and even religious values. It may seem contradictory, but voters want politicians to endorse religion in general without being specific about doctrinal issues: frequent church attendance is, after all, a political necessity for all presidential candidates and part of the unofficial code of American politics. This was as true in the 1950s—when prior to running for president, Eisenhower rediscovered his religious convictions after a long hiatus—as it is today. While it may be hypothetically possible for a self-proclaimed atheist or agnostic to rise to high political office, it also seems highly implausible.

Recent social flux has added a renewed urgency to these gestures. Politicians, particularly those on the right, found that "values" questions appealed to an increasingly worried electorate. In 1964, for example, Goldwater—an Episcopalian with a Jewish surname—was particularly effective in tapping into the sense of moral unease with the status quo. Richard Hofstadter noted that his themes of deteriorating family and community life perhaps played better to his core constituency than his hectoring tirades about rolling back communism.[10] Hofstadter further suggested that Goldwater's message played well among fundamentalists in both the south and west; indeed, Hofstadter, writing in 1964, implied that the rise of the New Right was a function of the growing political muscle of fundamentalist Christians themselves.

By 1966, the so-called counterculture had become a red-hot political issue—one that conservatives wisely exploited. The term "hippies," social nonconformists who let their hair and inhibitions down, entered the popular vocabulary; the young dropped out, tuned in and turned on; free speech became free love. Over time, the naive idealism of the folk revival gave way to the nihilistic indulgence and drug culture that permeated youth-based music. Psychedelia and tie-dye replaced the clean-cut image that seemed, to many, a type of corporate conformity.

Consequently, conservative politicians could play the "values" card in a general way that did not raise the specter of specific crusades built around specific policies. A large measure of Reagan's surprising success in his 1966 gubernatorial bid was in appealing to the cultural anxieties of middle-class Californians, who were understandably alarmed by campus unrest, urban riots and antiwar demonstrations. He appealed to those voters alarmed by trends and mystified by changing values. He reassured both bewildered conservatives and centrists alike.

Those same anxieties that rattled middle-class Californians in 1966 were magnified nationally in the 1968 elections. The demonstrations during the Chicago Democratic convention, as well as the assassinations of Martin Luther King Jr. and Robert F. Kennedy, left people feeling as if the very fabric of the American political order were tearing at the sides. Though less gifted in the art of reassurance than Reagan, Richard Nixon nonetheless tried, with some success, to fill that role. Making skillful use of themes he had touched on as early as 1961,[11] Richard Nixon in 1968 spoke of the "forgotten America" and the "silent majority"—the mass of the electorate that was allegedly ignored amid the agitation of discontented youth and radicalized dissent.[12]

The 1968 election established a pattern for Democratic-Republican presidential confrontations for the next two decades. In electoral terms, the so-called counterculture became a windfall for conservatives. Republicans adroitly identified themselves with mainstream values: patriotism, the work ethic, the family, organized religion, law and order and the military. The Democrats, by contrast, allowed themselves to be portrayed as the party of dissent, of welfare, of moral permissiveness, of values alien to the middle class. It was alleged to be the party, not of the silent majority, but of the vocal liberal minority at odds with mainstream morality. As with all stereotypes, the accusations against the Democrats combined elements of demagoguery and truth. As Christopher Lasch shrewdly noted, the left, which had penetrated the Democratic Party in the 1970s, seemed to have an intellectual quarrel with America.[13] The left, and by inference the Democrats, were on the wrong side of the cultural divide.

Many of the specific problems that had worried middle-class Americans gradually faded away. The issues that had dominated the election of 1968 had been contained by the mid-1970s. The riots had subsided, and the student protests petered out after the abolition of the military draft. Many of the ideas of the counterculture, however, permeated segments of American society and colored attitudes, particularly among the young—and this raised generalized questions about society's moral "health."

In these years, traditional institutions—the family, schools, organized religion, government—seemed to lose the prestige they once enjoyed. The root causes of this diminished authority were many. The war in Vietnam and the subsequent Watergate crisis, in which Nixon himself was forced to abdicate his office, contributed to a growing skepticism.[14] Affluence, with its attendant disaffection and ennui, also undermined older values; a degree of hedonism crept into American society. Recreational drug use rose among all sectors, traditional values were openly and deliberately flaunted, attitudes and mores that were previously taboo were celebrated and exhibited for public approval. Even the idea of what it meant to be "American" was subtly challenged, as it became fashionable to assert ethnicity, a hyphenated-Americanism.[15] Revisionist history, which became intellectually fashionable, predictably portrayed America as a corrupt and exploitive system. As they always do, revisionists themselves exaggerated and distorted their arguments in order to refute earlier biases.

For many, this culturally sanctioned "liberation" and the ethic of "doing one's own thing" blurred into an amoralistic culture of hedonism that stood in contrast to traditional morality inspired by Judeo-Christian values. Here we find a direct linkage between moral themes and policy drift. For many Americans, these unsettling trends merged with other concerns: a sense of declining power abroad, rising crime rates at home, a government that did not respond to their concerns yet taxed heavily. For conservatives, the failure of government and the sense of social drift merged into a rejection of the socially permissive agenda of the New Left. Indeed the New Left was a tempting target precisely because its proponents had been so openly dismissive of majoritarian values and the symbols of America's civil religion, such as the flag, the pledge of allegiance, the military and the courthouse.

Nathan Glazer argued that the "liberalizing trends" that emerged in the 1960s were somewhat deceptive[16] and not typical of majoritarian values in the 1970s and 1980s. Nonetheless, there was a significant divide, particularly in that American popular culture, that subtly glorified these "liberalizing" trends and undermined the older sources of tradition. Reflecting changing social mores, the media—films and television—seemed to offer increasingly graphic displays of violence, sex and even drug use, which would have been unheard of in the days of strict Hollywood censorship.

A cultural, if not political, backlash was perhaps inevitable, and it was Reagan's good fortune to be the ultimate political beneficiary of the trend. Indeed, the Watergate crisis left an unfortunate moral atmosphere that worked to Reagan's ultimate advantage. Alone among the devastated Republicans in 1974, Reagan manage to exude a sense of party purpose and conviction, even though he was half contemplating leaving the GOP. Reagan's strength was always in his capacity to sell his product and one of his products was the conservative message of "mainstream values." As biographer Lou Cannon noted, Watergate had brought America back to a reexamination of its first principles and these were the themes that Reagan, with his smiling and confident gift for anecdotes and his reverently patriotic gestures, handled so well.[17]

Nonetheless, Ford's appointment complicated Reagan's planned 1976 bid for the Republican nomination. This was the origin of his brief flirtation with the idea of challenging with a third party bid—an idea that Holmes Tuttle effectively squelched. Reagan was, after all, the darling of the GOP right wing; Ford had also chosen the centrist Nelson Rockefeller as his running mate and this was a red flag dangled in front of the Republican right wing. Rockefeller's problem was not simply that he was part of the East Coast establishment or that he was a centrist but, at bottom, a moral one. After his early 1960s divorce to marry his second wife, Rockefeller was always tainted with a hint of sexual innuendo and license; for the party faithful, compromised morals and dubious policies were a combustive combination.[18]

By 1976, Ford was compelled to change his vice presidential running mate from Rockefeller to Kansas senator Bob Dole, war hero, former Republican National Committee chairman and party loyalist par excellence. Ford's real problem was proximity to Richard Nixon. Never elected, appointed in conditions that to many seemed perilously close to a backroom deal, Ford lacked the stature necessary to be moralist in chief. A likable guy from Michigan, and a first-rate athlete, Ford also had a bumbling side that differed from Reagan's choreographed image and moral certainties. To compound matters, Mrs. Ford was politically tactless in her cavalier judgments about what was right and wrong: herself an admitted substance abuser, Betty Ford's casual pronouncements on so-called lifestyle matters, seemed to aggravate her husband's stature gap. Likable perhaps, Gerry Ford did not have the moralistic charisma that conservatives demanded. In 1976 Republicans had rallied around their man, but without great passion.

In 1976, Carter had won the presidential election in part by being an outsider to Washington, but also in part by his campaign against the secrecy and moral laxity that had characterized Nixon's and, by implication, Ford's administration. Honesty and integrity were to be hallmarks of the Carter presidency.

The Carter candidacy had actually been based on a repudiation of McGovern's 1972 campaign platform. Although he followed McGovern's outsider approach to capturing the party nomination, Carter nonetheless crafted a traditional Democratic strategy by forging an alliance between consumer and labor groups. Carter had thus tried to bridge the old gap between environmental lawyers and hard hats, between the Upper West Side and the Deep South. Carter's greatest trump card, however, was in the culture wars. With his conspicuous sanctimony, which soon became tiresome, he at least neutralized the charge against the McGovern forces—that of promiscuity and permissiveness—and drove a wedge into the opposing camp by linking Ford-Dole to the ethical compromises of the Watergate break-in, the lying, the phone taps, the slush fund, the CIA machinations in Chile, the bombings in Cambodia and the "un-American" diplomacy with the Soviets.

If Ford were somehow tainted, Carter was himself Mister Clean. A devout Southern Baptist, he was more sensitive than Ford to the moral dimensions of political reform. In 1976, Carter had mobilized those fundamentalists who had rejected politics and pursued "separatism"—a policy of isolation from the corruptions and compromises of the wider society. Entering the Baptist Church (which rejects infant baptism) at the age of eleven, Carter had taught Sunday school as an adult and served as a church deacon. After his Georgia gubernatorial bid in 1966 (the year Reagan was elected to the California state house), he experienced a personal crisis that led to his being "saved."[19]

Carter, in fact, had offered something for everybody in the Democratic coalition—he was tough on the Soviets but also wanted to stress human rights; he was the "born-again" politician who also wanted to give amnesty to Vietnam-era draft dodgers. In the broader political sense, Carter energized cultural conservatives, such as middle-class Roman Catholics, by emphasizing both family values and his opposition to abortion and mandatory busing. If elected, he promised to convene a conference on the family. It is easy to forget that, in 1976, Carter was supported by both televangelist Pat Robertson, himself the son of a Virginia senator, and conservative Roman Catholic activist Paul Weyrich, one of the founders of the Heritage Foundation and the Committee for a Free Congress.

The Carter years also marked the reemergence of fundamentalists—who had retreated after the 1920s—as a political interest group. With the changed moral climate in the 1960s and 1970s, and with the perception that traditional Judeo-Christian values were under siege, fundamentalists had become progressively politically active.[20] Although they had given unquestioned support to the Cold War, they took no direct leadership role nor did they challenge the basic premises of anti-Soviet containment. In domestic policy, by contrast, fundamentalists had become progressively alarmed by specific policy initiatives coming from Washington.

Through the 1970s, fundamentalists had put moral issues at the forefront of their agenda and did so in a way that was particularly appropriate to this time of vague and undefined moral crisis.[21] It would, however, be wrong to see the rise of the Religious or Christian Right as simply a replay of the 1920s experience, for both the message and messenger had changed in the half century between the Scopes Trial of 1925 and the election of Jimmy Carter in 1976. By the 1970s, fundamentalists had distanced themselves from the more unsavory associations of the past, such as the Klan, and adopted a more sophisticated and perhaps more subtle political argument that could appeal to conservative Roman Catholics who were also concerned about culturally sanctioned permissiveness and moral drift. In short, fundamentalists abandoned their old political liabilities.[22]

From Carter to Reagan: The Politics of Religion

Ironically, Carter's intimate connections to the newly politicized fundamentalist camp created a number of problems that gave Republicans the upper hand with the ascendant Religious Right. None of Carter's problems in isolation was truly significant, but taken as a whole they created a momentum in favor of Reagan, who outflanked Carter on cultural issues much as he outflanked him on the anti-Soviet stance.

One of Carter's problems was the style, not the content, of his religion. Although Americans want their politicians to obey the unwritten code of religion, there are certain styles that simply do not play in American politics and one of those was Carter's confessional style, which laid bare his moral failings. Garry Wills shrewdly described Carter and Reagan as fitting in to William James's typology of religious types.[23] Writing at the turn of the century, James had labeled Carter's style the psychology of the "sick soul"—a type more appropriate to Augustinian confessions rather than *Playboy* interviews. The spiritual wrestling of a Jimmy Carter creates doubts, not only in the voter himself, but also about the strengths of the leader. Carter's discussion of national malaise—a term he never used in the famous speech—nonetheless seemed to be a confession about the course of his own administration.

More congenial to democratic culture is James's "healthy-minded" religion—the superficially optimistic variant of salvation, as opposed to judgment religion. Americans want their political leaders to smile and reassure, to soothe and help overcome deeper anxieties in the body politic. Priggishly sanctimonious as a youth, inattentive to religion as an adult, Reagan had none of the doubts, introspection or even emotional commitment of the born-again Carter. Reagan exuded a sunny optimism. Indeed, the thought of Reagan reading Soren Kierkegaard or Reinhold Niebuhr, as Carter had done, seemed ludicrous. As with Franklin Roosevelt, Reagan was the proverbial healthy soul that did not enquire too deeply into spiritual matters.

Having drifted from his Disciples' background, Reagan's beliefs were always vague—but a reassuring vagueness was precisely what the public wanted. (He was, in fact, a member of the "society church," Bel Air Presbyterian.)[24] More to the point, Reagan's youthful religious pieties seemed to fade imperceptibly into political convictions that America was great, taxes too high, government wasteful, and communism wicked. Writing in 1969,

Garry Wills noted that Reagan's religion was simply "Goldwaterism." That was in large part the clue to his success—he spoke, not about the politics of religion, but about the religion of politics.[25]

Reagan spoke of politics with the authenticity of a heartfelt believer, which ironically put him beyond mere "politics." (Authenticity, rather than cleverly reasoned theology, was a cornerstone of the Religious Right.) Actually, he harbored some rather unorthodox beliefs: one about a nuclear Armageddon and another about astrology. Indeed, Ronald and particularly Nancy Reagan's interest in the astrological mumbo jumbo, which was used to determine the dates of both international summits and presidential debates, could also be seen as offensive to devout Christians. In religious matters, Reagan's handlers thus understood the importance of *not* "letting Reagan be Reagan."

Regardless, Reagan's greatest asset was not his personal religiosity but his perceived defense of religious values. Carter had never seemed to distinguish between the two, nor should he have in moral terms, but the packaging of a moral posture is quite different from moral reasoning itself. Consequently, fundamentalists were attracted to Reagan, not for the moral ardor of his faith, but for his perceived attack on social libertinism and the whole agenda of the 1960s. For the New Right, Reagan was a means to oust one of their own, Carter, who had strayed too close to liberal heresies. In politics, one tends to vote against rather than for, and the fundamentalist vote against Carter carried an element of political excommunication.

It would be wrong then to suggest, as the more histrionic observers on the left have, that Reagan had a symbiotic relationship with the New Right. With their fixation on ideology, liberal critics had failed to appreciate the nuances, and indeed tensions, within the American conservative movement. Liberal critics ignored the mundane calculations that politicians make in forging a coalition and then in conveniently dropping earlier pledges. The simple truth was that Reagan's relationship to the New Right rested on a few shared political instincts coupled to astute tactical endorsements. Indeed, campaign managers such as Jim Baker and Michael Deaver wanted Reagan to distance himself from too close an association with fundamentalists. Bucking their advice, Reagan did in fact speak at a Dallas convention of fundamentalists in April of 1980, but his speech was tepid and without rousing emotion. It was not vintage Reagan, but he already had their vote so there was no need to arouse moderates by stoking fundamentalist enthusiasm.

It was not so much that Reagan won over fundamentalists but that Carter had lost their support.[26] Indeed, one problem with Carter's courting of fundamentalists was the inevitable repercussion within his own Democratic coalition: it alienated liberals, who had failed to appreciate how necessary it was to make alliances with cultural conservatives in order for Democrats to win elections. Ronald Reagan and the Republican Party, by contrast, offered a more assertive and strident defense of traditional values for those fundamentalists who were themselves not enamored with left-wing Democratic activists. As in his support for anti-Soviet containment and cutting back the welfare state, Reagan's rhetoric on conservative moral themes was never ambiguous; supporters thus tended to endorse Reagan in a declaratory sense rather than in terms of specific policy initiatives.

Fundamentalists, however, were not simply a passive voting block to be won over; they themselves underwent something of a transformation in the years leading up to 1980. The Religious Right became, in the language of the time, a political action group, whose members came to play an influential role in the primary process and in local Republican organizations. Both Pat Robertson and Paul Weyrich, who had previously supported the then fiscally and culturally conservative Carter in 1976, actively campaigned for Reagan in 1980. The televangelist Jerry Falwell—head of the Lynchburg, Virginia-based Liberty Lobby—and political activists Richard Viguerie were both part of a broad cluster of religious conservatives who altered the political landscape in 1980. They helped register new voters; they organized at the local and state level; they followed the organizational methods that Gary Hart had utilized for McGovern in the early 1970s. The new religious conservatives were cohesive, disciplined and focused. They were highly sophisticated in the use of media and computerized mass mailings to propagate their message and raise money, and raise it they did.

In 1980, conservative Christian activists were also instrumental in targeting a number of liberal Democrats from the Senate, such as Birch Bayh of Indiana, Frank Church of Idaho, John Culver of Iowa, Warren Magnusson of Washington and George McGovern of South Dakota—all of whom lost their seats.[27] Gary Hart of Colorado was also heavily targeted but managed to hold on. These victories were instrumental in giving the Republicans control of the Senate in 1980—control that they had not enjoyed since 1952.

At the local level, religious conservatives had become energized by a cluster of issues, some of which had direct moral implications, whereas others simply touched on specific grievances of religious conservatives, such as tax exempt status of private schools and national education policy. In the largest sense, religious conservatives opposed those trends associated with the 1960s: the expansion of welfare services, greater government involvement in education policy, feminism, the "rights revolution," in which every vocal minority and interest group clamored for special status that set it apart from the "silent" but implicitly moral and conservative majority. This was a reinterpretation of old-fashioned populist themes in the context of the late 1970s: for New Right partisans, the people had become the repository of moral conservatism and culturally liberal elites and select minorities, who implicitly dominated the political process and pushed their own socially libertarian agenda. The "silent majority" of Goldwater and Nixon's speeches had, imperceptibly, become the "moral majority" of the 1980s

Unlike earlier fundamentalist jeremiads, which seemed like small-town ranting against big-city ways, this new suburban brand of religious conservatism was easy to pull into a wider coalition. In short, the moral critique of the Religious Right, against theological laxity and an aggressive social liberalism, blended in to a larger conservative offensive against waning moral fiber and intrusive government at home. How that played out in the policy realm during the Reagan years will form the subject of the next chapter.

Notes

1. Despite the language of frontier individualism, the West has been among the most strongly religious sections of the country. One need only look at the role of Mormonism and fundamentalist Christianity such as Reagan's own church, the Disciples of Christ. Given the loneliness and novelty of frontier life, religion and authoritarian values were necessary in the development of community. See Garry Wills, *Reagan's America: Innocents at Home* (Garden City, N.Y.: Doubleday and Company, 1987), 90.

2. Paul Allen Beck, "Incomplete Realignment: The Reagan Legacy for Parties and Elections," in *The Reagan Legacy*, Charles O. Jones, ed. (Chatham, N.J.: Chatham House Publications, 1988), 164.

3. Clinton's gushing moralistic enthusiasm masqueraded his moral inadequacies, but this too was part of the game. In 1992, Clinton played on the powerful themes of sin and moral confession. Whereas the Connecticut-born Bush—with his western boots and affected taste for pork rinds—seemed a sham westerner, Clinton's gaudy display of "imperfection" and "fallenness" on one hand and sugary displays of contrite redemption on the other made him the perfect Country and Western candidate for the 1990s. Improbably, Clinton actually turned "cheatin'" into a winning political formula.

By 1996, the endless repetition of song wore thin. Fortunately for the Democrats, Dole proved emotionally tone-deaf to the political possibilities of spiritual exhibitionism.

4. William Jennings Bryan, the old Populist warhorse, argued on behalf of the Creationists in the Scopes Monkey Trial.

5. In a more muted way, the "nativist"-immigrant divide played out within the Jewish and Roman Catholic communities. In the Jewish community, the divide pitted older "westernized" German Jews against the more recent immigrants from eastern Europe. In the Roman Catholic community, the divide pitted nineteenth-century ethnic groups—the Irish and Germans, both of whom controlled the church hierarchy—against more recent ethnic groups from eastern and southern Europe.

6. On the anti-Catholic bias of fundamentalism, see Richard Hofstadter, *The Paranoid Style in American Politics and Other Essays* (Chicago, Ill.: The University of Chicago Press, 1965: Phoenix Edition, 1973), 74.

7. The Temperance movement's energetic leader, Carrie Nation, was herself a member of the Disciples of Christ—Nelle Reagan's congregation.

8. Hofstadter, *Paranoid Style*, 78.

9. Hofstadter, *Paranoid Style*, 74.

10. Hofstadter, *Paranoid Style*, 116-117.

11. Garry Wills, *Nixon Agonistes: The Crisis of the Self-Made Man* (Boston: Houghton Mifflin, 1970), 25.

12. As Garry Wills suggested, Nixon was never a convincing moralist. Again, parentage offers clues. Neither the inward rectitude of Hannah Nixon's Society of Friends nor the "black-Irish" combativeness of Frank Nixon's "bible-thumping" Methodism played in the political arena, where rectitude appears distant and militancy raises anxieties.

Buoyant, positive thinking faith is what plays and, in this, Nixon never had the political "grace" necessary to make these themes come alive as Reagan could. Indeed, Nixon lacked Reagan's public voice but also stature as a cultural conservative. Nixon's defense of mainstream values—the silent majority, the forgotten America—had an element of siege to it. With his rhetorical flatness and the fact that his whole demeanor was given over to striving and an almost resentful struggle, Nixon subtly compounded the insecurities of the silent majority. Even before Watergate, Nixon lacked a halo.

13. Christopher Lasch, *The True and Only Heaven: Progress and Its Critics* (New York: W.W. Norton and Co., 1991), 35.

14. Lasch, *The True and Only Heaven*, 30.

15. Daniel Bell, "The End of American Exceptionalism," in The American Commonwealth, ed. Nathan Glazer and Irving Kristol (New York: Basic Books, 1976), 210.

16. Nathan Glazer, "The Social Agenda," *Perspectives on the Reagan Years*, ed. John L. Palmer (Washington, D.C.: Urban Institute Press, 1986), 18.

17. Lou Cannon, *Reagan*, (New York: G.P. Putnam's Sons, 1982), 188.

18. In terms of the generational morality play, Nelson Rockefeller had fallen from the godly discipline of his grandfather, John D., the strict Northern Baptist from Cleveland who taught Sunday school, gave heavily to his church and came to control the nation's oil industry by ruthlessly undercutting rivals. Americans have an abiding admiration for self-willed capitalists who make money the old-fashioned way—aggressively. Americans, however, have less admiration for passively inherited wealth as vaguely aristocratic and somehow ungodly. Unlike his grandfather, who seemed to personify Max Weber's idealization of the ascetic Protestant capitalist driven by an other-worldly desire to accumulate, Nelson Rockefeller seemed more interested in modern art and in being popular.

19. Personal redemption, being "born again," is a tenet of fundamentalism. After the "conversion," the believer accepts Jesus Christ, not church authorities, historical traditions, or intermediaries such as priests or pastors, as the only path to personal redemption.

20. As in the 1920s, fundamentalists in the 1970s railed against scriptural laxity and the political agenda of theological modernists. For many conservatives, religious

leaders were more interested in a liberal political agenda than in spreading the gospel of Jesus Christ. In a related vein, church membership in "mainline" Protestant denominations dwindled but rose significantly in those denominations that leaned to stricter biblical interpretations.

Trends within Protestant churches ran parallel to the renewed theological conservatism of the Vatican: in the late 1970s and early 1980s, Pope John Paul II demonstrated displeasure with "liberation theology," which was shot through with overtly political and redistributive concerns.

21. Glazer, "The Social Agenda," 23.

22. Glazer, "The Social Agenda," 24.

23. Wills, *Reagan's America*, 198.

24. Rowland Evans and Robert D. Novak, *The Reagan Revolution* (New York: E. P. Dutton, 1981), 209.

25. John B. Judis explored this point in *Grand Illusions: Critics and Champions of the American Century* (New York: Farrar, Straus and Giroux, 1992), 232-233.

26. By the summer of 1980, Carter was compelled to move further to the left in order to shore up support with party activists. Through the winter and early spring of 1980, Carter had to beat back the primary challenge of Ted Kennedy, the *bette noire* of the Religious Right, who shared with Rockefeller a mixture of moneyed background, liberal politics and sexual innuendo. In order to outflank Kennedy, the brother of two Democratic Party giants, Carter was forced to the left. In the process of becoming a "born-again liberal," Carter's conservative base increasingly left him.

27. Haynes Johnson, *Sleepwalking through History* (New York: W.W. Norton, 1991), 208; Schaller, *Reckoning with Reagan*, 23.

Chapter 15

The Reagan Years:
The Paradox of the Non-Revolution

Politicians often advertise their support for those issues near to the hearts of factions central to victory but they also phrase their support in general terms. The opponent's failings are always specified; counterproposals, however, are often couched in terms of platitude such as "cleaning up the mess" or the "building a bridge to the future..." Although one could trace Reagan's shifting positions on unrestricted abortion, homosexual rights and pornography,[1] his declaratory support for the social agenda was never meant to be specific. Instead, Reagan gave his official blessing to "family values"—a loose cluster of ideas that most American voters support in the abstract. As with Nixon, he arrayed himself on the right side of the cultural divide and portrayed his opponents as, not only out of touch with the people, but also as the intellectual prisoners of elite liberal academies.

It was a winning formula for conservative populism in the 1980s, but the White House handlers were not about to risk Reagan's national popularity by too close an identification with members of the New Right. Indeed, the only real member of the New or Religious Right in Reagan's cabinet was James Watt, who experienced a religious conversion in 1964 and sent his children to the Oklahoma fundamentalist school, Oral Roberts University. The cultural rift between Watt—personally abstemious, sanctimonious but relatively middle-class—and the other more affluent and sophisticated members of the cabinet was telling.

In fact, the de-emphasis of the social agenda was a deliberate policy on the part of both Jim Baker and Michael Deaver, who felt that social issues risked precious political capital and detracted from more important economic questions. The new Senate Majority leader, Howard Baker of Tennessee, endorsed the strategy—one that became a convenient excuse, if not smokescreen, for a White House that had no intention to commit the president to a bold legislative agenda addressing specific issues touching on potentially divisive moral themes. Nonetheless, there were a number of relatively simple gestures that Reagan could provide to placate the New Right—gestures that Jimmy Carter, captive to a center-left coalition, had not been able to provide.

Unlike previous chapters—where policy could be analyzed from a single agency or cabinet department or a cluster of related agencies—the moral dimensions of policy are not localized. There is no Department of Moral Affairs (although there is a supervisory office of ethics, which performs a limited role in internally policing the White House). Consequently, the study of the moral dimension of policy entails an examination of policy throughout the administration; it involves retreading ground covered in previous chapters but examining issues in a different light. The following examination is thus not so much a study of policy in various functional areas as a number of vignettes that examine how the moral argument and concerns played into judicial, educational, drug, foreign and economic policy.

Toward a Conservative Judiciary

Reagan's power to appoint federal judges was perhaps the most direct way to appeal to the Religious Right. In a society where the written constitution has become the semisacred scripture of America' civil religion, moral issues often become legal ones. Issues as diverse as school prayer, school choice, and abortion rights have both religious and judicial implications. Consequently, the push for a more conservative judiciary hit a chord with most conservatives—fundamentalists and nonfundamentalists alike.[2]

Indeed, for many religious conservatives, a strict interpretation of the constitution was tantamount to scriptural literalism against meddling modernists spreading an agenda that may have been fashionable in some circles but that also subtly subverted the moral order of society. Conservative judicial interpretations seemed to buttress conservative theological interpretations; put alternately, attacking judicial activism was a way to attack the cultural legacy of the 1960s.

Opposition to a liberal judiciary was thus one of the most potent political charges for a conservative candidate in the 1970s and 1980s. For conservatives in general, a liberal judiciary corresponded to an intellectual drift on the left that emphasized procedural, administrative and legal remedies to correct perceived social and political problems. For critics, this was a type of interference in the political process reminiscent of planning and statist paternalism. For more populist conservatives, it was a signal that liberals, who could not win elections, could nonetheless nullify their political unpopularity by "capturing" the judiciary. Indeed, many conservative critics hinted that a liberal judiciary was even antidemocratic, for liberal judges subverted the will of the implicitly conservative majority.[3]

For religious conservatives, opposition to a liberal judiciary thus hit on a number of overlapping themes. A liberal judiciary, after all, endorsed civil libertarianism and if this were pushed to extremes, it could allegedly undermine the values of the majority. Liberal jurists had outlawed school prayer—a prohibition that was tacitly ignored in many parts of the Deep South. Under the cover of legal rights, a liberal judiciary protected pornographers, abortionists and criminals, people whose ideas and activities were not simply un-American but indeed did damage to the moral traditions of society. These gut assumptions need not be sophisticated legal opinions, nor need they be gems of intellectual reasoning that often characterizes the legal opinions of the higher courts. They needed, however, to resonate with the populace and, in the 1970s and 1980s conservatives were far more mobilized in changing the nature of the courts than liberals were in defending those same courts. It would thus be a mistake to treat Reagan's pledge for a more conservative judiciary in issue-specific terms; the strength of his promise was in general political and even vaguely moral terms.

Ronald Reagan was eminently successful in appointing conservatives to the federal bench. After Franklin Roosevelt, he appointed a higher number of federal judges and a larger percentage of the federal judiciary than any other modern president.[4] Unlike Jimmy Carter, who appointed no Supreme Court justices, Reagan appointed three: Justices O'Connor, Scalia and Kennedy. He also appointed the Stanford-educated William Rhenquist of Arizona—a long-time Goldwater associate, a Nixon appointee and the high court's most conservative member—as chief justice. For the Reagan White House, this was the winning political formula: appoint a conservative judiciary and keep the White House out of the specifics of social legislation. In fact, the abortion issue provided the best example of this deliberate but politically rewarding strategy.

Neither Reagan nor his wife was avid pro-lifers.[5] As governor, Reagan had in fact signed the most liberal abortion law in California history and did so on the medical advice of his father-in-law, Dr. Loyal Davis. Nonetheless, he did so despite opposition from Roman Catholic leaders. In retrospect, Reagan claimed the bill was a terrible mistake. With his penchant for blaming others for his own choices and thereby evading issues, he claimed that California doctors had used the medical pretext as a ruse for providing abortion on demand. The real truth was that Reagan's later commitment to the pro-life position was probably typical of the type of gestures that Republicans had to make in order to cater to pro-lifers who carried a great deal of clout at the grassroots level and in the primaries. (George Bush, for example, switched positions in the 1980s and went from being pro-choice to pro-life.)

During the 1980 campaign, Reagan had appealed to the fundamentalist and Catholic vote by signaling his opposition to unrestricted abortion rights. The chronology is important. When George Bush had bested Reagan in the early Iowa primary, the Reagan campaign was running scared. Immediately, Reagan tried to appeal to pro-life forces who would play a key role in the upcoming primary in New Hampshire, a state with a strong pro-life contingent: Reagan pledged his support for a constitutional amendment to outlaw abortion.[6] After the election, however, James Baker and Michael Deaver were careful to distance Reagan from the pro-life movement. Reagan was never photographed with pro-life partisans nor did he ever attend a pro-life rally. There was no reason to believe that he was averse to this, but it helped to create a useful fiction that White House "handlers" were insulating Reagan from the pro-life grass roots that had helped put him in office.

The best example of the administration's calculated distance from the pro-life agenda came in the nomination of Sandra Day O'Connor, who actively supported abortion rights as expressed in the Supreme Court ruling, *Roe v. Wade*.[7] A Southwest native and a Stanford graduate, O'Connor also came from a well-established ranching family. Long associated with Arizona politics, she, along with Rhenquist, had been a volunteer in Goldwater's 1958 Senate campaign. It was perhaps inevitable that she and dilettante rancher Ronald Reagan would develop quick and cordial relations. On the 1980 campaign trail, Reagan had promised to appoint the nation's first female Supreme Court justice; in keeping his pledge he conveniently overlooked O'Connor's position on abortion rights.

The appointment alienated many who thought Reagan's commitment to rolling back abortion rights was genuine. Pro-lifers could see this as disingenuous and cynical, but Reagan also understood that the pro-life group, though strong in the Republican rank and file, was a minority voice in the electorate. They were expendable and, moreover, not about to bolt to the Democrats, the alleged party of the pro-choice feminists who wanted unrestricted abortion on demand. Given O'Connor's stand on abortion, Moral Majority leader Falwell suggested that every good Christian should be concerned. Defending his old protege O'Connor, Barry Goldwater retorted that "every good Christian should kick Falwell in the ass."[8]

In the end, the administration's coy opposition to unrestricted abortion rights in the abstract coupled to its studied avoidance of the issue was a shrewd move. Through its policy inaction, the administration actually pursued a compromise position between the extremes of the pro-choice and pro-life forces: in effect, a middle ground that most voters would fit in to. While many of these swing voters were turned off by Phyllis Schlafly, the pro-choice moral crusader, many were equally turned off by staunch feminists who opposed any restriction on abortion—parental warnings, third trimester operations—as an assault on women's rights and an alleged backlash against feminism. Indeed, many feminists became their own worst enemies by alienating family oriented women who may have been pro-choice but nonetheless resented the high-handed dismissal of conservative cultural concerns.

Education Policy: Putting Values Back in the Classroom?

Education is not normally considered a question directly touching on public morality, but by the late 1970s it became an issue of deep concern to fundamentalists and, to a lesser extent, Roman Catholics.

Throughout American history, the classroom played an important role in shaping the moral tone of society. In the earliest days of the Republic, schools trained both an educated clergy and a religiously literate lay population. Indeed, the origin of America's oldest and most esteemed universities was to train those who would propagate the Protestant gospel in the New Jerusalem. Although primary and secondary education was, by the nineteenth century, brought under the aegis of the state at the local level, it would be mistaken to suggest that state-supported education was thoroughly secularized. Bible study and moral teaching, derived from the Judeo-Christian tradition and colored by generalized Protestant assumptions, were part of the curriculum.

Private, religious schools, of course, continued to coexist alongside state-funded institutions. For Roman Catholic authorities, in particular, parochial schools provided an anchoring institution for dislocated immigrant groups. For the church, parochial education was a way of evangelizing to new groups, many of whom came from countries where Catholicism was relatively weak among the lower classes.[9]

At the turn of the century, fundamentalists themselves established a number of Bible colleges, and it was only later that they concentrated on the lower level of the education system. In a curious way, the same process by which Roman Catholics had created a private educational system played out among southern fundamentalists in the years after 1960—years when private, religious academies proliferated throughout the South. Critics have rightly pointed to this phenomenon as an example of "White flight" from federally mandated desegregation injunctions. In a deeper sense, however, the phenomenon was part of a larger trend: fundamentalists retreating from what they believed to be alien and permissive cultural values imposed on them. It was a move consistent with the idea of fundamentalist internal isolation of the 1920s and 1930s. For them, private education approximated the older Roman Catholic idea of private education as a form of autonomy and even resistance against the larger assimilative tendencies of the majority society. If the parochial schools had been bulwarks of conservative Catholicism against liberalizing "Americanization," fundamentalists academies had, by the 1970s, become shelters against a perceived "secularism" and against a public school system that prohibited prayer but fostered the teaching of evolution and even sexual behavior.

Complicating this situation was the issue of federally mandated school bussing as corrective policy to correct the legacy of racial segregation. For conservative critics, however, school bussing was not only of the type of social engineering that was symptomatic of the whole 1960s reform project, but the kind of legal-based remedy that liberal activists of the 1970s had favored. It also raised political tensions between both White ethnics and White southerners on one hand and Blacks on the other and helped further fragment the Democratic coalition and cement Republican gains. In a deeper sense, mandatory bussing was typical of the high-handed liberal reformism of the 1960s, for liberals had grown cavalier, not only about community values, but about the conservative attachment to neighborhood and community. Indeed, there was a pernicious class element to mandatory bussing since relatively liberal legislators, who tended to favor mandatory bussing in the abstract, often insulated their own children from the institutional upheavals that accompanied the transition by sending them to elite private schools.

Although there was indeed an element of racism in the antibussing movement, liberals misjudged the depth of conservative sentiment. Even Democrat Jimmy Carter, who did in fact send his daughter to an inner-city public school, opposed the policy. In a recoil against both bussing but also the waning discipline in the public schools, many tradition-minded parents chose private and often religious schools over public education. Inevitably, it was parochial schools and the newly created private academies in the South, many of which mandated Bible study, that absorbed the defection from the public schools.

The push for private, and religious, education raised another public policy issue and that was the tax-exempt status of private schools. Southern fundamentalists, rather than Roman Catholic authorities, were particularly energized by this issue. Here was where the issue of racial segregation, always latent in the "White flight," crept back in to the discourse. Indeed, during the Carter administration the Internal Revenue Service challenged the tax-exempt status of many southern private schools on the very grounds that they were discriminatory. One of the main cases involved Bob Jones University, a strictly fundamentalist school in Greenville, South Carolina. The Carter administration had urged that the institution be denied tax-exempt status because, on biblical grounds, it had prohibited interracial dating.[10]

Inevitably, fundamentalists interpreted this as an instance of harassment by the Carter-administration. Indeed, Carter had created a separate Department of Education in 1979 by expanding one branch of the older Department of Health Education and Welfare. For conservative critics, this was simply another example of an intrusive educational bureaucracy that told communities what to do and how to do it. Trying to shore up his Democratic coalition for the 1980 election, Carter could claim that he fulfilled a campaign promise—one made to the politically powerful teacher's union, part of the expanding service sector of union members—which favored the creation of an independent agency.

For his part, Reagan campaigned to abolish the Carter-era Department of Education. Reagan's maneuver was not simply a naked appeal to the Religious Right but one made to all cultural conservatives who felt that federal involvement in education involved interfering with community standards.[11] Attacking the Department of Education was thus a way of killing two birds with one ideological stone: it was a way to attack both interfering Washington bureaucrats but also liberal ideologues who forced a permissive social agenda on hardworking taxpayers. The strength of this emotional appeal was precisely in its all-consuming vagueness.

Nonetheless, Reagan's casual and almost cavalier promise to abolish the Carter-created Department of Education was typical of his campaign rhetoric. Although the White House did not eliminate the department, it cut the staff and scaled back the mandate. With prodding from David Stockman, the White House cut education block grants to the states from $5.5 billion to $1.5 billion.[12] Cutting funding was a simple and politically expedient way of whittling down the agency's scope without negotiating an alternative system with fifty different state governors. Nonetheless, it was one thing to attack Carter's big-government policies while on the campaign trail but quite another to dismantle agencies that, after all, exist because the federal government performs a function that, for better or worse, state and local agencies have come to depend upon. The Department of Education stayed.

Reagan was never terribly interested in education policy or who was appointed to the Education Department. In fact, the White House had actually angered the Religious Right by appointing the Utah educator Terrell Bell as education secretary. A veteran of the Nixon-Ford White House, Bell was an educator who favored school bussing and had even supported the creation of the cabinet level Education Department. The second choice of the administration, Bell's appointment was clearly not in keeping with Reagan's bold rhetoric of departmental rollback. Bell, however, was supported by two Utah senators, Jake

Garn and Orrin Hatch, both of whom were popular with the Religious Right, so there was at least the appearance of consensus-building in the appointment.

What the administration did offer the New Right was a key subcabinet post—the post that was devoted to nonpublic education. In this slot, the administration tapped the Reverend Robert Billings, a Baptist clergyman and an early founder of what later became the Moral Majority. Bell, however, resisted the appointment and later undercut Billings. Since Billings was not appointed until after the inauguration, Bell gave a Carter-era holdover control in the interim—and the interim continued indefinitely. With the probable encouragement of the White House handlers, Bell froze out Billings, whose appointment was actually opposed by most career bureaucrats at Education and indeed, by Roman Catholic educational authorities. Quite by coincidence, Billings came across an internal memo that indicated he was to be kept away from the undersecretary position. He subsequently resigned his post.

The sham appointment of Billings was typical of the tease and promise reform that the administration played with certain New Right groups. Although there may have been a good argument for reneging on casual promises to encourage educational autonomy of certain religious groups, or to promote policies such a school vouchers that might further erode public education, the manipulative tactics of the administration suggested a clear disjunction between flattery on the campaign trail and actual policies. Perhaps the administration was unwilling to have a genuine debate on education precisely because it might demonstrate the Reagan administration's continuities with Carter-era policy or, worse, the lamentable state of American education. In fact, the most damning criticism of the nation's schools came from a 1983 report, *A Nation at Risk*, the findings of a commission directed by Terrell Bell himself. In one sense, the report could be seen as a cry for help from the secretary of education, but beyond rhetorical concern, Reagan was uninterested in education policy and could just as easily ignore the issue, much as he had once carelessly pledged to abolish the whole agency.

In 1985, the administration appointed William J. Bennet as secretary of education to replace Bell, who had resigned his post. Bennet, who would go on to be drug czar in the Bush administration, was an articulate advocate for renewing traditional values as well as improving educational standards. A conservative, though not a member of the Religious Right, Bennet's appointment also illustrated the symbolic value of conservative appointments.

One could say that Education policy was consistent with Reagan's overall attitude about governing, that is, one of removing government involvement in social affairs and letting others fill in the gaps. Even a measure of institutional retreat, however, involves leadership. Candidate Reagan may have talked tough on Carter's educational policy, but once in Washington he gave it little thought nor did the White House staff view it as important. To do any more would involve a debate, negotiating with various groups and the expenditure of political capital if not energy. In absence of that, there was relatively little either Bell or Bennet could do other than dramatize the deteriorating conditions of U.S. education.

Drug Policy: The New Temperance?

In contrast to education, drug policy was an issue with a clear, unambiguous course of action—one that did not require political brokering or the expenditure of political capital. Concrete accomplishments would yield immediate political payoff and antagonize only extreme civil libertarians and perhaps the marijuana legalization lobby. Indeed, a concerted antidrug policy, aimed at reducing both supply and demand, was the type of issue that could appeal to both religious conservatives but also to suburban moderates worried about crime and public safety. In contrast to the abortion issue, an antidrug policy was without political controversy.

Under Attorney General William French Smith, the administration took an activist approach to drug interdiction. Part of Reagan's Kitchen Cabinet in Sacramento, Smith was widely dismissed by many as a society lawyer interested in the round of Washington cocktail parties and lining his resume. A crony of Frank Sinatra, Smith pleaded ignorance to the crooner's alleged ties to organized crime. Despite the negative press, Smith, a Harvard-trained lawyer, was a capable albeit low-key administrator who presided over a relatively effective drug enforcement policy. In the second Reagan term, Smith chose to return to California and was replaced by White House counselor Ed Meese, a former prosecutor in Alameda County, California, and generally thought to be one of the staunch conservatives within the Reagan entourage. Meese's migration from the White House inner sanctum to the cabinet mirrored Baker's move to Treasury. (Both men were, in fact, burned out by the constant demands of handling Reagan and the attendant daily need for political damage control.) While Meese supervised an ambitious series of drug hauls, his administration was itself mired in ethical problems that eventually forced him from office. Morale deteriorated and appointees resigned.

Overshadowing the Justice Department's policy to control the supply of illegal drugs entering American borders, Nancy Reagan's "just say no" campaign for drug temperance attempted to deal with the demand for drugs, particularly among the young. For conservatives, recreational drug use was one of the most pernicious legacies of the 1960s, when the inward oriented subculture of the day popularized the use of drugs as an antidote to middle-class conformity. The words and phrases "trip," "stoned," "tuning in," "grass" all imperceptibly entered popular culture, which increasingly celebrated socially nonconformist behavior.

When the full-blown excesses of the 1960s had subsided, when tie-dye and sandals disappeared and when the self-styled communards started re-entering the "system," the drug culture nonetheless remained. Indeed, it merged into the fashionable ethos of the 1970s, which was a time of hedonism without communal idealism, an Epicurean gratification of the senses in the name of the pleasure principle, not of some other cause. In a sense, it was the worst of the 1960s but without its nobler aspects. Drug, particularly "designer" drug, use seemed part of the new disco subculture.

With her "just say no" campaign and the pledge for "zero-tolerance," First Lady Nancy Reagan began to articulate a moral disapproval of drug use that had theretofore been absent from the White House. Public campaigns in the 1970s had still focused on kids as experimental glue sniffers, but the social problem was of a greater magnitude. In a subtle way, liberal elites also tended to frown on drug temperance as overtly moralistic or even alarmist. Although it would be wrong to suggest that drug use had been sanctioned, the social taboos against its use had, however, been eased.

The "just say no" campaign was an attempt to reimpose social taboos that had been loosened during the 1960s and 1970s. Nonetheless, the campaign was a flawed one. First, it was aimed at people who had not started to experiment, and ignored those who had. Second, it ignored the ghetto problem of drugs, where the penalties but also incentives for involvement in the drug business, were infinitely higher than in the safe, suburban world.

The suburban youth was, after all, rarely penalized for his peccadilloes; in the ghetto, by contrast, the price of such experimentation ran all kinds of risks, not only from the police but from gangs that performed surrogate social roles and became a perverse outlet for entrepreneurial behavior and thus accentuated a vicious circle of illegal activity and communal violence. These trends were aggravated in the mid-1980s when crack cocaine, a cheap form of the drug, flooded the market and created a new market niche. Crime, to paraphrase Daniel Bell, became a form of social mobility.

Critics could argue that Nancy Reagan's campaign was a socially useful, and perhaps necessary, form of preaching to an easy chorus—a first step, it is true, but hardly the stuff of substantive policy. It was easy to scoff at this type of official disapproval as a Band-Aid where radical surgery was required. As with education policy, the administration was frugal with funding, and funding was necessary to expand the institutional apparatus to wage the so-called war on drugs. Looked at in retrospect, however, Nancy Reagan's campaign represented something that has been absent from the subsequent two administrations. It perhaps is no accident that drug use, which fell during the years of "just say no" temperance, started to rise again in the late 1980s.[13]

Unlike his later successors, Reagan and his wife stood firm on the drug issue and "standing firm" counted for something in the cultural war against the celebration of marijuana and hard drugs that is often discreetly glorified in popular culture. Much of it may have been symbolic, but simple symbolism counts for much in politics—something that Bill Clinton understands on the issue of drugs, which he handled only by having an aggressive antitobacco campaign.[14]

Foreign Policy: The Good Fight

America's relation to the world has always played a complicated role in the conservative social vision of the domestic order. Colonial theologian Jonathan Edwards's "Shining City on a Hill," the idea of the New Jerusalem, was that America was the Promised Land, free of the moral compromises and the corrupt ambitions of the Old World. In a metaphorical sense, Americans were the new Hebrews who had made their covenant with the Lord and were, in some senses, His new "chosen" people.

Like British non-Conformists in the nineteenth century, fundamentalists have traditionally looked askance at balance of power politics and foreign entanglements. War and diplomacy was the sport of a frivolous aristocracy or an effete Diplomatic Corps; in America, or so fundamentalists alleged, it was the game played by the "Eastern establishment" types who were ignorant of the heartland, sported mock-British accents and wore "striped pants." The central point here was that certain groups—such as fundamentalists in the Midwest and South, and Irish- and German-American ethnics in the Midwest and Northeast—leaned toward isolationism in the first half of the twentieth century. It was telling that some of these groups lent their support to the Cold War and, more importantly, to the morally charged search for internal subversion that was associated with the career of Wisconsin senator Joseph McCarthy, himself a Roman Catholic who began his career representing a heavily Roman Catholic and German-American district.

Indeed, the Cold War helped break down the walls of mutual suspicion between culturally conservative fundamentalists on one hand and ethnic Roman Catholics on the other; it represented the type of domestic alliance politics that energized, rather than divided cultural conservatives. The political alliance of Richard Nixon, of mixed Quaker and Methodist background, and the Baltimore-based Roman Catholic priest Father Cronin in the early days of the Alger Hiss trial perfectly demonstrated this type of conservative alliance that cut across sectarian lines. Because of his Cold War credentials, Nixon had retained close ties to the Roman Catholic hierarchy. It was fitting that Cardinal Spellman, then the nation's leading Roman Catholic leader and a fervent supporter of anti-Soviet containment, openly endorsed Richard Nixon over John F. Kennedy in the 1960 presidential race.

Indeed, the Cold War crusade appealed to previously isolationist constituencies because it meant fighting the good fight against an atheistic, totalitarian foe: the Cold War conflict channeled the isolationist elements that were always latent in fundamentalism and among several Roman Catholic groups (Irish- and German-Americans) into a Manichean struggle against a militantly secular ideology. In doing so, Americans projected their own domestic order, and even tensions, abroad. In the words of Reinhold Niebuhr, the conflict involved the children of light fighting the totalitarian children of darkness. (The intellectually complex Niebuhr could be selectively quoted by both the left and the right.)

Anti-Soviet containment and permanent military alliance thus drew upon substantial bipartisan support in these years precisely because it brought together national security concerns in to a quasi-revivalist project that was shot through with those moralistic themes important to key interest groups. Indeed, American political leaders flattered the electorate with a sense of providential mission in the coming clash of civilizations. Harry Truman's secretary of state Dean Acheson, the son of the Episcopal bishop of Connecticut, had articulated a pseudo-messianic justification to American overseas commitment. Allen Welsh Dulles, head of the Central Intelligence Agency under Eisenhower and his brother, the moralistic secretary of state John Foster, were the sons of a New York Presbyterian clergyman; both of the Dulles brothers brought "high" Calvinistic rectitude to the world of cloak and dagger diplomacy. If anything, "lace-curtain" Roman Catholics played an even more prominent role in the Intelligence and National Security brotherhood—an almost Jesuit-like fraternity that required equal measure of patriotic zeal and clever casuistry.[15]

In different ways, the experience of Vietnam and the subsequent détente with the Soviets in the 1970s snapped the older connection between moral imperatives and foreign policy. The Vietnam War created divisions on the home front and even generated qualms about the moral rightness of American involvement in a war where the lines between military and civilian populations were blurred. Increasingly, the older language of the 1950s that was used to justify the Vietnam conflict rang hollow.

In a predictable change of tactics, both Nixon and Kissinger no longer spoke in terms of the Munich analogy, the domino theory, the moral imperatives of fighting a "Godless communism," but in the more sophisticated and pseudo-academic language of credibility, calibration, parallel-track negotiation and multilateral talks. Although Kissinger's language and style captivated many in the media, it also alienated those groups that found no moral resonance in this doctored up "geostrategy." Indeed, the whole trend of Nixon's conservative statecraft—an emotionally uninspiring type of operational balancing and even subtle moral equivalency between the United States and the Soviet Union—was directly offensive to many who had lent support to the Cold War crusade. This, more than anything, explained Reagan's success in the late 1970s, when he scored points against Ford and Carter for being "soft" on the Soviets and "selling America short." It was inevitable, then, that Reagan's stirring Cold War revivalism played to both conservative Roman Catholics and fundamentalists in 1980.

For Roman Catholic ethnic voters, Reagan's anti-Soviet stance had the double advantage of being identified with national liberation struggles in Soviet-occupied Poland, Hungary, Ukraine and the Baltics. In the 1980s, Reagan seemed to be one-half of the declaratory offensive against the Kremlin; the other half emanated from the Vatican, where the Polish-born pontiff waged a veritable moral crusade, not only against perceived Polish quislings installed after the 1980 coup d'etat, but also against the system of "atheistic Marxism."

Reagan also appealed to the fundamentalist block of voters with the same anti-Soviet rhetoric. Following the precedent of Senator Henry Jackson of Washington, Reagan championed human rights exclusively behind the Iron Curtain. Following Jackson, Reagan petitioned the Kremlin on behalf of Soviet Jews but also Soviet Pentecostalists and other groups. Indeed, Reagan's 1984 speech about the "evil empire" was made to Florida Evangelicals, not only to rev up fundamentalists for the campaign against Walter Mondale, but to make up for the administration's deliberate vagueness and even failure to offer tangible accomplishments in the domestic social agenda. Tone-deaf to the realities of coalition politics, most foreign policy commentators fixated on Reagan's caricature of Soviet communism and failed to realize that the speech, which was intellectually sophisticated and made references to both C.S. Lewis and Whittaker Chambers, was purely for domestic consumption. Predictably, most foreign policy analysts failed to understand how their own condescension and even intellectual contempt would play to Reagan's advantage among groups where foreign policy "experts" were vaguely anathema.

Second, Reagan's strident support for the state of Israel also carried resonance with fundamentalists who, far more than Roman Catholics, had become ardent supporters of biblically based, rather than secular-socialistic, Zionism. One might argue that such fundamentalist support was either a deliberate or even subconscious attempt to atone for the anti-Semitism so often latent within the fundamentalist movement or even an expression of guilt over the Holocaust in World War II—a war that many fundamentalists had opposed prior to the Pearl Harbor attack of December of 1941.

Such arguments, however, also ignore theology. Far more than with Roman Catholicism, fundamentalism is permeated with an Old Testament orientation; indeed, the thrust of fundamentalism is to strip away the thicket of Hellenistic accretions of the early church in order to get to the Hebraic "fundamentals" of early Christianity. Some Protestant eschatology has even emphasized the return of the Jews to Palestine as an unfolding of biblical revelation and, indirectly, this cemented fundamentalist support for Israel. In the broader sense, Israel was a democracy and, in terms of the culture wars, defending Israel was a way of defending the people of the Book against all perceived threats: terrorists, gun-toting radicals and advocates of "national liberation." Supporting Israel inevitably also sent a subtle message to American liberals, many of whom may have been "secular" Democratic Jews who attend Temple only on the High Holidays, that fundamentalists stood foursquare behind a persecuted Zion in a land of Philistines. (In this sense, fundamentalists tended to support a Likud- rather than a Labor-dominated Israel.)

Ultimately Reagan's moral defense of American values and his declaratory condemnation of atheistic Marxism was perhaps the easiest way to appeal to conservatives of all persuasions. It was easy to mock such crude simplicities as a hackneyed foreign policy but Reagan was also shrewdly playing to domestic groups; indeed, Reagan was trumping foreign policy as a way of keeping key culturally conservative groups on the party wagon and doing so without rupturing the coalition. There was thus something for everybody. It was an expedient substitute for the difficult domestic choices that the administration always, and perhaps wisely, avoided.

Moreover, when Reagan did pursue the new détente with the Soviets in the Gorbachev regime, it was under the guise of a new liberalism within the Kremlin and the corresponding assumption of renewed U.S. military confidence after the expensive arms buildup. Unlike his fellow Republican Richard Nixon, Ronald Reagan could claim that he had negotiated from strength, that the Soviet leadership had understood the conflict was over, and that the alleged forces of darkness had, at the last, understood both who won and why.

Morality and the Marketplace

Since American politics is about loose coalitions rather than ideological cohesion, it is not surprising that Reagan's professed aims contained contradictions. The sharpest contradiction—and perhaps the weakest political link in the Reagan platform—was between professed economic libertarianism, the conservatism of the marketplace, and a kind of moral communitarianism, the conservatism of the silent majority which allegedly stood for tradition.

Early in the twentieth century, social critics such as the German Max Weber or the Briton R. H. Tawney had been among the first to link religion with the beginnings of modern capitalism, but one need not delve in to the classics of social science literature to see how this played out in America. (Indeed, one suspects that Weber's own visit to America underscored his vision of the self-sacrificing Calvinist as the prototype capitalist.) Throughout much of the nineteenth century, economic accumulation had always been restrained by a semireligious ethic of discipline, frugality and thrift. To invest was godly, to consume was slothful. As with the New Testament parable of the talents, man was put in the world to husband his resources, to produce and be fruitful.

Of course, changes in American society eroded these older ideals. As Richard Hofstadter noted, the more business came to dominate American society, the less it needed to find references outside itself, and this trend accelerated in the so-called gilded age. By the twentieth century, ideals of sacrifice and personal frugality in the name of an almost otherworldly urge for success were cast aside as atavistic if not bad for business. In fact, one reason why the fundamentalist reaction was so strident in the 1920s was because this period inaugurated the modern cult of consumerism. Easy to belittle as small town rubes, fundamentalists directed their finely tuned moral antennae to social changes underway, to a new "worldliness." Operating through the fog of experience, fundamentalists nonetheless sensed a conflict that juxtaposed a relatively new and unfettered consumerism—the pursuit of material goods unjustified by even the veneer of moralism—against an older type of moral conservatism. In the old equation, men worked because it was godly; in the new equation, men work to enjoy the weekend. (Older assumptions, however, linger most pointedly in the idea that welfare, and even higher taxes, are an abrogation of this moral contract—one in which individual industry and economic perseverance are still signs, however unexpressed, of moral worth.)

In a curious way, the anticonsumerist movement of the 1960s built on both the moral disapproval of excessive consumption and the social depredations of big business that had been part of small-town fundamentalism, but that had also underscored the Populist movement. The New Left, however, exaggerated all the paranoiac faults of older western Populism and did so without connections to the popular culture of mainstream America—to church, to community, to the flag, to the forefathers and to the defense of a traditional "way of life" against alien influences. On the contrary, the 1960s critique of popular culture was tarred by association with those who rejected the moral virtue of work itself. Unlike the older Populist movement, which unified farmers and small shopkeepers with small-town moralists, the New Left was a campus movement with no larger resonance in the body politic.

By the 1970s, liberals had come to favor procedural and legal remedies to restraint the worst excesses of the market. There was, however, an almost secular-pharisaic quality about public-interest lawyers and consumer advocates demonizing American business, particularly at a time of growing economic difficulties due, in part, to changing conditions in the global economy.

It was perhaps predictable that Reagan—who had spent the 1950s speaking on behalf of corporate America—should flourish in a political environment where liberalism was colored by a growing skepticism of corporate America and the profit motive. Reagan's greatest success was always in attacking the excesses of liberalism by reminding Americans of older traditions and by finding vague moral justifications for pursuing alternative policies. He had an unerring sense for the emotional weak links in the opposition and for connecting his own policies to traditional values.

Even though Carter had, in 1976, seemed to embody the fiscal conservative as "born-again" moralist, he was the perfect candidate for Reagan to belittle as a "doom and gloom" candidate who could not see the moral redemption in positive economic growth. In the moral dimensions of economic policy, Reagan's "healthy soul" optimism reassured more than Carter's "sick soul" acknowledgment of limitations. Beyond that, Carter was forced to make alliance with the strongly center-left elements in his party and, to compound matters, suffered an economic downturn. Voters rejected, not so much Carter himself, but Carter's inability to inspire confidence and his inability to defend the moral rightness of a probusiness policy.

As in so many other aspects of his administration, Reagan's policy execution could never match the stirring rhetoric. To expect such correspondence is to perhaps look for the impossible, for the politics of opposition is fundamentally different from the politics of incumbency. Governing may not resolve irreconcilable tensions but it does involve finessing tensions, thereby denying the opposition an easy target. Reagan's economic policies revealed two tensions—the questions of fairness and consumption—and these were never satisfactorily finessed. In an interesting turn, the questions appealed to different groups within the culturally conservative Reagan coalition. First, the question of fairness.

It was perhaps predictable that two of the most trenchant critiques of Reagan's economic policies came from northeastern Democrats who themselves were finely attuned to the moral dimensions of public policy. Daniel Patrick Moynihan and Mario Cuomo, both New Yorkers, were heirs to a Roman Catholic cultural tradition of moral conservatism coupled to social welfare. Democrats like Moynihan and Cuomo expressed traditional concerns about the distribution, rather than simply the generation, of society's wealth. In some ways, the overtly free-market philosophy of "Reaganomics" contradicted the immigrant experience where municipal and state, rather than the federal, government had played an important role in tight-knit ethnic communities. (Moynihan had been highly critical of the drift of liberalism in the 1960s; his was not a criticism against state involvement but rather against the way that federal projects impinged on community.)

Traditionally, the Roman Catholic Church tended to favor the idea of distribution of goods and services—ideas that subtly converged with the assumptions of the New Deal Democratic Party. Roman Catholic authorities favored the union movement, for like their European counterparts, American Catholic authorities saw social welfare and a conservative labor movement as bulwarks against working-class socialism. It was doubly telling that most Roman Catholic authorities themselves came, not from the highest social strata, but from the working classes.

With a working-class, Irish-American and union background, Reagan could appeal to this constituency on cultural terms. His economic policies, however, raised concerns that shrewd Democrats, like House majority leader, Tip O'Neill could exploit by painting Reagan as a "country club Republican," whose policies favored the rich over "working Americans." Reagan never managed to fully dispel this notion, even though he himself carried a kind of populistic distrust of Wall Street. (Incidentally, this distrust created a bond between the president and his treasury secretary Don Regan—the Irish-America son of a South Boston cop who climbed his way up through Harvard, the Marine Corps and Wall Street.) Even the 1986 tax reform act, which Regan backed strenuously and which made taxes more progressive, could not overcome the perception that Reagan's 1981 tax cuts disproportionately favored the rich.

It is worth noting that in 1986, Don Regan, who had since become White House chief of staff, had recruited former Nixon and Agnew speech writer Pat Buchanan to craft communications for the White House. It was a clever move, since the Jesuit-educated Buchanan was skilled in articulating right-wing politics—populistic, culturally conservative and anticommunist—that played among Roman Catholic conservatives. Buchanan's commitment was always to conservative causes rather than Reagan, but he was useful in deflecting Democratic assaults by subtly reminding Roman Catholic ethnics why they should be loyal to the Reagan revolution.[16]

On the other hand, questions of economic fairness did not create rifts with the fundamentalists block, many of whom were southerners. For a variety of reasons, Reagan's economic platform played particularly well in the South—the home of the Boll Weevil Democrats who had been central to

Reagan's 1981 legislative successes. On the whole, one could argue that southerners and westerners, and among this a high proportion of fundamentalists, tended to look more favorably than Roman Catholic constituencies on the free-market aspects of the Reagan redirection.

It was in the second area of consumption, however, that the Reagan legacy raised troubling questions that might well have unsettled moral conservatives, particularly fundamentalists who had, in the 1920s, strongly reacted against the gaudy displays of the new consumerism. Indeed, economic events underscored the prominence of present-minded consumption, a kind of pleasure principle, over long-term investment. The vaunted business tax cuts went, not so much for reinvestment, but for mergers and acquisitions; the personal income tax cuts went not into long-term savings, which declined in the 1980s, but into a consumer spending-spree. Personal indebtedness grew as the national debt did and, compared to the seemingly woebegone 1970s, American economic productivity declined. For the first time since World War I, America had became a debtor nation, which proved unsettling to the moral conscience, particularly since that debt was not financing national development.

Critics even pointed to the conspicuous affluence within the Reagan White House but one suspects there was a double standard applied. Nancy Reagan was, after all, no different from Jackie Kennedy, and the Reagan years no different from "Camelot." Nonetheless, the critics did have a point. Although people wanted the political glamour of the Executive restored, particularly after the cloying sanctimony and vapidity of the Carter years, the Reagans, it seemed, did get carried away. The conspicuous consumption and Hollywood connection was subtly inappropriate, not only because the economy was far worse in the early 1980s than in the early 1960s, but because Reagan had promised a reform and austerity that Kennedy had not.

Symbolism counts for much and Reagan's first act as president was to freeze government hiring and new regulations. Unfortunately, symbolism can also undercut a putative reformer's moral authority to affect change. First, the transition process and the subsequent inauguration celebration—run by the organizationally challenged Meese—were the costliest to date. Always more consistent than Reagan in his conservatism, Barry Goldwater thought it grossly wasteful and unbecoming. The charge against "Queen Nancy" wearing Adolfo ball gowns coupled to the perception that Ronald Reagan was insensitive to the poor, to subsequent charges of Pentagon waste, and even to David Stockman's flippant confession of creative bookkeeping—all jeopardized Reagan's reformist reputation. After all, political reformers often have a puritanical, ascetic streak that may be politically tiresome but that nonetheless gives them the moral high ground in political confrontation. Though he professed his love of common things, nobody ever accused Reagan of being an ascetic. He had, effectively, squandered this asset—the moral high ground.

The troubling instances of ethical violations within the Reagan White House further undermined the administration's credibility. Having left the White House, Michael Deaver subsequently received a three-year suspended sentence for lying to a grand jury; Lyn Nofziger was found guilty on three counts of violating the Ethics in Government Act; Meese, while attorney general, had filed incorrect tax returns. Even the sanctimonious and outwardly abstemious James Watt was later charged for making an illegal call on behalf of a contractor who wanted a HUD deal—a phone call for which Watt received one hundred thousand dollars. Reagan acknowledged none of this. He himself had grown wealthy in state office, which put him in sharp contrast to fellow Republicans, Nixon and Bush.[17]

In an interesting way, the question of the corrupting consequences of money was even more troubling within the religious organizations that had expanded in these years. A series of scandals toward the end of the 1980s unsettled, and demoralized, the Religious Right. It was telling that the corruption came from the "televangelists"—the veritable financial empires based around television-based ministry. In 1987, the Oklahoma-based Oral Roberts claimed the Lord was going to "call him Home" if his followers would not contribute four and a half million dollars to his ministries.

The more bizarre story, however, opened up in 1988 when North Carolina televangelist Jim Bakker was alleged to have committed financial irregularities in his Praise the Lord (PTL) Ministries. The PTL Ministries included, of all things, a Christian-based theme park, which underscored not only the worldliness and even baroque gaudiness of televangelism but also the way that religion was infused by a consumerist, popular culture instead of the reverse. Bakker was, in many ways, a sympathetic figure who eventually went to jail and confessed, if not the absurdity of the whole endeavor, that it was at least misguided. Bakker had initially been condemned by the Louisiana-based televangelist, Jimmy Lee Swaggart. (The charismatic Swaggart was the cousin of the flamboyant 1950s rocker, and bible-school dropout Jerry Lee Lewis, who belted out lyrics like "great balls of fire" and "a whole lotta shakin'" but who subsequently ran afoul of popular opinion for legally marrying his thirteen-year-old cousin.) Despite Swaggart's casting the first stone, he himself was not without sin; indeed, it was revealed that he had a history of cavorting with Baton Rouge whores. His tearful and theatrical televised contrition was, itself, a caricature of the honky-tonk preacher-man down on his knees in front of the cameras.

Such corruption highlighted a problem within American fundamentalism and particularly within evangelism, which downplayed scriptural literalism in favor of ecumenical expansion; quite simply, it could degenerate into a form of crass hucksterism. One of the strengths of post-Reformation Protestantism has been in its independence from religious bureaucracy, a worldly and subtly political enterprise—one that often perpetuates its own prerogatives over the message itself and becomes a tyranny of tradition. By contrast, this rejection of tradition can itself lead to a type of antinomianism, whereby schism causes schism and produces a veritable multiplication of splinter sects. Indeed, the problem of money and temporal corruption thus reemerges anew, and in conditions where the institutional checks are correspondingly weaker.

This problem is particularly pointed in America, where the market-place metaphor dominates, and where many treat religion as a type of market choice. Traditionally, the worst excesses of denominationalism were somewhat checked when denominational loyalty was enforced, to some degree, by region, ethnicity and income; as old barriers eroded, the older checks have disappeared and the hucksterism and sham religion, always latent in American society, have increased. (It was for this very reason that Billy Graham, aware of these corrupting tendencies, had completely separated himself from the financial aspects of his ministry while still early in his career.)

Because of the adverse publicity, the Moral Majority seemed to disappear from the political arena in the late 1980s. True, Virginia televangelist Pat Robertson ran for the Republican presidential primary but his presence raised further suspicions about the political motives of the Religious Right, which did not play a prominent role in the relatively uneventful 1988 presidential election.[18]

The accumulated problems that tainted both the Religious Right and the Reagan White House were insufficient to unsettle conservative politicians when they ran against old-fashioned liberals, such as Michael Dukakis, a northeastern ethnic who lacked the common touch of Tip O'Neill, the intellectual range of Gary Hart or the moral passion of Mario Cuomo. Something of a technocrat in the Carter mold, Dukakis—a man who had consciously, and even bitterly, separated from his own Greek Orthodox faith—seemed to personify the bloodless legalism of 1970s centrist liberals who gravitated between Harvard's Kennedy School and political office.

The weakness of the Reagan legacy and his political coalition was, however, most evident in the Bush-Clinton contest of 1992. Indeed, former Reagan staffer Pat Buchanan had mounted a feisty primary challenge against Bush by trying to rebuild the Nixon-Reagan alliance between White ethnics and southern fundamentalists. Lacking Reagan's political touch and seeming too much a patrician, Bush was an easy target. Reagan's political vulnerabilities became Bush's undoing: the question of economic fairness, the legacy of debt and a pattern of reckless consumption were compelling issues for candidate Bill

Clinton, who brought back many of the Reagan Democrats and Southern fundamentalists to the Democratic Party.

Moralism and the Paradox of Inactivity

However shallow his prescription, Reagan nevertheless offered a compelling ideological formula that was essentially consistent with the larger message he had advocated since 1966, when his pollsters began to register voter anxieties. He was a staunch defender of the moral rightness of conservative values; he defended traditions that hearkened back to the pristine virtue of happier and perhaps more pious days. This type of reform-ism—arguably the most emotionally satisfying of all reform agendas—implies a rooting out of moral decay from society. Just as salvation religion cleanses sin from the individual, traditional reformism promises to cleanse corruption from the body politic and return to authentic values.

Political success, however, always comes with a price, and part of the problem in Reagan's appeal to the cultural conservatives, and to the religious groups that made up the New Right, was that his defense was tactical and, in the end, a superficial "sound-bite" reform agenda. Despite his strong convic-tions and stubborn streak, Reagan was a coached candidate surrounded by savvy advisors adept at reading the nation's pulse through continuous polling. New Right partisans were mesmerized by Reagan, who despite his rhetoric, was never "one of them." Like so many others, these religious conservatives could be gently nudged away once they performed their function of getting him to the White House.

Nathan Glazer thus argued that the Reagan policy on domestic and social issues may have been consistent but it was not terribly effective. For his part, Lou Cannon noted that the administration was simply not preoccupied with the social agenda.[19] Other than judicial appointments, and to some extent the antidrug policy, the administration was content to keep its policy confined to brave declaratory statements. It was a measure of political sophistication, if not cynical manipulation, that the White House endorsed the broad agenda of the cultural conservatives without brandishing specific plans for school prayer, anti-abortion legislation and school vouchers. The discrepancy was entirely consistent with Reagan's tenure as governor of California, in which his actions proved more pragmatic than his stridently conservative rhetoric suggested.

Ultimately, the discrepancy between vague promise and policy neglect was good politics and herein lies a paradox. Reagan gave the majority of voters what they wanted—no more and no less. Americans want an endorsement of these traditional values—the family, nation and religion—that liberal ideologues had neglected and even subtly disdained. In this light, Nathan

Glazer argued that the social agenda was not one of universal mandate but a defensive protection of traditional values perceived to be under siege.[20] Reagan brought these values back to the political dialogue and, through the symbolism of high office, put a break on the corrosive attacks against them. This might well have been one of his major contributions as president, and a subtle clue to his deep popularity.

There is, however, a limit to reformism as a purely symbolic enterprise. While it may have yielded results in restoring the nation's sense of patriotism, it glossed over profound problems. Family values are relevant when families are intact but futile when families have broken down. Reagan never addressed why these social pathologies linger in American society, even after the rebellious and even nihilistic values of the counterculture had subsided. As with the "New Federalism," policies of individual responsibility are meaningful only if the individuals and intermediaries are prepared to assume the task assigned to them. Indeed, transferring duties to those either unprepared or unwilling to assume them, and accordingly dismantling a host of programs, may even make a bad situation worse.

It is perhaps too early to determine the long-term political repercussions of the "Reagan redirection" in the social agenda. One thing, however, is certain: Reagan's popularity accelerated the rightward shift in the social debate. The faddishness of moral relativism, which had been embraced by liberals in the McGovern-Carter years, was pushed out of the mainstream political discourse by a greater emphasis on traditional patriotism and by declaratory commitments to traditional ethics based on Judeo-Christian precepts. It is also entirely conceivable to assume that this was all that Reagan intended to do and would be consistent with his gut belief of simply tearing down faddish innovations of the 1960s and, in its absence, letting a normal course of events reassert itself.

It took two trouncings for the Democrats to realize that they needed to absorb Reagan's language and the political symbolism of "family values" if they were to compete effectively at the presidential level. The success of the Reagan redirection was partly illustrated by Bill Clinton who won the presidency as a "new Democrat," that is, by extolling "values politics" and by speaking candidly of his own Baptist faith but with none of the embarrassing confessionalism of Jimmy Carter.

Up from Reaganism: The Future of Conservative Moral Critique

Hugh Heclo noted that, unlike earlier religious revivals in American politics, which were characterized by a social gospel, the latest reassertion of the public faith seemed shallow in comparison. In a similar vein, the late Christopher Lasch argued that the New Right never lived up to its expectations. It is indeed ironic that the promise of religious conservatives in the coming decades might well be measured in their capacity to distance themselves from the lure of politics and promote the deeper social transformation that no politician, however popular, can ever accomplish. Substantive moral reform is almost always contaminated by overtly political behavior.

One might well be skeptical about continued complaints of the nation's eroding "moral" order. After all, the moral order, like the nation's "soul" cannot be defined. Moreover, alarmists from the earliest days of the Republic have always issued jeremiads about the deteriorating nature of society, the rise in deviance and crime, the disrespect of the young and the alienation of those drifting without moral anchor. Such laments are in the nature of things. What is moral decline to the parents is moral freedom to the children: the fall from stoicism and frugality to moral indiscipline and indulgence, or alternately, from narrow Puritanism to expansive freethinking are, after all, the stock themes of literature.

There is, however, one difference that distinguishes the current debate from the traditional critique of American moralists: complaints about moral disorder are today framed within a culture where older, traditional checks and balances have been progressively removed from popular discourse. What troubles so many cultural conservatives is not the lack of religiosity in American society, but that the traditional values of the "majority" are somehow under assault from popular culture. Hence the moral confusion of so many who believe in the separation of church and state and yet demand some— any—validation of traditional morality. Nathan Glazer may have been right to suggest that the liberalizing trends of the 1960s did not fully permeate American society and are thus deceptive, but Glazer's same observation supports the contention that there is a large disjunction between the average lives of America's citizens and the behavior tacitly condoned by either articulate minorities or celebrated in popular culture. Given these tensions, it would seem that there are two principal challenges for American conservatives in the coming years.

The first challenge is to work out the tensions between the economic libertarianism of the market place and the moral conservatism of "values politics."

In a paradoxical way, the intellectual and emotional strength of the modern American Right comes from a rejection of extreme individualism and from the adoption of communal values, subsumed not so much in a common denominator of Christianity but in the defense of general principles that somehow seems part of the American fabric. Conservatives may talk of rugged individuals, but they really are referring to rugged—and implicitly pious—communities. Conservatives may talk about the market but, at their most compelling, they do not refer to a society of atomistic economic individualists but to an older, almost moralistic compulsion of wealth creation as the pursuit of virtue and discipline.

For his part, Reagan never understood the tension between the two branches of his conservative coalition: the failure to understand is an obstacle to reconciliation. He was content to remain in an untroubled never-land—disappearing even in the Dixon, Illinois, of his youth—in which making money was still somehow godly and praising the Lord involved a kind of easy defense of what seemed right without any of the difficult choices and clarifications of a maturing political coalition.

It is this tension, seldom acknowledged by proponents of the values-neutral free market, that gives religious conservatives their persisting voice in American politics. They represent an older, authoritarian and moralistic version of market economics—one that is culturally sustainable because the source of values lies outside the vacuous and quite uninspiring, marketplace metaphor. (One need only remember that, before he was an economist, Adam Smith was a moral philosopher; one could further argue that Smith's "invisible hand" is possible only in a society where the social, and implicitly religious, infrastructure has been firmly established.) The arguments of religious conservatives are further strengthened by the progressive libertinism and even nihilism within the hypertrophic popular culture of the fourth quarter of the twentieth century.

The second, and perhaps more pressing, tension is not one of competing foci of loyalty but one of procedure. Conservatives argue that moral renewal cannot come from the state but from social groups, and the history of American reformism would bear this out. This, however, leaves conservatives unsure about just what to do with political institutions. The state may not be godly but it can at least do a number of things to facilitate the moral well-being of society; one contribution may be the frank acknowledgement of the essential moral neutrality of governance in many issues. Conservatives have succeeded—perhaps beyond their wildest imagination—in breaking down what they saw as the corrosive cultural legacy of the 1960s; they have been less successful in articulating a conservative vision for social rehabilitation beyond the simply "negative" stance of the Reagan era. The failure to locate what is appropriate and inappropriate for public policy continues to confound conservatives.

Every political party, and every political movement, operates with tensions in its ruling coalition. Nonetheless, such disjunctions—whether between factions of a coalition or between professed principles and an unwillingness to be concrete—are corrosive over the long run if not corrected or channeled in to creative compromise. As with all religious leaders, the sense of charisma or blessedness begins to wear off if not matched by specific actions. Laboring in the vineyard of American conservatism requires a more serious foot soldier than Ronald Wilson Reagan, all heart and syrupy emotion but with no reflection. He played his role, and played it well, but cultural conservatives would do well to ponder the gap between promise and performance, to separate the wheat from the chaff, and in doing so, develop a maturing vision for the coming century and negotiate their agenda through the democratic system, which is one of compromise rather than crusades.

Notes

1. See: Nathan Glazer, "The Social Agenda," in *Perspectives on the Reagan Years*, John L. Palmer, ed. (Washington, D.C.: Urban Institute Press, 1986), 5.

2. Glazer, "The Social Agenda," 5.

3. The trouble with the argument was that many of the liberal jurists were themselves appointed by conservative Republicans. Indeed, the relatively liberal Burger Court contained a number of Nixon and Eisenhower appointees. In another sense, the objection was unimportant; what was central was that conservatives argued the judiciary, regardless of who appointed whom, needed to be pushed further to the right.

4. Lou Cannon, *President Reagan: The Role of a Lifetime* (New York: Simon and Schuster, 1991), 802.

5. Cannon, *Role of a Lifetime*, 812.

6. Rowland Evans and Robert D. Novak, *The Reagan Revolution* (New York: E.P. Dutton, 1981), 216.

7. See Cannon, *Role of a Lifetime*, 804.

8. Cannon, *Role of a Lifetime*, 805.

9. Parochial education played into another debate within the Roman Catholic community, namely, how far its communicants should become Americanized. Critics of Americanization argued that they would lose their moral cohesion through assimilation. As with fundamentalists in their assault on the liberal "mainline" denominations, Roman Catholic conservatives reasserted themselves early in the twentieth century. For them, parochial education proved a bulwark against absorption and ecumenical dialogue with reform-minded Protestants.

10. This was slightly ludicrous since Bob Jones University prohibited all dating, unless one considered a chaperoned conversation in a specified chat room a date.

11. One can make compelling arguments both for and against Washington involvement. On one hand, the federal government provides massive financial support to public education and tax breaks for private education. On the other hand, education has traditionally been the preserve of state and local governments.

12. Evans and Novak, *The Reagan Revolution*, 221.

13. The Reagan administration practiced as it preached. When Supreme Court nominee Douglas Ginsburg was revealed to have smoked pot as a Harvard law

professor, conservatives balked at his nomination. With the support of the White House, William Bennet asked him to withdraw his name from consideration. (It was telling that Senator Gore, then running for the Democratic nomination, tried to preempt potential questions by confessing that, in his younger and more foolish days, he too had "experimented.")

14. Both Clinton and Gore dodged their own history of marijuana use by waxing indignant against big tobacco, the new dope peddler preying on innocent children. For his part, Al Gore has mawkishly fought back tears when speaking of his sister's death from cigarette-related cancer but has neglected to add that he, too, took tobacco money for several years after her alleged martyrdom to the tobacco leaf.

15. James Forrestal, James Jesus Angleton, Vernon Walter and William Colby were Roman Catholics in the Intelligence brotherhood. Even William F. Buckley, the most prominent spokesman of old-fashioned Catholic conservatism, was himself a CIA operative for a time.

In some ways, fundamentalists were too parochial for foreign affairs, which required a sense of nuance, worldliness and sly craftiness not thought of as part of the fundamentalist style. It was not surprising that cadres for the Cold War intelligence apparatus came from the high end of the social spectrum, "high" Protestants and "lace-curtain" Roman Catholics. One might even suggest that a fundamentalist elite is a contradiction in terms, for once fundamentalists acquire higher economic status, they tend to migrate to society denominations, that is, Presbyterian, Episcopalian, Congregationalist and so forth.

By contrast, Roman Catholic doctrine prevents the social bifurcation characteristic of "low" and "high" Protestant denominations. When Roman Catholics migrate up the social ladder, they move to "society" parishes rather and abandon the neighborhood parish—with its ghetto-ethnic connotations. Nonetheless, the Roman Catholic elite retains a direct denominational tie to the lower end of the social spectrum.

16. Commentators have overemphasized Buchanan's anti-Semitism and tried to connect him to the 1930s radio priest, Father Coughlin. The connection is only half-right. Like Coughlin, Buchanan is best in pointing to the limitations of the market as an encompassing metaphor but weak in pointing out solutions. Buchanan, in fact, is particularly skilled in marshaling moral disapproval of social change. Himself a child of relative privilege, Buchanan can play the card of anti-elitism without evident class resentment or envy, which usually backfires in American politics. Whereas William F. Buckley's conservatism seems overtly scholastic and almost aggressively erudite, Buchanan's conservatism has a direct emotional appeal.

17. On ethics charges, see Cannon, *Role of a Lifetime*, 801-802; Haynes Johnson, *Sleepwalking through History* (New York: W.W. Norton and Company, 1991), 184-186.

18. In the 1990s, Robertson's group was perhaps better served by the low-key Ralph Reed, who softened much of the negative publicity, by astutely crafting a coalition of religious conservatives and giving it the shrewd and alliterative name, the Christian coalition—which indirectly signals an acknowledgement of political bargaining and negotiation.

19. Cannon, *Reagan* (New York: G.P. Putnam's Sons, 1982), 318.

20. Glazer, "The Social Agenda," 27.

Chapter 16

Conclusions: Ronald Reagan and the Promise of Reform

Ronald Reagan's conservative reformism was a response to several trends. In response to perceived U.S. weakness overseas, Reagan offered a political message of strident anticommunism and a policy of aggressive military buildup. In response to growing discontent with domestic policy, he urged scaling back the scope of government involvement. In response to perceived social drift, Reagan offered a sturdy defense of tradition. In the end, the reform vision that Reagan articulated was a peculiarly American phenomenon—one that was deeply rooted in both nationalism and a conservative skepticism of the federal government.

This idea had its roots in Anglo-American political thought, with its distinctions between "country" and "court" factions, but Americans, with their open frontier and federal system, took eighteenth-century constitutional traditions further than Britons ever could. Consequently, one of the strongest themes of American reformism is predicated on the idea of virtuous outsiders coming to the capital to save it from itself. It is an idea with strong roots in the antique world; Roman history eulogized the general Cincinattus who left his farm to save Rome, not for his own benefit, but for that of the republic.

Reagan's political strengths and credibility emerged in part from this tradition, one that he helped to cultivate. With his roots in the Middle- and then the Far West, Reagan was the virtuous and independent westerner who came to clean out the cosmopolitan capitol. His campaign messages were peppered with such references. In his 1976 bid against Ford, his campaign slogans advertised vague references to "Reagan country"—the range and the land of rugged

273

individuals. Sympathizers spoke of the "sagebrush rebellion" and Reagan himself spoke metaphorically of conservative ideas spreading like wildfire through the West. These are appealing political images, but as with so many images, they distort as much as they clarify.

Critics claimed that Reagan's political vision could hardly be reformist. Scaling back the size and scope of the federal government, they argued, was regressive and a fundamental step backwards. This negative verdict was perhaps understandable in a political system in which reform has most typically been associated with a strong federal presence: it is, however, also a biased value judgment. Two generations after the first experiments of the New Deal, opposition to a strong federal presence can indeed be called reformist for the simple reason that it is a radical change of policy and precedent that its proponents view it as a fundamental improvement. One many not endorse Reagan's policy predicated on scaling back the size and scope of the state, but one cannot objectively disqualify it as an illegitimate vision of political reform.

Those who remain skeptical of Reagan's reformist credentials criticize him for his fixation on the past—that he was backward-looking and, in a value-free sense, "reactionary." The most common cliche about Reagan was that he wanted to "turn back the clock," and in conventional wisdom, reactionaries cannot be reformers. This, too, is a false premise. Even if Reagan were a consistent reactionary (which he was not), nothing in that particular political equation would disqualify his reformist credentials. To make such a judgment is to mischaracterize reform politics, in which agendas may be made with reference to either the past or future. In fact, few self-styled reform politicians are consistent reactionaries or progressives: most accept the implicit need to preserve traditions in some instances and innovate in others.

One can, of course, talk like a reformer, but what counts in the politics of reform is acting like one. Reagan, critics argued, remained little more than a figurehead who endorsed certain reforms but left the difficult tasks to questionable subordinates who were often part of the Washington establishment he proposed to change. Critics charged that he was not only a popularizer of ideas rather than a practitioner of policy, but that he did not even understand the technical side of the reforms he proposed.

It is true that Reagan left policy implementation to others. In this, he was following the pattern of Franklin Roosevelt, who did not draw up New Deal legislation, but left the task to the "brain trusters" and few condemn Roosevelt for this. Historically, reform politicians rarely master the technical details of policies they endorse. In Britain earlier this century, David Lloyd George did not understand the details of either the health or tax reforms his subordinates devised. He did, however, understand the political impact of the measures and his judgment was not only that the public would support it but that the public expected it. If there is a truth about politicians who run on reform platforms, it is that politics comes first and then the technical details are teased out. Reagan's inattention to, and even disinterest in, policy was in keeping with this precedent.

If anything, Reagan was a rare figure among reform politicians: someone whose advocacy of reform and political change actually predated his career as an elected official by more than a decade. Most reform politicians, such as Gorbachev, endorse policy change after the political climate has made it timely, if not imperative. Politicians are seldom ideological risk-takers. Reagan, by contrast, spent much of the 1950s in a type of political wilderness, preaching ideas he would later popularize to wider audiences. His presidency was unlikely precisely because people from the political wilderness rarely make it to the top of a political order, in which astute politicians annex and co-opt popular ideas that develop on the fringes of the political spectrum. Reagan's political compromises appear exaggerated precisely because he had further to move toward the center than more conventional politicians.

Unlike Franklin Roosevelt or Woodrow Wilson, Reagan had fine-hewed his message when it was not fashionable in terms of the larger political climate. One need not call this courage of conviction; it was simply a tactical determination to swim against the prevailing tides. When the political currents begin to move in the direction of the fringe enthusiast, the previously marginal politician seems less a loner on the margins but a champion of "a new majority"—a political prophet of sorts. If he is astute, and if he softens his rhetoric while hinting at compromise, the fringe enthusiast can reap enormous political dividends by representing his ideological brethren while also mollifying centrists. "Party unity" is the name given to softening the previously strident rhetoric. All reform politics is thus a type of bargaining and deal-making writ large.

Critics argue that the putative reformer can only be judged by the degree to which he meets the standards he himself sets. If he has failed to meet his objectives, critics can claim that he has failed as a reform politician.

Such judgments, however, are both too simple and too sweeping to approximate the untidy realities of political life. No president can fulfill all his campaign pledges, not because of the careless and even manipulative character of these promises, but because campaign pledges are a tool of winning elections, not of governing. Most voters implicitly understand this. It is thus too easy to condemn Reagan for not living up to his promise of balancing the budget. Indeed, there is a precedent for Reagan's broken promise. In 1932, Franklin Roosevelt also campaigned to balance the budget, and few condemn him for his failure to do so. One can argue that the New Deal was an ad hoc policy appropriate to a moment of crisis and therefore the "promise gap" can be forgiven. To make such a qualification, however, is to implicitly acknowledge political contingency, and the importance of flexibility over initial promise.

The very same arguments one uses to exonerate Roosevelt's gap between policy and "reformist" performance can be used to exonerate Reagan. Politics is about adjustment, and Reagan, like Franklin Roosevelt, was a master of political judgment. Roosevelt's mandate was not framed in specifics as much as the general imperative of doing something positive—anything—to inspire a measure of confidence and stability. In the same spirit, Reagan's mandate was, not in the specifics of policy, but to do something to restore public confidence in a period of rampant inflation, perceived foreign policy drift and a vague pessimism about American institutions. Partisans of Reagan policies can use the same logic to defend the expensive "Reagan buildup" which eased Americans' doubts about their superpower status and helped bring the Soviets to the negotiating table thereby contributing to the end of the Cold War. Reagan's defenders can argue that he helped end inflation and restore business confidence. Huge budget deficits, it could be argued, were a secondary concern in the short-term.

Reagan thus resembled other successful politicians not in the specifics of his agenda, but by framing policy in a vague, often undefined need to do something. In reform, the details are often secondary to the imperative of action and purpose. Reform politics, like business, rests on a large measure of public confidence in both the message and messenger.

Having discounted too close a judgment based on campaign promise, the analyst does, however, have to look at the record and assess if the politician helped leave things better off at the end of the enterprise than at the beginning. Did the political stewardship represent a qualitative improvement over that of predecessors and did it leave a legacy to its successors?

Critics from both the left and right could say, with much justification, that in the end, Reagan failed to accomplish his chief domestic objective: reforming the federal government by scaling it back. He accomplished relatively little of the ambitious legislative agenda that he sketched out in the first two years of office. Countering his moves, congressional opponents managed to put a brake on his policies, which were never as coherent as the public was led to believe. Indeed, critics from the left can point to the irony that Reagan made big government somehow acceptable by maintaining the status quo, by not tackling entitlements, and by indirectly demonstrating the social and economic costs of radical budget-cutting.

Like most successful politicians, Reagan managed to split the difference; he got some but not all of what he wanted. Like all successful politicians, he created a "snowball effect" for actions that took on a momentum quite independent of his administration. Reagan did not roll back the New Deal but that was not his intention—he rolled back the Great Society, which was.

In the end, there is no formula dictating success or failure other than the subjective verdict of whether he left things better off at the end of his tenure than at the beginning. Since political life is shot through with ambiguities in which successes often contain the seeds of later problems and in which problems often have cathartic benefit, any assessment is bound to be precarious. Since political life is always a continuing ledger of both successes and failures, ironic reversals and surprises, any summing-up of the politician's career is bound to reveal the priorities and prejudices of the reviewer. This constant reassessment and reappraisal is, of course, the task of historians who operate in a discipline where many facts are indeed incontrovertible but in which the importance one assigns to those facts is highly subjective.

Consequently, there is a strange unwillingness in both the left and right to look at Reagan in a critical way. Many on the left think it inconceivable that Reagan be given credit for the new détente with the Soviets; Reagan, they say, had the good luck to be in office when the Soviets happened to collapse. For their part, many in the right still speak of the "Reagan revolution" even as they conveniently overlook the legacy of Reagan's rather nonrevolutionary domestic policy. It is important then to tally up the record, for though Ronald Reagan the politician remains something of an enigma, it is relatively easy to complete an historical audit of Reagan the putative reform politician.

Reagan's problems appeared most sharply on the domestic side of the political ledger. Though he campaigned for a new federalism, his policy was one of dumping responsibility on to the states. It proved, in the end, not very satisfactory and was all but abandoned. Despite heroic budget cuts in the first years, Reagan did not preside over a radically scaled back bureaucracy. The rate of government growth was slowed, but not reduced. In a similar vein, his helter-skelter plan for deregulation was ridiculed as a sellout to corporate America, which in fact it was, and inevitably raised bipartisan congressional opposition. Far from cleaning up the Washington mess, Reagan contributed to it as much as any twentieth-century president: the Savings and Loan debacle took place under his watch, and Americans will be paying to clean it up well into the twenty-first century. Most galling of all, Reagan presided over a tripling of the federal budget deficit during his eight years of office.

In the domestic sphere, Reagan was considerably more successful when little direct policy was required. This was, ironically, in keeping with his philosophy of governance. In his policy addressing family values, Reagan and his staff were successful in balancing the symbols of conservative cultural issues without taking direct action that might fragment his center-right coalition. He helped shift the debate toward long-running Reagan themes:

patriotism, family values, personal responsibility, community. Future historians might well put this as equal to his successful arms control negotiations. In effect, the eight years of Ronald Reagan buried the lingering remnants of the faddish New Left, which has all but disappeared in American politics in the tenth decade of the twentieth century. Reagan forced the left to annex his ideas and that is the ultimate form of political success.

Reagan was perhaps most successful on the foreign policy side of the ledger. Although he kept his campaign promise to increase defense spending, his peacetime buildup was nevertheless a flawed one that emphasized more acquisition than substantive reform: Carter's more modest approach might well have yielded the same results. Reagan's "big stick" approach was, however, politically satisfying and confirmed a general impression that Reagan made America strong again. Morale and perception are essential to statecraft. Whether it was the discrepancy between American technological wizardry and Soviet penury or Reagan's stubborn anticommunist instincts and flexible tactics, events pushed General Secretary Gorbachev to the negotiating table with Reagan. Either by luck, design or by the astute advice of his foreign policy staff, Reagan kept his word and did indeed negotiate with the Soviets from what would seem a position of military strength. Unlike all of his predecessors, Reagan was successful at both the negotiating table and in selling the new détente to an American public.

Although assessing Reagan's policies leads to inescapable questions of political prejudice and value judgment, charting Reagan's political success seems relatively straightforward.

First, Reagan was fortunate to have a governing entourage—those retainers who enter into a kind of modern vassalage in the expectation of some type of payoff. It was to Reagan's political credit that he had a coterie of these seasoned advisers who had served him throughout the 1960s, 1970s and 1980s. Despite their limitations and their often-parochial understanding of Washington, these men understood Reagan's strengths and limitations, but also his gut beliefs. They both protected the candidate and preserved his political assets. American democracy, in which the head of government does not assume office with a "shadow cabinet," makes such a coterie of advisors necessary in order to minimize the difficult transitions from the legislative to the executive or the state house to the White House.

Second, Reagan had the unusual ability to place his presidency in terms of what preceded it—both in a negative and a positive sense. In cleaning out the alleged thicket of recent bureaucratic corruption, he could return the republic to the glory days before such corrupting innovations. Skeptics argued that Reagan, who was rooted to the past, wanted to turn back the clock. This, however, is a misreading of politics, which is always based on past experience. When commentators are biased against a candidate, they condemn him for being nostalgic and escapist: when they are prejudiced toward him, they marvel that he has a sense of history. (Liberals, it would seem, are rarely condemned as nostalgic and conservatives are rarely praised for their sense of history.) Nonetheless, the fact remains that rhetoric that connects the past to the future is not only emotionally powerful but the stock trade of all great speakers.

Paradoxically, political futurism—where one assumes the future to be a tabula rasa—is in fact an actual instance of political escapism. It takes no tremendous leap of imagination to see political futurism as a kind of Gatsbyesque dodge whereby the politician evades his own record by claiming that it is only the future that counts: the future, however, is only known with reference to what preceded it.

Reagan's third asset was an extension of the second: he possessed a few core political values—less government, greater defense spending, less taxes— and repeated them consistently, almost programmatically. One can argue about the incompatibility of less taxes and more defense spending but that is a separate concern and, already, one is granting that Reagan had strong beliefs. By contrast, a president who lacks focus in his administration but campaigns with an almost driven focus is bound to raise doubts—that of cynicism and expediency and even subtle doubts about the candidate's ethical fitness for office; this was not Reagan's problem.

The corollary of this was that Reagan had a rather simplistic view of the world. In politics, complexity is not a virtue, nor is simplicity a weakness. Indeed, politicians who are overly intellectual are prone to hubris and arrogance, to disorder and disarray. Politics rewards, not so much intellect, but will, ambition and drive. Speaking of Franklin Roosevelt, the jurist Oliver Wendell Holmes Jr. noted that he had a second-class intellect but a first-class temperament, and this is the alpha and the omega of all politics. Abraham Lincoln said of himself that he knew only a few things but knew them well. Reagan, another Republican from Illinois, completely matched that description.

Since politics is based so strongly on compromise and maneuver, a simple and compelling message is necessary precisely so the politician does not appear too compromised or compromising. Even when he altered his positions, Reagan never appeared compromised.

Having strong beliefs, or the appearance of them, gives the politician believability, perhaps the most important trait in democratic politics. Reagan's intellect may have been suspect; his honesty was not. If anything, Reagan had an astonishing capacity for rationalization, but this only added to his believability. Though a glaring personality flaw, self-rationalization is a good one for politicians to possess. The obverse of self-rationalization is irony and politicians gifted with irony are often doomed in American politics.

Fourth, Reagan's legislative agenda was framed in terms of a consistent strategy, one that reflected his stated principles: that society and the economy, not the state, should be the engine of change. Reagan may have underestimated the role of government but he kept to his lines. As such, Reagan's consistency contrasted favorably with other presidents, who have failed to enunciate an overall vision of governance or have announced one, backed off and, in effect, endorsed the policies of the other party. Such parliamentary maneuvering brings short-term expediency but at the risk of larger vision.

Indeed, such maneuvering raises larger problems for a president. Although democratic politics almost always merges toward the center, and although politicians often pay tribute to the other party by annexing its ideas, there must also be an element of ideological discretion. Great politicians achieve their status because they have a vision to enunciate, not because they have co-opted the opposition. T.S. Eliot suggested that bad poets borrow whereas great ones steal, but politics is different from poetry, and ideological theft is a sign of unbecoming opportunism rather than leadership. It subtly violates our expectations that our political labels and parties—however loose they may be—must at least stand for something.

This leads to the sixth reason for Reagan's political success, which was based, not simply on his two presidential victories, but on how his party and how his ideological fellow travelers fared in terms of the larger political alignment. His coattails helped the Republicans win the Senate in 1980, and although they lost control six years later, it is not hard to see that Reagan's stewardship in the White House energized a whole generation of conservatives who were poised to take control of both houses in the 1990s.

At the end of the twentieth century, is too early to tell about the lasting effects of the Reagan coalition. This is particularly true in a period when political parties tend to be fragmenting and party loyalty diminishing. As such, it is almost unfair to use Franklin Roosevelt as the yardstick for success in building coalitions. Short of Roosevelt, however, it would seem that Reagan has done more than any subsequent president to help accelerate a shift in the slow-moving tectonic plates of American politics—and, in that, he must be considered a success.

The broader shift was not so much electoral as ideological—if one assumes ideology to be a loose cluster of related ideas rather than a programmatic doctrine. The rightward trend predated Reagan's presidency but he accelerated it as few could. What Reagan did was not so much enunciate conservative principles, but marginalize the type of liberalism that had been faddish in the 1960s and 1970s. As specific policies, Reagan's defense of big business, the military, anticommunist containment, a conservative judiciary, family values and the whole congeries of symbols that we associate with American "civil religion" may have been limited and even flawed, but as part of a larger political vision, they held together brilliantly. It would appear that most Americans did not share the values that permeated the New Left and Reagan's virtuosity as a politician was in reminding them why. For this reason, Reagan retained the support, and perhaps even affection, of so many who nonetheless disagreed with the details of his policy. Herein was the real Reagan revolution.

Chapter 17

Conclusions: The Conservatism
of American Reform

It would be hard to summarize Reagan's story other than to suggest that, like any life, it was a collection of stories. There are, however, a number of tentative generalizations that can be culled from the study of Reagan and the promise of reform.

First, reform politics always involves competing value judgments. Historians of American history long perpetuated an unfortunate dichotomy between reform (i.e., liberalism) and reaction (i.e., conservatism). That dichotomy has perhaps served its purpose and is no longer useful. The person who calls for scaling back government has as much claim to the reform mantle as the one who calls for expanding it. In political dialogue, it is impossible to abstain from value judgment, for political ideas are based on prejudice, that is, gut beliefs of what is good and bad. It is, for example, a prejudice to think that change is always for the better or, alternatively, that everything old has somehow stood the test of time. In our political analysis, however, we should be more critical and assume that, in the politics of reform, there are many paths to salvation. Observation need not lead to exhortation.

This leads to a second generalization: just because a policy is "reformist" does not make it an ipso facto "good." Misconceived reforms may make a bad thing worse: they may solve one problem but create another. If political reform rests on competing value judgments, it would stand to reason that, depending on one's perspective, there is sensible and there is misguided reform. The analyst's duty then is to examine the implementation of policy, weigh the beneficial and detrimental implications and gauge the political outcome.

The Politician and Reform

The politics of reform is, first and foremost about politics. It is not about the reform of politics, though proponents often pretend it is. Knowing the public preference for the idea of reform, politicians use the term liberally, almost recklessly. They even use their commitment to reform, that is to "changing the system," as a smoke screen for their own corruptions of judgment and practice.

Indeed, the promise of reform is perhaps the most important arrow in the politician's rhetorical quiver. Instead of aspiring to office for its own sake—which most politicians do—the putative reform politician has a ready-made objective, namely to clean up abuses, to correct wrongs, to make things work.... Since almost everything can be helped by improvement, the erstwhile reformer can pick and chose at will.

By implication, the retainers and advisors who fasten their own chances for promotion and employment to their candidate's prospects are no longer the "spoilsmen" reminiscent of gilded age politics, but associates of the reformer and therefore somehow touched by the charisma of the great one. The reformist mantle covers up the often-compromised clamor of outsiders to be insiders; the sense of outrage at corruption camouflages the self-seeking ambition and often astonishing mediocrity of the semipermanent political entourage within both parties.

The mantle of reform brings other subtle advantages. It advertises the challenger's outsider status, if the mood is one of anti-incumbency; conversely, by pledging to "reform the system," the putative reformer is implicitly suggesting he understands the nature of the problems—a tactic for deflecting questions of lack of preparation for office. One need not be too specific, which raises liabilities; vagueness, by contrast, is rarely penalized and is eminently understandable.

As such, the mantle of reform—which sounds good even if it is nothing more than vague pronouncements about change—is a way of dressing up the dreary and often compromising business of politics. It enables our politicians to sound courageous and forward thinking. It enables them to speak about things other than their own selves and herein is a paradox, for we personalize politics but we, as voters, do not want it too personal. In the same way, we want to know that the candidate is religious but do not want to know the details of his religion. We want to know that he stands for something, which we can identify within the spectrum of American politics, but that he is not too tied to his faction to be a leader "for all Americans." In advocating reform, one pays homage to precedent and the need for novelty; it satisfies our yearning for the periodic circulation of our political elites within the context of an established order.

The reform politician is, at best, a semiopportunistic facilitator of change already under way. There are sham reformers—and we can see them for what they are—but most politicians perform the useful function of bringing change but modifying it and thereby performing the tasks that make our civil society possible.

The Phases of Reform

Looking with a broader perspective, the process of political reform fits in to a fairly predictable pattern of problem, diagnosis, corrective policy and outcome. This simple, commonsense scheme is helpful in that it raises a number of corollaries.

The problem phase is not hard to fathom. If politics is a competing game of half-truths, then it is the business of the democratic opposition to focus on problems, which are ever present. It is in the nature of democratic life to search for problems and propose corrective remedies. Political debates are often waged over differing priorities and often at cross-purposes; when opposing factions debate policy, they are debating, not simply the specifics of policy or even the same issues, but rather the relative hierarchy of problems.

The phase of diagnosis, by contrast, is both more interesting but also more complex. We tend to think of reformist diagnoses as grounded in grand strategies, unified by a common political philosophy, with implications for all branches of the state apparatus. In short, we assume that intellectual "models," the unified visions of governance, lurk inside the brain of the political reformer who clamors for change. Like so many assumptions, it contains an element of half-truth.

Ultimately, the ideologically rigorous plan as a platform for change is appropriate only in two select instances. One, to rationalize change that has already taken place and thus give it an intellectual respectability congruent to political realities. We can see this trend with the enunciation of New Deal liberalism, that gave an intellectual respectability to the often ad hoc policies of the Roosevelt administration. The second instance is at the other end of the spectrum: when a political party or creed is marginalized in a changing political climate, it must fall back on ideology to regroup. This is not simply a return, or a collective reinvention, of so-called first principles but something deeper. In an age when a dominant governing assumption has squeezed its rivals out of the dialogue and when those representing the dominant assumptions constitute the majority party, the minority party has two choices. It can concede minority status, co-opt the dominant line and suggest that they can "get things done better." Alternately, partisans can aspire to majority status and, to do this, they must put forth their own creed. Wanderers in the political wilderness, must exaggerate to be heard—it is part of their sales pitch.

Reagan was of the latter, true believing camp—those who helped discredit the dominant post-war liberalism and make the world safe for conservatives. In Reagan, even more than in his predecessor Goldwater, we see the perfect example of the enthusiast progressively softening his rhetoric and, in doing so, spreading the gospel to a wider congregation.

If we push further, we see a number of subsidiary corollaries within this "dialogue phase" of reform politics.

The first has to do with "national discussion," a phrase that politicians blessed with a flare for empathy seem to fixate upon. For many, a "national discussion" connotes a kind of well-meaning encounter group that helps us transcend our parochial concerns. There could be nothing further from the truth. The real national discussion is within our own coalition of like-minded comrades. The left talks to the left and the right to the right, and never the twain shall meet, nor should it except in times of crisis. The real national discussion implies convincing the swing voters in the middle to join one discussion to the exclusion of the other. Partisans do this by stigmatizing the alternative, by ridiculing its core assumptions and by suggesting that the alternative philosophy leads, over time, to a corruption of practice.

Those most vociferous advocates of "national discussion" in the naive, unpolitical sense are invariably those whose parties have been on the losing end of national trends and thereby indirectly demonstrate their unfitness to win political debates in American politics. It is also telling that "national discussion" is an idea strongly supported by academics, whose prominent powers of political criticism are inversely proportionate to their low levels of political responsibility.

The second implication touches on the marketplace metaphor, and specifically the "marketplace" of ideas. We tend to assume that democracy is somehow congruent with this intellectual marketplace—one that offers a number of choices that magically lead to the most rational conclusions. While there maybe a marketplace of ideas, it a relatively closed store and, contrary to common assumptions, its strength is that it is something of an oligopoly. The range is limited and market-entry is relatively difficult. In fact, the success of a political idea comes to the extent that it can displace other products and, for a time, assume complete brand loyalty. The strength of New Deal liberalism was that it pushed laissez-faire economics and isolationism off the political shelf for a generation; the strength of modern American conservatism has been that it has pushed the New Left back to isolated enclaves, as it was in the 1950s. In reform, the triumph of ideas comes in the capacity to marginalize rivals.

This, however, leads to the paradox of success. In banishing the ideological pariahs, the new majority ironically loses the foe that had sustained them through the wilderness years or that had subsequently helped shift national momentum in their favor. The public loses memory of the "economic royalists" and old-fashioned fiscal conservatives of the New Deal rhetoric; it forgets about the unwashed, antiwar demonstrators who made us rally around the flag. Soon, the minority opposition co-opts the newly popular ideas, makes them their own, and this seems to subvert the natural order of things.

This, too, is part of the dialectic of reform. Politicians who are intellectually removed from, or subtly out of synch with, the main political trends are often more adept at playing the politics of practical maneuver for the simple reason that they have few intellectual inhibitions—and are thus free to be inconsistent. For the majority, the burdens are the obverse, particularly if its members are experiencing the dangerous giddiness of assuming power for the first time. The tight, and often untried principles of opposition that had sustained the faithful in the wilderness years often prove too parochial and too narrow for a broader coalition. Invariably, those politicians stigmatized as too accommodating of the old order—who were too content to remain a minority party—prove adept at forging a new consensus between the enthusiasts and pragmatists. This is also part of the implementation of reform, where the skills of political opposition are often not those of governance, where there is a rough intellectual division of labor between the proselytizer and the practical politician. The skills of the ideologue may mean survival in the harsh conditions of minority status but become a type of political clumsiness in keeping a new majority coalition together. This is why reform coalitions often fragment in the second generation when the galvanizing leader passes from the scene.

Observers are inclined to look sharply at Reagan's unfinished agenda as a failure of conservative reformism. In another sense, however, Reagan never fell into the trap of overreaching or in fragmenting his coalition—one that all but put his politically weak vice president in to office. Reagan's presidential career was, quite simply, an amazing feat of political coalition building.

Like so much in life, the politics of reform is an ironic enterprise, for defeat is an invitation to both reassessment and renewal, and victory the beginning of a set of responsibilities, headaches and heartaches. Nothing remains and the victorious coalition often grows so big that it, too, fragments. Fragmentation, however, is a sign of success, for it guarantees the triumph of principles, which often outlive coalitions and become entrenched in the political order.

The short-term goals of politics may indeed be to assume power and to win credit for victories but what sustains the whole process is principle. In times of political crisis and setback, it is to first principles that we must invariably return. To be great in politics, one needs more than strong convictions, but no politician can be great without principle and conviction—those things that make political life meaningful because they stand outside the kind of permanent and even sullied poker game of democratic politics. To repeat, a politician, however much a virtuoso in the art of maneuver, who cannot stand for something beyond annexing the opposition, has no claim to greatness.

The Conservatism of Reform Politics

It is not the intention of this author to endorse one faction over the other. Partisans of the left and right can make of things as they see appropriate and fitting. There will always be a dialogue, with its ups and down, with its victories and losses, with its changing assumptions and shifting coalitions. Political life goes on.

There is, however, one point that may be of some consolation to those conservatives of an intellectual rather than a purely partisan casting. The politics of reform in American democracy is a fundamentally conservative enterprise to the extent that it puts a premium on tradition over novelty, on practical experience over abstract reasoning, on legislative bargaining over executive fiat. The politics of American reformism is conservative to the degree that it is permeated with checks and balances that both wear down the intemperance of the young and frustrate enthusiasm and folly in the pursuit of political glory. The politics of American reform, by contrast, puts an emphasis on empiricism—the tried and the true that has already filtered its way through the political process. Our politics is fundamentally cautious, for caution belongs to those who know the frailty of things and the need for continuity in order to make change possible. It is better to be wrong in a small way than a spectacular way.

Whoever said that a little revolution is good for political stability was wrong; a little reform, here and there, is better. To place one's confidence in the possibilities of reform—within limits—is to acknowledge stability. This is why self-styled revolutionaries heap scorn on reform-minded liberals, who want to "work within the system," as crypto-conservatives. The radical is right: reformism is a way of rehabilitating and updating the dominant tradition. Reformism is, at bottom, a conservative enterprise, for even the task of maintaining traditions depends on creative adaptation and constant reappraisal.

It is said that the successful society makes room for the talented and upwardly mobile by assimilating them into the highest strata. The same is true of the political order and, reform is a way of assimilating both ideas and policy changes. Reform is, after all, about probabilities. Despite our professed preference for policy boldness, we do not want our politicians to experiment with the untried: to do so would be to risk failure, which is the greatest sin in political life. That is why we want our politicians to endorse changes that have already been debated about, modified, "market-tested" and, ideally, diluted. In the main, we want our politicians to endorse positions when they no longer require too much courage, for too much courage in politics is foolishness in all but the most extreme situations.

This inevitable lag time between truly original ideals and the subsequent implementation of policy change is a healthy one. It prevents wild oscillations of policy; it allows for a measure of trail and error; it implies more a ratification of change already underway rather than the proposal of bold new plans.

Our failure to look critically at the politics of reform and see it for what it is—a type of bargaining between shifting coalitions and a ratification of change that has already occurred—perhaps blinds us in to thinking that the only valid reform is the type of sweeping, administrative fiat determined in the first "one hundred days" of the new regime, the bold promise of change and renewal. Some analysts describe this sweeping reform as "revolution from above"—an absurdly contradictory term—whereas the more intellectually cautious call it "great" or "grand reform."

In the end, an undue fixation of grand reform leads to a number of unfortunate implications. In trying to make simple politics into "grand reform" we implicitly diminish the difficult, dreary but necessary business of running a government. The daily observance of difficult duties, Goethe reminded us, is all the revelation we need. In forgetting this, we tend to view the strength of the U.S. political order—the premium on institutional checks and balances to frustrate sweeping executive action—as a weakness. Misguided, we look for things that our policy makers cannot deliver. We expect dramatic jolts of policy—with flair and flamboyance—when a mundane incrementalism is the norm. We look for philosopher-legislators, for the superexecutives, with blueprints for change and plans of attack and then when they fail—as they invariably will—we ridicule them as ideologues or, worse, as intellectuals prone to abstraction.

Consequently, we spend out time pining for breakthroughs—from the left or the right—that will never materialize. Perversely, the ideology of opposition subtly encourages this wishful thinking—which creates political pitfalls for new majorities that must bring promised change but with utmost care. Legislative breakthroughs, such as the New Deal legislation, are inappropriate for most normal times and are, more often than not, products of crisis and upheaval. There are those who hanker for a crisis as a kind of therapy and testing but this is a folly of youth wholly unbecoming for political leaders. To compensate for personal political failings in the pursuit of some great national test is a very unwise proposition: it takes only a little reflection to see that, in mundane politics, only revolutionaries, little more than principled arsonists, should anticipate crisis with enthusiasm.

The grand vision of reform encourages our disillusionment with political life, for when we pitch expectations too high we subtly undermine the predictability of our political life and create a gap between promise and performance. When everything becomes reform, then nothing is reformist; as with the term "revolution," (the computer revolution, the industrial revolution, the information revolution, the managerial revolution, the military revolution, the green revolution, "revolution from above," etc.) the term becomes emptied of its meaning by overuse. Instead of dressing up politics as reform, real courage would entail accepting what politics is and articulating what it is not. Nationalism, it was once said, is the last refuge of scoundrel: reform, it would seem, has become the last refuge of politician. Accepting a conservative, rather mundane vision of reform puts some type of intellectual check on the inflation and subsequent deflation of expectations.

Accepting the conservative nature of American reformism helps dispel the illusion of grand reform as a viable, or even desirable alternative, in our political order. It would seem that a realization based on the conservative nature of reform statecraft would trim some of our more exuberant expectations and, although it may leave the political world a little less heroic, it would be a sign of maturity to suggest that, in politics, too much heroism, like too much passion is a dangerous thing. It is a sign of maturity to accept things for what they are and not make them what they should not be.

The point can be pushed even further. To accept the compromised, bargained and negotiated aspects of American politics is to finally dispel the notion of politics as a fundamentally noble endeavor. It was Augustine who defined the blessed as those who excel at what they do, who have found their vocation a calling, and that it be a noble one. To die for one's country is noble; to renounce one's life to a religious calling is noble; to risk censure, and the loss of property and freedom for justice and honor—all are indeed noble. A virtuoso politician is, however, not a blessed man because his task is not intrinsically noble. (This runs counter to the platitudes we often here in which even highly paid sports figures and celebrities become "role models" and, most implausibly, "heroic.") Politics is socially useful and essential to society's well-being, but to call it noble is, sadly, to make it something it is not. Of course, we implicitly think of Lincoln and Churchill as paragons of nobility but these are false analogies. What made Lincoln noble was not his grasping ambition as an Illinois legislator but his masterful leadership as a war leader presiding over a nation literally torn apart. What made Churchill noble was not his early political life, in which he was something of an erratic hack, but his rallying his nation at its darkest hour. Lincoln and Churchill were great, in spite of, not because of their earlier "political" careers. Public service is essential to our society, but it is not noble.

Reagan was a successful president but he was not a noble, nor a heroic one. Nobility does not come from rhetorical skill, legislative success, or of any of the real virtues Reagan brought to high office, but from traits in many ways distinct from, and even subtly inappropriate to, political life, which by necessity demands a certain level of salesmanship, glibness and manipulation. To say all this is not to diminish either Reagan or American politics but to do both justice by seeing them as they are. Reagan accomplished his goals; he left the country and the office of president better than he found them; he knew his strengths and limits and acted accordingly.

We have, at last, come to the end of the intellectual journey into Reagan's political career but also into those careers which, by design and by luck, were somehow linked to his. This work has been biographical without being, in the strictest sense, a biography. In fact, there has been an element of group biography, or prosporography, running through the various chapters. Now there are those who are skeptical about the inferences to be made through biographical studies, as if generalities are significant only if based on graphs and data and charts—those gimmicks that simplify but also camouflage the idiosyncrasies, contingencies and radical unpredictability of political life. At the close of this work, it should be evident to the reader that this author is not one of those skeptics.

The particular, noted Kierkegaard, is always higher than the universal. To view a political career in its entirety is to fathom the limitations of hypotheses superimposed on the trajectory of individuals; it is to come face-to-face with the twists and turns, the continuities and departures that are, by necessity, the marks of the politician's craft. Surveying the course of a political life implies scaling back judgment, assessing difficulties and contradictions, acknowledging the discipline of defeat and the radical incompleteness at the heart of every political success. The biographical study of politics is, above all, an exercise in political criticism, which involves praise as much as censure.

With their incessant urge for periodization, historians of the twenty-first century will surely look back on America in the ninth decade of the twentieth century as the "age of Reagan"—a term that might well cover the presidency from Carter to Clinton, both of whom may be destined to live under the long shadow of Ronald Wilson Reagan, a transitional figure it is true, but history is made of such "transitional" figures.

Bibliography

Ahlstrom, Sidney E. *Religious History of the American People.* New Haven, Conn.: Yale University Press, 1972.

Beck, Paul Allen. "Incomplete Realignment. The Reagan Legacy for Parties and Elections." In *The Reagan Legacy,* ed. Charles O. Jones. Chatham, N.J.: Chatham House Publications, 1988.

Bell, Coral. *The Reagan Paradox: American Foreign Policy in the 1980s.* New Brunswick, N.J.: Rutgers University Press, 1989.

Bell, Daniel. "The End of American Exceptionalism." In *The American Commonwealth,* ed. Nathan Glazer and Irving Kristol. New York: Basic Books, 1976.

Berman, William C. *America's Right Turn: From Nixon to Bush.* Baltimore, Md.: Johns Hopkins University Press, 1994.

Cannon, Lou. *Reagan.* New York: G. P. Putnam's Sons, 1982.

————. *President Reagan: The Role of a Lifetime.* New York: Simon and Schuster, 1991.

Dais, Vincent. "The Reagan Defense Program: Decision Making, Decision Makers, and Some Results." In *Reagan Defense Program: An Interim Assessment,* ed. Stephen J. Cimbala. Wilmington, Del.: Scholarly Resources, Inc., 1986.

Destler, I. M. "Reagan and the World: An 'Awesome Stubbornness.'" In *The Reagan Legacy,* ed. Charles O. Jones. Chatham, N.J.: Chatham House Publications, 1988.

Dunnigan, James F., and Raymond Macedonia. *Getting It Right: American Military Reforms after Vietnam to the Persian Gulf and Beyond.* New York: William Morrow and Company, 1993.

Eads, George C., and Michael Fix. *Relief or Reform: Reagan's Regulatory Dilemma.* Washington, D.C.: Urban Institute Press, 1984.

Evans, Rowland, and Robert D. Novak. *The Reagan Revolution.* New York: E. P. Dutton, 1981.

Glazer, Nathan. "The Social Agenda." In *Perspectives on the Reagan Years,* ed. John L. Palmer. Washington, D.C.: Urban Institute Press, 1986.

293

Goldberg, Robert Allan. *Barry Goldwater*. New Haven, Conn.: Yale University Press, 1995.

Haig, Alexander M. *Inner Circles: How America Changed the World*. New York: Warner Books, 1992.

Heclo, Hugh. "Reaganism and the Search for a Public Philosophy. In *Perspectives on the Reagan Years,* ed. John L. Palmer. Washington, D.C.: Urban Institute Press, 1986.

Heilbroner, Robert, and Peter Bernstein. *The Debt and the Deficit: False Alrarms/Real Possibilities*. New York: Norton, 1989.

Hill, Dilys M. "Domestic Policy in an Era of 'Negative Governance.'" In *Reagan Presidency: An Incomplete Revolution?* ed. Dilys M. Hill, Raymond A. Moore and Phil Williams: New York: St. Martin's Press, 1990.

Hoff, Joan. *Nixon Reconsidered*. New York: Basic Books, 1994.

Hofstadter, Richard. *The Paranoid Style in American Politics and Other Essays*. Chicago: The University of Chicago Press, 1965; Phoenix Edition, 1979.

Hunter, James Davison. *Culture Wars: The Struggle to Define America*. New York: Basic Books, 1991.

Johnson, Haynes. *Sleepwalking through History: America in the Reagan Years*. New York: W. W. Norton and Company, 1991.

Katz, Michael B. *The Undeserving Poor: From the War on Poverty to the War on Welfare*. New York: Pantheon Books, 1989.

Lash, Jonathan. *Season of Spoils: The Reagan Administration's Attack on the Environment*. New York: Pantheon Books, 1991.

Luttwak, Edward. *The Pentagon and the Art of War: The Question of Military Reform*. New York: Simon and Schuster, 1984.

Mayer, Jack A. "Social Programs and Social Spending." In *Perspectives on the Reagan Years,* ed. John L. Palmer. Washington, D.C.: Urban Institute Press, 1986.

Reagan, Ronald. *An American Life*. New York: Simon and Schuster, 1990.

———. *Speaking My Mind: Selected Speeches*. New York: Simon and Schuster, 1989.

Regan, Donald T. *For the Record: From Wall Street to Washington*. New York: St. Martin's, 1988.

Schaller, Michael. *Reckoning with Reagan: America and Its President in the 1980s*. New York: Oxford University Press, 1992.

Shultz, George P. *Turmoil and Triumph: My Years as Secretary of State*. New York: Maxwell Macmillan International, 1993.

Stein, Herbert. *Presidential Economics: The Making of Economic Policy from Roosevelt to Clinton*. 3d ed. Washington, D.C.: American Enterprise Institute for Public Policy Research, 1994.

Stockman, David. *The Triumph of Politics: The Inside Story of the Reagan Revolution*. New York: Harper and Row, 1986; Avon Paperback Edition, 1987.

Stubbing, Richard A. *The Defense Game: An Insider Explores the Astonishing Realities of America's Defense Establishment*. New York: Harper and Row, 1986.

Vistica, Gregory L. *Fall from Glory: The Men Who Sank the U.S. Navy.* New York: Simon and Schuster, 1995.

Watt, James G. *The Course of a Conservative.* New York: Simon and Schuster, 1985.

Weatherford, Stephen M., and Lorraine M. McDonnel. "Ideology and Economic Policy." In *Looking Back on the Reagan Presidency,* ed. Larry Berman. Baltimore, Md.: Johns Hopkins University Press, 1990.

Weinberger, Caspar. *Fighting for Peace: Seven Critical Years in the Pentagon.* New York: Warner Books, 1990.

Whicker, Marcia Lynn. "Managing and Organizing the Reagan White House." In *The Reagan Presidency: An Incomplete Revolution?* ed. Dilys M. Hill, Raymond Moore and Phil Williams. New York: St. Martin's Press, 1990.

Wicker, Tom. *One of Us: Richard Nixon and the American Dream.* New York: Random House, 1991.

Wills, Garry. *Reagan's America: Innocents at Home.* Garden City, N.Y.: Doubleday and Company, 1987.

————. *Nixon Agonistes: The Crisis of the Self-Made Man.* Boston: Houghton Mifflin, 1970.

Index

abortion rights, 249-51. *See also*
 religious, moral and social issues
academic experts, in government
 positions, 16-17. *See also specific
 person*
ADA. *See* Americans for Democratic
 Action (ADA)
administrative reform, Reagan and,
 113-27, 129-45
AFDC. *See* entitlement programs
Afghan rebels, U.S. support of, 62
Air Force, U.S.: in Cold War, 95-99;
 peacetime buildup of, 95-99
air-traffic controllers, 163-64
Americans for Democratic Action
 (ADA), 43
Andropov, General Secretary, 67-68,
 70
Andrus, Cecil, 175-76, 177-78
Antiballistic Missile Treaty, 68
anticommunism: Carter and, 82; and
 the Cold War, 43-44 (*see also*
 Reagan, Ronald, foreign policy
 of); Nixon and, 44; Reagan and,
 43-45, 64-70. *See also The
 Committee on the Present
 Danger;* communism

Army, U.S., 80-81; in Cold War, 94-
 95; peacetime buildup of, 94-95;
 in Vietnam War, 94
auto industry, regulation of, 163, 164-
 65

Baker, James: as Chief of Staff, 221-
 22, 255; as Reagan campaign
 manager, 241, 248, 250; and tax
 cuts, 214-15; as treasury
 secretary, 182-83, 222, 255
banking industry: deregulation of thrift
 industry, 179-84; regulation by F.
 Roosevelt, 180
Bell, Terrell, 253-55
Bennet, William J., 254-55
Blumenthal, Michael, 194-95
Borland Amendment (1982), 63
Boston Tea Party, 150
Bradley-Gephardt tax reform code, 222
Brezhnev, General Secretary, 66, 67,
 91, 96
Brown, Harold, 80-81, 91, 96-97, 99
Brown, Jerry, 176-77, 189
Bryan, William Jennings, 153, 154-55,
 230-31
Brzezinski, Zbigniew, 80-81
budget. *See* fiscal policy and reform

297

About the Author

Originally from San Francisco, John Karaagac has degrees from U.C. Berkeley, Cambridge and Johns Hopkins. This present work emerged out of his doctoral thesis—a comparative and historical study of political reform in the great powers. He now lives in Washington, D.C.